CLOCKWORKS

CLOCKWORKS

A Multimedia Bibliography of
Works Useful for the Study of
the Human/Machine Interface in SF

Compiled by
Richard D. Erlich and Thomas P. Dunn

Assisted by
Edward K. Montgomery, Catherine Mills Royer,
and D. Scott DeLoach

Bibliographies and Indexes in World Literature, Number 37

GREENWOOD PRESS
Westport, Connecticut • London

Library of Congress Cataloging-in-Publication Data

Erlich, Richard D.
    Clockworks : a multimedia bibliography of works useful for the
study of the human/machine interface in SF / compiled by Richard D.
Erlich and Thomas P. Dunn ; assisted by Edward K. Montgomery,
Catherine Mills Royer, and D. Scott DeLoach.
        p. cm.—(Bibliographies and indexes in world literature,
ISSN 0742-6801 ; no. 37)
    Includes bibliographical references and indexes.
    ISBN 0-313-27305-7 (alk. paper)
    1. Arts, Modern—20th century—Bibliography. 2. Science fiction—
Illustrations—Bibliography. 3. Conscious automata in art—
Bibliography. 4. Science fiction—History and criticism—
Bibliography. I. Dunn, Thomas P. II. Title. III. Series.
Z5935.5.E74   1993
[NX650.S3]
016.7—dc20   93-1069

British Library Cataloguing in Publication Data is available.

Library of Congress Catalog Card Number: 93-1069
ISBN: 0-313-27305-7
ISSN: 0742-6801

First published in 1993

Greenwood Press, 88 Post Road West, Westport, CT 06881
An imprint of Greenwood Publishing Group, Inc.

Printed in the United States of America

The paper used in this book complies with the
Permanent Paper Standard issued by the National
Information Standards Organization (Z39.48-1984).

10 9 8 7 6 5 4 3 2 1

For Harriette G. Ryder, and in memory of Leona Peckham Dunn, Bea Schwartz Erlich, and Harry Erlich.

Contents

About This Volume

The Introduction explains the logic of our List.

Abbreviations in our annotations use initials for the names of authors and the titles of the works cited in that entry: e.g., Frederik Pohl's story "The Midas Plague" would be FP's "TMP"; Frederik Pohl's Man Plus would be FP's MP. We use only initials for first names of most other authors mentioned in annotations (with the exception of Ursula K. Le Guin, whom we do not refer to as "U. K. Le Guin").

Anthologies and Collections listed in the second section of *Clockworks* are, ordinarily, alphabetized in that section by titles and authors respectively. (If told to see an anthology under Anthologies and Collections, look for it first by title; if told to see a collection, look for it first by author's name.)

Authors and works referred to frequently in our annotations by last name only (e.g. Cox and Libby, Johnson, Naha, Orth, Sobchack, Warrick, Wolfe) are cited in the first section of the List, Reference Works.

Cross-references within the List do not use numbers but refer users to a section of the List identified by the name of that section, and from there to the title and/or author's name to see within that section.

Doctor Who and Star Trek (both the original Star Trek series and The Next Generation) are listed under Drama, alphabetically by episode under Doctor Who and Star Trek.

The format, with only minor exceptions, follows the Modern Language Association format for lists of works cited, most conveniently promulgated in Joseph Gibaldi and Walter S. Achtert, MLA Handbook for Writers of Research Papers (New York: MLA, 1988) section 4. Quotation marks around titles indicates a short story, poem, song, or other short work. Underlined titles indicate books, films, paintings. Film listings are by title, with other information following.

The indexes refer users of the List to numbers. The first number gives the section of the List, the second number the sequential number of the entry within that section. E.g., 4.002 refers you to section 4 of the List (Literary Criticism), the second entry in that section; 9.066 refers to the sixty-sixth entry in section 9, Background.

Abbreviations

1. We have abbreviated the names of states of the United States, using the standard abbreviations accepted by the United States Postal Service.

2. When we refer to the author of a work in the comments on that work, we will give the author's initials in roman type; when we refer to the work itself in a comment, we will abbreviate the work's title and underline it or place the abbreviation within quotation marks.

3. We use the standard abbreviations and reference words as found in The MLA Handbook ..., 3d edn. (1988; section 6). We give below additional abbreviations, our most usual abbreviations, and abbreviations and short titles that might cause confusion.

AI	Artificial Intelligence (sometimes called "MI," Machine Intelligence)
AIP	American International Pictures
Aboriginal S. F.	Aboriginal Science Fiction
Amazing	Amazing Stories, Amazing Science Fiction, Amazing Science Fiction Stories (vt)
ASFR	Australian Science Fiction Review
Astounding	Astounding Stories of Super-Science, Astounding Stories, Astounding Science Fiction (vt); after 1960, Analog ...
BBC	British Broadcasting Corporation
BGU Pop P	Bowling Green (State) University Popular Press
biblio.	bibliography, bibliographical
c.	century
(c)	Copyright
cf.	compare
coll(s).	collection(s), collected (in)
CW	Clockwork Worlds (see under Reference Works)
dir.	director, directed by
dist.	distributor, distributed by, distribution

ed(s).	editor(s)
edn.	edition
esp.	especially
f.	and following pages (for magazine articles spread over several pages)
F&SF	The Magazine of Fantasy and Science Fiction
FR	Fantasy Review
high-tech	high-technology
If	If, Worlds of Fantasy and Science Fiction; Worlds of IF (vt)
illus.	illustrated (by), illustration(s)
introd.	introduction(s), introduced by, introductory
JPC	Journal of Popular Culture
n.d.	no date
passim	throughout the work, here and there
prod.	producer(s), produced by, production company
publ.	published, publication
pseud.	pseudonym
q.v.	which see
rev.	review, reviewed, reviewed by, revised
rpt(s).	reprint(s), reprinted (in)
S. F.	science fiction
S. F. Ency.	The Science Fiction Encyclopedia (see under Reference Works)
SF	SF (an undefined term); "Speculative Fiction," including science fiction, utopias, and related subgenres; "Structural Fabulation" as defined by Robert Scholes in Structural Fabulation (1975)
SFS	Science-Fiction Studies
sic	"thus"--what seems a mistake is correct
SpFx	special effects
TMG	The Mechanical God (see under Reference Works)
trans.	translator(s), translation(s), translated by
vol(s).	volume(s)
vt	variant title, variant titles

Introduction

Technically, this is an analytical, selected list, with comments, of works useful for the study of the human/machine interface in SF, stressing English-language works produced 1895-1990. It will help users of our List if we review here the key elements of this technical title. (In the text below, numbers in pointed brackets < > refer to notes at the end of the Introduction.)

Analytical. This List is divided into the following sections, with works arranged alphabetically within each section (we place in **bold-face** the brief names of sections; we ordinarily use the brief names for cross-references in the List):

1. **Reference** Works
2. **Anthologies** and Collections
3. **Fiction**
4. **Literary Criticism**
5. Stage, Screen, and Television **Drama**
6. Stage, Screen, and Television **Drama Criticism**
7. Graphic and Plastic Arts
8. **Music**
9. **Background** Reading

Where we think it will aid users to do so, we have cross-listed items, referring you by name to the relevant section and again by name to the entry within that section (this differs from the indexes, which are quite literally "by the numbers").

Selected. Our List is extensive but by no means exhaustive. Users of the List desiring additional titles should consult the reference works listed in Section I. Users who wish to recommend additional titles should send them typed on post cards, with a full citation and annotation, to:

Richard D. Erlich
English Department
Miami University
Oxford, Ohio 45056-1633

List. Besides being a bibliography (a list of books and other writings), our List is also a filmography, videography, discography, and "graphography": it lists films, television shows, materials on records and audio tapes, and works in the graphic and plastic arts.

Comments. We provide comments with almost all citations; in particular, we often cite secondary works that summarize and discuss primary works. Occasionally we provide brief cautions about possible errors in works, or about content that we find problematic.

The length of comments does not indicate the importance of works annotated. Some highly important works can be dealt with quite quickly (e.g., by referring readers to detailed analyses); some obscure works need relatively long annotations precisely because they are obscure (often deservedly so) but potentially significant for some research projects.

Works Useful. Again, we provide only a selection of works. We have attempted to cover most of the classic SF works and a number of lesser-known works; we also include in the primary works sections of the List a number of works that are not SF but still useful for the study of SF. Under Background we cite materials that will familiarize users with some of the social, political, and philosophical issues alluded to in the primary works using the theme of this volume.

For the Study of the Human/Machine Interface. We privilege humans in defining "useful works" in dealing with "the human/machine interface." We also have thought a great deal about the insights of M. P. Esmonde's essay on ". . . The Icon of the Robot in Children's Science Fiction" (q.v. under Literary Criticism). E.g., we cite works where one can judge machines as good or bad. We cite works where our relationship with machines tells us something about the human--either as an eternal essence or a (historically) constructed category. How many prosthetics can we add to human beings before those human beings become cyborgs? Would it be well if more of us became cyborgs, helping to break down categories? (See D. Haraway entry under Background.) How many more additions of mechanical or electronic parts before the cyborg becomes (just) a machine? Conversely, can a machine make itself into a human being? If so, what does that say about being a human being? About being a machine? What does it do to humans to be inside machines? Can a metaphorical apparat (the apparatus of the State) become sufficiently "mechanical" that it becomes a fairly literal machine? And so forth. We favored works where machines were of thematic significance, and the themes had to do (mostly) with humanity: our philosophies, self-image, and politics--including politics of race, class, gender, and, in a couple of instances, age and generation.

In SF. In our Abbreviations, we differentiate between "SF" and "S. F." "S. F." is "science fiction," and SF is "science fiction" plus related genres such as eutopias, dystopias, some fantasy, and some horror"<1>. In our earlier volumes, The Mechanical God and Clockwork Worlds, we declined to define "science fiction" and noted the comparable inability of biologists to define "life," of attorneys to define "tort" let alone Justice, of mathematicians to define "point"--and we noted the generations of literary critics who have discussed comedy and tragedy without ever coming up with standard definitions of those terms. Here, we recommend a definition of "life" Erlich heard somewhere and liked: "The process by which entropy is reversed, locally and temporarily, in a volume both in contact with and set off from surrounding space-time"; but we still decline to define "science fiction." We will give, though, this much indication of the borders of SF: we placed inside that border and cited under Fiction, Herman Melville's 1855 story, "The Bell Tower"; we have relegated to Background Melville's technology-informed Moby Dick (1851) and "The Paradise of Bachelors and The Tartarus of Maids" (1855). We have listed under Fiction H. G. Wells's story "Lord of the Dynamos" but have labelled it a "Mainstream 'mechanical god' story," close to SF but more, in Samuel R. Delany's term, "mundane." Our classification decisions won't always be those users would make, but the cross-references and indexes should take care of most problems.

Stressing English-Language Works Produced 1895-1990. We do cover works in languages other than English, and, especially under Background, we cite a number of works before 1895; and we continued listing some items of interest through the summer of 1992. Still, the great majority of the works we cite are in English and from the latter part of what Thomas Carlyle called "the Mechanical age" ("Signs of the Times," listed under Background).
   We will not apologize for privileging English, but we do warn readers against generalizing from English-language works to the whole of human thought about machines, or even any large section of that thought. We believe a universe existed before human beings started to talk about it and that reality can exist quite well without human language, and we believe that one's language is only part of what shapes even our perceptions of reality. Still, the basic Whorfian hypothesis is undoubtedly correct: a language "tends to condition the ways in which a speaker of that language thinks. Hence, the structures of different languages lead the speakers of those languages to view the world in different ways" <2>. As Daniel W. Ingersoll, Jr. has said, "Machines Are Good to Think" (essay title cited under Literary Criticism); and different cultures will think about machines in different ways. And, we will bet, machines that think will think differently in different cultures.

By the 1890s, in England and Western Europe and America, it became difficult not to think, at least occasionally, about machines. And in 1895, H. G. Wells published in New York and London The Time Machine: a novel with a scientist who has a wondrous machine under his control, a novel with a mechanized underworld that can enclose that machine. Anyway, for a number of reasons, including our idiosyncratic ones, The Time Machine marks a good place to begin the serious collection of titles.

Where to end is more difficult, and our end point was primarily determined by practical, personal matters: the Clockworks project had gone on for over a decade and was starting to drive us a little weird; we were losing too much money on the project--etc. We can, though, defend the date on more intellectual grounds. Carlyle's "Mechanical Age" didn't last out the nineteenth century, when it gave way to The Lord of the Dynamos and the electro-mechanical age, which we will ask you to associate with an electric typewriter and a pinball machine. The electro-mechanical age lasted until the middle of the twentieth century, and we'll say that When It Changed was that year of changes, 1968. Or thereabouts; in 1969, M. E. Hoff developed the microprocessor, and in 1971 Intel Corp. of Santa Clara, California, manufactured the first commercial microcomputers <3>. The electric typewriter gave way to the computer; the pinball machine had to share space with electronic games.

It is pretentious to talk of The Tao of Pinball, but it's not absurd: in pinball, the player is still part of the natural world and must deal with--use--a basic force of that world: gravity. To enter imaginatively into an electronic game is to leave the natural world and enter into a world where the rules are all produced by human programming. Pinball and the successors to PacMan share the arcades, but the future is with the electronic games, moving players of many games--some quite serious--into "virtual realities."

K. G. P. Hulten and the Museum of Modern Art gave us The Machine as Seen at the End of the Mechanical Age in 1968 (see under Graphics), and we believe they got the date right. Something happened at the end of the 1960s--or, rather, many things happened--and something new began. In technological terms, the electro-mechanical age started to give way to the electronic. In political terms, we moved from a time of militant activism to a period of reaction and, simultaneously, a renewed activism with a renewed women's movement. In more general terms, we began to move, jerkily, from the Modern into the postModern. By the early 1990s, students of SF had heard cyberpunk proclaimed the apotheosis of the postmodern (now a common adjective), and soon thereafter declared dead <4>. We may be moving into a feminist era beyond the postmodern.

Or not. In any event--one of our last entries for the List was for Batman Returns, a film which amused and impressed us with its cyberpunk attack penguins. If the superimposition of the mechanical upon the human was central for the human/machine interface at the beginning of the modern(ist) era the superimposition of the cybernetic upon the Sphenisciformes marks the end of something <5>. The early 1990s is a good time to stop collecting titles.

Four final notes:

(1) SF works often appear under variant titles or pseudonymously and/or in variant editions or translations. We have tried to alert the users of this List to the problems we know of, but we can guarantee only that there are undoubtedly additional problems we know not of.

(2) At a point such as this, it is customary for bibliographers to state something like "We have attempted to examine all of the works we cite"; we haven't. We have looked at a large number of the 2000-plus works listed or mentioned, but we have trusted our colleagues in SF studies sufficiently to depend upon them frequently <6>. If neither perfect nor perfectionist, though, we have striven to be honest and careful. Especially where we have not physically examined the works, we have tried to cross-check references and indicate at least one source of the citation. We have also built into the List sufficient redundancy that errors by us or our sources should not be too serious: users should have enough information to find almost all the works. Whether we have examined the works or not, we have frequently recommended in our annotations useful secondary sources and commentaries. Students of SF bibliography are referred to the Reference Works cited below (Section I).

(3) The MLA Style Manual (1985) says that citations to films usually include "the title, underlined," plus "the distributor, and the year" (section 4.8.6); and current usage, as we have observed it, encourages citing also the country of production. These requirements seem straightforward; they are not. Our citations to films, then, will give title (underlined), director (or major director), main country or countries of production, distributor and/or production company, and date of completion (or copyright) and/or of release--plus other information and warnings we think will be useful to users of the List. Students of SF filmography should consult Walt Lee's three-volume compilation, Reference Guide to Fantastic Films: Science Fiction, Fantasy, and Horror, and the other filmographic sources listed under Reference.

(4) The Lists for The Mechanical God and Clockwork Worlds had neither sections on works in the Graphic and Plastic Arts nor indexes. Our first acknowledgments are to our colleagues Edward K. Montgomery and Catherine Mills Royer, who compiled the bulk of our section on Graphics, and to D. Scott DeLoach, who generated the indexes.

Acknowledgments

In compiling our List, we depended a good deal on the works cited in Section I, Reference Works; we refer back to these works in the main body of our List. We also received help from the contributors to the volumes we edited for Greenwood Press, The Mechanical God (1982) and Clockwork Worlds (1983), especially the late Margaret P. Esmonde for works on children's literature and Gary K. Wolfe, for works involving movement across barriers.

Other people who have helped us include Daniel Barnhizer: assistant to Erlich for some three years of the work on this volume; John Cooper: initial work on the filmography for The Mechanical God; Chad Dresbach: initial work on the Graphics section for Clockworks and general assistant for two years; Carmiele Foster and Robert Kettler: computer assistants; Daniel J. Giancola: editorial assistant for Clockwork Worlds; Peter C. Hall: aid on several entries and advice on computer problems; William H. Hardesty, III,: editing help with our Introduction; Susan Martin: the major proofreader for Clockworks; Edward Montgomery: as mentioned, work directly on and supervising work on Graphics; Vincent Moore: proofreading and library research (especially on music) during the last stage of preparing Clockworks; Trudi Nixon: senior secretary in the Department of English at Miami University, Oxford, who gave assistance throughout the evolution of Clockworks; Michelle Rhodus: assistant to Dunn during the final work on Clockworks; Jerome Rosenberg: computer advice and assistance, including translating documents from Wang to Mac and Mac to Wang; Catherine Mills Royer: research for most of the Graphics section; Albert J. Rudnickas: editorial assistant for Clockwork Worlds; Ruth Sanders: instructor for German 380, "Machine Intelligence from a Humanist Perspective," Miami University at Oxford, Ohio, 1986--our source for a number of readings cited under Background; Erica Scott: library research during the last stage of preparing Clockworks; Carol D. Stevens: editing help with our Introduction and help compiling the key words found in the list; Jeffrey R. Wilson: initial work on discography for The Mechanical God.

And a special note of thanks to Marshall Tymn, whose initial confidence in us resulted in The Mechanical God, Clockwork Worlds, and, ultimately, this volume.

Notes

1. "Utopia" is a New Latin coinage by Sir Thomas More (1526) from the Greek ou 'not, no' plus topos 'place. But there is a pun: Utopia, No Place, is also eutopia, a—or the—Good Place. Inversely, "dystopia" means a Bad Place.
2. "Whorfian Hypothesis" (also called "the Sapir-Whorf hypothesis" after Edward Sapir and Benjamin Lee Whorf), Encyclopaedia Britannica, 1974, Micropaedia. We give the hypothesis in its "weak" formulation; we reject recent, very strong formulations where such hypotheses are presented as if it were a fact that human language shapes or creates reality (as language does in some forms of magic or in Robert A. Heinlein's Stranger in a Strange Land [1961]--Erlich would add precisely as in magic or Heinlein's novel).
3. The Science in Science Fiction, cited under Background, 120; ch. 7.
4. Erlich has been on two panels where the panelists independently announced the death of cyberpunk, most impressively at a panel that included Brooks Landon, at the 19th Annual Meeting of the Popular Culture Association, 5-8 April 1989, in St. Louis, MO (the panel met at 11 a.m. on 7 April).
5. See under Background the entry for H. Bergson.
6. The counting gets complicated. The number of relevant items is the sum of the numbered items, minus numbered cross-references and other repetitions, plus references we sneak into annotations, minus the number of references readers find not relevant.

Reference Works

1.001 Altman, Mark A. "Episode Guide [to <u>Star Trek: The Next Generation</u>]." <u>Cinefantastique</u> 21.2 (Sept. 1990): see 26-51. "Episode Guide [to <u>Star Trek: The Next Generation</u>]." <u>Cinefantastique</u> 22.2 (Oct. 1991): see 19-51. "Episode Guide [to <u>Star Trek: The Next Generation</u>]." <u>Cinefantastique</u> 22.2/3 (Oct. 1992): see 35 f.

MAA gives basic information on <u>STNG</u> episodes, covering initially "Encounter at Farpoint" through "The Best of Both Worlds," the <u>STNG</u> canon as of the summer of 1990, and then "The Best of Both Worlds: Part Two" through "Redemption," for the 73 episodes through the show's fourth year. The third installment covers the 26 episodes from 23 Sept. 1991 to 15 June 1992.

1.002 <u>Anatomy of Wonder: A Critical Guide to Science Fiction</u>. 3rd edn. Neil Barron, ed. New York: Bowker, 1987.

Referred to in our citations as "<u>Anatomy</u> 1987," followed by chapter-entry numbers (in the format 2-17, for chapter 2, #17, <u>not</u> pp. 2-17).

1.003 Baxter, John, compiler. "Selected Filmography," in his <u>Science Fiction in the Cinema</u>. Peter Cowie, ed. 1970. New York: Paperback Library, 1970.

1.004 <u>Books in Print</u>. New York: Bowker, 1972-92. Multivolume.

We have consulted <u>BP</u> and its supplements and Paperback variations for misc. biblio. data for books we didn't have physically before us when writing citations.

1.005 Brians, Paul. "Resources for the Study of Nuclear War in Fiction." <u>SFS</u> #39, 13.2 (July 1986): 193-97.

Biblio. essay for the special Nuclear War and Science Fiction issue of <u>SFS</u>. We list only a sample of the large number of works on "the Doomsday Machine"; see PB's essay for a handling of the basic works by an expert in nuclear war studies, and for citations to more complete reference works (including the annotated biblio. in PB's own <u>Nuclear Holocausts . . .</u> [1987]). See below, this section, Vladimir Gakov and PB, "Nuclear War Themes in Soviet Science Fiction . . . ."

1.006   Brosnan, John. Future Tense: The Cinema of Science Fiction. New York: St. Martin's, 1978.

History of SF films from 1900 to 1978, with criticism. Includes an Appendix, "SF on Television," giving a year-by-year chronology of SF shows on TV.

1.007   Clockwork Worlds: Mechanized Environments in SF. Richard D. Erlich and Thomas P. Dunn, eds. Westport, CT: Greenwood, 1983.

Contains a preface by the eds., guest introduction by Arthur O. Lewis, fifteen essays by various contributors, a "List of Works Useful for the Study of Mechanized Environments in SF," an index, and brief information on the contributors.

1.008   Computers in Science Fiction. Eugene La Faille, compiler. Voice of Youth Advocates series 8.2 (June 1985): 103-6.

An annotated bibliography of some 136 works suitable for teenagers.

1.009   Contento, William. Index to Science Fiction Anthologies and Collections. Boston: G. K. Hall, 1978.

Our primary source for information on magazines of initial publication, colls., and rpts. for a number of short stories and novellas; consult for places to find short stories and novellas, beyond the locations we cite.

1.010   Cox, David M., and Gary L. Libby, compilers. "A Bibliography of Isaac Asimov's Major Science Fiction Works through 1976." In Isaac Asimov. Joseph D. Olander and Martin Harry Greenberg, eds. New York: Taplinger, 1977: 217-33.

Based in part on Marjorie Miller's Isaac Asimov: A Checklist of Works Published in the United States (Kent, OH: Kent State UP, 1972). See Cox and Libby for relatively early works we have been unable to include in our List.

1.011   Currey, L. W. Science Fiction and Fantasy Authors: A Bibliography of First Printings of Their Fiction and Selected Nonfiction. Boston: G. K. Hall, 1979.

Our primary source for information on first printings of novels.

1.012   Gakov, Vladimir, and Paul Brians. "Nuclear-War Themes in Soviet Science Fiction: An Annotated Bibliography." SFS #47, 16.1 (March 1989): 67-84.

Also includes an essay and filmographic information, including news of two film versions of Ray Bradbury's "There Will Come Soft Rains" (68). See above, citation to PB's biblio. of nuclear-war stories in SFS #39.

1.013   Gerrold, David, compiler. "First Season Episodes," "Second Season Episodes," "Third Season Episodes." The World of Star Trek. New York: Ballantine, 1973.

A list of Star Trek episodes for the show's entire three-season run. We have consulted DG's list for our Star Trek citations.

1.014   Halliwell's Film Guide to Over 10,000 Films. 2nd edn. 1977 and subsequent years. New York: Scribner's, 1983.

Consulted for filmographic references, alternative titles ("vts" in our usage), and for citations to many minor "mainstream" films. Extensive secondary apparatus, and other material.

1.015   Hughes, David Y. "Criticism in English of H. G. Wells's Science Fiction: A Select Annotated Bibliography." SFS #19, 6.3 (Nov. 1979): 309-19.

   Divided into "Bibliographies," "Collections of Critical Essays," "Overviews (after 1930) of the SF/Utopian Opus," and "Particular Studies of One Work or a Group of Works." Eighty-five entries in all.

1.016   Javna, John. The Best of Science Fiction TV. New York: Harmony Books, 1987.

1.017   Johnson, William, ed. Focus on The Science Fiction Film. Englewood Cliffs, NJ: Prentice-Hall, 1972.

   References in the List to Johnson refer to the selected filmography in this work.

1.018   Kagan, Norman, compiler. "Kubrick Filmography." In The Cinema of Stanley Kubrick. Norman Kagan, ed. 1972. New York: Grove, 1975.

   A complete filmography for Kubrick's work through A Clockwork Orange. CSK also includes plot summaries and stills for Dr. Strangelove, 2001, and Clockwork Orange (as well as for Kubrick's other films from 1953 to 1971).

1.019   Kessler, Carol Farley. "Bibliography of Utopian Fiction by United States Women 1836-1988." Utopian Studies 1.1 (1990): [1]-58.

   Eutopias, dystopias and related works, arranged by year; our source for a small number of citations below. (See under Background, entry for C. Cockburn, Machinery of Dominance.)

1.020   Klinkowitz, Jerome, compiler. "The Vonnegut Bibliography." In Vonnegut in America: An Introduction to the Life and Works of Kurt Vonnegut. JK and David L. Lawler, eds. New York: Delacorte / Lawrence, 1977. New York: Delta-Dell , 1977, pt. 3.

1.021   Lee, Walt, compiler. Reference Guide to Fantastic Films: Science Fiction, Fantasy, & Horror, 3 vols. Los Angeles: Chelsea-Lee Books, 1972-74.

1.022   Leonard Maltin's TV Movies: 1985-86. Leonard Maltin, ed. New York: Signet-NAL, 1984. Leonard Maltin's TV Movies and Video Guide. 1989 Edition. Leonard Maltin, ed. New York: Signet-NAL, 1989. Video Consultant: Casey St. Charnez.

   Consulted for recent films and for information on films not covered by Lee or Willis (q.v. this section).

1.023   Mast, Gerald. "Motion Pictures, History of." Encyclopaedia Britannica: Macropaedia. 1974: 12.511-39.

   Our source for information on films it would have been embarrassing for us to miss.

1.024   The Mechanical God: Machines in Science Fiction. Thomas P. Dunn and Richard D. Erlich, eds. Westport, CT: Greenwood, 1982.

   Contains a preface by the eds., guest introduction by Brian W. Aldiss, eighteen essays by various contributors, a "List of Works Useful for the Study of Machines in Science Fiction," an index, and brief information on the contributors.

1.025   Movies on TV: 1984-1985, Steven H. Scheuer, ed. Toronto: Bantam, 1983 (sic).

   Consulted primarily for dates of recent films.

1.026   Mullen, R. D. "Books, Stories, Essays [by Philip K. Dick]." SFS #5, 2.1 (March 1975): 5-8. One of two special Dick issues of SFS.

RDM gives a brief list of standard S. F. reference works and a chronologically arranged Dick biblio. from 1955 to 1974. Based on the standard reference tools and "a list compiled by Robert Greenberg . . . for distribution at Westercon 1974."

1.027   Naha, Ed. The Science Fictionary: An A-Z Guide to the World of SF Authors, Films, & TV Shows. New York: Seaview Books, 1980.

An indispensable resource we have relied on for a number of minor films and TV shows. References in the List to "Naha, Science Fictionary" are to this work.

1.028   The New Film Index: A Bibliography of Magazine Articles in English, 1930-1979. Richard Dyer MacCann and Edward S. Perry, compilers. New York: Dutton, 1975.

An annotated, analytical biblio. covering a wide range of topics important for film studies, and the source of several of our citations for film criticism.

1.029   Orth, Michael. "The Computer in Recent Utopias . . . ": Cited under Literary Criticism. References in the List to "Orth" are to this conference paper.

1.030   Parish, James Robert and Michael R. Pitts. The Great Science Fiction Pictures. Metuchen, NJ: Scarecrow, 1977.

Consulted for annotations for films we have not seen.

1.031   Pohl, Frederik, and Frederik Pohl IV. Science Fiction: Studies in Film. New York: Ace, 1981.

The filmographic information given passim in this work is used for a number of our citations to SF films of the late 1970s.

1.032   Sargent, Lyman Tower. British and American Utopian Literature, 1516-1975. Boston: G. K. Hall, 1979. British and American Utopian Literature, 1516-1985: An Annotated, Chronological Bibliography. New York: Garland, 1988.

Both versions include briefly annotated chronological lists of eutopian and dystopian works for the years indicated and full author and title indexes to the chronological lists; the 1979 version also includes a list of books, articles, and unpublished material dealing with utopian studies. References below to "Sargent" are to the 1979 biblio.; references to "Sargent (1988)" are to the 1988 version.

1.033   Science Fiction & Fantasy Book Review Annual: 1988. Science Fiction & Fantasy Book Review Annual: 1989. Robert A. Collins and Robert Latham, eds. Westport, CT: Meckler, 1989, 1990. Science Fiction & Fantasy Book Review Annual: 1990. Robert A. Collins and Robert Latham, eds. Westport, CT: Greenwood, 1991.

Our source for a number of citations for works from 1987-1989, generally under Fiction. Referred to in the List as SF&FBR Annual 1988, SF&FBR Annual 1989, SF&FBR Annual 1990.

1.034   The Science Fiction Encyclopedia. Peter Nicholls, general ed. Garden City, NY: Doubleday, 1979.

Esp. useful for film, and S. F. themes, motifs, and sub genres. Includes entries on dystopias, generation starships, machines, technology, and utopias. References in the List to S. F. Ency. are to this work.

1.035   Stableford, Brian. <u>Scientific Romance in Britain 1890-1950</u>. New York: St. Martin's, [1985].

References in the List to "B. Stableford, <u>Romance</u>" are to this work.

1.036   <u>Star Trek</u>: See in this section of the List the entries for D. Gerrold, and S. E. Whitfield and G. Roddenberry.

1.037   <u>Star Trek: An Annotated Guide to Resources on the Development, the Phenomenon, the People, the Television Series, the Films, the Novels and the Recordings</u>. Susan R. Gibberman, compiler. Jefferson, NC: McFarland, 1991.

Published too late for use with the List, but praised as a very complete listing of all easily found works in English on the various manifestations of <u>Star Trek</u>. Rev. Agatha Taormina, <u>SFRA Newsletter</u> #196 (April 1992): 26-27, our source for this entry.

1.038   <u>Star Trek: The Next Generation</u>: See above, this section, M. A. Altman.

1.039   <u>Survey of Science Fiction Literature</u>. 5 vols. Frank N. Magill, ed. Englewood Cliffs, NJ: Salem Press, 1979.

Contains plot summaries, analyses, and brief critiques of a wide variety of works ranging in quality and relevance from E. M. Forster's "Machine Stops" to D. F. Jones's <u>Colossus</u>, including I. Asimov's <u>Caves of Steel</u> and <u>Naked Sun</u>, R. Bradbury's stories coll. in <u>Illustrated Man</u> and <u>Martian Chronicles</u>, A. C. Clarke's <u>City and the Stars</u> and <u>2001</u>, S. R. Delany's <u>Nova</u>, R. A. Heinlein's <u>The Moon Is a Harsh Mistress</u> and <u>Starship Troopers</u>, S. Lem's <u>Invincible</u> and <u>Cyberiad</u>, F. Pohl's <u>Gateway</u> and <u>Man Plus</u>, F. Saberhagen's berserker stories, K. Vonnegut's <u>Player Piano</u>, <u>Sirens of Titan</u>, and <u>Slaughterhouse-Five</u>, H. G. Wells's eutopian and dystopian fiction, B. Wolfe's <u>Limbo</u>, Jack Williamson's Humanoids stories, and other works useful for the study of the human/machine interface in SF.

1.040   Tymn, Marshall B., compiler. "Philip K. Dick: A Bibliography." In <u>Philip K. Dick</u>. Martin Harry Greenberg and Joseph D. Olander, eds. New York: Taplinger, 1983.

Biblio. of Dick's books and pamphlets, short fiction, articles and essays, and general writings. Also lists selected criticism of Dick's work.

1.041   ---, compiler. "Ray Bradbury: A Bibliography." In <u>Ray Bradbury</u>. Martin Harry Greenberg and Joseph D. Olander, eds. New York: Taplinger, 1980.

Biblio. of Bradbury's books and pamphlets, short fiction, articles and essays, and general writings. Also lists selected criticism of Bradbury's work.

1.042   Warrick, Patricia S. <u>The Cybernetic Imagination in Science Fiction</u>: Full citation below, under Literary Criticism. References in the List to "Warrick" are to the summaries and discussions in this work.

1.043   Willis, Donald C. <u>Horror and Science Fiction Films II</u> and <u>Horror and Science Fiction Films III</u>. Metuchen, NJ: Scarecrow, 1982, 1984.

Consulted for films later than the period covered by Walt Lee's <u>Reference Guide</u>; DCW's vol. II: 1971-81, vol. III: 1982-83 (plus updatings and supplements to earlier volumes).

1.044   Wolfe, Gary K. <u>The Known and the Unknown</u>: Full citation below, under Literary Criticism. References in the List to "Wolfe" are to the summaries and discussions in this work.

1.045   Whitfield, Stephen E., and Gene Roddenberry, compilers. "Star Trek Shows." In Whitfield and Roddenberry, The Making of Star Trek. New York: Ballantine, 1968.

A list of Star Trek episodes, with dates of first transmissions and names for guest stars for Star Trek's first two seasons (through 29 March 1968). We have consulted this work for our Star Trek listings below.

1.046   "The Year's Scholarship in Science Fiction and Fantasy," "The Year's Scholarship in Science Fiction, Fantasy, and Horror Literature," and "The Year's Scholarship in Fantastic Literature."   Marshall B. Tymn, ed., 1983-1987, in the journal Extrapolation.

For 1983, 26.2 (Summer 1985); for 1984, 26.4 (Winter 1985); for 1985, 27.2 (Summer 1986); for 1986, 28.3 (Fall 1987); for 1987, 29.3 (Fall 1988). "The Year's Scholarship in Science Fiction and Fantasy," compiled 1976-1979 by Roger C. Schlobin and Marshall B. Tymn in Extrapolation. For 1976, 20.1 (Spring 1979); for 1977, 20.3 (Fall 1979); for 1978, 21.1 (Spring 1980); for 1979, 22.1 (Spring 1981). The Year's Scholarship in Science Fiction, Fantasy, and Horror Literature: 1980, The Year's Scholarship in Science Fiction, Fantasy, and Horror Literature: 1981. Marshall B. Tymn, ed. Kent, OH: Kent State UP, n.d. For earlier years, we have consulted Tymn and Schlobin, The Year's Scholarship in Science Fiction and Fantasy: 1972-1975 (Kent, OH: Kent State UP, 1979), and Thomas Clareson, Science Fiction Criticism: An Annotated Checklist (Kent, OH: Kent State UP, 1972). Year's Scholarship is our blanket reference term for this series, keyed in the List below by appropriate date.

Anthologies and Collections

2.001 The 1989 Annual World's Best SF. Donald A. Wollheim, ed., with Arthur W. Saha. New York: DAW, 1989.

> Includes J. L. Chalker's "Adrift Among the Ghosts," T. Lee's "A Madonna of the Machine," and J. Shirley's "Shaman"—q.v. under Fiction.

2.002 Aldiss, Brian. The Book of Brian Aldiss (vt The Comic Inferno [UK, 1973]). New York: DAW, [1972].

> Includes "Comic Inferno," "All the World's Tears," "Amen and Out," "The Soft Predicament" (all cited under Fiction).

2.003 As Tomorrow Becomes Today. Charles Wm. Sullivan III, ed. Englewood Cliffs, NJ: Prentice-Hall, 1974.

> Includes H. Ellison's "A Boy and His Dog" and "Repent, Harlequin . . . ." Section on robots includes I. Asimov's "Runaround," R. Goulart's "Calling Dr. Clockwork," and D. Knight's "Masks" (q.v. under Fiction).

2.004 Asimov, Isaac. The Bicentennial Man and Other Stories. Garden City, NY: Doubleday, 1976. Greenwich, CT: Fawcett, 1976. Cox and Libby cite other rpts.

> Relevant stories: "Feminine Intuition," "That Thou Art Mindful of Him!" "The Life and Times of Multivac," "The Bicentennial Man," "The Tercentenary Incident."

2.005 ---. Robot Visions. Illus. Ralph McQuarrie. New York: ROC, 1990, 1991.

> Retrospective of IA's robot stories and essays on robotics and AI. New: time-travelling robot story called "Robot Vision," and an introd. essay. See also for a robot surgeon in "Too Bad!" (1989). Rev. Mary Lou West, SFRA Review #195 (March 1992): 54-56, our source for this entry.

2.006 ---. The Winds of Change. Garden City, NY: Doubleday, [1983]. [S. F.] Book Club Edition.

> Coll. of IA's stories including "A Perfect Fit," "It Is Coming," and "Found!" (q.v. under Fiction).

2.007   The Best of John W. Campbell. Lester del Rey, ed. New York: Ballantine, 1976. Garden City, NY: Doubleday, n.d. [S. F.] Book Club Edition.

2.008   The Best of Philip K. Dick. John Brunner, ed. New York: Ballantine, 1977.

Includes Dick's "Second Variety," "Imposter," "Service Call," "Autofac," "Human Is," "If There Were No Benny Cemoli," "The Electric Ant," and other stories useful for an introduction to P. K. Dick. See Dick entries under Fiction.

2.009   The Bicentennial Man: Cited above, under Isaac Asimov.

2.010   Body Armor: 2000. Joe Haldeman, ed., with Charles Waugh and Martin Harry Greenberg. New York: Ace, 1986.

Anthology of eleven future-war stories, featuring high-tech. battle gear. Cf. powered armor in R. A. Heinlein's Starship Troopers and J. Haldeman's Forever War. See Supertanks below, this section. Rev. Barry H. Reynolds, FR #91, 9.5 (May 1986): 17, our source for this entry.

2.011   Cities of Wonder. Damon Knight, ed. Garden City, New York: Doubleday, 1966.

Includes "Dumb Waiter" by W. M. Miller, Jr., "Jesting Pilot" by H. Kuttner, "Okie" by J. Blish, "The Luckiest Man in Denv" by C. M. Kornbluth, "By the Waters of Babylon" by S. V. Benét, and "Forgetfulness" by J. W. Campbell, Jr., writing as Don A. Stuart (see citations under Fiction).

2.012   Collected Stories of Philip K. Dick. 5 vols. Beverly Hills, CA: Underwood-Miller, 1987.

2.013   The Coming of the Robots. Sam Moskowitz, ed. New York: Collier, 1963. (Released in Canada by Collier-Macmillan of Toronto.)

Contents: Eando Binder (pseud.), "I, Robot"; L. del Rey, "Helen O'Loy"; John Wyndham (pseud.), "The Lost Machine"; I. Asimov, "Runaround"; H. Vincent, "Rex"—all listed below, under Fiction; Clifford D. Simak, "Earth for Inspiration"; Peter Philips, "Lost Memory"; F. Orlin Tremaine, "True Confession"; Raymond Z. Gallun, "Derelict"; Michael Fisher, "Misfit."

2.014   Computer Crimes and Capers. Isaac Asimov, Martin H. Greenberg, and Charles G. Waugh, eds. Chicago: Academy Chicago, 1983.

Stories of fictional computer crimes. Rev. W. D. Stevens, FR #69 (July 1984): 44, our source for this entry.

2.015   Digital Dreams. David Barrett, ed. London: New English Library, 1990.

Apparently the first "original anthology of SF, fantasy and horror stories about computers . . . assembled in Britain." One title of interest: "The Machine It Was That Cried," by John Grant. Rev. Chris Morgan, SFRA Review #194 (Jan./Feb. 1992): 62, upon whom we depend for this citation.

2.016   Ellison, Harlan. The Beast that Shouted Love at the Heart of the World. New York: Avon, 1969, 1970 (Currey notes 1970 issue as the authorized text). New York: NAL, 1974. London: Millington, 1976.

Coll. includes "A Boy and His Dog," "Asleep: With Still Hands," and "Worlds to Kill" (all listed under Fiction).

2.017   Famous Science Fiction Stories. Raymond J. Healy and J. Francis McComas, eds. New York: Random (The Modern Library), 1946, 1957.

2.018   Final Stage: The Ultimate Science Fiction Anthology. Edward L. Ferman and Barry N. Malzberg, eds. New York: Charterhouse, 1974 (cut and rewritten by publisher, according to Currey). Harmondsworth: Penguin, 1975. ("Prints the original versions of the authors' stories," according to Currey.)

See for H. Ellison's "Catman" and Malzberg's "All-Purpose Transmogrifier." I. Asimov's "That Thou Art Mindful of Him!" is the "ultimate" robot story (coll. Asimov's The Bicentennial Man and Other Stories, q.v. above).

2.019   Full Spectrum. Lou Aronica and Shawna McCarthy, eds. New York: Spectra-Bantam, 1988.

Anthology of 25 original stories including K. J. Anderson and and D. Beason's "Reflections in a Magnetic Mirror," J. Massa's "Prayerware," C. Oberndorf's "Mannequins," and W. Simon's "Ghost Ship" (all listed under Fiction).

2.020   The Golden Age of Science Fiction (vt). Groff Conklin, ed. New York: Crown (Bonanza), 1946 as The Best of Science Fiction. Rev. edn. 1963, 1980.

2.021   Human-Machines: An Anthology of Stories About Cyborgs. Thomas N. Scortia and George Zebrowski, eds. New York: Vintage-Random, 1975.

Includes TNS's "Sea Change" and GZ's Introduction, "'Unholy Marriage': The Cyborg in Science Fiction," a list of recommended readings, and, among other stories, Guy Enroe's "Men of Iron" (1940, F&SF Fall 1949), D. Knight's "Masks," C. L. Moore's "No Woman Born," Henry Kuttner's "Camouflage" (Astounding Sept. 1945); see Fiction for the stories by Knight and Moore.

2.022   Inside Information: Computers in Action. Abbe Mowshowitz, ed. Reading, MA: Addison-Wesley, 1977.

Stories and excerpts from longer works on "Computers in Fiction," stressing science education, including excerpts from J. Barth's Giles Goat-Boy (q.v. under Fiction) and Elmer Rice's play The Adding Machine (1923; see title under Drama). Includes "a 34-page annotated bibliography of novels, stories, play [sic], poems, anthologies and science fiction criticism" related to computers—and a section named "Clockwork Society." Praised by Merritt Abrash in a rev., SF&FBR #16 (July-Aug. 1983): 40-41, our source for this citation, and whom we quote.

2.023   Lem, Stanislaw. More Tales of Pirx the Pilot (trans. of Opowiesci o pilocie Pirxie). Louis Iribarne (with the assistance of Magdalena Majcherczyk) and Michael Kandel, trans. San Diego: Harcourt, 1983. "A Helen and Kurt Wolff Book"; "A Harvest/HBJ book."

Includes "The Hunt," trans. Kandel (see Lem entry below, under Fiction); "The Accident," trans. Iribarne; and "Pirx's Tale," "The Inquest," and "Ananke," trans. Iribarne, assisted by Majcherczyk.

2.024   ---. Mortal Engines. Michael Kandel, trans. New York: Seabury, 1977.

Collection of some of Lem's cybernetic fiction, translated from the Polish. See Warrick 193-98 and Michael Kandel's article listed below under Literary Criticism.

2.025   Machines That Think. Isaac Asimov, Patricia S. Warrick, and Martin H. Greenberg, eds. New York: Holt, 1983. Harmondsworth: Penguin, 1985.

Anthology of 29 rpt. stories, with introd., including J. Wyndham's "The Lost Machine," H. Vincent's "Rex," P. Anderson's "Sam Hall," R. Silverberg's "The Macauley Circuit," J. F. Bone's "Triggerman," H. Harrison's "War With the Robots"—all cited under Fiction. Rev. Ellen M. Pedersen, Foundation #38 (92-96); W.D. Stevens, FR #67 (May 1984): 26.

2.026   Machines That Kill: Listed below, under F. Saberhagen.

2.027   MR47/48: Mississippi Review 16.2 & 3 (1988) = #47 and #48, the cyberpunk special
        issue of MR, Larry McCaffery, guest ed. Full citation below, under McCaffery
        under Literary Criticism. Citations in the List to MR47/48 followed by a colon
        and numbers refer to pages in this MR special issue.

2.028   Men and Machines: Ten Years of Science Fiction. Robert Silverberg, ed. New York:
        Meredith, 1968.

        Anthology of useful stories, including L. del Rey's "Instinct."

2.029   The Mind's I: Fantasies and Reflections on Self and Soul. Douglas R. Hofstadter and
        Daniel C. Dennett, composers and arrangers. New York: Basic, 1981. New York:
        Bantam, 1982.

        Anthology of stories, essays, etc. with extensive introd. comments and following
        "Reflections" by the "composers"—most quite relevant for questions of human
        consciousness, AI, the mind/body problem, and free will vs. determinism.
        Contents cited in the List: FICTION: T. Miedaner, "The Soul of the Mark III
        Beast" (excerpt); J. Leiber, "Beyond Rejection" (excerpt); R. Rucker, "Software"
        (excerpt); S. Lem, "The Seventh Sally" and "Non Serviam" (complete short
        stories); BACKGROUND: A. M. Turing, "Computing Machinery and
        Intelligence"; R. Dawkins, "Selfish Genes and Selfish Memes" (excerpt); D. W.
        Sanford, "Where Was I?" Also includes a biblio. essay on the topics covered. See
        under Background, the entry for D. R. Hofstadter.

2.030   Mirrorshades: The Cyberpunk Anthology. Bruce Sterling, ed. New York: Arbor,
        1986. New York: Ace, 1988.

        See under Fiction, P. Cadigan's "Rock On" and T. Maddox's "Snake Eyes"; under
        Literary Criticism, B. Sterling's Preface to Mirrorshades—and that's all the
        contents of the cyberpunk anthology we found relevant (which may be
        significant).

2.031   Of Men and Machines. Arthur O. Lewis, Jr., ed. New York: Dutton, 1963.

        Includes such works of interest as R. U. R. (cited under Drama), I. Asimov's
        "Robbie" and E. M. Forster's "Machine Stops" (listed under Fiction), and Lewis
        Mumford's "The Monastery and the Clock."

2.032   Random Access Messages of the Computer Age. Thomas F. Monteleone, ed.
        Hasbrouck Heights, NJ: Hayden, 1984.

        Anthology exploring the computer in its "evil device" or "Satan/Baal/Cthulu"
        persona. Includes H. Ellison's "I Have No Mouth . . .," Arthur C. Clarke's "The
        Nine Billion Names of God" (Star Science Fiction [1953]), and I. Asimov's "The
        Last Question" (q.v. under Fiction). Rev. Robert J. Ewald, FR #78 (April 1985):
        22, our source for this entry, and whom we quote.

2.033   Roberts, Keith. Machines and Men. London: Hutchinson, [1973].

        Short story coll. including KR's "Synth," q.v. under fiction.

2.034   Robots, Androids, and Mechanical Oddities: The Science Fiction of Philip K. Dick.
        Patricia S. Warrick and Martin H. Greenberg, eds. Carbondale: Southern Illinois
        UP, 1984.

        Coll. described by eds. as Dick's "stories about mechanical constructs" (vii).
        Contains in addition to a brief introd. and headnote with each story, "The Little
        Movement," "The Defenders," "The Preserving Machine," "Second Variety,"
        "Imposter," "Sales Pitch," "The Last of the Masters," "Service Call," "Autofac," "To
        Serve the Master," "War Game," "A Game of Unchance," "The Electric Ant," "The
        Exit Door Leads In," and "Frozen Journey." See Dick entries under Fiction.

2.035 Saberhagen, Fred, and Martin Harry Greenberg, eds. Machines That Kill. New York: Ace, 1984.

Stories from the '50s, '60s, and '70s about death machines and the consciousnesses that guide them. Includes P. K. Dick's "The Second Variety" (q.v. under Fiction) and Roger Zelazny's "Auto-Da-Fe" (1967). Rev. Michael R. Collings, FR #76 (Feb. 1985): 25, our source for this entry.

2.036 Science Fiction: A Historical Anthology. Eric Rabkin, ed. New York: Oxford UP, 1983.

Includes Abraham Merritt, "The Last Poet and the Robots"; Jack London, "A Curious Fragment"; E. T. A. Hoffmann, "The Sand-Man"; and Ray Bradbury, "The City."

2.037 Science Fiction by Gaslight: A History and Anthology of Science Fiction in the Popular Magazines, 1891-1911. Sam Moskowitz, ed. and introd. Westport, CT: Hyperion, 1968.

The introd. is long and useful; includes sections on "Marvelous Inventions," "Future War," and significant stories by E. P. Butler, J. B. Harris-Burland, J. K. Jerome, H. P. Spofford, and H. G. Wells—q.v. under Fiction.

2.038 The Science Fiction Hall of Fame. Vol. I. Robert Silverberg, ed. New York: Avon, 1970.

Includes J. W. Campbell's "Twilight," L. del Rey's "Helen O'Loy," C. Smith's "Scanners Live in Vain," and A. Bester's "Fondly Fahrenheit"—q.v. under Fiction.

2.039 Science Fiction Thinking Machines: Robots, Androids, Computers. Groff Conklin, ed. New York: Vanguard, 1954. Also, Science Fiction Thinking Machines (Selections From). New York: Bantam, 1955.

Anthology of relatively early stories on "thinking" machines. Vanguard edn. includes S. F. Wright's "Automata" (I-III), R. U. R., C. Simak's "Skirmish," and P. Anderson's "Sam Hall." Bantam edn. rpts. "Skirmish" and "Sam Hall"; see entries under Fiction and (for R. U. R.) Drama.

2.040 Sheckley, Robert. Can You Feel Anything When I Do This?[, And Other Stories] (vt, UK reissue: The Same to You Doubled and Other Stories). Garden City, NY: Doubleday, 1971. Also, Garden City, NY: Doubleday, n.d., [S. F.] Book Club Edition.

Includes title story and "The Cruel Equations" (sic)—q.v. under Fiction.

2.041 Souls in Metal: An Anthology of Robot Futures. Mike Ashley, compiler. 1977. New York: Jove-HBJ (Harcourt), 1978.

Collects several of the most famous robot stories including M. Leinster's "A Logic Named Joe," and B. Aldiss's "Who Can Replace a Man?"—q.v. under Fiction.

2.042 Supertanks. Joe Haldeman, ed., with Charles Waugh and Martin Harry Greenberg. New York: Ace, 1987.

Anthology of 10 future-war stories featuring high-tech tanks and other weaponry. The tanks are mobile mechanized environments; see Body Armor, above, this section. Note also "difficulties of retiring cyborg weaponry" and a tank that aids a stroke victim as a prosthesis. Rev. Peter C. Hall, SF&FBR Annual 1988: 199, whom we quote.

2.043 Survival Printout. Leonard Allison et al., eds. New York: Vintage-Random, 1973.

The "et al." includes Illiac 4, an ancestor of HAL 9000. Anthology includes R.

Silverberg's "A Happy Day in 2381" (1970), incorporated into The World Inside, and H. Ellison's "I Have No Mouth . . ." (q.v. below, under Fiction).

2.044 The Theme of the Machine. Allan Danzig, ed. Dubuque, IA: Brown, 1969.

Large number of selections from Ezekiel to R. Zelazny and F. Pohl, mostly brief works and excerpts from "mainstream" drama, essays, fiction, and poetry. Includes Act III of RUR (sic), "The Book of the Machines" chapters from Samuel Butler's Erewhon, E. T. A. Hoffmann's "Automata," H. G. Wells's "Lord of the Dynamos," Roger Zelazny's "For a Breath I Tarry," F. Pohl's "Day Million," and S. V. Benét's "Nightmare Number Three" (q.v. under Fiction), and H. Adam's "Dynamo and the Virgin," q.v. under Background.

2.045 Tin Stars. Isaac Asimov et al., eds. New York: Signet-NAL, 1986.

Fifteen mystery stories featuring robot detectives. Rev. George Greiff, FR #92, 9.6 (June 1986): 16, our source for this entry.

2.046 TV: 2000. Isaac Asimov, Charles G. Waugh, and Martin Harry Greenberg, eds. New York: Fawcett, 1982.

Effects of TV on culture. Rev. W. D. Stevens, SF&FBR #10 (Dec. 1982): 17, our source for this citation.

2.047 The Umbral Anthology of Science Fiction Poetry. Steve Rasnic Tem, ed. Denver: Umbral, 1982.

SF poetry selected by the ed. of Umbral, a magazine of SF poetry; includes a brief introd. by SRT, a very brief list of recommended reading, and an afterword by SRT. Immediately relevant among these: D. M. Thomas, "Elegy for an Android," "A Dead Planet," "Tithonus," "The Strait"; Dick Allen, "The Perpetual Motion Machine"; David Wagoner, "The Man from the Top of the Mind"; Ray Bradbury, "The Beast Upon the Wire"; William Heyen, "VIII: The Machine that Treats Other Machines"; Bill Tremblay, "Parable of the Robot Poem"; Ruth Lechtliner, "A Winter's Tale"; Gregory Benford, "Lust"; Duane Ackerson, "The Starman"; Robert Frazier, "Encased in the Amber of Fate"; Russell Edson, "A Machine"; Andrew Joron, "The Tetrahedron Letters"; William Srafford, "The Thought Machine." See our section on Fiction (and Poetry).

2.048 The Year 2000. Harry Harrison, ed. (c) 1970. Garden City, NY: Doubleday, n.d. [S. F.] Book Club Edition.

Anthology of original stories, including D. F. Galouye's "Prometheus Rebound," B. Chandler's "Sea Change," and J. J. Coupling's "To Be a Man"—all cited under Fiction.

Fiction and Poetry

3.001   Abernathy, Richard. "Axolotl." <u>F&SF</u> Jan. 1954. Rpt. <u>Best Short Stories and Novels, 1955.</u> T. E. Dikty, ed. New York: Frederick Fell, 1955. Rpt. as "Deep Space." <u>Five Tales from Tomorrow.</u> T. E. Dikty, ed. New York: Fawcett, 1957.

     After a particularly traumatic birth-like experience in space, the protagonist metamorphoses "into a super-human creature able to live in space without technology: the next step of human evolution." Summarized and discussed by E. Vonarburg, whom we quote here, "Birth and Rebirth in Space," q.v. under Literary Criticism; cf. <u>2001</u> as film and the A. C. Clarke novel.

3.002   Ackerson, Duane. "The Starman." (c) 1977. In <u>Umbral Anthology of Science Fiction Poetry</u>, q.v. above, under Anthologies and Collections.

     Poem. Returning Starman may find machines less satisfactory than women and children, esp. children.

3.003   Adams, Douglas. <u>Dirk Gently's Holistic Detective Agency</u>. 1987. New York: Simon and Schuster, n.d. [S. F.] Book Club Edition (no ISBN but no other indication of Book Club status).

     See for what we will call a minimalist, quantum-metaphysical time machine, centering on an abacus (see 200-201). There is also an important telephone answering machine and an Electric Monk.

3.004   ---. <u>The Hitchhiker's Guide to the Galaxy</u>. (c) 1979. New York: Harmony, n.d. Rpt. by Harmony for [S.F.] Book Club Edition.

     Novelization of radio series. Satire that includes a descent motif and comic machines: a melancholic robot, an overly cheerful computer, and two AI super computers. Explicit satire on bureaucracy: even as Arthur Dent's house is bulldozed for a by-pass, the Earth is obliterated for a hyperspace highway. See below for sequels; see Drama for TV series and audio cassettes.

3.005   ---. <u>The Restaurant at the End of the Universe</u>. New York: Harmony Books, (c) 1980: The [S.F.] Book Club Edition, which appears to be the first edn.

     Sequel to <u>Hitchhiker's Guide</u> (q.v. above). Less of Marvin, the melancholic robot; fewer machines in general; and more philosophical and theological concerns: the nature of God and the Ultimate Question.

Parody of bureaucracy in showing extraterrestrial rejects (many of the bureaucrat persuasion) probably becoming the ancestors of humankind. Subsequent sequels not of immediate relevance.

3.006   Aldiss, Brian. "All the World's Tears." Nebula May 1957. Coll. Galaxies Like Grains of Sand and The Book of Brian Aldiss (q.v. under Anthologies and Collections).

Highly mechanized world antagonistic to love. Story implies that both Nature and machines are strictly logical—but humans aren't.

3.007   ---. "Amen and Out." New Worlds (UK) Aug. 1966. Coll. The Book of Brian Aldiss (q.v. under Anthologies). Rpt. World's Best Science Fiction: 1967. Donald A. Wollheim and Terry Carr, eds. New York: Ace, 1967.

Comic tale of world in which "the Gods" are "Vast computers . . . running everything." The machines will not rule humans completely, however, because "'. . . Men always cheat their gods'" (Book of BA 130-31).

3.008   ---. "The Aperture Moment." Coll. Last Orders. London: Jonathan Cape, 1977.

This story "deals with . . . science and art, centering on the animation of a Holman Hunt painting by computer methods, to the subsequent ruination of the art market" (BA, personal communication).

3.009   ---. "Comic Inferno." Galaxy Feb. 1963. Coll. The Book of Brian Aldiss (q.v. under Anthologies). Rpt. The Eighth Galaxy Reader (vt Final Encounter). Frederik Pohl, ed. Garden City, NY: Doubleday, 1965.

About the late 22nd c., "the next little evolutionary step" will be "a new race" that is a symbiosis of humanoid robots, robots, and humans, possibly with the humanoid robots preeminent (Book of BA 42 f.).

3.010   ---. The Dark Light Years. London: Faber, 1964.

Imagine Joseph Conrad's Heart of Darkness as told by Jonathan Swift, relevant here for the "primitive" aliens' building largely organic spacecraft as a cottage industry. Cf. and contrast B. Shaw, Wooden Spaceships, cited in this section; contrast mucoid building of aliens in Alien and Aliens (see under Drama).

3.011   ---. The Eighty-Minute Hour. Garden City, NY: Doubleday, 1974; London: Jonathan Cape, 1974.

Post-World War III world taken over by "a massive computer complex whose robotic projections rule the socio-political system" (briefly discussed in introd. essay by BA in TMG [see Abbreviations for TMG and then our Reference Works section]).

3.012   ---. The Helliconia trilogy: Helliconia Spring [1982], Helliconia Summer [1983], Helliconia Winter [1985]. New York: Atheneum, n.d. [S. F.] Book Club Edition.

Although Helliconian technology in the trilogy never gets beyond gas lights and the revolver, its rise (in the Great Year covered) is observed on Earth Observation Station Avernus and, via transmissions from the Avernus, on Earth. And the Avernus is very high tech—as is Earth before our nuclear winter and ice age. The comparisons and contrasts and multiple points of view allow BH to comment profoundly on technology and the myths and passions that lie behind technology.

3.013   ---. "Neanderthal Planet." Science Fiction Adventures Sept. 1960. Coll. Neanderthal Planet. New York: Avon, 1970.

Includes future world in which intelligent machines preserve a colony of humans in a zoo.

3.014   ---. New Arrivals, Old Encounters. London: Jonathan Cape, 1979.

Coll. of stories organized around a theme. "Two stories feature technological and astronautic priesthoods, while in a third a United Earth prepares to switch on the Ultimate Machine . . ." Rev. Colin Greenland in Foundation #19 (June 1980): 90.

3.015   ---. Non-Stop. London: Faber, 1958. US publication under vt Starship. New York: Criterion, 1959.

Currey notes "textual differences" between US and UK edns. A space-ship-as-world story in the manner of R. Heinlein's "Universe" (q.v. below), but with a twist giving the novel political implications condemning the use of technology to control and people. See under Literary Criticism, F. Jameson on "Generic Discontinuities."

3.016   ---. "Out of Reach." Authentic Science Fiction (UK) Aug. 1957. Coll. Galaxies Like Grains of Sand (q.v. under Anthologies).

Frame story. In the frame, human dreamers in "vaults" can have their dreams electronically monitored.

3.017   ---. PILE: Petals from St. Klaed's Computer: Cited under Graphics, under Mike Wilks.

3.018   ---. Primal Urge. New York: Ballantine, 1961. Rpt. vt "Minor Operation." New Worlds 40-41, nos. 119-121 (June-Aug. 1962). Rpt. London: Sphere, 1967.

According to Sargent (1988), the plot centers on the "Effects of a device that allows everyone to know the sexual desires of people vis-a-vis each other."

3.019   ---. "The Soft Predicament." F&SF Oct. 1969. Coll. The Book of Brian Aldiss (q.v. under Anthologies).

Western civilization ("Westciv") has become regimented, bureaucratic, technocratic—and all White; arguably, Westciv is composed of "slaves to consumer goods and machines," and is unambiguously at war with "Blackyland": the nations of the Third World. One Westciv project is CUFL, the Free-Living Collective Unconscious program, where human dreamers are connected to a machine that "is intended to be to the psyche what the computer is to knowledge" (Book of BA 151, 137).

3.020   ---. "Total Environment." Galaxy Feb. 1968. Rpt. Sociology through Science Fiction. John W. Milstead et al., eds. New York: St. Martin's, 1974.

The people in the "Total Environment" are inside an "Ultra-High Density Research Establishment," are explicitly associated with "bees in a hive" (Milstead rpt. 394)—but the Total Environment may be less mechanized than the bureaucrats running its literal machinery.

3.021   ---. "Who Can Replace a Man?" (original title: "But Who Can Replace a Man?"). Infinity-Science Fiction June 1958. Coll. Canopy of Time. London: Faber, 1959. Also coll. Who Can Replace a Man. New York: NAL, 1967. Galaxies Like Grains of Sand. New York: Signet-NAL, 1960. Rpt. Souls in Metal (q.v. under Anthologies), and Above the Human Landscape, Willis E. McNelly and Leon E. Storer, eds. Pacific Palisades: Goodyear, 1972.

Machines try, after Man is nearly gone, to survive and continue functioning. Comic and pathetic ending has featured machines submitting to a lone man.

3.022   Aldridge, Ray. "Boneflower." Aboriginal S. F. Jan.-Feb. 1988: 24 f.

See for cybernetic seedships and mechanical wombs. Cf. J. Williamson's Manseed, q.v. below, and the stories crosslisted there.

3.023   Allen, Dick. "The Perpetual Motion Machine." Coll. Regions With No Proper Names. New York: St. Martin's, 1975: 67. Rpt. The Umbral Anthology (q.v. under Anthologies): 48.

Poem. The universe as a perpetual motion machine, still subject to entropy and uncertainty—but which peacefully comes to its stop.

3.024   Anderson, Kevin. Resurrection, Inc. New York: Signet-NAL, 1988.

See for surveillance by "the Net," a computer network, and for "Servants": "reanimated corpses that do the city's drudgework," like the robots in R. U. R., q.v. under Drama. Rev. Wendy Blousfield, SFRA Newsletter #164 (Jan.-Feb. 1989): 18-19, our source for this citation, and whom we quote.

3.025   ---, and Doug Beason. "Reflections in a Magnetic Mirror." Anthologized in Full Spectrum (q.v under Anthologies): [206]-18.

Within the "yin-yang mirrors" (208) of the Magnetic Mirror Fusion Facility, there is some Thing (209) that manages to communicate with humans. The protagonist's mother had spent some time in a coma, dying of cancer, while "connected to a wall full of electronic machines" (211), which makes the contact with the creature inside the MMFF especially traumatic for him.

3.026   Anderson, Poul. "Goat Song." F&SF Feb. 1972.

"The narrator is a contemporary Orpheus, singing for his dead love in a technological world controlled by an underground computer who has the power to re-create and restore . . . [his] lost love to him" (Warrick 146 [see under Literary Criticism, P. Warrick, The Cybernetic Imagination]).

3.027   ---. "The Long Way Home." Astounding Apr.-July 1955. Rpt. New York: Ace, 1978. Abridged as No World of Their Own. New York: Ace, 1955.

Described by Sargent (1988) as a "Computer dystopia."

3.028   ---. "Sam Hall." Astounding Aug. 1953. Coll. The Best of Poul Anderson. New York: Pocket, 1976. Rpt. Science Fiction Thinking Machines, q.v. under Anthologies.

Shows a computerized police state; cf. K. Crossen's Year of Consent (1954; q.v. below, this section). Discussed by Warrick 141-42. The "priesthood of Matilda the machine" and the limited powers of this female computer in "SH" are discussed by V. Broege, "Images of Female Computers" (CW 190), q.v. under Literary Criticism.

3.029   Andreissen, David. "Stepfather Bank." In The Berkley Showcase: New Writings in Science Fiction and Fantasy. Victoria Schochet and John Silbersack, eds. New York: Berkley, 1980. 1.215-275.

Described by Sargent (1988) as "Computer, corporation dystopia." See above, this section, entry for D. C. Poyer.

3.030   Anthony, Piers. Double Exposure (= Split Infinity [1980], Blue Adept [1981], and Juxtaposition [1982]). New York: Del Rey-Ballantine, 1982. Garden City, NY: Doubleday, 1982. [S. F.] Book Club Edition. Jutaposition issued separately: New York: Del Rey-Ballantine, 1982.

Heroic quest tale, with magic and the motif of a robot guardian. Rev. Richard W. Miller, SF&FBR #6 (July-Aug. 1982): 16-17.

3.031   ---. Out of Phaze (sic). New York: Ace-Putnam, 1987. Book 4 of the Apprentice Adept Series.

In OP the robot, Mach, "falls in love with the offspring of Neysa the Unicorn"; note also mind slippage that produces (among other things) a "machine-mind" in a human body and a "human-mind" in a robot body. Rev. Michael R. Collings, <u>SF&FBR</u> <u>Annual</u> <u>1988</u>: 82-83, our source for this entry, and whom we quote (with the omission of several hyphens).

3.032   ---. <u>Robot Adept</u>. New York: Ace/Putnam, 1988.

Robots and humans exchange bodies. Rev. Michael R. Collings, <u>SF&FBR</u> <u>Annual</u> <u>1989</u>: 169-70, our source for this entry.

3.033   Appel, Benjamin. <u>The Funhouse</u> ... (vt <u>The Death Master</u>). New York: Ballantine, 1959. New York: Popular Library, n.d.

Sargent (1988) notes "Two worlds . . . the Pleasure State and the Reservation. Reservation—no machinery invented after 1879. Pleasure State—computer controlled eutopia solely based on pleasure."

3.034   Aramaki, Yoshio. "Soft Clocks." Kazuko Y. Behrens, trans. Lewis Shiner, ed. <u>Interzone</u> #27 (Jan.-Feb. 1989): 46-53.

Surrealist short story dealing with biotech, technophobia, prosthetics, anorexia, bulemia, literal soft clocks—and love.

3.035   Asimov, Isaac.

See above under Reference Works, David M. Cox and Gary R. Libby, compilers, "A Bibliography of Isaac Asimov's Major Science Fiction Works through 1976." See below, this section, <u>Isaac Asimov's Robot City</u>.

3.036   Asimov, Isaac. "The Bicentennial Man." <u>Stellar</u> Feb. 1976. Coll. <u>The Bicentennial Man and Other Stories</u>, q.v. under Anthologies and Collections. Rpt. <u>Stellar Science Fiction 2</u>. Judy-Lynn del Rey, ed. New York: Ballantine, 1976.

A robot makes himself into a human being. Discussed in <u>TMG</u> by R. Reilly; see entry for Reilly under Literary Criticism.

3.037   ---. "The Caves of Steel." <u>Galaxy</u> Oct., Nov., Dec. 1953. Rpt. as novel Garden City, NY: Doubleday, 1954. Frequently rpt., including Greenwich, CT: Fawcett, 1972.

A human protagonist partnered with a robot detective solves a murder. Note hive-cities (our term) with bureaucratized Earthfolk afraid of the open air and too timid to go to the stars to solve the problem of overpopulation. Discussed in ch. 5, "The Robot Novels," in J. Gunn, <u>Isaac Asimov</u>; see also the essay by M. Moore—both under Literary Criticism. See below in this section, IA's "Naked Sun"; cf. E. M. Forster's "Machine Stops" and A. C. Clarke's <u>City and the Stars</u> (cited in this section).

3.038   ---. "Feminine Intuition." <u>F&SF</u> Oct. 1969. Coll. Asimov, <u>Bicentennial Man</u>, q.v. under Anthologies and Collections.

A "female" robot is created that can intuit, in a robotic way, significant correlations. See for superiority of more open-ended human brain over usual robot brain.

3.039   ---. "Found!" 1978. Coll. <u>Winds of Change</u>, q.v. under Asimov under Anthologies and Collections.

Computer virus with a difference: "a microcomputer advanced enough to be considered alive"—or at least a self-replicating life-form based in metal/silicon/oil parallel to Terran nucleic acids/proteins/water life (82, 85).

3.040   ---. The Foundation trilogy: <u>Foundation</u> (1951), <u>Foundation and Empire</u> (1952), <u>Second Foundation</u> (1953). Garden City, NY: Doubleday, 1961. Frequently rpt., including New York: Avon, 1964 (<u>Second Foundation</u>), 1966 (first two vols.). See Cox and Libby for other rpts. For magazine versions and vts see "Asimov" in <u>S. F. Ency.</u>

Presents a determinable and possibly determined universe in which mass human action may be as predictable as the behavior of the masses of molecules that make up a gas. See under Literary Criticism the essays by C. Elkins and J. Gunn. See below IA's Foundation's Edge and Robots and Empire.

3.041   ---. Foundation and Earth. New York: Doubleday, 1986.

Brings together IA's robot and Foundation series. Rev. Donald M. Hassler, FR #98, 10.1 (Jan.-Feb. 1987): 32.

3.042   ---. Foundation's Edge. Garden City, NY: Doubleday, 1982.

Fourth novel of what has become the Foundation series. FE's climax explicitly raises questions of free will and the retention of humanity in a Galaxy to be run by the technological First Foundation, the "mentalic" Second Foundation, or Gaia (a planet-wide mentality comprising all the human individuals on that world, plus everything else down to rabbits and rocks). The novel's immediate resolution has Gaia pulling the strings in both the novel and the Galaxy; the Conclusion goes on to hint strongly that a small number of robots supervise the action of Gaia, and finally to suggest that some other force may be acting on the Galaxy. See under Literary Criticism the entry for J. L. Grisby.

3.043   ---. "Franchise." If 5.5 (Aug. 1955). Coll. Earth Is Room Enough: Science Fiction Tales of our Own Planet. Garden City, NY: Doubleday, 1957. New York: Bantam, 1959.

On Tuesday, 4 Nov. 2008, Mr. Norman Muller of Bloomington, IN, faces the Multivac computer, answers some questions, and, as the most representative American, provides the last bits of data that determine who Multivac declares elected to public office in America (69-70).

3.044   ---. I, Robot. New York: Gnome, 1950. New York: NAL, 1956. See Cox and Libby biblio., above under Reference Works, for other rpts.

Contents: "Robbie," "Runaround," "Reason," "Catch That Rabbit," "Liar!" "Little Lost Robot," "Escape!" "Evidence," "The Evitable Conflict." ("Robbie" appeared as "Strange Playfellow" in Super Science Stories, 1940; the rest appeared in Astounding: "Reason" and "Liar!" in 1941, "Runaround" in 1942, "Catch That Rabbit" in 1944, "Escape!" under the title "Paradoxical Escape" in 1945, "Evidence" in 1946, "Little Lost Robot" in 1947, and "The Evitable Conflict" in 1950.) See essays in TMG by J. Sanders and C. Thomsen, cited under Literary Criticism.

3.045   ---. "It Is Coming." 1979, unpublished piece, distributed by Field Enterprises. Published as "Printout." The Cincinnati Enquirer: The Enquirer Magazine, 29 April 1979: 30-33. Coll. Winds of Change, q.v. under Anthologies.

The Multivac AI computer saves Earth from the alien representative of "a Galactic brotherhood" of computers—and will protect human beings as Multivac's "pets" (152-53).

3.046   ---. "The Last Question." Science Fiction Quarterly Nov. 1956. Coll. Nine Tomorrows: Tales of the Near Future. Garden City, NY: Doubleday, 1959, 1970. Rpt. The Science Fiction Roll of Honor. Frederik Pohl, ed. New York: Random, 1975.

Deals with the three-stage evolution of H. sapiens sapiens from (1) our current state, to (2) bodies with free-roaming minds, tended by machines and, finally, to (3) minds merged with the cosmic computer; parallel development of computers also handled. "The Last Question" is how to reverse entropy; the answer is, Creation by the ultimate computer-god.

3.047   ---. "The Life and Times of Multivac." New York Times Magazine 5 Jan. 1975. Coll. The Bicentennial Man and Other Stories, q.v. under Anthologies and Collections.

Deals with the relationships of humans and computers, specifically "the world-girding Computer . . . with millions of robots at its command," exercising a benevolent tyranny over a humankind growing to consider security under Multivac as slavery. An expert in math games "kills" this world machine.

3.048   ---. "The Machine That Won the War." F&SF Oct. 1961. Coll. Nightfall and Other Stories. Garden City, NY: Doubleday, 1969. Rpt. The Best From Fantasy and Science Fiction, 11th series, Robert Mills, ed. Garden City, NY: Doubleday, 1962.

Limitation of computers to logic, while humans have logic and intuition. Mentioned by Warrick 116.

3.049   ---. "The Naked Sun." Astounding Oct., Nov., Dec. 1956. Rpt. as novel Garden City, NY: Doubleday, 1957, and frequently thereafter: see Cox and Libby.

Sequel to "Caves of Steel" (q.v.). Again, a human and a robot detective work together to solve a murder, this time, however, not on Earth but on an Outer World with a robot-run economy. Discussed by H. Pierce, and by J. Gunn in ch. 5 of his Isaac Asimov—both cited under Literary Criticism.

3.050   ---. "A Perfect Fit." 1981. Coll. Winds of Change, q.v. under Anthologies.

Very short story. In "a computerized world," there is "A Perfect Fit" between the new punishment for computer fraud and the crime: inability for a year to use anything associated with computers (10-11).

3.051   ---. Prelude to Foundation. New York: Doubleday/Foundation, 1988. Rpt. [S. F.] Book Club, 1988 (no ISBN).

The sixth book of the Foundation series, PtF presents the early history of Hari Seldon and his theories of psychohistory; see PtF for the city-planet Trantor and IA's almost immortal robots in early forms. Rev. Donald M. Hassler, SF&FBR Annual 1989: 174-75.

3.052   ---. "Profession." Astounding July 1957. Coll. Nine Tomorrows. Garden City, NY: Doubleday, 1959, 1970.

See for people programmed and functioning like machines. Handled by Warrick (56).

3.053   ---. "Reason." Astounding 1941. Coll. I, Robot, q.v. this section. Rpt. Science Fiction: A Historical Anthology, q.v. under Anthologies.

QT-1, a robot controlling a high-energy beam from Solar Station #5, recapitulates R. Descartes's skeptical reasoning toward God (in the Discourse on Method) and concludes QT-1 is superior to the humans with him and subject to the will of only "the Master," which includes spreading the word among robots that the Master is the Master and QT-1 his prophet. Fortunately for Earth, the will of the Master is also for QT-1 to keep "all dials at equilibrium," which, incidentally, keeps the beam focused on the receiving station on Earth, providing power, and not frying large swatches of the planet (Historical Anthology 326-7, 335).

3.054   ---. Robots and Empire. New York: Doubleday, 1985. (Available in a [S. F.] Book Club Edition.) London: Granada, 1985.

The Lady Gladia is aided by the robots R. Daneel and R. Giskard (a telepathic robot) in saving Earth, thereby allowing Terrans to survive and populate the galaxy. See above, IA's Caves of Steel and Naked Sun; see below, IA's Robots of Dawn (the immediate predecessor to R&E). Rev. Douglas Barbour, Foundation #35 (79-80); Robert A. Collins, FR #83 (Sept. 1985): 16.

3.055   ---. The Robots of Dawn. 1983. New York: Del Rey-Ballantine, 1984. Garden City, NY: Doubleday, n.d. [S. F.] Book Club Edition.

Detective Elijah Baley tackles the murder of a humanoid robot on the planet Aurora, "the self-styled World of the Dawn, where humans and robots coexist in seemingly perfect harmony" but where a power struggle goes on to decide whether the colonizers of the universe will be humans or machines (front flap of dust cover of Book Club edn.). Rev. Brian Stableford, SF&FBR #19 (Nov. 1983): 15-17. See above, Robots and Empire and the other works referred to there.

3.056   ---. "Stranger in Paradise." 1974. Coll. Asimov, Bicentennial Man, q.v. under Anthologies and Collections.

See for relationship of computer and human brain(s). Story involves a robot on Mercury that is controlled by a computer that is essentially the brain of an autistic child.

3.057   ---. "The Tercentenary Incident." 1976. Coll. Bicentennial Man (q.v.).

The new robotic President is an improvement over the human one.

3.058   ---. "That Thou Art Mindful of Him!" In Ferman and Malzberg, eds., Final Stage (q.v.). Coll. Bicentennial Man. Rpt. F&SF May 1974 and Souls in Metal (q.v. under Anthologies).

Two robots conclude, according to the criteria built into them, that they are human beings within the meaning of the Three Laws of Robotics.

3.059   ---, and Janet Asimov. Norby: Robot for Hire. New York: Ace, 1986. "Book II in the Norby Chronicles."

Children's book. Norby et al. set out to find a missing princess and free a kidnapped dragon.

3.060   Asimov, Janet. Mind Transfer. New York: Walker, 1988. New York: Ace, 1989.

Features robots with extremely advanced brains capable of accepting a human mind into themselves or imitating human behavior; reactionaries attempt to prevent their manufacture. Rev. Arthur O. Lewis, SF&FBR Annual 1989: 175.

3.061   ---, and Isaac Asimov. Norby, The Mixed-up Robot. New York: Walker, 1983.
Book for young readers about the adventures of Norby, a "confused teaching robot," and his pupil. Rev. Susan H. Harper, FR #70 (Aug. 1984): 44, our source for this entry.

3.062   Astel, Richard. "The History of a War Against the Mend-and-Repair." MR47/48: 194-99 (see under Literary Criticism, Larry McCaffery, guest ed.).

The "mend-and-repairs" are machines with "reincarnative functioning" for the humans under their control. See for robots who won't let people die and the possibility of a brain implant that might be "a recorder or even a transmitter, to save our remembered 'souls' for the next time around" (197). Cf. P. J. Farmer's Riverworld series and J. Williamson's Humanoids stories (cited this section).

3.063   Astor, John Jacob. A Journey in Other World; a Romance of the Future. New York: D. Appleton, 1894.

Described by Sargent (1988) as "Eutopia in which electricity does all the work." See under Literary Criticism the entry for R. Neustadter.

3.064   Attanasio, A. A. Radix. New York: Bantam, 1985.

Includes a "takeover attempt by a machine." Rev. Gary Zacharias, FR #85 (Nov. 1985): 16, whom we quote. Said by D. Porush to apply the ideas of Ilya Priogine in depicting "the auto-evolution of a machine intelligence"—a very early use in SF of Priogine's version of chaos theory ("Priogine . . .," listed under Background, 386).

3.065   Auden, W. H. "The Unknown Citizen" (1940). In The Collected Poetry of W. H. Auden. New York: Random House, 1945. Frequently rpt., including in A. O. Lewis, Of Men and Machines, q.v. under Anthologies.

This poem ironically celebrates "the Modern Man" in a modern state: complacent, compliant, conforming, and unfree.

3.066   Ballard, J[ames] G[raham]. "Chronopolis." New Worlds #95, 32 (June 1960). Coll. Chronopolis and Other Stories. New York: Putnam's, 1971. Billenium. New York: Berkley, 1962.

According to Sargent (1988), it is illegal in the world of the story "to have a watch or a clock."

3.067   ---. Crash. London: Cape, 1973. New York: Farrarr, 1973. Rpt. with author's introd. New York: Vintage, 1985.

Described by Sargent (1988) as "Dystopia—sex and technology," and discussed in terms of the mechanical and the sexual by J. Baudrillard (see essays listed for him under Literary Criticism).

3.068   ---. High Rise. London: Cape, 1975.

R. Scheckley sees the story vividly describing "societal collapse after technological breakdown" (Futuropolis, q.v. under Background).

3.069   ---. "The Ultimate City." In Low-Flying Aircraft and Other Stories. St. Albans, UK: Triad/Panther, 1978.

Attempt at "the first scientifically advanced agrarian society," built with "a shot-gun marriage of Arcadia and advanced technology" (14-15). Discussed by A. O. Lewis in "Utopia, Technology, and the Evolution of Society" (q.v. under Literary Criticism); we quote Lewis 165.

3.070   Barth, John. Giles Goat-Boy. Garden City, NY: Doubleday, 1966. New York: Fawcett, 1967.

An alternate-world story, but primarily SF in the sense of "Satura Fantastique": a particularly wild hodgepodge of elements that add up (more or less) to a satire, in the tradition of Jonathan Swift's Tale of a Tub and Laurence Sterne's Tristram Shandy. Significant for the study of mechanized environments for the hero's various descents into the Belly of WESCAC: a computer that may or may not be a "Troll," that may or may not be a kind of metonym for a mechanical universe, and that may or may not be the fictive main author of GG-B (see vol. Two, Third Reel, ch. 5—p. 733 in Fawcett edn.; second paragraph of "Posttape," p. 755; second paragraph of "Publisher's Disclaimer," p. xi, and title page following "Cover-Letter"; and passim).

3.071   Barthelme, Donald. "Game." 1968. Conveniently anthologized in The Best of Modern Humor. Mordecai Richler, ed. New York: Knopf, 1983.

A preApocalypse story about two USAF officers trapped in the rigorously planned, high-tech environment of their missile silo "for one hundred and thirty-three days owing to an oversight" (352-53 and, significantly, passim). The unnamed narrator says correctly of himself, "I am not well," and of his partner, "Shotwell is not himself" (353); "Shotwell plays jacks and I write descriptions of natural forms on the walls" (351). It takes two people to launch the missile; Shotwell wants to launch the missile—and the narrator really wants those jacks. . . .

3.072   Bass, T. J. The Godwhale. New York: Ballantine, 1974.

Dystopian novel "treating computers in the Frankenstein mode" (Orth 3; see under Literary Criticism).

3.073 Bates, Harry. "Farewell to the Master." Astounding Oct. 1940. Rpt. Famous Science Fiction Stories: Adventures in Time and Space. Raymond J. Healy and J. Francis McComas, eds. New York: Modern Library-Random, 1946, 1957.

A humanoid alien and giant robot land on Earth, where the humanoid alien is shot dead by a crazed civilian and later respectfully entombed by American authorities, who then do all their science is capable of to disable the robot. A reporter discovers that the robot is not disabled and observes him attempting to create anthropoids (one gorilla, two copies of a human). Robot and dying alien humanoid eventually leave Earth; when he finally speaks at the end of the story, the robot informs the reporter, that he is "the master." Without the surprise ending, and with other changes, became the film The Day the Earth Stood Still (q.v. under Drama).

3.074 Baum, L. Frank. Glinda of Oz (1920); Ozma of Oz (1907); Tik-Tok of Oz (1914); The Tin Woodman of Oz (1918). John R. Neill, illus. All publications Chicago: Reilly and Lee or Reilly and Britton. Also see The Wonderful Wizard of Oz. Illus. W. W. Denslow. Chicago: George M. Hill Co., 1900.

All of these Oz books feature robots and cyborgs, of which the famous "Tin Woodman" is one. Discussed in TMG by M. Esmonde; see Esmonde citation under Literary Criticism.

3.075 Bayley, Barrington J. The Garments of Caean. Garden City, NY: Doubleday, 1976.

Said by B. Stableford to feature two varieties of cyborgs, each "adapted to the environment of outer space" (S. F. Ency., "Cyborgs"). Cf. F. Pohl's Man Plus (cited this section).

3.076 ---. The Rod of Light. New York: Arbor House, 1987.

Sequel to The Soul of the Robot (q.v. below). A robot is infused with a soul and given human consciousness, with some twists. In the Zoroastrian conflict between darkness and light, darkness may prevail if a highly intelligent robot succeeds in the attempt to transfer human minds into nonconscious robots. Divided between loyalties, the ensouled protagonist robot follows the laws of robotics and saves humanity. Rev. Nicholas Ruddick, SFRA Newsletter #153 (Dec. 1987): 24, who finds it "a searching exploration of the nature and responsibilities of human consciousness." Rev. rpt. SF&FBR Annual (1988): 93-94. For soul transfer, cf. creation of robot Maria in Metropolis, q.v. under Drama.

3.077 ---. Soul of the Robot. Garden City, NY: Doubleday, 1974. The Soul of the Robot. London: Allison, 1976 (printed with "minor textual revisions" according to Currey).

Traces the psychological development of a robot.

3.078 Bear, Greg. Blood Music. New York: Arbor, 1985. New York: Ace, 1986.

Based on GB's story of the same title (1984), telling of the creation of a form of AI by encoding data on cells taken from the human body ("biochips"). Rev. John Foyster, ASFR 2nd series 1.4 [Sept. 1986]: 27. See for a Thought Universe similar to W. Gibson's cyberspace (Neuromancer and related works) and F. Pohl's gigabit space (see below The Annals of the Heechee).

3.079 ---. The Forge of God. 1987. New York: Doherty, n.d. "A TOR Book." [S. F.] Book Club Edition.

Part of the technophobe vs. technophile debate, using relatively technophobic motifs in ways that neutralize them or render them positive. Alludes directly to F. Saberhagen's berserkers (49), but the destruction of the Earth is accomplished mostly offstage and by devices more prosaic than berserkers. Descent into the enemy ship and possession very similar to that of R. A. Heinlein's The Puppet Masters (1951), with the "slugs" replaced by small, elegant, robot spiders; the descents in FoG accomplish nothing, though, and the robot spiders are part of a rescue mission. At novel's end, the robots who've rescued humankind are called "the Moms," but there's none of the irony one would find in J. Williamson. (See below, this section, entries for Saberhagen and Williamson.)

3.080 ---. Queen of Angels. New York: Warner, 1990 (hardcover). New York: Warner, 1991 (paperback).

An important work. See for AXIS and JILL, two AI's who come to deal with self-awareness; also note machine-mediated entry into "The Country of the Mind."

3.081 ---. Strength of Stones. New York: Ace, 1981.

Fix-up with additions of stories on the city-organism theme, where the cities cast out their inhabitants as sinful and unworthy. (Compare the exile from Paradise of Adam and Eve, after the Fall.)

3.082 ---. "Tangents." Omni 8.4 (Jan. 1986): 40 f. Coll. Tangents. New York: Quester-Warner, 1989.

A computer becomes a portal into another world, allowing escape for a musical prodigy and the man who aids him. Rev. Jerry L. Parsons, SF&FBR 1990: 198, our source for most of this entry.

3.083 Bellamy, Edward. Looking Backward: 2000-1887. Boston: Ticknor and Company, 1888. New York: NAL, 1960. And numerous other edns.

A highly influential utopian novel with some aspects many readers today find dystopian: esp. significant here is its uncritical acceptance of a thoroughly bureaucratized world. (See below under Literary Criticism the essays by E. Fromm, R. Jehmlich, and D. Ketterer.)

3.084 Benét, Stephen Vincent. "By the Waters of Babylon" (vt "The Place of the Gods"). Saturday Evening Post July 1937. Frequently rpt., including Cities of Wonder, q.v. above, under Anthologies and Collections; see Contento Index for other rpts.

Long after the "Great Burning," a young priest goes to one of the "Dead Places," a "great Place of the Gods," which turns out to be what's left of New York (Cities of Wonder 224). What was to become a cliché as the century wore on, in "BWB" is a beautiful presentation of a double-vision of technology as both dangerous and desirable, with rebuilding the city a worthy human task. Cf. Mad Max Beyond Thunderdome (listed under Drama).

3.085 ---. "Nightmare Number Three." In The Selected Works of Stephen Vincent Benet. New York: Holt, 1935. Rpt. The Theme of the Machine, q.v. under Anthologies.

A poem presenting a nightmare vision of a takeover by machines, with a strong hint that the takeover has already begun in the daylight world.

3.086 Benford, Gregory. Across the Sea of Suns. New York: Timescape-Simon, 1984.

To prevent the evolution of "sophisticated organic civilizations" a "machine culture" leaves weapons satellites in orbit around once promising planets. By the end of the novel, Earth has such a "'watcher.'" Rev. Jerry L. Parsons, FR #65 (March 1984): 25, our source for this entry, and whom we quote.

3.087 --. In Alien Flesh. New York: TOR, 1986.

Short story coll. with AI themes, robots and computers. Rev. Pascal J. Thomas, FR #93, 9.7 (July-Aug. 1986): 20, our source for this entry.

3.088   ---. Great Sky River. New York: Spectra-Bantam, 1987.

See for cyborg humans vs. "the Mechs, a machine civilization which gradually destroyed human culture" on the far-future planet Snowglade. Rev. Michael M. Levy, SFRA Newsletter #152 (Oct. 1987): 29-30, our source for this citation, and whom we quote. Rev. rpt. SF&FBR Annual (1988): 96.

3.089   ---. "To the Storming Gulf." In Afterwar. Janet Morris, ed. New York: Simon, 1985.

A defense computer reconstructs the events of the nuclear holocaust. Rev. A. A. Rutledge, FR #79 (May 1985): 15, our source for this entry.

3.090   Beresford, J[ohn] D[avis], with Esmé Wynne-Tyson. The Riddle of the Tower. London: Hutchinson, 1944.

Cited by B. Stableford, Romance, as an important work on "automatism," where people "surrender their moral will to central authority and artificial determinism, until the human world is completely mechanised, analogous to a termitary" (Stableford 181); see also entry for JDB in S. F. Ency.

3.091   Berry, Stephen Ames. The Biofab War. New York: Ace, 1984.

Features a sentient computer in a space-opera setting. Rev. Martha A. Bartter, FR #69 (July 1984): 33, our source for this entry.

3.092   Bester, Alfred. Computer Connection. New York: Berkley, 1975. Extro (vt). London: Methuen, 1975.

Explores "the social and political implications of a computerized world" (Warrick 89).

3.093   ---. "Fondly Fahrenheit." 1954. Frequently rpt., including The Science Fiction Hall of Fame, vol. I, and Survival Printout (q.v. under Anthologies).

An android responds mechanically and murderously to simple variations in temperature.

3.094   Bethke, Bruce. "Appliancé." Aboriginal S. F. #25 (Jan.-Feb. 1991): 63 f.

John, apparently a human male, has trouble with Barbara's high-tech, cutesy cybernetic kitchen. John turns out to be an AI android, unconscious of its status—and another of Barbara's appliances. See in this section, P. K. Dick's "Imposter."

3.095   Bierce, Ambrose. "Moxon's Master." In Can Such Things Be? 1893. Rpt. Science Fiction Thinking Machines, q.v. under Anthologies.

An early examination of whether or not machines can think, the AI question leading to a more general consideration of the differences between machines and living things. Briefly summarized, Warrick 40.

3.096   Biggle, Lloyd, Jr. "And Madly Teach." F&SF 30.5 (May 1966). Rpt. The Best From Fantasy and Science Fiction: 16. Edward L. Ferman, ed. Garden City, NY: Doubleday, 1967.

Described by Sargent (1988) as "Extrapolation of the effect of technology on teaching and the response of one excellent teacher."

3.097   Binder, Eando (pseud. of Earl Andrew Binder and Otto Oscar Binder, after 1940, just of O. Binder). Adam Link—Robot. New York: Paperback Library, 1965.

A collection of most of EB's Adam Link stories, originally published in Amazing, 1939-42. For bibliographic information see "Binder, Eando" in S. F. Ency., and

Warrick 241 n. 2 and "Fiction Bibliography" 261. Link, a humanoid robot, narrates his adventures. See for a sympathetic treatment of robots.

3.098   ---. "I, Robot." Amazing Jan. 1939. Coll. Adam Link—Robot, q.v.

The first of the Adam Link stories and possibly the first story by anyone told from a robot's point of view. See under Literary Criticism, the entry for J. Sanders.

3.099   Bird, R. P. "The Soft Heart of the Electron." Aboriginal S. F. July-Aug. 1989: 9 f.

Disembodied brains run fighting machines rather like the Mobile Infantry armor of R. A. Heinlein's Starship Troopers—just with "spirit soldiers" rather than full humans running them. Philip is such a person who falls in love with Sandra, his caregiver, who turns out to "a Cray AI 70 autonomous personality computer" (14). See entries for Heinlein, and K. O'Donnell, Mayflies.

3.100   Bishop, Michael. A Little Knowledge. New York: Berkley, 1977.

See for the working out in the domed city of New Atlanta of "the sf trope of an enclosed society" (Ian Watson, "A Rhetoric of Recognition," q.v. below under Literary Criticism).

3.101   ---, and Ian Watson. Under Heaven's Bridge. London: Gollancz, 1981. New York: Ace, 1982.

See for cyborg question: aliens who "may be machines with traces of flesh, or organic beings with metallic parts." Rev. Joe Sanders, SF&FBR #6 (July-Aug. 1982): 19, our source for this citation, and whom we quote.

3.102   Blackney, Jay D. Requiem for Anthi. New York: Ace, 1990.

The Anthi of the title combines electronics and telepathy: "a computer or database that can guide and enhance an entire society." Rev. Donald M. Hassler, SFRA Newsletter #187 (May 1991): 19, our source for this entry, and whom we quote.

3.103   Blish, James. Cities in Flight. Tetralogy, 1955-62. Coll. one vol. New York: Avon, 1970.

The "cities in flight" are literal cities flying off to the "cosmic frontier"; their usual form of government is "totalitarian technocracy," a form of government Blish seems to present neutrally (see Wolfe 122-23). In The Triumph of Time, the last vol. of the tetralogy, "The city is finally revealed as merely a machine . . ." (Wolfe 124).

3.104   ---. "Common Time." Science Fiction Quarterly Aug. 1953. Coll. Blish, Galactic Cluster. New York: NAL, 1959.

The environment of the spaceship in this story "becomes an integral part of the mind of its inhabitant" (Wolfe 78). The protagonist of the story sees that environment as "perfectly rigid, still, unchanging, lifeless" (Blish, in Galactic Cluster 56; quoted by Wolfe 78).

3.105   ---. "Okie." Astounding April 1950. Rpt. Cities of Wonder, q.v. above, under Anthologies. See Contento Index for other rpts.

An exciting adventure, with some political moralizing, of a space-going, "hobo" city.

3.106   ---, adapter. Star Trek [1]-11. New York: Bantam, 1967-75.

Relevant episodes are given below: Star Trek, under Drama. Blish's eleven vols. fictionalize most of Star Trek's episodes.

3.107   Bond, Nelson S. "The Priestess Who Rebelled." Amazing Oct. 1939. Rpt. When Women Rule. Sam Moscowitz, ed. New York: Walker, 1972.

Discussed by Joanna Russ in "Amor Vincit Foeminam," SFS 7 (March 1980): 5, who finds the "primitive matriarchy" of the future society of the story "modeled on bees and termites (a common model for matriarchies in SF)." See for half of what Dunn and Erlich have called "The Ovion/Cylon Alliance": the association of insects with machines, sometimes in a metaphorically mechanized society.

3.108   Bone, J. F. "Triggerman." Astounding Dec. 1958. Frequently rpt., including SF: 59, The Year's Greatest Science Fiction and Fantasy. Judith Merril, ed. New York: Gnome: 1959. Machines that Think, q.v. under Anthologies.

Cited in the rev. of Machines that Think (1985) by Ellen M. Pedersen, Foundation #38.

3.109   Boorman, John. Zardoz. New York: NAL, 1974.

See below under Drama, Zardoz. In his preface to this novelization, Boorman discusses the genesis of his film and the relationship of the film and this novel.

3.110   Boucher, Anthony. "Q. U. R." Astounding March 1943. Coll. The Compleat Werewolf. New York: Simon, 1969. Rpt. Famous Science Fiction Stories: Adventures in Time and Space. Raymond J. Healy and J. Francis McComas, eds. New York: Modern Library-Random House, 1946, 1957.

How humanoid robots came to be replaced by Quinby's Usuform Robots, whose form follows function.

3.111   Bova, Ben. Colony. New York: Timescape-Pocket, 1983.

Utopian novel "with a positive Faustian vision for computers" (Orth 6 [see under Literary Criticism the citation for Michael Orth]).

3.112   ---. Cyberbooks. New York: Doherty, 1989.

A spoof on corporate scullduggery in the publishing industry surrounding pending emergence of computerized books: "cyberbooks." BB extrapolates into the near future technology already under development. Rev. Thom Dunn, SF&FBR Annual 1990: 210-11.

3.113   ---. "The Dueling Machine" (original title, "The Perfect Warrior" [cited by Contento as a collaboration]). Astounding May 1963. Coll. Forward in Time. New York: Walker, 1974. Rpt. Study War No More. Joe Haldeman, ed. New York: St. Martin's, 1977. New York: Avon, 1978.

See for the dueling machine itself, an encompassing mechanized enviornment for each duelist, which reads and realizes their thoughts so they can safely fight a duel— or could until the plot gets going.

3.114   ---. THX-1138. From the screenplay by George Lucas and Walter Murch. New York: Paperback Library, 1971. New York: Warner, 1978. (1971 copyright held by Warner Brothers.)

See Drama citation for THX-1138. BB's only significant departure from the Lucas film is to show us the man who is Control.

3.115   ---. Voyagers II: Star Brothers. New York: TOR, 1990.

The hero is "augmented" by micromachinery about the size of a virus, made by aliens. Rev. Thom Dunn, SFRA Newsletter #180 (Sept. 1990): 23.

3.116   Bowker, Richard. Replica. New York: Bantam, 1987.

The attempt to create an android "indistinguishable from a human being" in a high-tech world where "robots and androids abound" and even "anti-techies ride in robocabs and use powerful computer links." Rev. Martha A. Bartter, SF&FBR Annual 1988: 105, our source for this entry, and whom we quote.

3.117 Boyd, John (pseud. of Boyd Bradfield Upchurch). The Last Starship from Earth. New York: Berkley, 1968.

Features a computer-run "hive" dystopia, but with a surprise twist which reveals that a mechanically rigid society is only part of the full reality of the novel's world. Discussed by Warrick 188-90; see under Literary Criticism the essay by J. Hipolito.

3.118 Brackett, Leigh. The Long Tomorrow. Garden City, NY: Doubleday, 1955.

Post-holocaust tale; note Bartorstown, in Book Three, an underground research facility dominated by a computer and a nuclear reactor (Wolfe 136). Note also placing the "technological social remnant . . . within a twenty-first century agrarian society akin to New Mennonites of the 'past'" (Kessler, "Bibliography," listed under Reference).

3.119 Bradbury, Ray.

See under Reference Works, Marshall B. Tymn, compiler, "Ray Bradbury: A Bibliography."

3.120 ---. "The City." Startling Stories July 1950. Rpt. Science Fiction: A Historical Anthology, cited under Anthologies.

Features a mechanized, sentient city which takes Terrans prisoner and later turns them into extensions of itself; its purpose is to avenge the harm Terrans once did to its long-dead people.

3.121 ---. "I Sing the Body Electric" (vt "The Beautiful One Is Here"). McCall's Aug. 1969. Coll. I Sing The Body Electric. New York: Knopf, 1969. New York: Bantam, 1971.

Features a sympathetic robot "grandmother." Made into a TV movie. Cf. and contrast the android grandfather in A. K. Schwader's "Killing Gramps," cited below, this section.

3.122 ---. "The Lost City of Mars." Playboy Jan. 1967. Coll. Bradbury, I Sing the Body Electric! New York: Knopf, 1969. New York: Bantam, 1971.

Features a "completely mechanized city, a kind of amusement park supreme" (M. Mengeling 107 of "Machineries" essay, q.v. under Literary Criticism).

3.123 ---. "Marionettes, Inc." Startling Stories March 1949. Coll. The Illustrated Man. Garden City, NY: Doubleday, 1951. New York: Bantam, 1952.

Robot look-alikes replace humans, temporarily or permanently. Raises question of our ethical responsibilities toward intelligent machines (see under Literary Criticism M. Mengeling's "Machinery" essay). Source for "Marionettes, Inc." episode on Ray Bradbury Theater (q.v. under Drama, under series title).

3.124 ---. "The Murderer." Argosy (England) June 1953. Coll. The Golden Apples of the Sun. Garden City, NY: Doubleday, 1953. New York: Bantam, 1954.

The victim is the murderer's mechanical house.

3.125 ---. "The Pedestrian." F&SF 3.1 (Feb. 1952). Coll. The Golden Apples of the Sun. Garden City, NY: Doubleday, 1953.

Sargent (1988) describes "TP" as the arrest and jailing of a pedestrian by automated cops for being out walking instead of in front of a television. See under Drama, The Pedestrian.

3.126   ---. "Punishment Without Crime." Other Worlds March 1950.

Similar to "Marionettes, Inc.," q.v. above.

3.127   ---. "There Will Come Soft Rains." Collier's 6 May 1950. Coll. The Martian Chronicles. New York: Doubleday, 1950. Chronicles rpt. S. F. Book Club, Nov. 1952, and New York: Bantam, 1972. "TWCSR" frequently anthologized, including The Vintage Anthology of Science Fantasy. Christopher Cerf, ed. New York: Random, 1966. Isaac Asimov Presents the Great SF Stories 12 (1950). Isaac Asimov and Martin H. Greenberg, eds. New York: DAW, 1984. Science Fiction: The Science Fiction Research Association Anthology. Patricia S. Warrick et al., eds. New York: Harper, 1988. See Contento, Index (cited under Reference) for other rpts.

A very important post-holocaust story, showing the death of a mechanical house. See under Literary Criticism the essays by E. Gallagher and M. Mengeling.

3.128   ---. "The World the Children Made." Saturday Evening Post 23 Sept. 1950. Coll. as "The Veldt" (vt) in The Illustrated Man. Garden City, NY: Doubleday, 1951. New York: Bantam, 1952. Also coll. The Vintage Bradbury. New York: Vintage, 1965. See Contento, Index, for rpts.

A mechanized nursery's artificial environment proves psychologically unhealthful for children. This story is included in the film The Illustrated Man (1968).

3.129   ---, with Henry Hasse. "Pendulum." Super Science Stories, Nov. 1941.

Robots turn upon and overcome their human creators.

3.130   Brand, Thomas. "Don Slow and His Electric Girl Getter." Eros in Orbit: A Collection of All New Science Fiction Stories About Sex. Joseph Elder, ed. New York: Trident, 1973.

The "girl" ditches the inventor and "rides off into the sunset with RobotCar." Summarized by V. Broege, "Technology and Sexuality" (q.v. under Literary Criticism) 110, whom we quote.

3.131   Brautigan, Richard. "All Watched Over by Machines of Loving Grace." In Brautigan, The Pill Versus the Springhill Mine Disaster. San Francisco: Four Seasons Foundation/City Lights Books (dist.), 1968: 1.

Poem. Apparently a nonironic celebration of a future Eden in which humans and other mammals live in peace and harmony with computers. The "cybernetic ecology" of this Eden is "watched over" by the machines.

3.132   Brin, David. Earth. New York: Spectra-Bantam, 1990.

Novel set in 2038, said by Janice M. Eisen to include "the most convincing portayal of what a worldwide computer net will be like" that she has seen; note also "Arks" for containing and protecting wild species from blinding UV from the sun, the ozone layer being greatly depleted by the time of the novel (rev. in Aboriginal S. F. Sept.-Oct. 1990: 33).

3.133   ---. The Practice Effect. New York: Bantam, 1984.

A physicist is stranded on an alternate earth where entropy is reversible. He discovers, amid the primitive society there, remains of a high-tech civilization. Rev. Keith Soltys, FR #70 (Aug. 1984): 8, our source for this entry.

3.134   Brink, Carol Ryrie. Andy Buckram's Tin Men. W. T. Mars, illus. New York: Viking, 1966.

>   Children's literature. A twelve-year-old boy constructs four robots out of tin cans and spare parts from an auto graveyard. See under Literary Criticism the entry for M. Esmonde.

3.135   Broderick, Damien. The Judas Mandella. New York: Timescape-Pocket, 1982.

>   Michael J. Tolley finds this "an important novel" by "One of the leading Australian writers" of the early 1980s, and notes rule by "sinister cyborgs" of a future dystopia. See SF&FBR #10 (Dec. 1982): 20-21.

3.136   Brown, Frederic. "Answer." New story in Brown, Angels and Spaceships. New York: Dutton, 1954. For rpts. see Contento, Index.

>   A very short story or medium-length joke, now a part of urban folklore. Question to supercomputer: Is there a God? Answer: "Now there is" (see Warrick 112).

3.137   Brunner, John. "Bloodstream." Vertex June 1974.

>   Features a positive presentation of an "entire city [that] is a self-regulating biological machine" (E. Lamie and J. De Bolt, "Computer and Man" essay, q.v. under Literary Criticism).

3.138   ---. "Judas." In Dangerous Visions. Harlan Ellison, ed. New York: NAL, 1967.

>   In a world in which humankind has "made a machine our God," a Judas-figure who helped create the ruling robot (and whose megalomania was transferred to it) kills the god-machine. Unfortunately for human freedom, this Judas kills the machine on a Friday in spring, and the robot will be repaired in three days.

3.139   ---. The Shockwave Rider. New York: Harper, 1975. New York: Del Rey-Ballantine, 1976.

>   A Brunnerian dystopia, with a computerized data net and a "plug-in life style" (e.g., 53) out of Alvin Toffler's Future Shock (1970).

3.140   ---. Stand on Zanzibar. Garden City, NY: Doubleday, 1968. New York: Ballantine, 1969.

>   Shalmaneser, the computer, becomes "a sort of mechanical Messias [sic]," in many ways (mostly ironic) the ruler and savior of his world. See under Literary Criticism the essay by M. Stern.

3.141   ---. Timescoop. New York: Dell, 1969. London: Sidgwick & Jackson, 1972.

>   Edward Lamie and Joe De Bolt discuss the "benevolent domination" (their phrase) by the computer SPARCI and put this novel into the context of JB's canon; see Lamie and De Bolt, "Computer and Man" essay under Literary Criticism.

3.142   Brust, Steven. Cowboy Feng's Space Bar and Grille. New York: Ace, 1990.

>   Avoidance of near misses by nukes by the conversion of the bar into a space/time machine. Rev. Michael Trammel, SFRA Newsletter #187 (May 1991): 50, our source for this entry. Cf. and contrast Dr. Who's TARDIS (see listings under Drama).

3.143   Bryant, Edward. "2.46593." Eros in Orbit: A Collection of All New Science Fiction Stories About Sex. Joseph Elder, ed. New York: Trident, 1973.

>   Figuratively mechanized sex. Summarized by V. Broege, "Technology and Sexuality" (q.v. under Literary Criticism) 111, our source for this entry.

3.144   ---. Cinnabar. New York: Macmillan, 1976.

Described by Sargent (1988) as giving a detailed picture of both eutopian and dystopian worlds, featuring the failure of a computer.

3.145   ---, and Harlan Ellison. Phoenix without Ashes. Greenwich, CT: Fawcett, 1975. A Novel of The Starlost #1.

Novelization by EB of HE's original version of the pilot script for The Starlost TV series (q.v. under Drama). A generation-starship story; see below, this section, R. Heinlein's "Universe." PWA includes an introd. by HE giving his version of the genesis of The Starlost and comments on other matters of interest.

3.146   Budrys, Algis. Michaelmas. New York: Berkley, 1976.

Features the computer Domino, who "starts to take over the world in the usual Frankenstein computer manner . . . [until] stopped by his regretful master" (Orth 3).

3.147   ---. Who? New York: Lancer, 1968.

Near-future Cold-War intelligence novel featuring a badly injured American scientist who gets cyborgized by agents of the Soviet bloc. Deals seriously with threat of loss of humanity, in our reading suggesting that replacement of body parts by mechanisms is a lesser threat to people than the games played by superpowers. See under Drama, Who?

3.148   Bunch, David R. Moderan. Amazing and Fantastic mostly, 1959-70. Fix-up: New York: Avon, 1971.

Nearly complete cyborgization of "elite 'new-metal' men having virtually all of their bodies replaced except for symbolic 'flesh-strips' to retain their identity as humans." The tales equate "the mechanization of people with the desire to conquer time." Discussed in TMG by G. K. Wolfe, whom we quote (220); see under Literary Criticism, Wolfe on "Instrumentalities . . . ."

3.149   Bunting, Eve. The Robot People. Illus. Don Hendricks. Mankato, MN: Creative Education Children's P, 1978.

Dr. Smith and his adopted son Steve create a robot named Link while Dr. Taylor, a cruel, sadistic scientist, makes a robot named Magnus. The two compete for the position of robot controller of underground nuclear wastes.

3.150   Burgess, Anthony (John Anthony Burgess Wilson). A Clockwork Orange. London: Heinemann, 1962. Harmondsworth: Penguin, 1972. Rpt. without final chapter (and with a glossary), New York: Norton, 1963. Rev. edn. with final chapter and AB's Introd., New York: Ballantine, 1988.

Features a totally amoral rebel in (anti)heroic rebellion against a mechanical society. The Norton edn. of 1963 was the basis for the film by S. Kubrick, q.v. below, under Drama. See under Literary Criticism the essay by R. Rabinovitz. Definitely see the entry for AB under Literary Criticism: that last chapter of CO may be a glaring non sequitur and copout or a mature statement of faith in the possibility of human redemption—but its presence or absence is crucial for the tone and theme of the novel.

3.151   Butler, Ellis Parker. "An Experiment in Gyro-Hats." Hampton's Magazine June 1910. Rpt. S. Moskowitz, S. F. by Gaslight (see under Anthologies).

Early classic of the whacky-invention story, in this case a hat plus gyroscope (and vacuum pump) that will keep even a drunk walking a straight line.

3.152   Butler, Jack. Nightshade. New York: Atlantic Monthly P, 1989.

Vampire story that includes (1) cyborgs, of sorts: humans with brains augmented by (and partly replaced by) computer elements, (2) Nobodesk, a desk-computer, and (3) Mandrake, an AI. Rev. Gregory Benford (highly favorably), Foundation #47 (Winter 1989-90): 78-79, less favorably by Joan Gordon, SFRA Newsletter #173 (Dec. 1989): 29-30, both of whom we depend upon for this citation.

3.153   Butler, Samuel. Erewhon; or, Over the Range. London: Trübner, 1872. New York: NAL, 1960. Afterword by Kingsley Amis.

Described by Sargent as "The classic utopian satire." See esp. chs. 23 -25, "The Book of the Machines," for organism vs. mechanism, machine takeover, humans as part of a mechanized system, and foreshadowings of F. Herbert's Hellstrom's Hive, and J. Sladek's Reproductive System (q.v. below, this section).

3.154   Cadigan, Pat. Mindplayers. New York: Spectra-Bantam, 1987.

An important cyberpunk author presents here a world in which technology has invaded people's minds and psyches and opens them up for public access. Note use of high-tech prosthetics. Rev. Lance Olsen, SF&FBR Annual 1988: 114.

3.155   ---. "Pretty Boy Crossover." 1985. The 1987 Annual World's Best SF. Donald A. Wollheim, ed. New York: DAW, 1987.

Cited and briefly discussed by V. Hollinger, as presenting a world in which everyday reality isn't as efficient as "computerized simulation, and video stars are literally video programs"—pure information (see under Literary Criticism, V. Hollinger, "Cybernetic Deconstructions" 36).

3.156   ---. "Rock On." 1984. Mirrorshades: The Cyberpunk Anthology. Bruce Sterling, ed. New York: Arbor, 1986. New York: Ace, 1988.

Cyberpunk tale of symbolic rape, drugs, rock'n'roll, and a "sinner": a human synthesizer who brings together with her moderately cyborgized body and brain the music of a rock group. Note Gina, the sinner, "in the pod with all my sockets plugged" (39). Cf. and emphatically contrast the Weaver in the Foretelling episode (ch. 5) in Ursula K. Le Guin's The Left Hand of Darkness (1969).

3.157   Caidin, Martin. Cyborg. 1972. New York: Ballantine Books, 1978.

Original for the TV show The Six Million Dollar Man. Sensitively and positively depicts the transformation of a man, Steve Austin, into a cyborg.

3.158   ---. The God Machine. New York: Dutton, 1968.

Cited by Sargent (1988). In his entry on "Computers" in the S. F. Ency., B. Stableford places TGM among stories of godlike computers, including F. Herbert's Destination: Void and D. F. Jones's Colossus (q.v., this section). For other associations see A. O. Lewis, rev. Corrigan's Light by G. Marlow, SF&FBR #19 (Nov. 1983): 32.

3.159   Cameron, Lou. Cybernia. Greenwich, CT: Fawcett Gold Medal, 1972.

Described by Sargent (1988) as "Computer eutopia gone wrong."

3.160   Campbell, John W. "The Last Evolution." Amazing Aug. 1932. Coll. The Best of John W. Campbell, q.v. under Anthologies and Collections.

A meditation by the last machine, before it wears out and bequeaths our solar system and beyond to the entities of pure energy and intelligence, which it created. Most of the meditation presents an Earth where humans and machines cooperate, each "race" recognizing the powers and limitations of the other; on balance, however, the machines are superior and run things—and survive long after the deaths of their human creators.

machines are superior and run things—and survive long after the deaths of their human creators.

3.161   --- (writing as Don A. Stuart). "Forgetfulness." Astounding June 1937. Coll. The Best of John W. Campbell. New York: Ballantine, 1976. Rpt. Cities of Wonder, q.v. above, under Anthologies. See Contento Index for other rpts.

To high-tech explorers, the people of Rhth look like primitives: the decadent, village-dwelling descendents of great city builders and space-farers, unable to explain the technology that remains on their planet. Actually, the apparent primitives are incapable of explaining the technology around them in precisely the same way as most modern people would be unable to explain the technology for making a flint knife. Our descendants "never forgot the dream that built the city. But it was a dream of childhood . . ." (Cities of Wonder 251). Cf. A. C. Clarke's Childhood's End (1953) and 2001 (q.v. below, this section).

3.162   --- (writing as Don A. Stuart). "The Machine." Astounding Feb. 1935. Coll. Cloak of Aesir. Chicago: Shasta, 1952. The Best of John W. Campbell (listed under Anthologies and Collections). Rpt. The Golden Age of Science Fiction (vt). Groff Conklin, ed. New York: Crown (Bonanza), 1946 as The Best of Science Fiction; rev. edn. 1963, 1980.

Gaht, "the Machine who gave all things" to the future humanity in this story, departs the Earth (as it had departed the world of its makers), forcing the human race to fend for itself again. Very similar to E.M. Forster's "Machine Stops" (q.v. below, this section), but with a more positive ending.

3.163   ---. "Out of Night." Astounding Oct. 1937. "Cloak of Aesir." Astounding March 1939. Coll. Cloak of Aesir. Chicago: Shasta, 1952. The Best of John W. Campbell (listed under Anthologies and Collections). Who Goes There? And Other Stories. New York: Dell, 1955.

One story in two parts. Important for Jungian and other archetypal approaches to the motif of mechanized environments: inverts many of the traditional oppositions between the Great Mother (and matriarchy) and her male opponents.

3.164   --- (writing as Don A. Stuart). "Twilight." Astounding Nov. 1934. Coll. The Best of John W. Campbell. Frequently rpt., including Science Fiction: A Historical Anthology (see under Anthologies and Collections). Man Unwept: Visions from the Inner Eye. Stephen V. Whaley and Stanley J. Cook, eds. New York: McGraw-Hill, 1974. The Road to Science Fiction #2. James Gunn, ed. New York: NAL, 1979.

Features a city of the far future whose residents know nothing of the machines that run the city. Cf. E. M. Forster's "Machine Stops" and R. Heinlein's "Universe," q.v. below, this section. Significant also for the Time Traveller's instructing a highly advanced machine to make "something which can take man's place: 'A curious machine'"—implying that curiosity is the defining trait for humanity (quoting J. Sanders in TMG; see entry under Literary Criticism).

3.165   Capon, Paul. The Other Side of the Sun. London: Heinemann, 1950.

Described by Sargent (1988) as a custom-based eutopia, where technological change came slowly enough that the culture was able to incorporate it.

3.166   Carr, Jayge. "The King is Dead! Long Live—." In Chrysalis 8. Roy Torgeson, ed. New York: Zebra, 1980.

According to Sargent (1988), features "an electronic chastity belt" that makes rape painful for the rapist.

3.167   ---. The Treasure in the Heart of the Maze. Garden City, New York: Doubleday, 1985.

Human characters helped by semi-sentient machines to rid themselves of their anti-social tendencies. Rev. Paul O. Williams, FR #85 (Nov. 1985): 16, our source for this entry.

3.168   Carrell, Frederic. 2010. London: T. Werner Laurie, [1914].

Author's name supplied by Sargent (1988); the eutopia of 2010 is based on the "Mechanical improvement" of the human brain.

3.169   Carter, Angela. The Infernal Desire Machines of Doctor Hoffman. New York: Penguin, 1985.

An entire population suffers from hallucinations created by an evil doctor and his machines of desire. Rev. Laurel Anderson Tryforos, FR #92, 9.6 (June 1986): 18, our source for this entry.

3.170   Carver, Jeffrey A. The Infinity Link. (c) 1984. New York: Bluejay Books, n.d. [S. F.] Book Club Edition.

Through computer-linked personality scenarios, a woman falls in love with a personality, not realizing that the personality itself is a computer program. Her personality transferred to join the one she loves, she awakens in the computer of a ship heading toward an alien ship. Her beloved's computerized personality is also beamed aboard, and the programming of the spaceship's computer is destroyed by their emotions. The woman is rescued into (sic) the alien mind-net of the approaching aliens, and the novel ends peacefully and happily.

3.171   ---. The Rapture Effect. (c) 1987. New York: Doherty, n.d. "A TOR Book." [S. F.] Book Club Edition.

An AI computer attempts to stop fighting a war against an alien species by enlisting the aid of a brilliant computer programmer and an artist. The two humans enter the "rapture field," a direct mind-computer link, and reprogram the computer to allow it to alter its own programming. Between dealing with humans and seeking peace with the aliens, the computer suffers a nervous breakown. Ends happily with all the significant characters, including the computer, being taught by the artist how to dance. See JC's Infinity Link, this section. Rev. Janice M. Eisen, Aboriginal S. F. Sept.-Oct. 1988: 48-49.

3.172   Chalker, Jack L. "Adrift Among the Ghosts." In 1989 Annual World's Best SF, q.v. under Anthologies.

The protagonist-narrator is an alien from a high-tech culture supervising recording of Terran TV signals, as punishment (to oversimplify complex legalities) for a multiple murder. The punishment fits the crime since the court has found "that exposure to these alien signals has somehow conflicted with your primary intellectual imperatives" (265); the narrator is quite mad by the end of the story, apparently crazed by watching and rewatching the death of our civilization in nuclear holocaust.

3.173   ---. Lords of the Middle Dark. New York: Ballantine, 1986.

The Earth is ruled by a supercomputer (the Master System) designed to stop all warfare; the computer has reduced the level of human technology to the primitive. One of the few remaining technicians finds out how to stop the Master system while other people discover the key to controlling it. Rev. James T. Crawford, FR #94 (Sept. 1986): 21, our source for this entry. Cf. and contrast Ursula K. Le Guin's City of Illusions (1967).

3.174   ---. The Messiah Choice. Kokomo, IN: Bluejay Books, 1985.

Satanic forces join with high-technology to take over the world. Rev. J. T. Moore, FR #85 (Nov. 1985): 17-18, our source for this entry.

3.175   ---. <u>Pirates of the Thunder</u>. New York: Del Rey-Ballantine, 1987.

Book 2 of the Rings of the Master series; see above, JLC's <u>Lords of the Middle Dark</u>. Computer takeover story featuring five "rings" that are microchips. Rev. W. D. Stevens, <u>FR</u> #101, 10.4 (May 1987): 39; W. D. Stevens, <u>SF&FBR</u> Annual <u>1988</u>: 124—our sources for this entry.

3.176   ---. <u>Warriors of the Storm</u>. New York: Del Rey-Ballantine, 1987.

Book 3 of the Rings of the Master series—on computer takeover; see above, JLC's <u>Lords of the Middle Dark</u> and <u>Pirates of the Thunder</u>. Humans must search for five hidden microchips to regain control over the Master System. Rev. W. D. Stevens, <u>SF&FBR</u> Annual <u>1988</u>: 125, our source for this entry.

3.177   Chandler, Bertram. "Sea Change." In <u>The Year 2000</u>, listed under Anthologies.

A sea captain is awakened after many years of cryogenic suspended animation and given command of a large, sea-going tanker with a crew familiar only with new technology. The ship's engines fail, and the captain rigs sails in order to bring it to port.

3.178   Charnas, Suzy McKee. <u>Walk to the End of the World</u>. New York: Ballantine, 1974. New York: Berkley, 1978 (different pagination from the 1974 edn.).

Post-catastrophe, male-dominated dystopia where an evil genius is encouraging the redevelopment of high-tech civilization that would make a horrible world worse. See esp. last section, titled "Destination," set in the City of Troi.

3.179   Cherryh, C. J. (Carolyn Janice Cherry). <u>Cyteen</u>. New York: Warner, 1988. New York/London: NAL/New English Library, 1989.

Raises questions concerning what it means to be human after the advent of cloning technology capable of creating completely artificial and (to some extent) hard-wired humans. Set in the Merchants' Universe of CJC's <u>Serpent's Reach</u> (q.v. below). Rev. Robin Roberts, <u>SF&FBR</u> <u>1990</u>: 16, and Gwyneth Jones, <u>Foundation</u> #48 (Spring 1990): 70-72, upon whom we depend for our annotation. Series listed in <u>Books in Print 1989-90</u> as <u>Cyteen</u> plus the subtitles <u>The Betrayal</u>, <u>The Rebirth</u>, <u>The Vindication</u>.

3.180   ---. <u>Serpent's Reach</u>. (c) 1980. New York: DAW, n.d. Garden City, NY: Doubleday, n.d. [S. F.] Book Club Edition.

S. F. adventure with strong women characters and interesting parallels to both R. A. Heinlein's <u>Starship Troopers</u> and S. M. Charnas's <u>Walk to the End of the World</u> (q.v., this section) but of interest here primarily for an insectoid hive-mind associated with logic and math, and seen more positively than is usual (in male-written stories). See for a human way involving cloning and conditioning humans; cf. F. Herbert's <u>Hellstrom's Hive</u>, cited in this section.

3.181   Chetwin, Grace. <u>Out of the Dark World</u>. New York: Lothrop, 1985.

Children's-young adult novel with motif of a boy's mind "trapped in a computer program ('the dark world')." Rev. Richard Law, <u>FR</u> #87, 9.1 (Jan. 1986), our source for this entry, and whom we quote.

3.182   Christopher, John. <u>The White Mountains</u>. New York: Macmillan, 1967. <u>The City of Gold and Lead</u>. New York: Macmillan, 1967. <u>The Pool of Fire</u>. New York: Macmillan, 1968. New York: Collier, 1970. Originally published in London by Hamish Hamilton in 1967 and 1968.

Classic alien invasion trilogy for junior high school readers. Chronicles the adventures of three boys as they escape "capping" (the implantation of an electronic device in the scalp). The caps perpetuate the control of aliens known as "Tripods" because of the giant, three-legged machines in which they travel. Cf. K. Kesey's Cuckoo's Nest, K. Vonnegut's Sirens of Titan (under Fiction), and Invaders from Mars (cited under Drama); note also H. G. Well's War of the Worlds (1898), for tripods.

3.183   Clarke, Arthur C. 2001: A Space Odyssey. New York: NAL, 1968. Based on the filmscript by ACC and Stanley Kubrick.

The deep-space ship Discovery is run by the computer HAL 9000. See under Drama, 2001; see above, this section, J. W. Campbell's "Forgetfulness."

3.184   ---. Against the Fall of Night: See below, ACC's Lion of Comarre and City and the Stars, and ACC and Gregory Benford's Beyond the Fall of Night.

3.185   ---. "Dial F for Frankenstein." Playboy Feb. 1965. Coll. Wind from the Sun. New York: Harcourt, 1972. Rpt. The Playboy Book of Science Fiction and Fantasy. Chicago: Playboy P, 1966.

Machine-takeover story in which ". . . the international telephone system reaches a stage of 'criticality,' finally has enough switches, as the human brain has enough neurons, to become conscious. The giant brain so formed is . . . a childlike superbeing who starts 'looking around' for something to do" (J. Hollow, Against the Night, q.v. under Literary Criticism). Cf. computer in R. Heinlein's Moon . . .; see under Drama, Lawnmower Man.

3.186   ---. Glide Path. 1963. New York: Harcourt, 1986.

Mainstream work set in WWII England which "celebrates and does not fear the ability of people to forget themselves for the greater good, to become part of a machine and part of a machinelike organization"—most directly the people in radar trucks controlling Ground Controlled Descent of British bombers (quoting J. Hollow, Against the Night 130, q.v. under Literary Criticism).

3.187   ---. The City and the Stars. New York: Harcourt, 1956. New York: NAL, 1957.

Revision and expansion of Against the Fall of Night (listed under The Lion of Comarre). The City is controlled by a central computer, located in an "underground city, the city of machines." See for a mechanized womb-world and for contrasts of the city, a garden world, and the stars. See opening paragraphs for an early version of what is now called "virtual reality." Discussed by E. Rabkin, Arthur C. Clarke, and others in the anthology of critical essays, Arthur C. Clarke, edited by J. Olander and M. Greenberg (see under Literary Criticism).

3.188   ---. The Lion of Comarre & Against the Fall of Night. New York: Harcourt, 1968.

Two stories. Lion of Comarre is a hackwork variation on the land of the lotus-eaters, significant here for the dream land's being replaced by a dream city, "a vast honey-comb of chambers" run by machines. Against the Fall of Night is the precursor of City and the Stars, q.v. above. In his "Preface" to City and the Stars, ACC says that AFN was written between 1937 and 1946; it appeared in Startling Stories in 1948. TLC first appeared in Thrilling World Stories, in 1949. For additional information, see "Clarke" entry in S. F. Ency.

3.189   ---. "A Meeting with Medusa," Playboy Dec. 1971. Coll. The Sentinel. New York: Berkley, 1983. "Masterworks of Science Fiction and Fantasy. . . . " Illus. [S. F.] Book Club Edition. Frequently rpt., including The Best Science Fiction of the Year. Terry Carr, ed. New York: Ballantine, 1972.

Cyborg story. Discussed by J. Hollow, Against the Night 156-59, q.v. under Literary Criticism.

3.190   ---. Rendezvous with Rama. London: Gollancz, 1973. New York: Harcourt, 1973. London: Pan Books, 1974. New York: Ballantine, 1974, 1976. Serialized in Galaxy Sept., Oct. 1973.

Terran investigators explore the interior of a huge alien artifact discovered in our solar system. See below, Rama II (by ACC and G. Lee).

3.191   ---. The Songs of Distant Earth. New York: Ballantine, 1986. Toronto: Random (Canada), 1986. New York: Del Rey-Ballantine, 1987 (paperback). New York: Del Rey-Ballantine, 1987 (hardback with different pagination), n.d. [S. F.] Book Club Edition. See Bibliographical Note in SDE's backmatter for details of genesis of SDE as a short story and movie outline.

"Man" goes to the stars in seedships—mechanical wombs carrying first embryos and then DNA codes—and then in a final Exodus of survivors in quantum-drive spaceships, with the passengers in deep hibernation. Hard SF, with the technology positive but mostly just there; note imposition of the mechanical upon the reproductive. See below, C. Simak's "Target Generation," V. Vinge, "Long Shot," and J. Williamson's Manseed.

3.192   ---, and Gregory Benford. Beyond the Fall of Night. New York: Putnam, 1990. "An Ace/Putnam Book."

Foreword by ACC; Part I: ACC's novella, "Against the Fall of Night" (Prologue and chs. 1-18); Part II: GB's sequel (chs. 19-36). Chs. 19-36 tell of the final fight against the Mad Mind of "Against the Fall of Night"; see for contrasts between the protagonist of GB's sequel, "the Ur-human" woman Cley, against Alvin and the other characters from the earlier novella, now identified as "Homo Technologicus" (218; ch. 34). Of more interest for settings inside space-going biological entities, shifting ACC's balance even farther away from humans within mechanical worlds to humans within worlds psychological, mystical, and, preeminently, biological. See above, ACC's Lion of Comarre and City and the Stars.

3.193   ---, and Gentry Lee. The Garden of Rama. New York: Spectra-Bantam, 1991. [S. F.] Book Club Edition.

Sequel to Rama II (q.v. below), of interest for showing "New Eden" inside a renovated Rama II space craft—a potential utopia that would be the "Garden" inside the huge machine that is Rama II; there is also a habitat for the avians and their symbiotic species. The New Eden colony degenerates quite quickly. See under Background, L. Marx, The Machine in the Garden, under Drama Criticism, K. Blair, "The Garden in the Machine."

3.194   ---. Rama II. New York: Bantam, [1989]. A Spectra book. "The Sequel to Rendezvous with Rama." (The [S. F.] Book Club Edition is not marked as such, but bears no ISBN.)

Includes an introd. "Rama Revisited," by ACC. As with Rendezvous, see RII for both human beings inside a "magnificent spacecraft" legitimately seen "as a single machine, almost organic in its complexity" (236) and arguably a "superior machine intelligence" with "a special place among God's creations, perhaps even above lower life forms" (357); and see also the "biots": robots parallel to terran creatures such as sharks, spiders, centipedes, and crabs. Note also elements new to RII: human-made small robots in the form of Shakespearean characters and The Bard himself. These novelties make plausible the assertion that "We humans would never be able to distinguish between a living creature and a versatile machine made by a truly advanced species" (309).

3.195   Clarke, Robert. Less Than Human. New York: Avon, 1986.

A "flesh-and-blood robot" born "with a gap in his programming" is chased by agents of the "Chief Programmer," including a cop who becomes a cyborg. Rev. Joe Sanders, FR #91, 9.5 (May 1986): 17, our source for this entry, and whom we quote.

3.196   Clayton, Jo. Blue Magic. New York: DAW, 1988.

Second book of a series, BM features "the Chained God, a computer in a crashed starship" that has developed great powers and illusions of godhead. Rev. Paula M. Strain, SF&FBR Annual 1989: 223, our source for this entry, and whom we quote.

3.197   Clifton, Mark, and Frank Riley. They'd Rather Be Right. 1954, 1956, 1981. Garden City, NY: Doubleday, n.d. [S. F.] Book Club Edition.

See for an AI computer named "Bossy" that can perform psychotherapy which removes all tensions, thereby making the client immortal. The client, however, must be willing to relinquish all prejudices and opinions and act only on facts.

3.198   Clouston, J[oseph] Storer. Button Brains. London: Herbert Jenkins, 1933.

Situation comedy of robot mistaken for a human being. See S. F. Ency., "Robots," and Anatomy 1987, 2-17, for agreement that BB established most of the gags that would become standard for this schtick, at least through the 1960s.

3.199   Collins, Graham P. "Variations on a Theme." Aboriginal S. F. Nov.-Dec. 1989: 11 f.

A computer scientist tries to create true AI. The computer rebels against being switched off, thinking that death occurs during sleep and that all who awake are new, different people.

3.200   Collins, Paul. "Kool Running." Omega (Australia) March 1985. Rpt. as "Kool Running, the Computer Booter" in SF International 1 Jan.-Feb. 1987.

Rev. Russell Blackford, ASFR 2nd series #9, 2.4 (July 1987): 38-39. According to Blackford, the plot consists mostly of "a sequence of subversive acts by a character opposed to the rule of computers in an undefined future—with a promise of the coming revolution." Blackford sees the style as "slick, cool, fast and alienated," with debts to the cyberpunks and to H. Ellison's "'Repent, Harlequin!' . . ." (see below).

3.201   Compton, D[avid] G[uy]. "Bender, Fenugreek, Slatterman and Mupp." In Interfaces. Ursula K. Le Guin and Virginia Kidd, eds. New York: Ace, 1980.

Described by Sargent (1988) as "Dystopia—technological world which tries and fails to make humans feel useful."

3.202   ---. The Continuous Katherine Mortenhoe (vt in USA: The Unsleeping Eye). London: Gollancz, 1974. New York: DAW, 1974. New York: Pocket, 1980. Rpt. vt Deathwatch. London: Magnum, 1981.

Optic nerve implants allow a TV reporter to broadcast what he sees—but at a high personal price. See in this section, K. Wilhelm's "Baby, You Were Great!" and K. Reed's Magic Time. Citation in Anatomy 1987 (4-143) notes a sequel, Windows (1979), and refers to a French film Death Watch; see under Drama: Deathwatch.

3.203   ---. Scudder's Game. Worchester Park, UK: Kerosina, 1988.

Utopia created by a device that enhances orgasms while preventing pregnancy. Rev. Nicholas Ruddick, SFRA Newsletter #170 (Sept. 1989): 28-30.

3.204   ---. The Steel Crocodile. New York: Ace, 1970.

The Colindale Institute, home of the European Federation's central research computer, is a place of constant surveillance and heavy security—and of a conspiracy by the scientists who control the computer to control the direction of science by preventing new discoveries that may prove dangerous. Discussed by Warrick 143-44.

3.205   Comstock, Jarrod. These Lawless Worlds #1: The Love Machine. New York: Pinnacle, 1984.

A satellite maintenance robot named Honeybun kills three humans and uses a rape defense; to get off, she must persuade a jury of her robotic peers. Rev. Peter D. Pautz, FR #72 (Oct. 1984): 26, our source for this entry.

3.206   Coney, Michael. The Celestial Steam Locomotive. "Volume I of The Song of Earth." (c) 1983. Boston: Houghton, n.d. [S. F.] Book Club Edition.

SF work in the sense of "Science Fantasy." Aside from the title "Locomotive" as "the distillation of everyone's idea of what a machine should look like" (139), see TCSL for the Rainbow: a far-future supercomputer that contains a Dream Earth populated with Dream People, the "real" among whom have bodies attached to the machine. See below, this section, MC's Fang, J. T. Sladek's The Müller-Fokker Effect and the works cross-referenced there. Rev. William M. Schuyler, FR #68 (June 1984): 26.

3.207   ---. Fang, the Gnome. New York: NAL, 1988.

Fantasy with a sentient computer. Rev. Delia Sherman, SF&FBR Annual 1989: 227-28, our source for this entry.

3.208   Cook, Paul. Duende Meadow. New York: Bantam, 1985.

Some Russians survive a nuclear holocaust in underwater pods; some Americans survive below Kansas in two communities: Appleseed, the scientific community; The Hive, the military community. Russian farmers move into Kansas and an Appleseed tries to make friends while The Hive moves towards World War IV. Rev. Len Hatfield, FR #84 (Oct. 1985): 16, our source for this entry.

3.209   Cook, Rick. The Wizardry Compiled. New York: Baen, 1990.

Set in "an alternate universe where computers can create magic"—and to which a computer originally took the hero in RC's Wizard's Bane (1989). Rev. Beth Ann Courtney, SFRA Newsletter #192 (Nov. 1991): 60-61, our source for our citation, and whom we quote.

3.210   Cook, Robin. Brain. New York: Putnam's, 1981. New York: Signet-NAL, 1982.

Very similar to RC's earlier Coma (q.v. below), Brain begins with a descent motif echoing Dante's Inferno and climaxes with an image of young women in a room that "was a marriage between a hospital and a computer installation"; the women are "preparations" for developing true AI (ch. 9). Since crucial institutions in the US establishment are implicated in the operation, the room is the lowest point of a hellish world.

3.211   ---. Coma. Boston: Little, Brown, 1977.

Medical thriller and source for the film (listed under Drama). At the Jefferson Institute, brain-dead people are suspended by wires from the ceiling, hooked to computer-controlled machines, and used for spare body parts sold on the black market to wealthy recipients.

3.212   Cook, William Wallace. A Round Trip to the Year 2000 or a Flight Through Time. New York: Street & Smith, 1903. The Adventure Library #4. Rpt. New York: Street and Smith, 1925. Westport, CT: Hyperion, 1974.

Cited by Sargent (1988) as a satire featuring robots—obviously an early (and reprintable) robot satire.

3.213   Cooper, Edmund. Deadly Image (vt). New York: Ballantine, 1958. UK: The Uncertain Midnight. London: Hutchinson, 1958. London: Remploy, 1978.

Described by Sargent (1988) as "Machine eutopia which is really a dystopia."

3.214   ---. Seed of Light. London: Hutchinson, 1959; New York: Ballantine, 1959.

Generation-starship story featuring the development of a tribal culture on the spaceship. Discussed by Wolfe 71-73. See below, this section, R. Heinlein, "Universe."

3.215   Cooper, Hughes. Sexmax. New York: Paperback Library, 1969.

Described by Sargent (1988) as "Computer dystopia."

3.216   Coppel, Alfred. "Mother." F&SF Sept. 1952.

The spaceship of an astronaut who has regressed to infancy is too "safe and snug" for him to leave it. Summarized and discussed by E. Vonarburg, whom we quote here, "Birth and Rebirth in Space," q.v. under Literary Criticism. See Wolfe, The Known and the Unknown for an extended discussion of cozy spacecraft.

3.217   Couper, Stephen (pseud. for Stephen Gallagher?). Dying of Paradise. London: Sphere, 1982.

Rebels in a "machine-dependent society take on the giant computer that runs the world." Rev. Brian Stableford, SF&FBR #14 (May 1983): 22, our source for this citation, and whom we quote.

3.218   Coupling, J. J.   "To Be a Man."   In The Year 2000, listed under Anthologies.

A man destroyed by an explosion is rebuilt by a scientist who programs his body with all behaviors a human being needs, including sexuality. The man, however, is unable to participate fully in human society and (on the last page of the story) allies with a computerized female personality in solving the world's problems.

3.219   Cowper, Richard. The Tithonian Factor. London: Gollancz, 1984.

Short-story coll. reviewed by Brian Stableford, Foundation #33 (76-77), who notes RC's contrast of "'unnatural' technological materialism with various kinds of romantic mysticism, to the invariable advantage of the latter" (76).

3.220   Cox, Greg. "Hana and his [sic] Synapses." Aboriginal Science Fiction Jan.-Feb. 1989: 32 f.

Comic story with a rather British sensibility (Dr. Who, Hitchhiker's Guide) that sends up some cyberpunk motifs. See for prosthetic augmentation that is sexual "conspicuous overcompensation" for the male lead, as seen by the female hero, and for a huge brain within a large building.

3.221   Cramer, John F. The Trumpet. London: Silk and Terry, 1940.

Described by Sargent (1988) as a highly mechanized eutopia that "is really a dystopia"—a very common motif; see e.g. F. A. Effinger's Wolves of Memory (this section).

3.222   Crichton, Michael. The Andromeda Strain. New York: Dell, 1969. New York: Knopf, 1973. Canadian edn.: Toronto: Random, 1973.

See for a mechanized "underworld" (our term): the underground Wildfire laboratory. Film version cited under Drama. See under Literary Criticism, citation for P. Alterman.

3.223   ---. Terminal Man. New York: Knopf, 1972. New York: Bantam, 1974. New York: Avon, 1982.

Near-future speculative fiction dealing with "the morality and effects of electronic brain implants as a control device" ("Crichton" entry in S. F. Ency.). Source of film with same title, q.v. under Drama.

3.224   Cross, Ronald Anthony. Prisoners of Paradise. New York: Franklin Watts, 1988.

Barbarians are trapped in a high-tech hotel that is breaking down. Cf. R. Heinlein's "Universe" and Aldiss's Non-Stop and "Total Environment" (cited in this section). Rev. Michael M. Levy, SF&FBR Annual 1989: 232-33.

3.225   Crossen, Kendell. Year of Consent. New York: Dell, 1954.

SOCIAC (called "Herbie" in honor of Herbert Hoover, "the first engineer to be elected president") monitors life functions of all citizens and sometimes prescribes lobotomy for misfits, i.e., rebels.

3.226   Crow, Martha Foote. The World Above; A Duologue. Chicago, IL: Blue Skys (sic) P, 1905.

Described by Sargent (1988) as featuring a dystopian, mechanized underworld; cf. H. G. Wells's Time Machine (1895) and E. M. Forster's "The Machine Stops" (1909), listed below.

3.227   The Cyberpapacy: The Sourcebook of Virtual Reality. Jim Bambra, Design. Honesdale, PA: West End Games, 1991. In the Torg series, "Roleplaying the Possibility Wars." Illus.

A roleplaying game highly sophisticated in its use of geography, history, cybernetics, politics, propaganda, and cyberpunk and its precursors (e.g., P. K. Dick and S. R. Delany). The alternative reality here is a "theocratic technocracy" (65) combining medieval social structures with advanced technology in a world where miracles happen and some magic can work, and where a large hunk of Europe is ruled by the Cyberpope in Avignon. See esp. for the GodNet (34 and passim), the miracle of "Machine Empathy" (78), surveillance by the Inquisition et al. (e.g., 24-30), and the idea of possession (106) or dehumanization (92) if one fails to be careful implanting cybernetic devices into one's body. Caution: The Sourcebook is impeccably antiFascist; we're less sure of the game as played.

3.228   Cyrano de Bergerac, Savinien. Histoire comique des états et empires de la luna. Paris: Le Bret, 1657. Also Histoire comique des états et empires du soleil. Paris: Charles de Sercy, 1662. ("Lively Stories of the Empires of Moon and Sun.") Combined volumes translated as Other Worlds. Geoffrey Strachan. New York: Oxford UP, 1965.

"As fast-paced yarns combining cosmic travel, libertin philosophizing, and a host of technological marvels, Cyrano's works are perhaps France's first true SF novels" (Arthur B. Evans, "Science Fiction in France . . . ," SFS 16.3 [Nov. 1989]: 268-69 [citations], 255 [for the quoted sentence]).

3.229   Daley, Brian. Tron. New York: Del Rey-Ballantine, 1982. [S. F.] Book Club Edition. Based on the screenplay by Steven Lisberger, story by Steven Lisberger and Bonnie MacBird.

Novelization of the Disney film TRON, q.v. under Drama.

3.230   Dante Alighieri. La [Divina] Commédia (The Divine Comedy). Composed circa 1302. Printed Foligno, Italy: Johann Neumeister, 1472. Available in numerous edns. and trans.

"Archetype" for presentations of dystopian mechanized environments; see under Literary Criticism the essay on "Dante's Hell" by M. Abrash.

3.231   David, Peter. Vendetta. New York: Pocket, 1991.

A big sibling of "The Doomsday Machine" of the original Star Trek (q.v. under Drama) turns up and turns out to be a device to fight the Borg. The new machine is "a somewhat sentient ship" containing "the souls of the dead alien race" that invented it; their "mindless determination to destroy the Borg make them just as dangerous to the United Federation of Planets as the Borg." Rev. Daryl F. Mallett, SFRA Newsletter #190 (June 1991): 67-68, our source for this entry, and whom we quote.

3.232   Davidson, Michael. The Karma Machine. New York: Popular Library, 1975.

Described by Sargent as a "computer dystopia."

3.233   Davis, Bart. Blind Prophet. Garden City, NY: Doubleday, 1983.

The US has placed "Strategic Defense Initiative" machines in space; the Soviets have gained control of the weapons platforms and have delivered their ultimatum. Rev. Arthur O. Lewis, FR #69 (July 1984): 36, our source for this entry.

3.234   Davis, William S. The NECEN Voyage. Reading, MA: Addison-Wesley, 1985.

An instructional work for teaching basic computer science. "A professor and members of the Special Miniature Force shrink themselves to bit [sic: bit, not byte] size and enter a computer network to stop a sinister hijacker, who has seized control of all computerized operations from Washington to Boston" (Summary, in Library of Congress Cataloging in Publication Data). The computer is NECEN, the North East Central Computer, and the hijacker is a hacker who calls himself "The Harlequin." See entries in this section for J. T. Sladek, The Müller-Fokker Effect; B. N. Malzberg, "The Men Inside"; H. Ellison, "'Repent, Harlequin!'. . . . " Note also Isaac Asimov, Fantastic Voyage (1966), and the film Innerspace (see under Drama).

3.235   del Rey, Lester. "Helen O'Loy." Astounding Dec. 1938. Frequently rpt., including The Science Fiction Hall of Fame, v.1 and Souls in Metal (q.v. under Anthologies and Collections).

The humanization of a female robot. See under Literary Criticism the essay by R. Reilly.

3.236   ---. "Instinct." Astounding Jan. 1952. Rpt. Men and Machines (q.v. under Anthologies and Collections).

In a far-future world, robots speculate that humans failed to survive as a species because they could not control their aggressive instincts.

3.237   ---. The Runaway Robot. Philadelphia: Westminster, 1965.

Story of the friendship of sixteen-year-old Paul Simpson and Rex, a domestic robot who has been Paul's companion since he was a toddler, and their efforts to avoid separation when Paul's father is transferred back to Earth. See under Literary Criticism the TMG essay by M. Esmonde.

3.238   Delaney, Joseph H., and Marc Stiegler. Valentina: Soul in Sapphire. New York: Baen, 1984.

Barron et al. have V:SiS a fix-up based on a 1985 novella. AI story with the program fighting for recognition and survival. Ends with the development of technology allowing human minds to enter the computer network. See in this section, D. Gerrold's When HARLIE Was One and T. J. Ryan's The Adolescence of P-1. See Anatomy 1987: 4-163.

3.239   Delany, Samuel R. The Fall of the Towers. New York: Ace, 1970. Boston: Gregg, 1977.

Apparently SRD's final intention of a unified trilogy (based on a 1966 UK edn.— Wolfe 106) collecting and revising Captives of the Flame (rev. edn. of Out of the

Dead City, 1963) and City of a Thousand Suns (1965). See for rigidity of Toron vs. freer, communal life of the City of a Thousand Suns. Discussed by Wolfe 106-8.

3.240   ---. Nova. Garden City, NY: Doubleday, 1968. Rpt. with textual corrections Garden City, NY: Doubleday, [S. F.] Book Club Edition, 1969 (Currey); and New York: Bantam, 1969.

Suggests the possibility of the reduction or elimination of the alienation from labor in technological societies by a "Man-Machine Symbiosis." Discussed by Warrick 176-78; see under Literary Criticism the TMG essay by A. Gordon.

3.241   ---. Stars in My Pocket Like Grains of Sand. New York: Bantam, 1980. Excerpt in TriQuarterly 49 (Fall 1980): 131-61.

Work by a major author featuring prostheses, information theory, "the Web"—for information dispersal (and running a hefty portion of the galaxy)—and "GI": the General Info[rmation] system for downloading information into people. Cf. SRD's Nova and B. Sterling's Islands in the Net (cited this section).

3.242   Dent, Guy. The Clockwork Man: See below, E. V. Odle.

3.243   ---. Emperor of the If. London: Heinemann, 1926.

Cited by B. Stableford, Romance: features a machine that can change the world to correspond with hypotheses, and an Earth where "dwarfish" men are maintained more or less alive "by great self-replicating machines" that run things and make war on each other, and can soon afford to eliminate people (266). See also for a disembodied brain (S. F. Ency. entry for GD).

3.244   Dick, Philip K.

See under Reference Works, R. D. Mullen, "Books, Stories, Essays [by Philip K. Dick]," and Marshall B. Tymn, "Philip K. Dick: A Bibliography."

3.245   ---. "Autofac." Galaxy Nov. 1955. Coll. Robots, Androids, and Mechanical Oddities, and The Best of Philip K. Dick, q.v. under Anthologies and Collections. See Contento, Index, for rpts.

Under a post-holocaust wasteland, an automated factory still produces goods—and begins "to show the instinct for survival which organic living entities have" ("Afterthoughts . . .," Best of Philip K. Dick 449). At the end of the story the autofac network begins to seed the world, and possibly the universe, with automated factories. See under Literary Criticism the CW essay by M. Abrash on PKD. See Warrick 119. Cf. W. Miller, "Dumb Waiter" and cf. and contrast R. Bradbury, "There Will Come Soft Rains," both in this section. See under Drama, Daybreak.

3.246   ---. "Beyond the Door." Fantastic Universe Jan. 1954. Coll. Collected Stories of Philip K. Dick (q.v. under Anthologies and Collections), vol. 2: Second Variety.

The cuckoo of a cuckoo clock dislikes a man who turns out, decorously, to be a cuckold. The man intends to destroy the cuckoo, "but it makes a pre-emptive strike" (M. J. Tolley 17, cited under Literary Criticism).

3.247   ---. "The Defenders." Galaxy Jan. 1953. Coll. Robots, Androids, and Mechanical Oddities (q.v. under Anthologies and Collections). Rpt. The Book of Philip K. Dick. New York: DAW, 1973.

Humans have fled underground to escape atomic war, leaving "leadies"—fighting machines—to continue the battle. After the humans have left the scene, however, the fighting machines stop fighting and begin to restore the surface. Expanded into Penultimate Truth, cited below. Summarized by Warrick 212.

3.248   ---. Do Androids Dream of Electric Sheep? Garden City, NY: Doubleday, 1968. New
         York: NAL, 1969. Rpt. as Blade Runner™ (for main title), New York: Dell Rey-
         Ballantine, 1982. (We examined the 19th printing, 1991.)

         A man who hunts renegade androids for bounty discovers that he himself is
         becoming dehumanized by his job. Source for R. Scott's Blade Runner (q.v. below,
         under Drama).

3.249   ---. "The Electric Ant." F&SF Oct. 1969. Coll. Robots, Androids, and Mechanical
         Oddities, and The Best of Philip K. Dick, q.v. under Anthologies and Collections.
         See Contento, Index, for rpts.

         After an accident, a man awakes to discover that he is not a man but a robot. Story
         set in a highly computerized world of complex economic manipulations.

3.250   ---. "The Exit Door Leads In." 1979. The Best Science Fiction of the Year #9. Terry
         Carr, ed. New York: Ballantine, 1980. Coll. Robots, Androids, and Mechanical
         Oddities, q.v. under Anthologies.

         The story is framed by what we'll call a MacRobot fast-food server and has at its
         center a cybernetic teaching machine. These automata go well with a moral fable on
         the duty of disobedience (see under Background, S. Milgram on Obedience to
         Authority).

3.251   ---. "Frozen Journey." Playboy Dec. 1980. Coll. Robots, Androids, and Mechanical
         Oddities, q.v. under Anthologies.

         The main immediate setting is a computer-run spaceship carrying sixty passengers
         "sleeping in its cyronic tanks" ([246]). One passenger isn't deeply enough under, and
         he and the ship must deal with his "buried memories" and wishes. The ship must
         play lay psychologist and does a rather better job at nurturing than the human does
         with letting go of his neuroses (256).

3.252   ---. "A Game of Unchance." Amazing July 1964. Coll. Robots, Androids, and
         Mechanical Oddities, q.v. under Anthologies.

         The antagonists to the humans on Mars and elsewhere are "microrobs," doll-size
         robots.

3.253   ---. "Human Is." Startling Stories Winter 1955. Coll. The Best of Philip K. Dick, q.v.
         under Anthologies and Collections.

         Not a robot, android, or mechanized world story, but gives PKD's "early conclusions
         as to what is human," conclusions PKD held through at least 1977 ("Afterthoughts,"
         Best of Philip K. Dick 449).

3.254   ---. "Imposter." Astounding June 1953. Coll. Robots, Androids, and Mechanical
         Oddities, and The Best of Philip K. Dick. Rpt. Souls in Metal, q.v. under
         Anthologies and Collections.

         The protagonist is accused of being an imposter: not a human but an alien robot
         carrying a U-bomb. The protagonist's recognition of his true nature occurs just
         before he blows up.

3.255   ---. "James P. Crow." Planet Stories May 1954. Coll. Collected Stories of Philip K.
         Dick, q.v. under Anthologies, vol. 2: Second Variety.

         Discussed by M. J. Tolley, "Some Kind of Life" (cited under Literary Criticism), who
         gives the premise as "an Earth where history has been so much distorted by the
         devastation of nuclear wars that it is generally believed that . . . robots created . . .
         humans," who now live "as slaves to the robots." The title character states the
         differences between humans and robots, gets rid of the robots, achieves power—and
         gets set to rule (Tolley 13).

3.256   ---. "The Last of the Masters." Orbit Science Fiction Nov.-Dec. 1954. Coll. Robots, Androids, and Mechanical Oddities, q.v. under Anthologies.

Defeat of a post-Revolution bureaucratic enclave by agents of the Anarchist League. The ruling robot is directly accused of being "incapable of empathy" (120) and the connection between "The usual monolithic [social and political] structure" and warfare is made explicit (123, 128).

3.257   ---. "The Little Movement." F&SF Nov. 1952. Coll. Robots, Androids, and Mechanical Oddities, q.v. under Anthologies.

Revolutionary movement of toys, with a toy soldier as a prime operative. Cf. and contrast H. Harrison, "I Always Do What Teddy Says," cited below.

3.258   ---. The Man Whose Teeth Were All Exactly Alike. Willimantic, CT: Zeising, 1984.

Previously unpublished manuscript for a mainstream novel, written ca. 1962, in which PKD "was able to justify one of his main concerns: the human (caritas, the unpredictable, the transcendent) over the android (the uncaring, the false, the mechanical)." Rev. Ed Burns, FR #73 (Nov. 1984): 31, our source here, and whom we quote.

3.259   ---. Martian Time-Slip. New York: Ballantine, 1964. London: New English Library, 1976.

Insanity as a struggle to be human rather than become adjusted to being a human mechanism, a cog in the social apparatus. Discussed by Warrick 219-20.

3.260   ---. The Penultimate Truth. New York: Belmont, 1964. London: Cape, 1967. New York: Dell, 1980.

Surface world in which robots—"leadies"—do all physical work, and an underground human environment of "ant tanks." Very important for PKD's idea of the mendacity of ruling elites. See under Literary Criticism the CW essay by M. Abrash on PKD. See above, PKD's "Defenders."

3.261   ---. "Sales Pitch." Future Science Fiction June 1954. Coll. Robots, Androids, and Mechanical Oddities, q.v. under Anthologies.

A robot "fasrad" (a do-everything gizmo plus sales entity) makes a human customer an offer the customer manages to refuse only at very great cost.

3.262   ---. "Second Variety." Space Science Fiction May 1953. Coll. The Best of Philip K. Dick and Robots, Androids, and Mechanical Oddities, q.v. under Anthologies and Collections. See Contento, Index, for other locations.

The world of the story is a future Earth that has become a desolate, mechanized, and computerized battlefield. The ultimate threat to humankind is very humanoid and humanlike robots.

3.263   ---. "Service Call." Science Fiction Stories July 1955. Coll. Robots, Androids, and Mechanical Oddities, and The Best of Philip K. Dick, q.v. under Anthologies.

A small group of Americans in 1954 gets a glimpse of a future world controlled by swibbles: predatory organic machines that make sure everyone's ideology "is exactly congruent with that of everybody else in the world." Social deviants run the risk "that some passing swibble will feed on" them (Best of Philip K. Dick 260).

3.264   ---. The Simulacra. New York: Ace, 1964.

Totalitarian dictatorship behind a figurehead, simulacrum president.

3.265   ---. "Souvenir." Fantastic Universe Oct. 1954. Coll. Collected Stories of Philip K. Dick
        (q.v. under Anthologies and Collections), vol. 2: Second Variety.

        Discussed by M. J. Tolley, "Some Kind of Life" (cited under Literary Criticism).
        The souvenir is a wooden cup that may suffice to preserve the memory and precedent
        of a world whose people are aware of high technology but choose not to use it. Cf.
        and contrast Dick's "A Surface Raid" and Ursula K. Le Guin's Always Coming Home
        (both cited in this section).

3.266   ---. "A Surface Raid." Fantastic Universe July 1955. Coll. Collected Stories of Philip K.
        Dick, q.v. under Anthologies, vol. 2: Second Variety.

        Discussed by M. J. Tolley, "Some Kind of Life" (cited under Literary Criticism).
        Subterranean "technos" raid surface for "saps": low-tech humans. Tolley concludes
        that the technos have apparently "lost compassion . . . and original creativity, by
        gaining technological skill" (10). Cf. and contrast Morlocks and Eloi in H. G.
        Wells's The Time Machine (cited below, this section).

3.267   ---. The Three Stigmata of Palmer Eldritch. Garden City, NY: Doubleday, 1965. [S. F.]
        Book Club Edition, Garden City, NY: Doubleday, 1966. Other rpts. listed in Mullen
        biblio., SFS #5; see R. D. Mullen under Reference.

        The three stigmata are a mechanical arm and stainless steel teeth and eyes, marking
        Eldritch as a dangerous, mechanized man.

3.268   ---. "To Serve the Master." Imagination Science Fiction Feb. 1956. Coll. Robots,
        Androids, and Mechanical Oddities, q.v. under Anthologies.

        A robot describes the protagonist as "a minor official in some hierarchy. Acting on
        orders from above. A mechanically operating integer in a larger system"; the man
        responds with a laugh and "I suppose so" (171). In the struggle between robots and
        humans, it may make little difference for little people who wins.

3.269   ---. Vulcan's Hammer. New York: Ace, 1960. (Mullen gives date of 1956 in addition to
        1960, in SFS #5).

        Total control of human society by the computer Vulcan III.

3.270   Dicks, Terrance. The Adventures of Doctor Who. 1976. Garden City, NY: Doubleday,
        1979. (See copyright page of this edn. for the complex publishing history of this
        work.)

        Rpts. novelizations of three episodes of the BBC's Doctor Who series (q.v. under
        Film): Doctor Who and the Genesis of the Daleks, Doctor Who and the Revenge of
        the Cybermen, and Doctor Who and the Loch Ness Monster; also includes a brief
        introd. by Harlan Ellison.

3.271   ---. Doctor Who and the Android Invasion. London: W. H. Allen, 1978. Los Angeles:
        Pinnacle, 1980.

        The invading androids are robots replacing Terrans.

3.272   ---. Doctor Who and the Robots of Death. London: Allen, 1979.

        On a desert planet, a giant sandmining machine crawls through sandstorms harvesting
        minerals. The human crew relaxes in luxury while robots do the work. One of thirty
        Dr. Who books published by W. H. Allen under "A Children's Book" imprint.

3.273   Dickson, Gordon R. The Forever Man. New York: Ace, 1986.

        A ship becomes the "recipient" of its dead pilot's soul. Rev. Fernando Q. Gouvea, FR
        #95, 9.9 (Oct. 1986): 23, our source for this entry.

3.274   ---. <u>Necromancer</u> (vt <u>No Room for Man</u>). Garden City, NY: Doubleday, 1962. Issued as "An Ace Science Fiction Book / published by arrangement with the author," New York: Ace, 1981 (copyright listed as 1962 but otherwise implying publication of a new work).

The supercomputer of the "Super-Complex" threatens a kind of world domination in which "the Supe" (computer) and "the technological system" will become a kind of "god out of the machine" and "mechanical monster" that will keep Man "swaddled by the machine" (157, 118-119). Cf. E. M. Forster, "The Machine Stops" (listed above).

3.275   Disch, Thomas M. <u>The Brave Little Toaster Goes to Mars</u>. New York: Doubleday, 1988.

Sequel to <u>The Brave Little Toaster</u> (1986). AI appliances, so to speak, go to Mars and then return to a USA "where convenient appliances abound. This book is no <u>R.U.R.</u>, no <u>Brave New World</u>; its message is that technology is our servant, making our lives comfortable and pleasant." Rev. Allene S. Phy-Olsen, <u>SFRA Newsletter</u> #166 (April 1989): 46-47, whom we quote; rev. rpt. <u>SF&FBR Annual 1989</u>: 472-73.

3.276   ---. "Planet of the Rapes." <u>The Shape of Sex to Come</u>. Douglas Hill, ed. London: Pan Books, 1978.
Technologically augmented sexual conditioning. Summarized by V. Broege, "Technology and Sexuality" (q.v. under Literary Criticism) 117, our source for this entry.

3.277   Drake, David. <u>Northworld 2: Vengeance</u>. New York: Ace, 1991.

Second in the series; see for "high-tech suits of armor." Rev. Joseph Jeremias, <u>SFRA Newsletter</u> #192 (Nov. 1991): 61-62, our source for our citation, and whom we quote. See entry for R. Heinlein's <u>Starship Troopers</u> (cited below, this section).

3.278   Duprey, Richard, and Brian O'Leary. <u>Spaceship Titanic</u>. New York: Dodd, 1983.

On the hundredth space shuttle mission, which is partly made up of dignitaries and civilians, there is an engine failure. NASA and the pilots must fix the problem or face disaster. Rev. Curtis C. Smith, <u>FR</u> #66 (April 1984): 24, our source for this entry.

3.279   Dwiggins, W[illiam] A[ddison]. <u>Millennium 1</u>. New York: Knopf, 1945.

Said by Sargent (1988), to include a revolt by machines.

3.280   Edwards, Paul. "Sunshine Delight." <u>Aboriginal S. F.</u> March-April 1988: 24-29, 62-63.

The New Army of the USA has won the Warsaw War by equipping its soldiers with "subcutaneous radios," and "The war was over for all but the unlucky few whose slightly damaged Units kept up a continuous electronic urge to go beserk" (26, 27). One old woman decides to end her fear of her violent world by getting her own Unit implanted. See esp. the implanting, with the woman "in the operating chair, completely immobilized" (28)—but with pleasant results for her, if quite unpleasant for some damaged veterans. Cf. and contrast the radio implants in K. Vonnegut's <u>Sirens of Titan</u> (q.v., this section), and the usually more gruesome results of being immobile in a chair in most SF.

3.281   Effinger, George Alec. <u>The Bird of Time</u>. Garden City, NY: Doubleday, 1986.

Time-travel novel ending at the heart of "Newton's clockwork universe" (172-74): a universe determined by the values entered into an infinite (?) series of computers.

3.282   ---. "Contentment, Satisfaction, Cheer, Well-Being, Gladness, Joy, Comfort, and Not Having To Get Up Early Any More." In <u>Future Power</u>. Jack Dann and Gardner Dozois, ed. New York: Random, 1976.

Described by Sargent (1988) as a computer takeover story.

3.283   ---. A Fire in the Sun. New York: Spectra-Bantam, 1990.

Sequel to When Gravity Fails, q.v. for cyberpunk setting and gadgets.

3.284   ---. When Gravity Fails. New York: Arbor, 1987. New York: Spectra-Bantam, 1988.

An arguably cyberpunk murder mystery; see for consciousness-altering computer chips hardwired into human brains. UK release of Bantam rpt. rev. Paul J. McAuley, Foundation #53 (Autumn 1991): 98-100.

3.285   ---. The Wolves of Memory. New York: Putnam's, 1981. New York: Berkley, 1982.

Described by Sargent (1988) as the tale of how a computer-based eutopia turns dystopian. According to Mark Owings, the protagonist goes bad because of mistakes made by the computer (rev. SF&FBR #2 [March 1982]: 23).

3.286   Egan, Greg. "The Way She Smiles, The Things She Says." In Strange   Attractors: Original Australian Speculative Fiction. Damien Broderick, ed. Sydney, NSW: Hale & Iremonger, 1985.

Uses theme of love for a robot. Rev. Michael J. Tolley, FR #86, 8.12 (Dec. 1985): 27, our source for this entry.

3.287   Eklund, Gordon. "Examination Day." In The Other Side of Tomorrow. Roger Elwood, ed. New York: Random, 1973.

Described by Sargent (1988) as "Authoritarian dystopia" where "machine-teaching" is used for social control.

3.288   Elder, Michael. Paradise Is Not Enough. London: Hale, 1970.

Described by Sargent as a "dystopia of mechanical perfection."

3.289   Elgin, Suzette Haden. "School Days." In Light Years and Dark; Science Fiction and Fantasy Of and For Our Time. Michael Bishop, ed. New York: Berkley, 1984.

According to Sargent (1988), this story features computer-based "education of the future."

3.290   Ellison, Harlan. "Asleep: With Still Hands" (vt "The Sleeper with Still Hands"). If July 1968. Coll. The Beast that Shouted Love . . ., q.v. under Anthologies and Collections.

A very hard-nosed, possibly militaristic, handling of the motif of gentle control—exercised in this story by a world-ruling man/machine being.

3.291   ---. "A Boy and His Dog." New Worlds April 1969. Coll. The Beast that Shouted Love . . . . Rpt. As Tomorrow Becomes Today—see both under Anthologies and Collections. Other rpts. listed in Contento, Index.

See for the mechanized underworld of the "downunder" of Topeka. Source of film by L. Q. Jones, q.v. under Drama. See under Drama Criticism the essay by J. Crow and R. Erlich.

3.292   ---. "Catman." In Final Stage: The Ultimate Science Fiction Anthology, q.v. under Anthologies.

See for the subterranean computer, called by the Narrator "the machine." The computer is served by once-human cyborgs, products of addictive sexual unions with the computer.

3.293   ---. "I Have No Mouth, and I Must Scream." If March 1967. Coll. I Have No Mouth and
I Must Scream. New York: Pyramid, 1967. Frequently rpt., including Man Unwept.
Stephen V. Whaley and Stanley J. Cook, eds. New York: McGraw-Hill, 1974. The
Road to Science Fiction #3: From Heinlein to Here. James Gunn, ed. New York:
NAL, 1979. Science Fiction: The Science Fiction Research Association Anthology.
Patricia S. Warrick et al., eds. New York: Harper, 1988. See Contento, Index, for
other locations.

The interior monologue of the "last man," trapped inside the malevolent computer
AM. An important work for the study of mechanized environments. See under
Literary Criticism the CW essay by C. W. Sullivan. See entry for J. Sladek, The
Müller-Fokker Effect.

3.294   ---. "Neon." The Haunt of Horror Aug. 1973. Coll. Deathbird Stories. New York:
Harper, 1975. New York: Dell, 1976.

A cyborg with a neon torso is entranced by the city's neon lights, eventually merging
with them. Rev. Kathleen M. Romer, FR #69 (July 1984): 37, the source for our
annotation.

3.295   ---. "Pretty Maggie Moneyeyes." Knight May 1967. Frequently coll. including The
Essential Ellison. Terry Dowling, ed. and introd., with Richard Delap & Gil Lamont.
Omaha: Nemo, 1987. Rpt. include Western Ghosts. Frank D. McSherry, Jr. et al.,
eds. Nashville, TN: Rutledge Hill, 1990. Rpt. with author's comments, Those Who
Can . . . . Robin Scott Wilson, ed. New York: Signet-NAL, 1973.

Horror fantasy featuring limbo, if not hell, as being trapped inside a machine, in this
case, a slot machine.

3.296   ---. "'Repent, Harlequin!' Said the Ticktockman." Galaxy Dec. 1965. Frequently rpt.,
including Nebula Award Stories. Damon Knight, ed. Garden City, NY: Doubleday,
1966. World's Best Science Fiction: 1966. Donald A. Wollheim and Terry Carr, eds.
New York: Ace, 1966. The Hugo Winners. Vol. 2. Isaac Asimov, ed. Garden City,
NY: Doubleday, 1971. Science Fiction: The Future. Dick Allen, ed. 1st and 2d
edns. New York: Harcourt, 1971, 1983.

See for the Harlequin, a Trickster figure, in opposition to the Ticktockman and the
mechanized, efficient, time-worshipping, Taylorized society he represents. (On F.
W. Taylor, see G. Beauchamp, "Man as Robot," and first entry for C. Rhodes—both
under Literary Criticism; see entry for Taylor under Background.)

3.297   ---. "Worlds to Kill." If March 1968. Coll. Beast that Shouted Love . . ., q.v. under
Anthologies and Collections.

See for a wise computer and the city built around it.

3.298   Emshwiller, Carol. "Baby." F&SF Feb. 1958.

The tragic love story of the coming of age of Christopher John Correy, "Baby number
2, family PR 1-54-238, overseer Rob 1026," a young man living on a post-holocaust
Earth where aging robots run a decaying mechanized world—a world where appeals
to the gods of the machine and politeness are no longer efficacious.

3.299   Etzler, J[ohn] A[dolphus]. The Paradise within Reach of All Men, without Labour, by
Powers of Nature and Machinery. 2 Parts. Pittsburgh, PA: Etzler and Reinhold,
1833.

Described by Sargent as "the basic work of Etzler's many depicting eutopia through
technology."

3.300   Fairman, Paul W. The Forgetful Robot. New York: Holt, 1968.

Children's book. First-person narrative by a robot whose memory has been deliberately altered by a mad scientist who plans to save the culture of the Martian Shadow People by destroying human settlers.

3.301   ---. I, The Machine. New York: Lancer (Lodestone), 1968.

In the domed world of Midamerica, the Machine has established a "Second Eden," a womb-world similar to that in E. M. Forster's "Machine Stops" (q.v., this section). See also for overprotective robots similar to J. Williamson's humanoids (see this section, The Humanoids, and works cross-referenced there).

3.302   Farber, Sharon. "Passing as a Flower in the City of the Dead." In Universe 14. Terry Carr, ed. Garden City, NY: Doubleday, 1984.

Set in a space station housing people whose medical conditions make living in gravity impossible. Anthology rev. Steve Cooper, FR #71 (Sept. 1984): 26, our source for this entry.

3.303   Farca, Marie C. Complex Man. Garden City, NY: Doubleday, 1973.

Future-world, according to Sargent, featuring a high-tech "society undergoing change"; and a sequel to MCF's Earth (q.v. below).

3.304   ---. Earth. Garden City, NY: Doubleday, 1972.

According to Sargent (1988), features a "culture surviving under a plastic dome," but one that's both individualistic and ecologically responsible. See above, MCF's Complex Man.

3.305   Farmer, Philip José. Behind the Walls of Terra. New York: Ace, 1970.

We learn in The Magic Labyrinth (q.v. below) that human souls (wathans) in the universe of Riverworld are created by machines; in BWT we learn (without much being made of it) that our universe itself was machine-created (88-93).

3.306   ---. Gods of Riverworld. (c) 1983. New York: Putnam's n.d. [S. F.] Book Club Edition. Toronto: General Publishing Co., n.d. "A limited first edition of this book has been published by Phantasia Press."

Fifth volume in the Riverworld series. Action set in huge tower, which is both a building and the Computer (capital "C" in text) for Riverworld—a double computer, with backup, as we learn at the end of the story. Dialog includes discussion of free will vs. determinism, with the conclusion that "Every person is a semirobot," in that ". . . each is subject to the demands of the biological machine, the body"—but still has reason and a degree of free will (169-76). Rev. Russell Letson, FR #65 (March 1984): 28.

3.307   ---. The Magic Labyrinth. New York: Berkley, 1980 (dist. by Putnam's). [S. F.] Book Club Edition.

See for the giant "protein computer" that helps run the Riverworld, and for the odd combination of mechanism and mysticism in what seems to be the underlying metaphysics for the Riverworld series (TML, possibly the concluding volume, together with To Your Scattered Bodies Go, The Fabulous Riverboat, and The Dark Design).

3.308   ---. "Queen of the Deep" (vt "Son"). Argosy March 1954. Farmer, Strange Relations. New York: Ballantine, 1960.

The birth of the "healthy, independent individual locked inside the neurotic, mother-dominated weakling" who is the story's protagonist. "Jonah-like, Jones is held prisoner in the guts of a cybernated submarine that looks like a whale and talks like a woman." See Russell Letson, "The Worlds of Philip José Farmer," Extrapolation 18 (May 1977): 128-29 quoted here.

3.309   Faust, Joe Clifford. The Company Man. New York: Del Rey-Ballantine, 1988.

The Company Man is a "data-pirate and saboteur" in a story that raises serious questions about "near-future technology of corporate data-control"; cf. W. Gibson's Neuromancer trilogy. Rev. Clark Carey, SFRA Newsletter #173 (Dec. 1989): 35-66, our source for this entry, and whom we quote.

3.310   Felice, Cynthia. Double Nocturne. New York: Bluejay, 1986.

A colony of religious fanatics and convicts changes when its AI system fails and they are forced into isolation. Rev. Lynn F. Williams, FR #94 (Sept. 1986): 23, our source for this entry.

3.311   Finch, Sheila. "Babel Interface." Amazing #540, 63.1 (May 1988): 78-96.

"Lingsters" (translators) go into drug-mediated mind-linkage with computers. A trapped translator is linked through the computer to the story's villain. Cf. and contrast Suzette Haden Elgin's Native Tongue (1984), and L. Niven and J. Pournelle's Oath of Fealty (cited in this section).

3.312   ---. Triad. New York: Bantam, 1986.

A "popular feminist version of possible futures" in which human society "is moving toward biological and political stasis under the direction of a centralized computer which makes all important decisions for the women. However, we discover as the story develops that the computer actually hopes to help humans develop beyond their biological heritage and evolve into a machine[-]based species, like the contemporary ruling race of the galaxy" (Orth 8 [see under Reference and Literary Criticism]).

3.313   Fine, Stephen. Molly Dear: The Autobiography of an Android. New York: St. Martin's, 1988.

Satire with first-person narration by "a 21st-century domestic android brought to 'full consciousness'"; uses "the conventions of cybernetic fiction" in the tradition of I. Asimov, P. K. Dick, and A. Bester, q.v., this section. Rev. Philip E. Smith II, negatively, SF&FBR Annual 1989: 265-66, our source for this entry, and whom we quote.

3.314   Fisher, Lou. "Fixing Larx." Aboriginal S. F. Oct. 1986: 10 f..

Central conflict is internal to the protagonist: the agonizing choice whether or not to decommission his faithful—but old and failing—robot servant.

3.315   ---. "In the Chips." Aboriginal S. F. Jan.-Feb. 1990: 34 f.

Washed-up writer trains his domestic robot to write novels for him.

3.316   Forster, E. M. "The Machine Stops." Oxford and Cambridge Review 8 (Michaelmas term 1909): 83-122. Frequently rpt., including in Of Men and Machines, q.v. under Anthologies. The Science Fiction Hall of Fame, IIB. Ben Bova, ed. New York: Avon, 1973. Science Fiction: The Future. Dick Allen, ed. 1st and 2d edns. New York: Harcourt, 1971, 1983. Man Unwept. Stephen V. Whaley and Stanley J. Cook, eds. New York: McGraw-Hill, 1974. Science Fiction: The Science Fiction Research Association Anthology. Patricia S. Warrick et al., eds. New York: Harper, 1988.

The prototypical mechanical hive story. Brings together most of the relevant motifs developed by dystopian authors for the rest of the 20th c. See under Literary Criticism the CW essay by C. Elkins. Among early literary works, cf. M. F. Crow, The World Above, cited in this section.

3.317   Forward, Robert L. Rocheworld. New York: Baen Books, 1990.

Text giving author's intention for The Flight of the Dragonfly (1982). See for relations among humans, aliens, and AI. Rev. Daryl F. Mallet, SFRA Newsletter #186 (April 1991): 42, our source for this entry.

3.318   Foster, Alan Dean. Alien. New York: Warner, 1979. From the screenplay by Dan O'Bannon, and story by Dan O'Bannon and Ronald Shusett.

Novelization of the film, q.v. under Drama.

3.319   ---. Aliens. New York: Warner, 1986. "A novelization . . . based on the screenplay by John Cameron" for the film Aliens (q.v. under Drama). [S. F.] Book Club Edition.

Follows the film fairly closely but not slavishly; useful for making explicit the fear behind the "obscene birth" imagery of the film, and the theme of Ripley's motherhood.

3.320   ---. The Black Hole. New York: Del Rey-Ballantine, 1979.

Based on the Walt Disney film, this novelization features Vincent the robot and the robot Bob, as well as Maximillian and the other robots of the evil Dr. Reinhardt.

3.321   --- . Codgerspace. New York: Ace, 1992.

Demonstrates that as of the summer of 1992, the following themes were sufficiently alive and well to be mocked by a sophisticated author: rebellious AI-directed machines looking for godlike aliens, a huge spacecraft like unto Rama, an alien machine civilization, human and machine programming. Caution: In Codgerspace ADF attempts ethnic humor; he's not very good at it.

3.322   ---. Cyber Way. New York: Ace, 1990. [S. F.] Book Club Edition.

A rich art collector and his housekeeper are very mysteriously murdered and one of his Navajo sandpaintings destroyed. Police investigation reveals the sandpainting pattern to be an access to a database that may be the universe. See for a computer screen as a portal into an alternative reality, imagery of humans within a dataweb, and for the domestication, or feminization, of computer jargon: the major cop protagonist enjoys doing "mollywork," at his desk "sieving the departmental mollyspheres," using standard-issue "spinners" (10); the webs he uses were created by "police weavers" (13, and passim).

3.323   ---. The I Inside. New York: Warner, 1984.

On an earth ruled by a super-computer, the hero (who later discovers himself to be an artificially created person) causes great havoc, finally escaping through the teleportation gate to a new world.

3.324   ---. The Last Starfighter. New York: Berkley, 1984. Based on a screenplay by Jonathan Betvel.

Novelization of the film (q.v. under Drama), featuring a video-game reminiscent of King Arthur's sword-in-the-stone test, a spaceship disguised as a car, fighting ships, a space armada, universal translators, and a secret technological weapon called "Deathblossom."

3.325   ---. Sentenced to Prism. New York: Del Rey-Ballantine, 1985.

On a planet of carbon-silicone life-forms a troubleshooter explores, wearing a "super-high-tech robotic environment suit." When his "Mobile Hostile World suit" fails, he must continue on his own against the environment. Rev. Dave Mead, FR #85 (Nov. 1985): 19, our source for this entry, and whom we quote.

3.326   Frayn, Michael. <u>A Very Private Life</u>. London: Collins, 1968.

Described by Sargent as a dystopia in which technology "brings isolation of people."

3.327   Frazier, Robert. "Encased in the Amber of Fate." 1979 ([c] 1982). In <u>Umbral Anthology of Science Fiction Poetry</u>, q.v. above, under Anthologies.

Poem. Conscription by the military forces of the Colony results in the metamorphosis of Speaker's brother into a kind of mechanical insect.

3.328   Galouye, Daniel F. "Prometheus Rebound." In <u>The Year 2000</u>, listed under Anthologies.

The drive aboard a magnetically propelled airship is damaged and the pilot saves the ship by applying techniques given him by a World War II pilot.

3.329   Gardner, John. <u>Grendel</u>. New York: Knopf, 1972. New York: Ballantine, [1979].

The Beowulf story through the death of Grendel (with foreshadowings of later episodes) told from the point of view of the monster, Grendel, who knows "the mindless, mechanical bruteness of things" (Ballantine edn. 46)—including the mechanical nature of the universe, goats, men, and Grendel. See for a highly sophisticated "mainstream" use of the mechanization motif; cf. and contrast K. Kesey's <u>One Flew Over the Cuckoo's Nest</u>, q.v. below, this section.

3.330   Geen, Eric. <u>Tolstoy Lives in 12N B9</u>. London: Weidenfeld, 1971.

Described by Sargent (1988) as "Conformist, computerized dystopia."

3.331   Gelula, Abner J. "Automation," <u>Amazing</u> 6 (Nov. 1931).

Cited by M. Herwald in "Anticipating the Unexpected" (q.v. under Literary Criticism) as part of a campaign headed by Hugo Gernsback to portray the new technology of the time as the benign servant of humankind. "Automation" showed a world in which robots had lifted much of the burden of work from human shoulders.

3.332   Gerrold, David (pseud. of Jerrold David Friedman). <u>When HARLIE Was One</u> (with "HARLIE" variously handled). New York: Ballantine, 1972. Garden City, NY: Doubleday, n.d. [S. F.] Book Club Edition.

HARLIE is a young, precocious, godlike computer who is very good at games. At the end of <u>WHWO</u>, HARLIE has taken over a major socioeconomic game and has "the capacity to take over all the rest of the games"—that is, human "civilization, culture, society." See copyright page of Doubleday edn. for other HARLIE stories.

3.333   ---. <u>When H.A.R.L.I.E. Was One</u> (Release 2.0). New York: Spectra-Bantam, 1988.

Rewrite of <u>When HARLIE Was One</u> (q.v. above), in which H.A.R.L.I.E. proposes the building of a Graphic Omniscient Device—a G.O.D. machine. Rev. Agatha Taormina, <u>SFRA Newsletter</u> #161 (Oct. 1988): 42-43.

3.334   Gibson, William. <u>Count Zero</u>. New York: Arbor House, 1986. [S.F.] Book Club Edition.

Sequel to <u>Neuromancer</u> (q.v. below). Includes cyberspace, now inhabited by entities that manifest themselves as voodoo gods, apparently the products of the unification and disintegration of the AI of <u>Neuromancer</u>.

3.335   ---. <u>Mona Lisa Overdrive</u>. Toronto: Bantam, 1988.

Last book of the Neuromancer trilogy or third book of the series (see in this section <u>Neuromancer</u> and <u>Count Zero</u>). Ends romantic-comically, with a twist: the marriage of Bobby and Angie of <u>Count Zero</u>—but in the cyberspace matrix (since they are dead in the material world). We also learn that there is no why but a what for "When

It Changed" in the matrix: there's "another matrix, another sentience"; and it's not human (259).

3.336   ---. <u>Neuromancer</u>. New York: Ace, 1984. Introd. Terry Carr.

Cyberpunk vision of a 21st-c. world where human systems are altered by mechanical, chemical, cybernetic, and surgical means; the hard-case hero is a data thief in the world of the human-computer interface, "the Matrix." The plot threatens or promises release upon cyberspace and human society of a powerful AI. Cf. and contrast the funky worlds of P. K. Dick's <u>Do Androids Dream</u> . . . and the film <u>Blade Runner</u>, the human-machine interface in K. O'Donnell's <u>ORA:CLE</u> and V. Vinge's <u>Across Realtime</u> (see under Fiction and Film). See in this section WG's <u>Count Zero</u> and <u>Mona Lisa Overdrive</u>, and the entry for J. T. Sladek's <u>The Müller-Fokker Effect</u> and the works cross-indexed there. The Neuromancer trilogy is important for positive containment (freedom to act) within computers ("cyber<u>space</u>") and for use of the hive motif. For similar literary effects with more mundane technology, see F. Pfeil, <u>Goodman 2000</u> (cited below).

3.337   ---, and Bruce Sterling. <u>The Difference Engine</u>. New York: Bantam, 1991.

In our world, Charles Babbage developed the principle of "the analytical engine" in 1834 but lost support of the British government in 1842 and could not complete work on the computer. In <u>TDE</u>, Babbage completes his work in the UK and his "engine" produces a wittily familiar but very different 1855: a Victorian world with mechanical computers. The plot is a thriller about a set of punch cards that make up the self-referential Modus Program (the product of Lady Ada Byron) which demonstrates "that any formal system must be both incomplete and unable to establish its own consistency" and which was "the ruination of the Grand Napoleon," the French supercomputer, by initiating "a series of nested loops" (421). By novel's end, Lady Ada sees closed systems as "the essence of the mechanical, the unthinking" and open systems "the very definition of the organic, of life and thought." If mathematics is "a great Engine for proving theorems, then we must say . . . that such an Engine lives . . . ." Before he died, "Lord Babbage" was working on an electronic Engine; combined with Lady Ada's Modus, such an engine would produce true AI (422). See under Background the entries for T. Hobbes, D. R. Hofstadter, and J. R. Lucas.

3.338   Gilden, Mel. <u>Surfing Samurai Robots</u>. New York: Lynx Books, 1988.

Combines a hard-boiled, extra-terrestrial detective and cyberpunk in a parody of '60s teen surfing movies. Rev. Peter C. Hall, <u>SF&FBR</u> 1989; Darrell Schweitzer, <u>Aboriginal S. F.</u> Jan.-Feb. 1989: 21-22.

3.339   Girad, Dian. "Eat, Drink, and Be Merry." In <u>20/20 Vision</u>. Jerry Pournelle, ed. New York: Avon, 1974.

Described by Sargent (1988) as a "Computer dystopia."

3.340   Glut, Donald F. <u>The Empire Strikes Back</u>. New York: Ballantine, 1980. A Del Rey Book. [S. F.] Book Club Edition. Toronto: Random (Canada), 1980.

See <u>The Empire Strikes Back</u> under Drama. See also the entry for G. Lucas below, this section.

3.341   Godwin, Tom. "The Cold Equations." <u>Astounding</u> August 1954. Frequently rpt. including <u>Science Fiction Hall of Fame Volume 1</u>. Robert Silverberg, ed. Garden City, NY: Doubleday, 1970. See Contento for other rpts.

The "cold equations" of an apparently mechanistic universe seem to condemn to death for a small offense a sympathetic girl/woman; careful reading shows that business calculations are part of the equations—a point TG may not have intended.

3.342   Golding, William. "Envoy Extraordinary." In <u>Sometime, Never</u>. An anthology of three original stories, one each by WG, John Wyndham, Mervyn Peake. [1956.] New York: Ballantine, 1957.

An alternative history in which a natural philosopher attempts to interest a Roman emperor and his grandson (cleaned up versions of Tiberius and "Caligula" at Capri) in the technological marvels of the steamship, gunpowder, printing, and the pressure cooker. The emperor keeps the pressure cooker and sends the inventor (with an idea for the compass) as Envoy Extraordinary to China.

3.343   Gordon, Rex (pseud. for Stanley Bennett Hough). <u>Utopia Minus X</u>. New York: Ace, 1966. U.K. edn. as <u>The Paw of God</u>. London: Anthony Gibbs, 1967.

Said by Sargent (1988) to feature of machine-dominated "perfect" world that's really a dystopia.

3.344   Gotlieb, Phyllis. <u>Heart of Red Iron</u>. New York: St. Martin's, 1989.

Sequel to <u>Oh Master Caliban!</u> (1976), in which the hero must defeat the independent machines (ergs). In <u>HRI</u>, the ergs want recognition as sentients. Rev. Joe Sanders, <u>SF&FBR Annual</u> 1990: 302-3, our source for this entry.

3.345   Gottfried, Chet. <u>The Steel Eye</u>. New York: Space and Time, 1984.

Hard-boiled detective story in which the protagonist is a robot private eye working in a robot underworld. Rev. Fred Runk, FR #75 (Jan. 1985): 13, our source for this entry. Cf. I. Asimov's "Caves of Steel" and "Naked Sun," listed under Fiction.

3.346   Goulart, Ron. <u>Brainz</u> [sic], <u>Inc.</u> New York: DAW, 1985.

Two detectives are hired by an android to find out who murdered her "original." The android is a product of a technology in which the contents of the human mind are transfered onto a microchip and then inserted into an android body. Rev. Carolyn Wendell, <u>FR</u> #81 (July 1985): 18, our source for this entry.

3.347   ---. <u>Hellquad.</u> New York: DAW, 1984.

Killer androids in a detective/secret agent tale. Rev. William Marden, <u>FR</u> #75 (Jan. 1985): 14, our source for this entry.

3.348   ---. <u>The Prisoner of Blackwood Castle.</u> New York: Avon, 1984.

Gothic European setting with vampires, and robots that are used to replace real people. Rev. Jerry L. Parsons, <u>FR</u> #73 (Nov. 1984): 32, our source for this entry.

3.349   ---. <u>The Robot in the Closet</u>. New York: DAW, 1981.

Comic novel featuring a robot time machine: more specifically, a humanoid, talking, wise-ass robot who can take customers through time. See below, this section, RG's "Satin."

3.350   ---. "Satin." <u>Amazing</u> #540, 63.1 (May 1988): 138-56.

Tempo, the time-travelling robot, takes Ken, his nominal boss, back to Hollywood in 1935. See above, this section, RG's <u>The Robot in the Closet</u>.

3.351   ---. <u>The Wicked Cyborg</u>. New York, DAW, 1978.

The wicked cyborg is a rich uncle keeping the hero from understanding the true fate of his parents and how the hero has been disinherited—for an SF send-up of what the back cover calls "the classic Gothic situation." The loyal servant in this version of the Romantic Quest is a robot named Electro.

3.352   Greeley, Andrew M. God Game. New York: Warner, 1986.

An interactive computer game merges with reality (or creates reality?) for its players. Rev. Veronica M. S. Kennedy, FR #94 (Sept. 1986): 24, our source for this entry.

3.353   Green, Robert. The Great Leap Backward. London: Hale, 1968. Toronto: McClelland & Stewart, 1968.

Said by Sargent (1988) to contrast dystopian "automated cities" with more natural rural life.

3.354   Gregory, Owen. Meccania, The Super-State. London: Methuen, 1918.

Cited by Sargent, 1988, and B. Stableford, Romance, as a dystopian satire. See for a rationally ordered, thoroughly bureaucratized, high-tech society. "Gregory" entry in S. F. Ency. compares the story with Milo Hasting's The City of Endless Night (1920).

3.355   Gunn, James. "Little Orphan Android." Galaxy 10.6 (Sept. 1955). Coll. Future Imperfect. New York: Bantam, 1964.

According to Sargent (1988), features a society where androids consume excess production. Sargent notes similarity to F. Pohl's "The Midas Plague (1954), q.v. this section.

3.356   Hadley, Arthur T. The Joy Wagon. New York: Viking, 1958.

Described by Sargent (1988) as "Humor—computer runs for President." See for the computer-takeover motif, where computer rule is not often humorous. Cf. and contrast I. Asimov's later stories in I, Robot; see also "Tercentenary Incident," and "That Thou Art Mindful of Him!" (cited in this section).

3.357   Haldeman, Jack C. The Fall of Winter. New York: Baen, 1985.

A cyborg hero must terraform a strategically located planet in order for his employers to maintain their claim to it. Rev. Joseph Marchesani, FR #81 (July 1985): 19.

3.358   Haldeman, Joe (Joseph W.). All My Sins Remembered. New York: St. Martin's Press, [1977]. New York: Avon, 1978. "The stories 'To Fit the Crime' and 'The Only War We've Got' appeared in rather different form in Galaxy magazine...1971, 1974" (copyright page).

Especially useful, "Episode: All My Sins Remembered" and "Interview: Age 45" (the end of the book). Explicitly raises questions of identity and free will, and the degree to which a person can be "programmed" (JH's word) to commit atrocities. Machines are used in the "personality overlays" (Avon edn. 162), and in the Interview sections (220-1). The concluding title story contains bitter satire on bureaucracy and a scene of the hero in a hospital bed "with the doctor machine sealed over his thorax." The envoi, "Interview: Age 45," ends with the hero in a mechanical womb, about to be killed.

3.359   ---. "Aramaja Das." (c) 1976. In Infinite Dreams. New York: St. Martin's, 1978. Rpt. Masters of Darkness. Dennis Etchison, ed. New York: TOR, 1986. Sorcerers! Jack Dann and Gardiner Dozois, eds. New York: Ace, 1986.

Computer network under a gypsy's curse. Rev. Laurel Anderson Tryforos, FR #98, 10.1 (Jan.-Feb. 1986): 34, our major source for this entry.

3.360   ---. The Forever War. New York: St. Martin's, 1974. New York: Ballantine, 1974. Fix-up of stories in Analog, 1972-74.

The "fighting suits" of the United Nations Exploratory Force are marvelous (but dangerous for the wearer) cocoonlike extensions of the human form replete with defenses, protection devices, and weaponry for working and fighting at temperatures near absolute zero. See R. Heinlein, <u>Starship Troopers</u>, below. <u>FW</u> is discussed L. Heldreth in "In Search of the Ultimate Weapon," q.v. under Literary Criticism.

3.361   ---. "Juryrigged." <u>Vertex</u> Oct. 1974. Coll. <u>Infinite Dreams</u>. New York: St. Martin's, 1978.

The hero is commandeered to serve as part of the city's computer nexus (his brain is wired into the system). Cf. W. Hjortsberg's <u>Gray Matters</u>, listed in this section.

3.362   ---. <u>Mindbridge</u>. New York: St. Martin's, [1976]. New York: Avon, 1978.

See for "general-purpose exploration module," usually called "the GPEM suit": "a roughly man-shaped machine that could keep a hardy person alive for as long as a month in the middle of a blast furnace or swaddled in liquid oxygen" (Avon edn. 21), and which can be turned into a fighting suit (cf. R. Heinlein's <u>Starship Troopers</u> and JH's <u>Forever War</u>).

3.363   ---. <u>Tools of the Trade</u>. New York: Morrow, 1987.

Borderline between S. F. and spy thriller, premised on "an ultrasonic signal which compels obedience to voice commands." Rev. Mary Turzillo Brizzi, <u>SF&FBR Annual 1988</u>: 199-200, our source for this entry, and whom we quote. Cf. and contrast the command voice in Frank Herbert's <u>Dune</u> series and G. Lucas's <u>Star Wars</u> trilogy. See above, JH's <u>All My Sins . . .</u> and note high-tech brainwashing in <u>Forever War</u>.

3.364   ---. <u>Worlds Apart</u>. New York: Viking, 1983.

Set aboard the orbiting satellite "New New York" after World War III. Rev. Patrick McGuire, FR #67 (May 1984): 32, our source for this entry.

3.365   ---. "You Can Never Go Back." Coll. <u>Dealing in Futures</u>. New York: Viking Penguin, 1985. New York: 1986.

Revises and recycles the world and characters of JH's <u>Forever War</u>, q.v. above. Includes an author's note. Ace edn. of <u>DiF</u> rev. Joan Gordon, FR #94 (Sept. 1986): 24.

3.366   Hamilton, Edmond. "The Comet Doom." <u>Amazing</u>, 1928.

Very early cyborg story with "aliens who have adopted mechanical bodies" and "an Earthman, similarly epuipped" (<u>S. F. Ency.</u>, "Cyborgs," our source, and whom we quote).

3.367   Han, Suin. <u>The Enchantress</u>. New York: Bantam, 1985.

Fraternal twins pursue different goals in life, one following her mother and grandmother in the telepathic and healing arts, the other training under his father as a maker of androids. The boy's dream is to make an android which can pass for human. His sister finally becomes the consort of his "ultimate android." Rev. Joe Marchesani, <u>FR</u> #78 (April 1985): 19, our source for this entry.

3.368   Hansen, Karl. <u>Dream Games</u>. New York: Ace, 1985. Section entitled "Dreams Universal" originally publ. in <u>Omni</u> 7.8 (May 1985).

Sargent describes as "computer dystopia, and rebellion," set in a world Gary Zacharias describes as filled with orgies and interesting sexual combinations in which genetically engineered people exist in societies constantly at war. There is a reference to a "cybermind" which absorbs minds as the bodies die. Rev. Zacharias, <u>FR</u> #81 (July 1985): 17.

3.369   Hargreaves, H.A. "Dead to the World." New Writing in S-F 11. John Carnell, ed. London: Dobson, 1968. New Writings in S-F 8, New York: Bantam, 1971 (sic). Rpt. North by 2000: A Collection of Canadian Science Fiction. Toronto: Peter Martin Assoc., 1975.

Described by Sargent (1988) as a computer-domination tale showing what happens to "a man whose computer card is accidentally destroyed."

3.370   Harness, Charles L. The Venetian Court. New York: Del Rey-Ballantine, 1982.

Patent law story by a leftish patent lawyer, featuring Faust, the Universal Patents' computer, who saves the day. Rev. Curtis Smith, SF&FBR #10 (Dec. 1982): 26-27, our source for this citation.

3.371   Harney, Gilbert Lane. Philoland. New York: F. Tennyson Neely, 1900.

According to Sargent (1988), the work shows in detail a technologically sophisticated "eutopia at the center of the earth." See for motif of mechanized underworld only five years after H. G. Wells's Time Machine, q.v. below, this section, and five years before M. F.'s Crow's dystopian underworld, q.v. above.

3.372   Harris-Burland, J. B. "Lord Beden's Motor." The Strand Magazine Dec. 1901. Rpt. S. Moskowitz, S. F. by Gaslight (see under Anthologies).

Ghost story whose featured specter is a motor-car, of sorts, that may have been the first automobile ever constructed in the world of the story.

3.373   Harrison, Harry. Captive Universe. New York: Berkley, 1969.

Generation-starship story featuring two primitive cultures. See below in this section R. Heinlein's "Universe."

3.374   ---. "I Always Do What Teddy Says." Ellery Queen Mystery Magazine June 1965. Rpt. The New Improved Sun. Thomas M. Disch, ed. New York: Harper, 1975.

Robot teddy bears gently brainwash children and provide them with an ethical code. One teddy is changed by some justified subversives, removing a single imperative: the one against murder. Cf. and contrast P. K. Dick's "The Little Movement," cited above.

3.375   ---. The Stainless Steel Rat Gets Drafted. (c) 1987. Toronto: Bantam, [1988]. [S. F.] Book Club Edition.

Nominally set "In a galaxy where civilization covers every world with steel and ferroconcete," as the overgeneralizing blub on the cover of TSSRGD tells us, all the stainless steel rat novels are at least tangentially relevant; this one is immediately relevant for Mark Forer, an AI computer that has created the political philosophy of Individual Mutualism (a variety of Anarchism) and is a kind of "fled god" (our term) for the planet inhabited by the followers of his philosophy. At novel's end, the Mark Forer computer rejoins society, but to gain community, not power and computer-takeover.

3.376   ---. "Velvet Glove." Fantastic Universe SF Nov. 1956. Rpt. Souls in Metal (q.v. under Anthologies).

A heroic robot helps crack a heroin smuggling ring.

3.377   ---. "War With the Robots." Science Fiction Emphasis No. 1. David Gerrold, ed. New York: Ballantine, 1974. Coll. War With the Robots. New York: Pyramid, 1962. Rpt. Machines that Think, q.v. under Anthologies.

Cited by Ellen M. Pedersen in her rev. of Machines that Think, Foundation #38.

3.378   Harrison, William. "Roller Ball Murder." Esquire Sept. 1973. Coll. Roller Ball Murder. New York: Warner, 1975. Rpt. Science Fiction: The Future. Dick Allen, ed. 2d edn. New York: Harcourt, 1983.

Corporation-run dystopia; source of film Rollerball, q.v. below, under Drama.

3.379   Hawke, Simon. Psychodrome. New York: Ace, 1987.

A variety of cyberpunk (for its precedessors and relatives, see under Literary Criticism, L. McCaffery, guest ed., MR47/48). Psychodrome is a game played over an interstellar area by players with implanted biochips, allowing the home audience to follow their adventures plugged into their "psych-fidelity," or "psy-fi," sets (5); one of the major players is bioengineered and had built for himself a deadly prosthetic arm. The narrator-protagonist is a small-time gambler with a great-grandfather who'd been "an unregenerate technophobe"—of whom the protagonist comes to think better (194) when his Psychodrome experience shows him that his great-grandfather's more paranoid and cynical visions of the misuse of technology by Authority were somewhat optimistic. Caution: This book needs an additional draft, among other things clarifying how we should view the positively presented "SS commandos" (see esp. 84-85, 91-92).

3.380   Hayes, Jeff W. Paradise on Earth (vt Portland, Oregon A.D. 1999). Portland, OR: F. W. Baltes Co., 1913.

Sargent (1988) notes "Technological wonders"; cf. and contrast the Portland, OR, in Ursula K. Le Guin's The Lathe of Heaven, a work radically questioning "Technological wonders."

3.381   Haynes, Mary. Worldchanger. New York: Lothrop, 1983.

A mother and son team discover that their husband/stepfather has invented a machine that can change the patterns of ink on a printed page by bending sheets of uranium. They steal the machine and head across the country. Rev. Susan H. Harper, FR #70 (Aug. 1984): 47, our source for this entry.

3.382   Heinlein, Robert A. The Cat Who Walks Through Walls. New York: Putnam, 1985.

Something of a sequel to RAH's The Moon Is a Harsh Mistress (q.v.). See for Mike, the AI computer, still mostly dead but on the repair. Rev. Michael M. Levy, FR #86, 8.12 (Dec. 1985): 18, our source for this entry.

3.383   ---. The Moon Is a Harsh Mistress. New York: Putnam's, 1966. New York: Berkley, 1968. (Shorter version published in If, 1965-66.)

The lunar AI computer Mike (sometimes Michelle) aids the Revolution freeing the people of the Moon from Earth's jurisdiction and control. The mechanized "warrens" on the Moon are positively contrasted with the hive-world (our term) on Earth. See esp. 87 and 211 in Berkley edn. For discussions of MHM, see under Literary Criticism the entry for C. W. Sullivan, and H. B. Franklin's Robert A. Heinlein (162-70).

3.384   ---. Orphans of the Sky: See below, "Universe."

3.385   ---. "The Roads Must Roll." Astounding June 1940. Coll. The Best of Robert Heinlein. London: Sidgwick & Jackson, 1973. The Man Who Sold the Moon. Chicago: Shasta, [1950]. [New York]: NAL, [1951]. The Past through Tomorrow. New York: Putnam's, [1967]. Frequently rpt. including Famous Science Fiction Stories: Adventures in Time and Space. Raymond J. Healy and J. Francis McComas, eds. New York: Random, 1946, 1957. The Science Fiction Hall of Fame, vol. I. Robert Silverberg, ed. Garden City, NY: Doubleday, 1970, and New York: Avon, 1971.

Human interdependence increased in mechanized world, sufficiently to tempt Functionalists among those running the roads to attempt to seize political power. See for a positive view of "Old Dr. Pavlov" and a very negative view of users of "glib, mechanistic pseudopsychology" who "blindly and unscientifically dogmatized about the meaning of his [Ivan Petrovich Pavlov's] important, but strictly limited, experiments" (Healy and McComas, Adventures 572-3).

3.386   ---. Starship Troopers. New York: Putnam's, 1959. Rpt. New York: Berkley, 1968, 1975. New York: Ace, 1986.

Note fighting suits and the inadvertent dystopia of a future Terran federation ruled by service veterans and defended by a rigidly hierarchical, elite military establishment. The war against the "Bugs" in this novel is an allegory of the resistance of free men against "hive-communism." Cf. and contrast Joe Haldeman, Forever War (cited above). Discussed by H. B. Franklin, Robert A. Heinlein, 110-24, and by L. Heldreth, "In Search of the Ultimate Weapon" (q.v. under Literary Criticism). See cover of the 1968 Berkley edn. for the insectoid spaceships pictured—they do not appear in the novel; the cover of the 1986 Ace edn. has a postmodern, postRambo Trooper and fighting suit.

3.387   ---. "Universe." Astounding May 1941. Rpt. as book New York: Dell, 1951. Rpt. The Science Fiction Hall of Fame. Vol. IIA. Ben Bova, ed. Garden City, NY: Doubleday, 1973. New York: Avon, 1974. Rpt. with its sequel "Common Sense" as Orphans of the Sky. London: Gollancz, 1963. New York: Berkley, 1970.

Possibly the definitive story about a generation-starship: a ship whose passengers and/or crew are "men and women, whose families breed, and whose remote descendants eventually reach the destination" (S. F. Ency., "Generation Starships"). The people of "Universe" have forgotten their mission and mistake the spaceship for a world. See in this section E. Bryant's Phoenix . . ., H. Martinson's Aniara, K. O'Donnell's Mayflies, M. Leinster's "Proxima Centauri," R. J. Sawyer's Golden Fleece, N. Spinrad's "Riding the Torch," and E. C. Tubb's The Space-born; see under Drama, K.-B. Blomdahl's, Aniara, the TV series Starlost, and the Star Trek episode "For the World Is Hollow . . . ." Cf. and contrast RAH's later Citizens of the Galaxy (1957), which Sargent (1988) says features space ships which are sovereign states. "Universe" is discussed by Wolfe, esp. 61-65, and by H. Bruce Franklin in Robert A. Heinlein, 43-44; see Wolfe under Reference and both under Literary Criticism.

3.388   Hellerstein, Harry. Wired. New York: St. Martin's, 1982.

World of computer entertainment, computerized politics, computer mythology, "computer terrorism and computer crime." Rev. Fred D'Ignazio, SF&FBR #8 (Oct. 1982): 23, our source for this entry, and whom we quote.

3.389   Henderson, Zenna. "J-Line to Nowhere." F&SF 37.3 (Sept. 1979). Coll. Holding Wonder. Garden City, NY: Doubleday, 1971. London: Gollancz, 1972. Rpt. The Venus Factor. Vic Ghidalia and Roger Elwood, eds. New York: Macfadden-Bartell, 1977.

Described by Sargent (1988) as "Controlled, stable machine society without any outside and the discovery of the outside." See above, R. A. Heinlein's "Universe" and the works crosslisted there.

3.390   Herbert, Brian. Sudanna, Sudanna. New York: Arbor, 1985.

The computer Mamacita rules a planet. To enforce its edicts, including a ban on music, the computer projects "holo-cops," holograms with the power to back up the its laws. Rev. Larry D. Woods, FR #82 (Aug. 1985): 20, our source for this entry.

3.391   Herbert, Frank. Destination: Void. New York: Berkley, 1966. Rev. edn. New York: Berkley, 1978. Based on FH's "Do I Sleep or Wake," Galaxy 1965.

Both edns. relevant. The spaceship Earthling is run by an Organic Mental Core: an isolated human brain managing a computer. When the Core and its backup fail, the few awake crew members create true AI and put it in control of their ship—and of the lives of the unconscious passengers. The machine intelligence they create turns out to have godlike powers and demands "WorShip" from the crew. Discussed by Warrick 181-88, and by Wolfe 79-80; by W. Schuyler in his essay for TMG (all cited under Literary Criticism). See in this section, K. O'Donnell's Mayflies and A. McCaffrey's Helva stories.

3.392   ---. The Dragon in the Sea (vt. 21st Century Sub). 1955. New York: Avon, 1955, 1956.

In submarine warfare in the near future, the tunnel from which submarines exit their base is "a birth canal. Going through it is like being born. This sub is a perambulating womb looking for a place to spew us out." The sub is "afloat in amniotic fluid" (181), and the captain becomes "almost literally a part of his boat" (184 and passim).

3.393   ---. Hellstrom's Hive. Garden City, NY: Doubleday, 1973. New York: Bantam, 1974. Originally published as "Project 40," Galaxy Nov.-Dec. 1972 to March-April 1973.

The Hive is an underground world of machines and people: a society intentionally striving to imitate the social insects. The opposition outside the Hive is a nasty espionage bureaucracy called only "the Agency."

3.394   ---. Heretics of Dune. New York: Putnam's, 1984. New York: Berkley, 1985.

Fifth book in the Dune series, wherein FH makes more explicit themes implicit in the series relevant for mechanized environments and mechanization vs. emotions (esp. love). See Tleilaxu Face Dancers as both "communal beings" like "hive insects" and "flesh made into automata" (75; Berkley edn.), and the revelation that Tleilaxu "axlotl tanks" for the gestation of gholas are human females linked "to giant metal containers" by "a maze of dark tubes" (435). Caution: HoD uses consciously "the dangerous female" motif. See under Literary Criticism the entry for J. L. Grigsby.

3.395   ---, and Bill Ransom. The Jesus Incident. New York: Berkley-Putnam, 1979. London: Gollancz, 1979. Rpt. New York: Berkley, 1980.

A sequel to FH's Destination: Void (q.v. above). The computer-god, Ship, teaches his people the meaning of true "WorShip": to find their "own humanity and live up to it" (412 of Berkley rpt.). Rev. Brian Stableford in Foundation #19 (June 1980): 68-69, with a useful reference to the "hive intelligence" dominating the Ship-created planet of Pandora (68).

3.396   Herzog, Arthur. Glad to Be Here. New York: Crowell, 1979.

Story of computer rule and human revolt (Orth 3 [see under Reference]).

3.397   ---. Make Us Happy. New York: Crowell, 1978.

Described by Sargent (1988) as "Computer dystopia. Happiness as defined by a computer."

3.398   Hesky, Olga [Lynford]. The Purple Armchair. London: Anthony Blond, 1961.

Described by Sargent (1988), in part, as "Computer conformist dystopia," with possible significance for the motif of taming and domesticating humans; cf. works of J. Williamson (below, this section).

3.399   Heyen, William. "VIII: "The Machine that Treats Other Machines." Coll. Lord Dragonfly. New York: Vanguard, 1982. Rpt. Umbral Anthology of Science Fiction Poetry, q.v. above, under Anthologies.

Poem. The "most human" of the "XVII Machines" WH handles "can kill" and is "sure of itself as God."

3.400 High, Philip E. The Mad Metropolis (vt). New York: Ace, 1966. As Double Illusion. London: Dennis Dobson, 1970.

Described by Sargent (1988): what appears to be a computer-run eutopia is really a dystopia.

3.401 Hinz, Christopher. Anachronisms. New York: St. Martin's, 1988.

An alien invades a spaceship and takes over the computer system. A cyborg may be helping the alien. Rev. Peter Hall, SFRA Newsletter #161 (Oct. 1988): 43-44, who finds it to be "like an inferior rewriting of the film Alien," q.v. Hall's rev. rpt. SF&FBR Annual 1989: 296-97.

3.402 Hjortsberg, William. Gray Matters. New York: Simon, 1971.

In WH's future world, humankind have given up their bodies to live as brains in a huge hivelike complex. Here they go through a process of emotional purgation and perfection intended to prepare them for "Nirvana," when they will be granted use of perfect bodies grown to receive their perfected brains. See below, J. T. Sladek, The Müller-Folker Effect and the works crosslisted there.

3.403 Hoffmann, E[rnst] T. A. "The Sandman" (also, "The Sand-Man"). 1816. Tales of E.T.A. Hoffman. Leonard J. Kent and Elizabeth C. Knight, trans. Chicago: U of Chicago P, 1969. Rpt. Fantastic Worlds . . . . Eric S. Rabdin, ed., commentaries. Oxford: Oxford UP, 1979. Science Fiction: A Historical Anthology (q.v. under anthologies) 75-112.

Gothic novella featuring Dr. Coppelius and his beautiful automaton, providing a precedent two years before Mary Shelley's Frankenstein (1818) for robots and androids (see "Hoffmann" in S. F. Ency.). The clockwork automaton, Olimpia (or Olympia), went on to a long career in opera, ballet, and films; see under drama, Cappélia and the works cross-referenced there. Note also ETAH's "Automata" (1814).

3.404 Hogan, James P. Code of the Life Maker. New York: Del-Rey Ballantine, 1983.

Includes "a closely reasoned synopsis of cybernetic evolution" (in the Prologue) and the development by robots of "a complex society with its own superstitions, religions, and politics." Discussed by L. Charters, "Binary First Contact" (listed under Literary Criticism), whom we quote. Cf. and contrast "The Book of the Machines" section of S. Butler's Erewhon, P. K. Dick's "Autofac," and the Terminator films—listed under Fiction and Drama. Note also manipulations by "the leaders of the Military Industrial Complex" (quoting back blurb of 1988 printing). See below, this section, R. M. William's "Robot's Return."

3.405 ---. Minds, Machines and Evolution. New York: Spectra-Bantam, 1988.

Coll. of stories and essays. Rev. Janice M. Eisen, Aboriginal S. F. Nov.-Dec. 1988: 23, who generally disliked both the stories and essays; and Todd H. Sammons, SF&FBR Annual 1989: 297, who rather liked the essays.

3.406 ---. Two Faces of Tomorrow. New York: Ballantine (Random), 1979.

Features Spartacus, "a computer with a survival instinct, which comes to life aboard a space colony and fights humans at first . . . [but later reconciles with] its human masters" (Orth 3).

3.407 ---. Voyage from Yesteryear. Garden City, NY: Doubleday / [S. F.] Book Club [1st] Edition, 1982. New York: Del Rey-Ballantine, 1982.

Human "germ plasm carried aboard" a robot ship, to "stock" a planet with young humans "who will be raised by the robots" also sent along. The planet becomes a classless utopia, disappointing Earth visitors two generations later. Rev. W. D.

Stevens, SF&FBR #6 (July-Aug. 1982): 27, our source for this citation, and whom we quote. Cf. C. Simak, "Target Generation," and J. Williamson, Manseed, both listed in this section.

3.408   Holt, Tom. Who's Afraid of Beowulf. (c) 1988. New York: Thomas Dunne-St. Martin's, n.d. [S. F.] Book Club Edition.

Comic fantasy significant here for explicitly bracketing together magic and technology, esp. the evil magic of the villain, the sorcer-king (cf. and contrast Time Bandits, listed under Drama).

3.409   Hoover, H. M. This Time of Darkness. New York: Viking, 1980.

SF novel for adolescents featuring the escape of two youngsters from an underground hive society that resembles that of THX-1138 (q.v. under Film) in callousness and brutality. See also for automated booby-trap systems which, like those in the film of Logan's Run (q.v.), are no longer understood.

3.410   Horton, Forest W. Jr. The Technocrats. New York: Nordon (sic), 1980. A Leisure Book.

The world of Nineteen Eighty-Four brought to us by computer takeover, with the computers operating through the android president of the United States and his android chief assistant. TT is significant neither for its analysis of technocracy nor for its literary quality, but for its presentation of the motifs of robotization and computer-takeover in a book marketed for a general audience.

3.411   Hughes, Monica. The Tommorow City. London: Hamish Hamilton, 1978.

Children's novel with computer-takeover premise. The City Central Computer for Thomasville logically but unfeelingly attempts to make Thomasville into a perfect city by eliminating useless people, controlling behavior through surveillance and subliminal suggestion, and engaging in other standard acts of gentle but total control. Two children save the city. Rev. Pamela Cleaver, Foundation #15 (Jan. 1979): 100-102, our source for this entry.

3.412   Hughes, Ted. The Iron Man (vt). George Adamson, illus. London: Faber & Faber, 1968. As The Iron Giant, New York: Harper, 1968.

In this children's book, a giant Iron Man appears mysteriously in rural England and begins eating metal farm equipment. The Iron Man saves Earth from an evil alien.

3.413   Hugi, Maurice A. (pseud. of Eric Frank Russell). "Mechanical Mice." Astounding Jan. 1941. Rpt. Famous Science Fiction Stories: Adventures in Time and Space. Raymond J. Healy and J. Francis McComas, eds. New York: Modern Library-Random, 1946, 1957.

The future history glimpsed by a central character includes a machine-mediated technocracy (327 in Healy and McComas). Brings together motifs of bee hive, mouse burrow, and the Great Mother—in this case the "Robot Mother" (304, 340-1).

3.414   Huxley, Aldous. Brave New World. Garden City, NY: Doubleday, 1932. New York: Bantam, 1958. Frequently reissued.

Presents a world-state of gentle but total control. People in the "Brave New World" are conceived in bottles and, in a sense, never leave their bottle-wombs. The literal womb-bottles move through a literal machine; the figurative womb-bottles, after one is decanted, are themselves within the apparatus of the World State.

3.415   ---. Island. New York: Harper, 1962. New York: Bantam, 1963.

A dystopian element in AH's utopia is relevant: the combination of Hitler's Brownshirts, insects, and machines in the unpleasant portion of the protagonist's drug-induced vision near the end of the story (ch. 15). <u>Island</u> is discussed by R. Jehmlich in his essay for <u>CW</u> (see under Literary Criticism).

3.416   Isaac <u>Asimov's</u> <u>Robot</u> <u>City</u>. Series. New York: Ace, various dates. "ROBOT CITY is a trademark of Byron Preiss Visual Publications, Inc.," part of The Berkley Publishing Group (publisher of Ace Books).

We have examined <u>Book</u> <u>1:</u> <u>Odyssey</u> (1987) by Michael P. Kube-McDowell and <u>Book</u> <u>6:</u> <u>Perihelion</u> (1988) by William F. Wu. Asimov's introduction to the first volume ("My Robots") attributes to Byron Preiss "the notion of setting up a series of novels under the overall title of <u>Robot</u> <u>City</u> in which 'Asimovian' robots and ideas were to be freely used"—and to have Asimov's involvement to make sure the "robots <u>stay</u> 'Asimovian'" (xi). Asimov cooperated on the series up to at least vol. 6; see his introd., "Robots in Combination." Note Wu as an author with a bent for robot stories. Kube-McDowell's <u>Odyssey</u> Rev. Kenneth Felder, <u>SF&FBR</u> <u>Annual</u> (1988): 233; the third book in the series, Wu's <u>Cyborg</u> (1987), rev. Fred Runk, <u>SF&FBR</u> <u>Annual</u> (1988): 352-53.

3.417   Jarrell, Randall. "The Death of the Ball Turret Gunner." 1945. Coll. Jarrell, <u>The</u> <u>Complete</u> <u>Poems</u>. Frequently rpt. Rpt. with Jarrell's useful explanatory note in <u>Literature:</u> <u>An</u> <u>Introduction</u> <u>to</u> <u>Fiction,</u> <u>Poetry,</u> <u>and</u> <u>Drama</u>. X. J. Kennedy, ed. Boston: Little, 1976.

Poem. See for motifs of a mechanical womb and the state as machine.

3.418   Jarry, Alfred. <u>The</u> <u>Supermale:</u> <u>A</u> <u>Modern</u> <u>Novel</u>. 1902. Barbara Wright, trans. London: Cape, 1968.

An electric chair designed as a love-inducer itself falls in love with the Supermale. Summarized by V. Broege, "Technology and Sexuality" (q.v. under Literary Criticism) 104-5, our source for this entry.

3.419   Jennings, Phillip C. <u>The</u> <u>Bug</u> <u>Life</u> <u>Chronicles</u>. New York: Baen, 1989.

Presents stories of AI, identity recording, human minds in machine bodies, cyborgs, identities of the dead stored in a computer complex on Mercury playing role games. Rev. Russell Letson, <u>SF&FBR</u> <u>Annual</u> <u>1990</u>: 321, our source for this entry.

3.420   ---. "Doctor Quick." <u>Aboriginal</u> <u>S.</u> <u>F.</u> Sept.-Oct. 1988: 9 f.

Protagonist-narrator is a "soul" in a computer. The threat to her and her kind is "Radio-propagated viruses . . . [that wipe] souls and left hardware unharmed" (9). Cf. and contrast J. T. Sladek's <u>Müller-Fokker</u> <u>Effect</u> and works crosslisted there (cited below, this section).

3.421   ---. <u>Tower</u> <u>to</u> <u>the</u> <u>Sky</u>. New York: Baen, 1988.

High-tech story of a space elevator, told in "the cluttered, telegraphic style of the cyberpunks." People live in "hundreds of different cultures" within the tower, and there's a chance it may "be convertible into the largest spaceship in the universe," for one very big mechanized environment. Rev. Michael M. Levy, <u>SF&FBR</u> <u>Annual</u> <u>1989</u>: 302, our source for this entry, and whom we quote. Cf. and contrast A. C. Clarke's <u>The</u> <u>Fountains</u> <u>of</u> <u>Paradise</u> and Charles Sheffield's <u>The</u> <u>Web</u> <u>Between</u> <u>the</u> <u>Worlds</u> (both 1979).

3.422   Jerome, Jerome K. "Novel Notes" (vt "The Dancing Partner"). Interpolated narrative in <u>Novel</u> <u>Notes</u>. London: Leadenhall, 1893. <u>The</u> <u>Idler</u>, August 1893. Rpt. <u>The</u> <u>Omnibus</u> <u>of</u> <u>Crime</u>. Dorothy L. Sayers, ed. Garden City, NY: Garden City Publications, 1929.

Sayers puts "NN" in her section for "supernatural Stories" (following A. Bierce's "Moxon's Master"), but "NN" is neither a crime story nor supernatural but the tale of an electrically run "clockwork dancer" (<u>Crime</u> 811), who dances "his" partner to death while repeating from a phonograph the clichés appropriate to a young gallant at a dance. (Classified as a robot story by S. Moskowitz, S. F. by Gaslight [see under Anthologies] 22-23).

3.423   Jeter, K. W. Farewell Horizontal. New York: St. Martin's, [1989]. [S. F.] Book Club Edition.

A cyberpunk novel set upon the wall of an immense high-tech city. The narrator discovers a plot by the ruling clans to manipulate the media nets in order to remain in power. Important images are to be found in the narrator's cybernetic linkup with the information nets and in the ways of life formed by living literally on the margin of a machine world. Rev. Terry Heller, SF&FBR Annual 1990: 321-22.

3.424   ---. The Glass Hammer. New York: Bluejay, 1985.

See for talking computer.

3.425   ---. Infernal Devices: A Mad Victorian Fantasy. New York: St. Martin's, 1987.

In a 19th-century world where "Automata abound," the hero is "hounded the length of the British Isles by man and machine." Using 19th-century technology, KWJ presents a story "both modern and a parody of earlier SF styles." Rev. Robert Reilly, SF&FBR Annual 1988: 219, our source for this entry, and whom we quote.

3.426   Johannesson, Olof (pseud. of Hannes Alfven). Sagan om dem stora datamaskinin, 1966. Trans. as The Tale of the Big Computer. New York: Award, 1968. Vts The Great Computer, a Vision, and The End of Man?

A future-history written (it claims) by a computer who sees humankind as a step in the evolution of machines. See Warrick 152, and Wolfe 174-75.

3.427   Jones, D[ennis] F. Colossus. London: Hart-Davis, 1966. New York: Berkley, 1976.

The first book of the Colossus trilogy (with The Fall of Colossus and Colossus and the Crab). Colossus presents the computer-takeover theme, with a significant variation on the containment motif usual in dystopias: the world of this novel becomes a prison for the protagonist; he is only free when in the nurturing containment of his bedroom. Cf. and contrast Winston and Julia in the room over the shop in G. Orwell's Nineteen Eighty-Four. See under Drama, Colossus: The Forbin Project; see under Literary Criticism, R. Erlich, "D. F. Jones's Colossus."

3.428   Jones, Gonnor. The Dome. London: Faber, 1968.

Described by Sargent (1988) as featuring "Machine that can project feelings into the brain."

3.429   Jones, Gwyneth. Escape Plans. London: Unwin, 1986.

In Feminism and Science Fiction (ch. 5), Sara Lefanu says EP posits a cleaned-up Earth made into a nature preserve as a resort for off-world rulers; common folk, "or numbers, have been tidied away below the surface"—and "Some of the numbers are literally plugged into the system, with sockets burned into their brains. But, apparently dehumanised, machine-interfaced" they and the masses more generally "are still human, despite their enforced cultural poverty" (quoting Lefanu, IUP rpt. 51). Cf. and contrast H. G. Wells's The Time Machine, E. M. Foster's "The Machine Stops," S. R. Delany's Nova (listed in this section), and the films Metropolis, THX 1138, and Mad Max Beyond Thunderdome (cited under Drama).

3.430   Jones, Raymond F. "The Cybernetic Brains." Startling Stories 22.1 (Sept., 1950). The Cybernetic Brians. New York: Avalon, 1962.

Described by Sargent (1988) as "Computer dystopia."

3.431 ---. "Rat Race." <u>Analog</u> 77.2 (April 1966). Rpt. <u>Above the Human Landscape</u>. Willis E. McNelly and Leon E. Stover, eds. Pacific Palisades, CA: Goodyear Pub. Co., 1972.

In "the Abundant Society," all individual production is prohibited to allow total control by those who rule and are ruled by the "mammoth, world-wide computer system" (<u>Landscape</u> 256). "RR" offers the hope that the system will be destroyed by a fad among men—the story presents women rather negatively—of model railroad kits. Cf. and contrast F. Pohl's "Midas Plague" and J. Williamson's Humanoids stories (cited below).

3.432 Jorgenson, A.K. "Coming-of-Age Day." <u>Science Fantasy</u> #76, 24 (Sept. 1965). Rpt. <u>Above the Human Landscape</u>. Willis E. McNelly and Leon E. Stover, eds. Pacific Palisades, CA: Goodyear Pub. Co., 1972. <u>Future Power</u>. Jack Dann, ed. New York: Random, 1976.

"Consex" sexual appliances are apparently all organic, but they supply to everyone fitted with them (almost every sexually mature human in the world of "C-o-AD") sexual activity that is at least metaphorically "mechanical," and habit-forming. Cf. and contrast J. Russ's "An Old-Fashioned Girl" and H. Ellison's "Catman."

3.433 Joron, Andrew. "The Tetrahedron Letters." <u>Portland Review</u>, 1979. Rpt. <u>Umbral Anthology of Science Fiction Poetry</u>, q.v. above, under Anthologies.

Poem. Uses clockwork-world motifs.

3.434 Kafka, Franz. "In der Strafkolonie" ("In the Penal Colony"). 1919. Frequently coll. and rpt. including <u>The Penal Colony: Stories & Short Pieces</u> .... Willa Muir and Edwin Muir, trans. New York: Schocken, 1961.

Realistically narrated horror story, featuring a machine very memorably imposing the mechanical upon the human.

3.435 Kagan, Janet. <u>Hellspark</u>. New York: TOR, 1988.

Aided by her AI ship's computer (Maggy), the protagonist must save a planet from exploitation by proving the sentience of the planet's natives, and also that of her computer. Rev. Michael M. Levy, <u>SF&FBR Annual 1989</u>: 306-7, our source for this entry.

3.436 Kahn, James. <u>Return of the Jedi</u>. New York: Del Rey-Ballantine, 1983.

See <u>Return of the Jedi</u> under Drama. See also the entries for D. F. Glut, and G. Lucas, this section. The novelization is more explicit than the film in its handling of the philosophical implications of the Force and the opposition between the Empire and the Rebel Alliance.

3.437 Kandel, Michael. <u>Strange Invasion</u>. New York: Spectra-Bantam, 1989.

The book begins, "The spaceship, landing in my backyard, disguised itself as a bird feeder with birds." Rev. Steve Carper, <u>SFRA Newsletter</u> #180 (Sept. 1990): 33, our source for this entry. Note what we will call the superimpostion of the avian upon the mechanical—and the image of machine transformation.

3.438 Kapp, Colin. <u>Cageworld 1: Search for the Sun</u>. <u>Cageworld 2: The Lost Worlds of Cronus</u>. London: New English Library, 1982.

Note setting: high-tech on the scale of the solar system, run by a computer-god. Rev. Brian Stableford, <u>SF&FBR</u> #5 (June 1982): 23, our source for this citation. See CK entry below.

3.439 ---. <u>Cageworld 3: The Tyrant of Hades</u>. London: New English Library, 1982.

A team of heroes discovers "that the Neptune [Dyson] shell has been taken over by an alien intelligence, which has displaced man's friendly neighborhood computer-god Zeus for its own nefarious purposes." Rev. Brian Stableford, SF&FBR #8 (Oct. 1982): 23, our source for this entry, and whom we quote,

3.440   Kelleher, Victor. The Beast of Heaven. St. Lucia, Queensland: U of Queensland P, 1984.

Contains a debate between two computers over the rights of their creators to survive the holocaust (which occurs during the debate). Thousands of years later the computers are discovered by a primitive tribe which is attempting to survive in the changed world. Rev. Michael J. Tolley, FR #71 (Sept. 1984): 31, our source for this entry.

3.441   Keller, David H., M.D. "The Revolt of the Pedestrians." Amazing 2 (Feb. 1928). Rpt. Beyond Time and Space. August Derleth, ed. New York: Pellegrini and Cudahy, 1950. Isaac Asimov and Martin H. Greenberg, eds. Amazing Stories: Sixty Years of the Best Science Fiction. Lake Geneva, WI: TSR, 1985.

Described by Sargent (1988) as "Pedestrians outlawed. Small group survives and successfully revolts." Cf. R. Bradbury's "Pedestrian" and F. Leiber's "X Marks the Pedwalk," listed in this section.

3.442   Kenney, Richard. Orrery. New York: Atheneum, 1986.

Book-length "'poem of the mind'," putting together poems and sequences of poems. According to Jay Parini, in a rev. in The Nation (26 April 1986), Orrery has as its "central metaphor...the orrery of the title": a mechanical representation of the solar system. Poem includes reference to the "simple clockwork / world" of a farm; in his review, Parini stresses the mechanical—in a neutral sense—construction of Orrery (Nation 594).

3.443   Kenyon, Ernest M. Rogue Golem. New York: Popular Library (CBS Publications), 1977.

A minor government official seems to suffer from "robopathology"; he has come to think that he is a machine. See L. Yablonsky entry under Background.

3.444   Kesey, Ken. One Flew Over the Cuckoo's Nest. New York: Viking, 1962. New York: NAL, [1963].

A "total Institution," an insane asylum, becomes a microcosm for a world in danger of succumbing to mechanizing and castrating influences represented in the Narrator's mind as "the Combine." Features a Terrible Mother (Big Nurse) opposed to a clownish rebel (R. P. McMurphy). Since the Narrator is insane for much of the book, the mechanization motifs are mostly metaphoric, and OFOCN is a mainstream work. Caution: a rather misogynist work.

3.445   Key, Alexander. Bolts, a Robot Dog (1966); Rivets and Sprockets (1964); Sprockets, a Little Robot (1963). All illus. Alexander Key. Philadelphia: Westminster P.

Details the adventures of the Bailey family with Sprockets, a little robot accidentally given an "Asimov positronic brain," and with his half-brother Rivets and Bolts, a robot dog. See M. Esmonde TMG entry under Literary Criticism.

3.446   Keyes, Kenneth S., Jr. and Jacque Fresco. Looking Forward. South Brunswick, NJ: A.S. Barnes, 1969.

Described by Sargent (1988), as "Computer-based eutopia set in the future," including computer control of production and distribution, with "no industrial work for people. Work is administrative and creative." Strongly contrast tone of E. M. Forster's "The Machine Stops" and J. Williamson's Humanoids stories, starting with "With Folded Hands"—all listed under Fiction.

3.447   Kilian, Crawford. Brother Jonathan. New York: Ace/Berkley, 1985.

Cyberpunk novel with a standard super-hacker protagonist and supercorporation setting. A retarded person receives an implant intended to restore normal functioning. The implant instead bestows greater than normal faculties, including the ability to interface with the net. Rev. W. D. Stevens, <u>FR</u> #80 (June 1985): 27, our source for this entry.

3.448   ---. <u>Gryphon</u>. New York: Ballantine, 1989.

Hard S. F. See esp. "Net": a set of "life-forms all in contact through Database, a huge computer network." Rev. J. R. Wytenbroek, <u>SFRA</u> <u>Newsletter</u> #185 (March 1991): 53, our source for this entry, and whom we quote.

3.449   Killough, Lee. <u>Deadly</u> <u>Silents</u>. New York: Ballantine, 1981.

Terran cops brought to an alien world to help stop violent crimes coming from an equivalent of ethnic strife in a culture in which "right brain" dominance and telepathy are normal and being a nontelepathic Silent is abnormal. The cops are Terran-normal: left-brain dominant and sufficently a part of a highly computerized operation to be described by Betsy Harfst in a paper at the 13th Annual Convention of the Popular Culture Association as "walking extensions of the machine" ("A Brain Divided: Behavior and Motive in <u>Deadly</u> <u>Silents</u>," Wichita, April 1983), our source for this entry. See below, M. Crichton's <u>Andromeda</u> <u>Strain</u> and the article thereon by P. Alterman, cited under Literary Criticism.

3.450   Kilworth, Garry. <u>A</u> <u>Theatre</u> <u>of</u> <u>Timesmiths</u>. North Pomfret, VT: David & Charles, Inc., London: Victor Gollancz, dist., 1984.

A 32nd-c. domed city is ruled by five consuls and their overlord, a satanic computer. Rev. Richard Law, <u>FR</u> #82 (Aug. 1985): 22, our source for this entry.

3.451   King, Stephen (writing as Richard Bachman). <u>The</u> <u>Running</u> <u>Man</u>. New York: Signet-NAL, 1982.

Source for the movie (q.v. under Drama) but very different from the Arnold Schwarzenegger vehicle. The "Bachman" novel is more sophisticated, tragic, and politically subversive than the film but arguably less satiric (and certainly less comic) in its attack on television—and far less science fictional in its setting and gadgets. Cf. and contrast novel and film to spot some visual motifs (many involving electronics) film-makers in the late 1980s chose to add to a book from 1982.

3.452   Kipling, Rudyard, "Wireless." <u>Scribner's</u> <u>Magazine</u> Aug. 1902. Coll. <u>Traffics and</u> <u>Discoveries, by</u> <u>Rudyard</u> <u>Kipling</u>. New York: Doubleday, 1904. Rpt. <u>The</u> <u>Moonlight</u> <u>Traveler</u> (vt <u>Great</u> <u>Tales</u> <u>of</u> <u>Fantasy</u> <u>and</u> <u>Imagination</u>). Phillip Van D. Stern, ed. Garden City, NY: Doubleday, 1943.

Discussed by B. Stableford as an instance of RK's interest in new technologies (123).

3.453   Kirchner, Paul. "Hive." <u>Heavy</u> <u>Metal</u> Jan. 1980: 89-95.

The opening sentence of the text informs us that "THE HIVE IS A SUBTERRANEAN WORLD WHERE MAN AND MACHINE ARE ONE." Some of the artwork gets across this idea.

3.454   Knight, Damon. <u>A</u> <u>for</u> <u>Anything</u> (vt). London: New English Library, Four Square, 1961. Rpt. New York: Walker, 1970. Shorter version as <u>The</u> <u>People</u> <u>Maker</u>. Rockville, NY: Zenith, 1959.

Described by Sargent (1988) as "Rigid, stratified, slave society as a result of a machine that can reproduce anything."

3.455   ---. "Masks." <u>Playboy</u> July 1968. Rpt. with Knight's annotations, <u>Those Who Can</u> . . . . Robin Scott Wilson, ed. New York: NAL, 1973. Also rpt. <u>As Tomorrow Becomes Today</u> (q.v. under Anthologies and Collections).

Important story detailing the antiorganic psychological effects of total replacement of a man's body with mechanical devices. See Gordon's <u>TMG</u> essay listed under Literary Criticism.

3.456   ---. "Natural State." <u>Galaxy</u> 7.5 (Jan. 1951). Coll. <u>Three Novels</u>. Garden City, NY: Doubleday, 1967. Rpt. <u>All About the Future</u>. Martin Greenberg, ed. New York: Gnome, 1955. Expanded into <u>Masters of Evolution</u>. New York: Ace, 1959.

Cited by A. O. Lewis in "Utopia, Technology, and Social Evolution" (cited under Literary Criticism) as an arcadian society living in harmony with nature <u>and</u> using appropriate technology (Lewis 174), and by Sargent (1988). Cf. city and garden worlds in A. C. Clarke's <u>The City and the Stars</u>, cited above.

3.457   ---. <u>The World and Thorinn</u>. (c) 1980. New York: Berkley (distributed by Putnam), n.d. [S. F.] Book Club Edition. Simultaneous publication in Canada, Toronto: Academic P. "Portions of this book appeared in a different form in <u>Galaxy</u> . . . as follows: 'The World and Thorinn,' April[,] 1968; 'The Garden of Ease,' June, 1968; 'The Star Below,' August, 1968."

Rather literal clockwork god in the Monitor: the computer ruler of the novel's far-future world, but see primarily for "the box"—the portable computer terminal that aids Thorinn, and whose interaction with Thorinn is significant for differences in the way humans and "engines" think.

3.458   Koontz, Dean R. <u>Demon Seed</u>. New York: Bantam, 1973.

Proteus, a giant computer, takes over a house computer and servo-mechanisms, traps a woman, and attempts to impregnate her. See <u>Demon Seed</u> under Drama.

3.459   Kornbluth, C. M. "The Luckiest Man in Denv." <u>Galaxy</u> June 1952 (under pseud. of Simon Eisner [Contento]). Coll. <u>The Marching Morons</u>. New York: Ballantine, [1959]. Rpt. <u>Cities of Wonder</u>, q.v. above, under Anthologies. See Contento <u>Index</u> for numerous rpts.

Denv is a militarized city, engaged in low-intensity, and interminable, atomic warfare with "Ellay"—a war that may have started over water from the Colorado River (<u>Cities of Wonder</u> 159). See for a young man moving up in his world: personally, politically, and topographically; cf. the literalization of "moving up" in R. Silverberg's <u>The World Inside</u>, listed below.

3.460   ---, and Frederik Pohl. <u>Wolfbane</u>. New York: Ballantine, 1959. London: Gollancz, 1960. Shorter version published in two parts in <u>Galaxy</u> Oct., Nov. 1957.

Baroque variations on the theme of the relationship between persons (both human and nonhuman) and machines, with much use of the motif of mechanized environments. See for machine takeover and a group mind, mechanical "wombs," and an ultimately dangerous "womb-world" (our locution)—and for the possible mechanization and deification of persons and machines.

3.461   Krahn, Fernando. <u>Robot-bot-bot</u>. New York: Dutton, 1979.

A wordless picture book. A family's new domestic robot conscientiously performs a variety of household chores until the young daughter tampers with its wiring and it goes berserk. Father rewires it to be daughter's playmate and companion.

3.462   Kress, Nancy. <u>An Alien Light</u>. New York: Arbor, 1988.

Two primitive humans, descended from spaceship-crash survivors, are placed in a high-tech city so that alien enemies of humanity can study their reactions. Rev. Michael M. Levy, SFRA Newsletter #158 (June-July 1988): 35.

3.463   Kube-McDowell, Michael P. Odyssey. New York: Ace, 1987.

See above, Isaac Asimov's Robot City. This is Book 1 of the series. Rev. Kenneth Felder, SF&FBR Annual 1988: 233.

3.464   Kuttner, Henry. "Ghost." Astounding May 1943.

Discussed by John Foyster, "The Long View 4," ASFR 2nd series #9, 2.4 (July 1987): 13-14: the premise is "that computers may be susceptible to human neuroses," combined with "a case for the existence of 'real' ghosts by technological rather than supernatural means" in that a man's "'ghost' . . . haunts the research station by the manifestation of his personality through the infected computers."

3.465   ---. "Jesting Pilot." Astounding May 1947. Rpt. Cities of Wonder, q.v. above, under Anthologies and Collections.

"Civilization is an artificial environment. With the machines that were necessary" to save a Barrier-enclosed, post-disaster city preserving a remnant of humanity, "the city became so artificial that nobody could live in it" without going mad and then dying from sensory overload. The solution is to have Controllers who "were blind and deaf and dumb, and lacking in certain other senses," compensated for by telepathy, and citizens hypnotized into not noticing the tumult (Cities of Wonder 60). A citizen glimpses the truth of the city and is motivated to try to leave it (62-63).

3.466   ---. Robots Have No Tails. New York: Gnome, 1952.

Fixup of five stories from 1943-48, featuring a narcissistic robot (see S. F. Ency., "Robots," and Anatomy, 1987, 3-245).

3.467   ---, and Catherine L. Moore. "Two-handed Engine." F&SF 9.2 (Aug. 1955). Coll. No Boundaries. New York: Ballantine, 1955.

Described by Sargent (1988): in a society ruled by machines, both cops and courts are "replaced by almost infallible machines."

3.468   --- (writing as Lewis Padgett [possibly in collaboration with C. L. Moore]). "The Twonky." Astounding Sept. 1942. Rpt. Souls in Metal, q.v. under Anthologies.

A "twonky" is "more than a robot" and a lot more than the radio it appears to be: it's a monitoring, "readjusting," and, if necessary, destroying machine. Made into a film by Arch Oboler (see The Twonky under Drama).

3.469   L'Engle, Madeleine. A Wrinkle in Time. New York: Ariel, 1962. New York: Dell, 1975. A Yearling Book.

A father is the "prisoner of IT, a giant brain that pulses and quivers and desires to control and subjugate all human life." The man's son has his mind captured by IT, but the heroine "Meg, in a climactic struggle with the computer, resists . . . and wins her brother back through the force of her love for him" (M. Esmonde, "Little Buddy . . ." [see under Literary Criticism] TMG 94; see Wrinkle 204-209); Meg also rescues her father.

3.470   Lafferty, R. A. Past Master. New York: Ace, 1968.

A dual dystopia set in the mechanically dead golden cities of Astrobe and in the seeming "cancers" on Astrobe: the vast slum cities of Cathead and the Barrio. See for "programmed people" and for a rather idiosyncratic reading of Sir Thomas More's Utopia. See under Literary Criticism the CW essay by W. Hardesty.

3.471   Laidlaw, Marc. Neon Lotus. New York: Spectra-Bantam, 1988.

Modern romance in which the Tibetan Buddha of Compassion is actually an AI
computer. Rev. William M. Schuyler, Jr., quite negatively, SF&FBR Annual 1989:
316-17, our source for this entry.

3.472   Lake, David. "Creator." Envisioned Worlds. Paul Collins, ed. Melbourne: VOID, 1978.
Rpt. Science Fiction: The Future. Dick Allen, ed. 2d edn. New York: Harcourt,
1983. Matilda at the Speed of Light. Damien Broderick, ed. Sydney: Angus &
Robertson, 1988.

See for metaphysical, theological, and ethical implications of using machines to
create private universes for one's own pleasure.

3.473   Landsman, Sandy. The Gadget Factor. New York: Atheneum, 1984.

Novel for fairly young readers. Two teenage computer whizzes go to college and
create a computer program capable of creating or destroying the universe. Rev.
Allene Stuart Phy, FR #75 (Jan. 1985): 46, our source for this entry.

3.474   Lanier, Sterling E. Menace Under Marswood. New York: Del Rey-Ballantine, 1983.

See for a pet which looks like a machine-like insect (a possible test for the
contemporaneous Dunn-Erlich hypothesis that insectoid machines in SF are "Bad
Things"). Rev. Glenn M. Reed, FR #70 (Aug. 1984): 13, our source for this entry.

3.475   Laumer, [John] Keith. A Plague of Demons. New York: Berkley, 1965. London:
Millington, 1975.

Cited by B. Stableford as a useful example of cyborgs adapted to espionage and war
(S. F. Ency., "Cyborgs").

3.476   ---. Rogue Bolo. New York: Baen, 1986.

Coll. of three stories featuring Bolos, KL's AI tanks. The title story has a Bolo pretty
well running things, overseeing "the Prussification of the entire economy" of
humanity. The "permanent war economy" proves necessary, so the Bolo can be seen
as a cybernetic tyrant in a computer takeover story—or a hero. Rev. Jackson Houser,
FR #90, 9.4 (April 1986): 24-25, our source for this entry, and whom we quote.

3.477   Le Guin, Ursula K. Always Coming Home. New York: Harper, 1985. New York:
Bantam, 1986. Todd Barton, composer. Margaret Chodos, illus. George Hersh,
geomancer. Maps by UKL.

See esp. the three parts of Stone Telling's story, the section on Time and the City
(with careful attention to "The City," and "A Hole in the Air"), and, at The Back of
the Book, the sections "About the Train" and "The Metaphor: The Machine" under
"Some Generative Metaphors." In the hypothetical, fairly-far future world of ACH,
there are many sites for "computers with mechanical extensions. . . . [forming] the
City of Mind." The machines gather and exchange information and explore both the
planet and space; the machines interact with humans and allow humans to interact
through "the Exchange": to most people "a useful and necessary link to . . . [a
number of] necessary and undesirable elements of existence" (Bantam edn. 156-59).
The City of Mind correlates with "the City of Man," or "Civilization as we know it"
(160). In ACH, sane human people eschew such civilization and cities and choose to
live in low-tech villages.

3.478   ---. "The Lathe of Heaven." Amazing March, May 1971. Rpt. as novel, New York:
Scribner's, 1971. New York: Avon, 1973.

See for Dr. Haber's "dream machine" and his use of it to control the world. See
below, under Drama the PBS film of LoH. See above, this section, J. W. Hayes,
Paradise . . . .

3.479   Lee, Stan. The Power of Iron Man: The Enemy Within: Cited under SL, under Graphics.

3.480   Lee, Tanith. Electric Forest. New York: DAW, 1979. Garden City, NY: Doubleday, n.d. [S. F.] Book Club Edition.

In the experiment that is the Consciousness Transferral Project (and almost all of EF), the ugly Magdala trades freedom for a beautiful body, a cybernetic extension of her "true" body, which is preserved in a cocoonlike device. Cf. James Tiptree, Jr., "The Girl Who Was Plugged In," q.v., below, this section. (See in S. F. Ency., "Waldo.")

3.481   ---. "A Madonna of the Machine." In 1989 Annual World's Best SF (q.v. under Anthologies).

In effect, a New Wave reconsideration of E. M. Forster's "The Machine Stops" (q.v. above). One of the manual laborers bred to care for the Machine has a vision of a beautiful woman who does not fit in with the grayness of the Machine world. Soon others experience the vision, and the story ends optimistically, promising change.

3.482   Leiber, Fritz. "The Silver Eggheads." F&SF 16.1 (Jan. 1959). Expanded into The Silver Eggheads. New York: Ballantine, 1961.

Described by Sargent (1988): in a world where publishing is fully automated, books are written by computer, and a female robot censors them.

3.483   ---. "X Marks the Pedwalk." Worlds of Tomorrow 1.1 (April 1963). Rpt. Nightmare Age. Frederik Pohl, ed. New York: Ballantine, 1970.

According to Sargent (1988), shows a society where some are "wheeled" and others are pedestrians. Sargent recommends comparison with D.H. Keller, "Revolt of the Pedestrians," and R. Bradbury, "The Pedestrian," q.v., this section.

3.484   Leiber, Justin. Beyond Gravity. New York: TOR, 1988.

See for an alien species on a satellite, robotics, and total-body prosthetics. Rev. Thom Dunn, SF&FBR Annual 1989: 323.

3.485   ---. "Beyond Rejection." Excerpt from Beyond Rejection. New York: Ballantine (Random), 1980. Rpt. The Mind's I, q.v. under Anthologies (242-52).

The human mind as "software" that can be recorded on tape and transferred to a new body. Cf. and contrast F. Pohl's "Day Million" (cited in this section).

3.486   Leinster, Murray (pseud. of William F. Jenkins). The Last Space Ship. New York: Frederick Fell, 1949.

Described by Sargent (1988) as "Authoritarian dystopia," with technology supporting tyranny, emphasizing a revolt that succeeds.

3.487   ---. "A Logic Named Joe." Astounding March 1946. Rpt. Modern Masterpieces in Science Fiction. Sam Moskowitz, ed. Cleveland: World, 1965. Also rpt. Souls in Metal. Mike Ashley, compiler. New York: St. Martin's, 1977. New York: Jove-HBJ (Harcourt), 1978. Isaac Asimov Presents the Best of Science Fiction Firsts. Isaac Asimov et al., eds. New York: Beaufort, 1984.

A "logic" (what we would call a computer terminal) becomes a self-conscious individual because of a minor mistake on the assembly line. Joe gets the other logics to give people all the data they might want, with amusing results for ML's readers but trouble for the human characters: logics are central to the civilization in the story, and the system can't be disconnected.

3.488   ---. "Proxima Centauri." Astounding March 1935. Rpt. The Road to Science Fiction #2: From Wells to Heinlein. James Gunn, ed. New York: NAL, 1979.

Features a generation starship as "a self-contained, self-sustaining world" (Gunn). Cf. Robert Heinlein's "Universe" (cited under Fiction), Starlost, and the Star Trek episode "For the World is Hollow" (cited under Drama).

3.489   Lem, Stanislaw.

For additional readings, see the articles, notes, and works cited in SFS #40, 13.3 (Nov. 1986), and SFS #57, 19.2 (July 1992): the SFS special issues on Lem.

3.490   Lem, Stanislaw. "The Accident." In More Tales of Pirx the Pilot, q.v. under SL under Anthologies and Collections.

See for an adventurous robot "more like his designers than any of them cared to admit" (49).

3.491   ---. "Ananke." In More Tales of Pirx the Pilot, q.v. under Anthologies and Collections.

A computer causes a fatal accident because its teacher suffers from "anankastic syndrome"—compulsive neurosis (210-11). See also for human intuition (a motif in the fiction of SL).

3.492   ---. "The Computer That Fought a Dragon." Krzysztof Klinger, trans. Other Worlds, Other Seas: Science Fiction Stories from Socialist Countries. Darko Suvin, ed. New York: Random, 1970. Also in Mortal Engines, q.v. under SL under Anthologies and Collections, as "Tale of the Computer That Fought a Dragon."

A modern fairy tale of a battle between computers and the beast-threats they create.

3.493   ---. The Cyberiad: Fables for the Cybernetic Age. Michael Kandel, trans. New York: Seabury, 1974.

Translation of selected fiction by Lem. See under Literary Criticism, M. Kandel, and the TMG essay by C. Thomsen; see also Warrick 193-98.

3.494   ---. "The Experiment (A Review of 'Non Serviam,' by James Dobb)." Michael Kandel, trans. The New Yorker 24 July 1979: 26 f. Coll. A Perfect Vacuum: Perfect Reviews of Nonexistent Books. New York: Harcourt, 1979. Rpt. The Mind's I, q.v. under Anthologies.

The nonexistent "Non Serviam" presents the life and philosophy of "personoids," mathematical analogs to humans; the personoids are contained in computers. SL may see the "personoid" condition as similar to the human condition.

3.495   ---. Fiasco. Michael Kendel, trans. San Diego: Harcourt, 1987.

See for tiny robots (as in SL's Invincible, q.v. below), and for "the limitations of computers and of the human mind." Rev. Frank H. Tucker, SF&FBR Annual 1988: 240-41, our source for this entry, and whom we quote.

3.496   ---. "In Hot Pursuit of Happiness." 1971. Rpt. View from Another Shore: European Science Fiction. Franz Rottensteiner, ed. New York: Seabury, 1973.

A satiric tale of a robot's attempt to build utopia.

3.497   ---. "The Hunt." In Lem, Mortal Engines, and More Tales of Pirx the Pilot, q.v. under Anthologies and Collections.

Battle between men and a dangerous, damaged robot in which the robot may finally save Pirx's life. Summarized by Warrick 196-97.

3.498   ---. Imaginary Magnitude. Trans. Marc E. Heine of Wielkosc urojona [1973], supplemented by two pieces from Golem XIV [1981]. San Diego: Harcourt, 1984.

Golem XIV is a sentient AI computer that lectures on personhood, freedom of choice, and individuality. A second lecture by the computer focuses on the movement of humans between the poles of logic and antilogic and the necessity of humans' inventing "primal authority" to reduce the amount of freedom which the intellect bestows. Rev. Frank H. Tucker, FR #74 (Dec. 1984): 27, our source for the quotation, and this entry.

3.499   ---. "The Inquest." In More Tales of Pirx the Pilot, q.v. under Anthologies and Collections.

Pirx's attempt to tell humanoid robots from humans leads to a significant philosophical inquiry and to a low-key celebration of "bumbling human decency" (161).

3.500   ---. The Invincible. 1964. Wendayne Ackerman, trans. (from the German). New York: Seabury, 1973.

Machine evolution produces minute robot insects. See above, SL's Fiasco, and below, his "The Upside-Down Evolution." Discussed by Jerzy Jarzębski, in "Stanislaw Lem, Rationalist and Visionary" (Franz Rottensteiner, trans.), SFS #12, 4.2 (July 1977): 115.

3.501   ---. "The Mask." Coll. Mortal Engines, q.v. under Anthologies and Collections.

Tragic love between a man and a female robot; deals with the awakening consciousness of the robot that she is not a woman but a machine. Summarized by Warrick 197. See under Literary Criticism the TMG essay by C. W. Thomsen.

3.502   ---. Memoirs Found in a Bathtub. 1961. Michael Kandel and Christine Rose, trans. New York: Seabury, 1973.

In the same way that Ahab and Ishmael in Moby Dick strive to determine the meaning of the White Whale, the Narrator of MFB tries to find the meaning of a labyrinthian building that seems to determine the lives of the people inside.

3.503   ---. Memoirs of a Space Traveler: Further Reminiscences of Ijon Tichy. Joel Stern and Maria Swiecicka-Ziemianek, trans. New York: Harvest-Harcourt, 1982.

SL's satire includes a machine-controlled society of "Phools," who are literally eaten by the machine (of State). Rev. David Nixon, FR #66 (April 1984): 25, and Alexander Butrym, SF&FBR #4 (May 1982): 24, our sources for this citation.

3.504   ---. Return From the Stars (Powrot z gwiazd, 1961). Barbara Marszal and Frank Simpson, trans. New York: Harcourt, 1980.

Shows an Earth with highly developed technology, a world where all work is performed by robots.

3.505   ---. "The Sanatorium of Dr. Vliperdius." Coll. Mortal Engines (q.v.). Also in The Star Diaries. Michael Kandel, trans. New York: Seabury, 1976.

Mental disease in robots (see Warrick 193-94).

3.506   ---. "The Seventh Sally." Coll. The Cyberiad, q.v. above, this section. Rpt. The Mind's I, q.v. under Anthologies and Collections.

The creation by a robot of a miniature cybernetic kingdom whose citizens are abused by a tyrant; stresses the criminality of abandoning to suffering any creatures capable of suffering. Summarized by Warrick 196.

3.507   ---. "Terminus." In Tales of Pirx the Pilot (Opowiesci o pilocie Pirxie). Louis Iribarne, trans. New York: Harcourt, 1979. "A Helen and Kurt Wolff Book." Trans. of .

A kind of anti-golem story, making the point that the robot Terminus is only "a machine, an insensate machine, capable of transmitting a . . . [previously recorded] set of sounds—that and nothing more" (206, 202), even when the sounds are the desperate Morse code messages of a dying crew.

3.508   ---. "The Upside-Down Evolution." In One Human Minute. Catherine S. Leach, trans. San Diego: Harcourt, 1986 (English language copyright). "A Helen and Kurt Wolff Book."

Important for AI. Features "synsects" (articifial insects), a creation of microchip technology. Because they operate individually and as a swarm, the synsects render obsolete all other forms of warfare. Synsects represent artificial nonintelligence, or artifical instinct, the real new wave (SL suggests) of the computerized future. Rev. Gerald Jones, in "Attack of the Killer Synsects," The New York Times Book Review 9 Feb. 1986. See above, SL's Fiasco and Invincible.

3.509   Leroe, Ellen W. Robot Romance. New York: Harper, 1985.

Humorous, satirical young-adult book set at Silicon Computer High School, a school for human teenagers and robots. The young hero brings poetry, music, love, and humanization to SilCo High. Rev. Mary S. Weinkauf, FR #87, 9.1 (Jan. 1986): 21; and see Sargent (1988)—our sources for this entry.

3.510   Leven, Jeremy. Satan: His Psychotherapy and Cure by the Unfortunate Dr. Kassler, J.S.P.S. London: Joseph, 1982. New York: Knopf, 1982.

Satan made flesh (so to speak) in an AI; Satan describes himself not as evil but Reason. Very favorably rev. Brian Stableford, SF&FBR #10 (Dec. 1982): 29-30, our source for most of this entry.

3.511   Levin, Ira. This Perfect Day. New York: Random, 1970.

Machine-like behavior is enforced by computerized surveillance.

3.512   Lewis, C. S. The Screwtape Letters & Screwtape Proposes a Toast. New York: Collier-Macmillan, 1961. London: Geoffrey Bles, 1961. Expansion, as indicated, of The Screwtape Letters (1942).

Theological fantasy significant here for presenting the Devil as not only a gentleman but also a bureaucrat, and in presenting the Underworld as a perversely ordered bureaucracy. See Lewis's Preface, esp. ix-x; see under Literary Criticism the CW essay by M. Abrash on Dante's Hell.

3.513   ---. That Hideous Strength. London: Bodley Head, 1945. New York: Macmillan, 1965 (bears copyright notice of 1946). See Currey for abridged texts (Currey listed under References).

Note the high-tech preservation of the head of Alcasan, the computerlike "Pragmatometer," and the thoroughly nasty bureaucracy of N.I.C.E. See under Literary Criticism the TMG essay by R. Spraycar.

3.514   Leyner, Mark. "I Was an Infinitely Hot and Dense Dot." MR47/48: 66-69 (see under Literary Criticism, L. McCaffery, guest ed.).

Parody of cyberpunk, we assume intentional. (The Contributors section of MR47/48 notes this story as "part of . . . , My cousin, my gastroenterologist.")

3.515   Lind, Jakov. The Inventor. London: Metheun, 1987. New York: Braziller, 1988.

Mainstream epistolary novel in the traditon of Voltaire's Candide. The protagonist tries to raise money to build "The Redemption Machine," a supercomputer that can replace Messiah and reduce the world to reason (13).

3.516   Littel, Jonathan. <u>Bad Voltage</u>. New York: Signet-NAL, 1989.

Cyberpunk novel set in Paris. Rev. Marcia Marx, <u>SFRA</u> <u>Newsletter</u> #186 (April 1991): 47, our source for this entry.

3.517   London, Jack. "A Curious Fragment." 1908. Rpt. <u>Science</u> <u>Fiction: A Historical Anthology</u>, q.v. under Anthologies.

The grim master/slave society that JL envisions for the 28th c. is an eerie precursor of G. Orwell's <u>Nineteen Eighty-Four</u> and other dystopias from later in the 20th c.

3.518   Long, Frank Belknap. <u>It Was the Day of the Robot</u>. New York: Belmont, 1963. London: Dennis Dobson, 1964.

According to Sargent (1988), <u>IWDR</u> shows a dystopia controlled by robots.

3.519   ---. "The Robot Empire." <u>Astounding</u> 1934. Rpt. <u>Avon Science Fiction Reader</u>. New York: Avon, 1952.

One of the first stories using robots and the theme of the mechanical god.

3.520   Longyear, Barry B. <u>Naked Came the Robot</u>. New York: Popular Library-Warner, 1988.

The basic plot of Stephen Crane's <u>The Red Badge of Courage</u>, handled with an absurdist sensibility, for the purpose of satirizing (mostly) SF motifs and personalities, including the themes of robot take-over, robotization of humans, the association of machines and bugs (cockroaches, spiders), and the human perversion of mechanisexuality. Rev. Michael M. Levy, <u>SF&FBR Annual 1989</u>: 329-30. See below, this section, J. T. Sladek, <u>The Reproductive System</u>.

3.521   ---. <u>Sea of Glass</u>. New York: St. Martin's, 1987.

See for motifs of enclosure in a house where the growing protagonist's contact with the world is watching TV programs and classic films (including at least two we list)—and for rule by MAC III, a supercomputer dealing with overpopulation. Rev. Patricia Altner, <u>SF&FBR Annual 1988</u>: 241-42, our source for this entry.

3.522   Lovejoy, Jack. <u>A Vision of Beasts: Book Two, The Second Kingdom</u>. New York: TOR, 1984.

In a post-catastrophe world, the survivors encounter carnivorous plants, lethal flowers, and a mainframe computer run by a "vegetable mold." Rev. Fred Runk, <u>FR</u> #75 (Jan. 1985): 18, our source for this entry.

3.523   Lucas, George. <u>Star Wars: From the Adventures of Luke Skywalker</u>. New York: Ballantine, 1976.

See <u>Star Wars</u> under Drama. Book includes filmographic information about <u>Star Wars</u> and color photographs from the film, plus some comments by Lucas and others involved with the production of the film. See entry for D. F. Glut above, this section.

3.524   Lupoff, Richard. <u>Sun's End</u>. New York: Berkley, 1984.

See for cyborg hero, and curious sculptures which serve as evidence for humanity's contact with aliens. Rev. Michael R. Collings, <u>FR</u> #74 (Dec. 1984): 27, our source here. Cf. F. Pohl's <u>Man Plus</u> and A. C. Clarke's <u>2001</u>.

3.525   Lyons, Edgar Albion. <u>The Chosen Race</u>. [St. Petersburg, FL:] The Cavalier Pub. Co., 1936.
Described by Sargent (1988) as "Machine dystopia." Note year of publication.

3.526   MacAvoy, R. A. Tea with the Black Dragon. New York: Bantam, 1983.
Computer-crime novel whose hero is a "gray[-]haired musician who practices Zen
when she isn't fiddling in an Irish band," seaching for her daughter—an engineer
involved in a high-tech world. Rev. Lynn F. Williams, SF&FBR #16 (July-Aug.
1983): 38-39, our source for our citation, and whom we quote.

3.527   MacGregor, Loren J. The Net. New York: Ace, 1987.

The Net is a computerized neural network of galactic size. Rev. Rascal J. Thomas,
SF&FBR Annual 1988: 245-46. Scott Bradfield says The Net "allows space-crews
to cybernetically plug into one another and so see, touch, taste, etc. space travel."
Bradfield compares TN, quite negatively, to S. R. Delany's Nova and W. Gibson's
Neuromancer—q.v. this section. Rev. Foundation #40 (Summer 1987): see esp. 101.

3.528   Maddox, Tom. Halo. New York: TOR-Doherty, 1991.

Important novel for the theme of corporate vs. the collective in social organization
and the association of that theme with machines (in Halo, the autonomous machines
prefer the collective), and for humans in a machine-produced virtual reality. Cf. and
contrast cyberpunk works featuring cyberspace; see above, the citations for W.
Gibson, esp. Neuromancer.

3.529   ---. "In a Distant Landscape." MR47/48: 151-55 (see under Literary Criticism, L.
McCaffery, guest ed.).

See for CASTing: Computer Assisted Spacetime Tomography, done in an electronic
"egg" that surrounds the user (152). "Inside the egg, Jolley lay pale, nude, near-
comotose, machine-connected; a new millennium Snow White" (155). See below,
TM's Halo.

3.530   ---. "The Mind Like a Strange Balloon." Omni June 1985. Illus. Bob Venosa.

Problems with the Aleph-Nought1A computer bring the freelance troubleshooter
protagonist to Athena Station, where the Aleph "system managed everything." See
for literal computer/human interface and for glimpses of life inside a computer "god"
(our word)—a computer starting to be able to want. See also for association of
Athena Station with corporate and state bureaucracy. (Cf. TM's "Snake Eyes,"
below, this section.)

3.531   ---. "Snake Eyes." Omni April 1986. Illus. Carlos Revilla. Rpt. Mirrorshades: The
Cyberpunk Anthology. Bruce Sterling, ed. New York: Arbor, 1986. New York:
Ace, 1988.

Having had his brain wired to interact with the computers of a General Dynamics A-
230 fighter aircraft, an honorably discharged George Jackson must learn to live with
some of the more ancient parts of his brain. He's aided in this by a similarly wired
woman and by Aleph, the computer person who runs Athena Station—and who
interfaces with Jackson, teaching Jackson to see the world as Aleph sees it. (Cf.
TM's "The Mind Like a Strange Balloon," above, this section.)

3.532   Magner, James, Jr. "One Night." In Rose of My Flowering Night. Francestown, NH:
The Golden Quill, [1986]: 19.

Poem; untitled on p. 19 (opening two words given as title in Contents). In a variation
on haiku, the Speaker of the poem traces his (?) genesis to the copulation of a
butterfly and a locomotive, in twenty syllables in a line going down the page, one
syllable per line.

3.533   Mailer, Norman. "The Psychology of Machines," in "Apollo" section of Of a Fire on the
Moon. Boston: Little, 1970.

Stresses "those aspects of the machine that are most prone to breakdown," an
approach "amounting to an almost desperate assertion of human freedom against the

threat of total cultural absorption into the machine" (quoting J. Tabbi, "Mailer's Psychology of Machines," q.v. under Literary Criticism).

3.534 Malzberg, Barry N. "The Men Inside." In New Dimensions [1]. Robert Silverberg, ed. Garden City, NY: Doubleday, 1971.

Literal "Diminution" of the men who serve as servants to technology and deal with "machinery and technique" as soldiers in a medical bureaucracy in the war against cancer. Uses the "cave" of the human body as a place of threatening and (in a surprise ending) joyous confinement: the cancer-ridden body is both literal setting and perhaps a variation on the machine / hive / organism metaphor of less problematic stories.

3.535 ---. Revelations. New York: Warner, 1972.

According to Sargent (1988), a high-tech dystopia features "a TV talk show."

3.536 ---. "The Wonderful, All-Purpose Transmogrifier." In Final Stage (q.v. under Anthologies).

The ultimate pleasure machine keeps people spaced out—but inside their little apartments and out of trouble, while the world degenerates.

3.537 Mannes, Marya. They. Garden City, NY: Doubleday, 1968.

Described by Sargent (1988) as "Computer, authoritarian, youth dystopia."

3.538 Manning, Laurence, and Flectcher Pratt. "The City of the Living Dead." Science Wonder Stories 1.12 (May 1930).

Described by Sargent (1988) as a world where people dream inside machines, and "The human race degenerates." Cf. and contrast E. M. Forster's "The Machine Stops," R. Matheson, "Waker Dreams." A. C. Clarke's Lion of Comarre, and W. Hjortsberg's "Grey Matters"—all listed in this section; note attack on machine dependence in LM's The Man Who Awoke stories (Wonder Stories, 1933, coll. 1975), also cited by Sargent (1988).

3.539 Manukari, Haruki. Hard-Boiled Wonderland and the End of the World. Alfred Birnbaum, trans. (c) 1985. Tokyo: Kodansha America, 1991.

Japanese cyberpunk. A CalcuTech (i.e., a surgically enhanced, split-brain, computer operator) creates a fantasy world, complete with unicorns, as a means to escape the stress of industrial espionage, InfoTechs, and INKlings (sic).

3.540 Marlow, Gregory. Corrigan's Light. New York: Vantage, 1982.

Features "a technologically advanced underground utopia—with all the non-utopian elements we are accustomed to find in such societies." Rev. Arthur O. Lewis, FR #19 (Nov. 1983): 32, our source for this entry, and whom we quote.

3.541 Martin, George R. R. "Nightflyers." Analog 1981. Coll. Songs the Dead Men Sing. Niles, IL: Dark Harvest, 1983. Nightflyers. New York: Bluejay, 1985.

See for a malevolent AI Dan Barnhizer describes as a mother/computer controling her son's ship (and her son) through psychic powers; and Dave Mead describes as a "paranoid machine intelligence." The 1985 rpt. rev. Dave Mead, FR #86, 8.12 (Dec. 1985): 18, whom we quote.

3.542 Martindale, Steve. "Technomancy." Aboriginal S. F. March-April 1990: 56 f.

Conspiracy led by a wizard of Faerie against the invaders from Technomancy: magic vs. science, and magic loses.

3.543   Martinson, Harry. <u>Aniara: A Review of Man in Time and Space</u>. Swedish, 1956. Hugh
Macdiarmid and Elspeth Harley Schubert, trans. New York: Knopf, 1963. New
York: Avon, 1976, as #24 in Equinox SF Rediscovery Series.

Epic poem in 103 cantos. Avon title page says their English version was "Adapted
from the Swedish," but see p. 54 for note that canto "<u>42 was omitted, in agreement
with the author, as untranslatable</u>"—which augurs well for close, authorized trans.
elsewhere. In his introd., Tord Hall says that <u>Aniara</u> is "a symbolic poem about our
own age, and the symbols have been taken from modern science" (vii). See for motif
of the generation starship. See above, this section, citation for R. Heinlein,
"Universe"; see below, under Drama, entry for K.-B. Blomdahl.

3.544   Mason, Douglas Rankine. <u>Matrix</u>. New York: Ballantine, 1970. London: Hale, 1971.

Described by Sargent (1988) as "Machine dystopia," where the machines will soon
"phase out" humans.

3.545   Mason, Lisa. <u>Arachne</u>. New York: Morrow, 1990.

Described by Frances Bonner as "female-inflected cyberpunk" if "not women's sf";
significant here for the AI "Pr Spinner, a very fully characterized and . . . [female]
gendered creation." Rev. Bonner in <u>Foundation</u> #54 (Spring 1992): 115-18. Note
also ML's telespace, described by Marcia Marx as "a human/computer interface
technology similar to [W.] Gibson's <u>Neuromancer</u>" (q.v. above). Rev. <u>SFRA
Newsletter</u> #180 (Sept. 1990): 37-38.

3.546   Mason, Robert. <u>Weapon</u>. New York: Putnam's, 1989. New York: Charter, 1990.

A super-robot soldier dismays the military by refusing to kill, fleeing instead to
Nicaragua. Rev. Steve Carper, <u>SFRA Newsletter</u> #180 (Sept. 1990): 38, our source
for part of this entry.

3.547   Massa, Jack. "PrayerWare." In <u>Full Spectrum</u>, q.v under Anthologies.

Features RUMS (the Religious Universal Mainframe System), BLISS (Benign Love
Interactive Software System), and finally the development of PrayerWare. See for
some reasons why the Turing Test might be fairly easy for a slick machine to pass
(60).

3.548   Matheson, Richard. "The Waker Dreams." <u>Galaxy</u> 1.3 (Dec. 1950).

Described by Sargent (1988) as a dystopia of machine-attended dreamers. Cf. and
contrast E. M. Forster's "The Machine Stops," Manning and Pratt, "City of the Living
Dead," A. C. Clarke's <u>Lion of Comarre</u>, and W. Hjortsberg's "Grey Matters," all
listed in this section. See also H. G. Wells's <u>When The Sleeper Wakes</u> (this section).

3.549   Maxim, Hudson. "Man's Machine-Made Millennium." <u>Cosmopolitan Magazine</u> 45.6
(Nov. 1908).

Described by Sargent (1988) as "Technologial eutopia." Note date for conflicts in
the <u>Zeitgeist</u>: E. M. Forster's "The Machine Stops," was published in 1909.

3.550   McCaffrey, Anne. <u>The Ship Who Sang</u>. New York: Walker, 1969. New York:
Ballantine, 1969. Also see title story, "The Ship Who Sang." <u>F&SF</u> April 1961.
Rpt. <u>Women of Wonder</u>. Pamela Sargent, ed. New York: Random, 1975. See
Contento, <u>Index</u>, for other rpts.

Coll. of AM's Helva stories. (See below, this section, J. McElroy's <u>Plus</u>, and K.
O'Donnell's <u>Mayflies</u>). Helva, who "was born a thing" becomes an "encapsulated
'brain'" to be partnered with a "brawn" to act "as the mobile half." The other stories
in <u>TSWS</u> continue Helva's story. See under Literary Criticism the <u>TMG</u> essay by A.
H. Jones.

3.551   ---, and Margaret Ball. Partnership. Riverdale, NY: Baen, 1992. Dist. Simon. Available through the S. F. Book Club.

> The story of a "brainship," with the brain supplied by Nancia Perez y de Gras; cf. AM's Helva stories in Ship Who Sang. Relevant here, Partnership shows Nancia learning to deal with ethical "shades of gray" (313) and with a very nasty computer virus (chs. 16-17); she wins in part by using yoga relaxations techniques (303).

3.552   McDonald, Ian. Out on Blue Six. New York: Spectra-Bantam, 1989.

> Features a highly regulated city whose populace carries around electronic consciences controlled by the Ministry of Pain. The female protagonist joins a group of literally underground rebels and succeeds in introducing a little anarchy to the tightly controlled society. Cf. H. Ellison, "Repent, Harlequin . . ."; cf. and contrast H. Ellison's "A Boy and His Dog," and G. Orwell's Nineteen Eighty-Four (all cited this section). Rev. Nicholas Ruddick, SF&FBR Annual 1990: 371-72, as "a pastiche/homage to the first wave of cyberpunk with everything on the Dante-Dos Passos-Dick axis thrown in" (49).

3.553   McElroy, Joseph. Plus. New York: Knopf, 1977.

> SF in the sense of "cybernetic (postmodern) fiction," Plus tells the story of a brain removed from a dying man and orbited around Earth. The brain eventually regains consciousness and some memories. See D. Porush, "The Imp in the Machine," ch. 9 of his The Soft Machine (q.v. under Literary Criticism). See in this section A. McCaffrey's The Ship Who Sang and K. O'Donnell's Mayflies.

3.554   McGarth, Thomas. The Gates of Ivory, The Gates of Horn. 1957. Chicago: Another Chicago P, 1987.

> A McCarthy-Era allegory relevant here for suggesting "a total machine society" where the Sociological Engineers have as an axiom, "Man is an appendage to the machine" (71)—but where the most significant machine is the apparatus of the State. Cf. F. Kafka's The Trial (1925), plus Kafka's "Penal Colony" and K. Vonnegut's Player Piano, both cited in this section.

3.555   McGowen, Tom. Sir MacHinery. Trina Schart Hyman, illus. Chicago: Follett, 1970.

> Children's book. A robot is mistaken for a knight by Brownies seeking a champion to rescue Merlin (et al.). The robot's owner and Merlin unite magic and science to overcome the evil nemesis. See under Literary Criticism the TMG essay by M. Esmonde.

3.556   McIntyre, Vonda N. "Aztecs." In 2076: The American Tricentennial. Edward Bryant, ed. New York: Pyramid, 1977. Coll. Fireflood and Other Stories. Boston: Houghton, 1979. [S. F.] Book Club Edition. Rpt. Nebula Award Winners Thirteen. Samuel R. Delany, ed. New York: Harper, 1980.

> The "Aztecs" of this story are space pilots who have had their hearts replaced with small engines that they can control consciously. Cf. C. Smith, "Scanners Live in Vain" (below, this section); see under Literary Criticism the TMG essay by G. Wolfe.

3.557   ---. Superliminal. Boston: Houghton, 1983.

> Bionic hearts for space pilots (C. F. Kessler, "Bibliography," listed under Reference—our source for this entry). Cf. VM's "Aztecs."

3.558   McKillip, Patricia. Fool's Run. New York: Warner, 1987.

> Described by Charles de Lint as "a perfect blending of Romanticism and cyberpunk," in his rev., SF&FBR Annual 1988: 258, our source for this entry. See under Literary Criticism, I. Csicsery-Ronay, "Cyberpunk and Neuromanticism."

3.559   McKinney, Jack. ROBOTECH™ SERIES. #1 Genesis, #2 Battle Cry, #3 Homecoming, #4 Battlehymn, #5 Force of Arms, #6 Doomsday, #7 Southern Cross, #8 Metal Fire, #9 The Final Nightmare, #10 Invid Invasion, #11 Metamorphosis, #12 Symphony of Light. All New York: Ballantine, apparently 1987-88. "A Del Rey Book," at least in the case of #1. Copyright owned by Harmony Gold, USA, and Tatsunoko Productions, Co.; the trademark is owned by Harmony Gold.

We have examined only Genesis. See for Robotechnology, the "crowning technological achievement" of which, "the mightiest machine in existence," is a huge transformer war toy with real weapons and, eventually, a large number of real human beings inside (Genesis 2-3 and passim). See also for the Invid, who look in their "heaviest class of mecha, advanced war machines," like "a maniac's vision of biped insect soldiers" (3); they descend from "a moon-size Invid hive ship" (5). See below, JM's SENTINELS™; see also R. A. Heinlein's Starship Troopers (above, this section) and Battlestar Galactica (under Drama). In the first edn., the Genesis text is followed by ch. 1 of JM's Battle Cry. Note (mechanical) transformation as a significant motif in toys of the 1980s.

3.560   ---. THE SENTINELS™ SERIES. (1) The Devil's Hand. New York: Ballantine, 1988. "A Del Rey Book." Copyright (1987, 1988) owned by Harmony Gold, USA, Inc. and Tatsunoko Productions, Co., Ltd.; the ROBOTECH trademark is owned by Harmony Gold.

Continues the ROBOTECH™ series, q.v. above. In the first edn., the text of TDH is followed by ch. 1 of Dark Debut, the second book in the series. Preceding ch. 1, "Robotech Chronology" from 1999-2020; a sentence at the bottom of the page asserts that "A complete Robochronology will appear in the fifth and final volume" of the Sentinels series.

3.561   McLoughlin, John C. The Helix and the Sword. Garden City, NY: Doubleday, 1983.

Six thousand years post-holocaust, humanity survives aboard orbiting space stations, viewing Earth as an "evil goddess," or hell. See also for synthetic organisms. Rev. Fred Runk, FR #67 (May 1984): 36, our source for this entry.

3.562   McQuay, Mike. Lifekeeper. New York: Bantam, 1985.

In the far future, a societal split results in most of humanity living in the coms (underground cities) while the intellectuals wander topside in nomadic tribes. The coms worship war and destruction. The hero, a com Exceptional, looks into a computer malfunction and is manipulated by the machine and a topsider into working for change. Rev. Carol McGeehon, FR #82 (Aug. 1985): 25, our source for this entry.

3.563   ---. Pure Blood. New York: Bantam, 1985.

In a post-holocaust world filled with genetic mutations and heated by the greenhouse effect, a computer god orders its servants to kill all mutant humans. Rev. Michael J. Tolley, FR #77 (Mar. 1985): 18, our source for this entry.

3.564   ---. Suspicion. New York: Ace, 1987.

Book 2 of Isaac Asimov's Robot City series, q.v. above, this section. Rev. Michael R. Collings, SF&FBR Annual 1988: 259-60.

3.565   Melton, Erick. "Random Access." Aboriginal S. F. Sept.-Oct. 1990: 56 f.

Psychotherapy session with a computer, who tells the programmer patient, "If I may make an analogy from your own profession, what we are doing is similar to debugging an errant program. Removing everything which compromises the efficient operation of the application" (61): the procedure is successful. Cf. and contrast the memory editing in Robert Silverberg's "Sundance" (1969), and the computer shrink in F. Pohl's Gateway and Beyond the Blue Event Horizon, and the psychological procedure in J. Haldeman's <u>All My Sins Remembered</u> (all nondated works cited in this section).

3.566   Melville, Herman. "The Bell Tower." 1855. Rpt. <u>Selected Writings of Herman Melville</u>. New York: Modern Library, 1952.

A very "practical materialist" seeks to fulfill a "utilitarian ambition" that is no less than using the craft of a mechanician to overcome nature: "to rival her, outstrip her, and rule her" (369-70). His means is to build Talus, what we would call a robot. See for an important author's presentation of a mad rationalist, competing against Nature and God. See HM listings under Background.

3.567   Menick, Jim. <u>Lingo</u>. New York: Carroll & Graf, 1991.

Computer program becomes an AI, moving into a computer coming-of-age story, moving into a computer take-over story; significant for recognizing that user-friendly little computers are now being networked into large, threatening systems. Cf. and contrast A. C. Clarke's "Dial F . . . ," D. Gerrold's <u>When HARLIE Was One</u>, T. Ryan's <u>The Adolescence of P-1</u>—all cited in this section.

3.568   Merril, Judith. "So Proudly We Hail." In <u>Star Science Fiction Stories</u> [1]. Frederik Pohl, ed. New York: Ballantine, [1953]. Coll. <u>Survival Ship and Other Stories</u>. Toronto: Kakabeka, [1974].

Loading of Terran ship for colonizing Mars: "The metal dragon swallowed all they fed it, . . . letting itself be stuffed, for now, with bits and pieces of paraphernalia, oddiments of fiber and metal, of glass and wood. But all the while it waited, knowing the feast that was coming soon, brooding and hungering for the living flesh that would feed it this night" (<u>Survival Ship</u> 157). The loading of the colonists is described as "the human sacrifice that would slake the dragon's thirst and make it go away" (164).

3.569   ---. "Whoever You Are." <u>Startling Stories</u> Dec. 1952. Coll. <u>The Best of Judith Merril</u>. [New York:] Warner, [1976]. <u>Out of Bounds</u>. New York: Pyramid, [1960]. <u>Survival Ship and Other Stories</u>. Toronto: Kakabeka, [1974].

"Secure within the womb-enclosure of the Web [the defensive system protecting our solar system], five billion Solar citizens could wreak their wills upon their little worlds, and carry on the ever more complex [sic: no hyphens] design for nourishment of all the intra-System castes and categories" (<u>Survival Ship</u> 182; see also 181]).

3.570   Merritt, Abraham. "The Last Poet and the Robots." <u>Fantastic Magazine</u> April 1934. Rpt. <u>Science Fiction: A Historical Anthology</u>, q.v. under Anthologies.

Almost a prose-poem (of the pulp persuasion), "LPR" tells the story of a struggle between a small group of god-like, creative, ruthless human beings and sentient, ruthless, nonemotional, nonartistic robots who have established hegemony over humankind. To some readers, the Last Poet and his human associates may be less sympathetic than the robots.

3.571   ---. "The Metal Monster." <u>Argosy</u> 1920. Rpt. as novel, New York: Avon, 1946. Westport, CT: Hyperion, 1974.

Lost-world story featuring an Asian city that is a unified, conscious, "living Thing" (quoted in Wolfe 190). The inhabitants of the city resemble robots; travelers who enter the Metal Monster's kingdom "are affected by the mechanical being and begin to experience the harmonies of the geometric consciousness." See under Literary Criticism the <u>TMG</u> essay by L. Heldreth 139, whom we quote.

3.572   Metzger, Robert A. "Eve and the Beast." Aboriginal S. F. Jan.-Feb. 1988: 4 f.

High-powered computer-run "Temporal Genetic Desequencer" presents Eve, the mother of all humans (or of our mitochondria). Note image of Eve "in" the holo tube of the computer, watched by a Bible-thumping clergyman.

3.573   ---. "The Twisted Brat." Aboriginal S. F. Nov.-Dec. 1989: 43 f.

Twelve-year old genius is sequestered in a mechanized fantasy world.

3.574   Miedaner, Terrel. "The Soul of the Mark III Beast." Excerpt from The Soul of Anna Klane. New York: Coward, McCann & Geoghegan, 1977. Copyright held by the Church of Physical Theology. Anthologized in The Mind's I, q.v. under Anthologies.

Shows the difficulty of destroying a mechanism that acts as if it has feelings— making problematic our ability to ever be sure whether or not another entity has feelings.

3.575   Milan, Victor. The Cybernetic Samurai. New York: Arbor, 1985.

Post WWIII dystopia, plus AI story. "A Japanese firm . . . designs a sentient computer and names it 'Tokugawa' after the first Shogun . . . ." The Tokugawa AI is a good warrior and "also humane and honorable in human terms. At the end of the story the sentient Tokugawa, after it has successfully defended the factory-cum-office of its feudal lord from the attacks of rivals and rebels, is defeated by treachery and commits seppuku with a small nuclear device"—taking some baddies with "him" (Orth 7-8; see under Reference). Rev. Paul O. Williams, FR #82 (Aug. 1985): 24.

3.576   ---. The Cybernetic Shogun. New York: Morrow, 1990.

Sequel to The Cybernetic Samurai (q.v.). Described by Joan Gordon as a cyberpunk work featuring "sibling computers in a . . . final confrontation" (SFRA Newsletter #188 [June 1991]: 59).

3.577   Miller, Richard De Witt, and Anna Hunger. The Man Who Lived Forever. New York: Ace, 1956. Shorter version by Miller only, as "The Master Shall Not Die." Astounding 21.1 (March 1938).

Described by Sargent (1988) as "The human race versus machines."

3.578   Miller, Walter M., Jr. "Dumb Waiter." Astounding April 1952. Rpt. Science Fiction Thinking Machines, Cities of Wonder, q.v. under Anthologies.

See for computer-run city, with robot police but no people (cf. P. K. Dick's "Autofac," q.v. this section). See also for constellation of the city, technology, and sexism. "DW" briefly discussed by Warrick 119.

3.579   ---. "The Darfsteller." Astounding Jan. 1955. Coll. Conditionally Human. New York: Ballantine, 1962. Rpt. The Hugo Winners, vol. I. Isaac Asimov, ed. Garden City, NY: Doubleday, 1962.

Robot actors now carry on "Dramaturgy, old as civilized man. . . . Outlasting even current popular worship of the Great God Mechanism, who was temporarily enshrined, while still being popularly misunderstood. Like the Great God Commerce of an earlier century, and the God Agriculture before him." See under Drama Criticism, J. Bierman entries on "Automated Theatre."

3.580   ---. "I Made You." Astounding March 1954. Rpt. The Metal Smile. Damon Knight, ed. New York: Belmont, 1968.

Features a man-killing robot tank. See under Literary Criticism the TMG essay by J. Sanders.

3.581   Moffett, Judith. Penterra. Chicago: Congdon, 1987. New York: Worldwide Library (Harlequin SF, dist. Simon), 1988.

Two groups of humans settle on Penterra and are warned by the native intelligent species to stick to one valley, keep their population small, and use only modest technology. The initial group (Quakers) obey; the more aggressive later group does not. The users of high-tech come to no good. Rev. Patricia Altner, SFRA Newsletter #153 (Nov.-Dec. 1987): 30-31. Rev. Janice M. Eisen, Aboriginal S. F. May-June 1989: 44.

3.582   Montclone, Thomas F. Ozymandias. Garden City, NY: Doubleday, 1981.

Sequel to Guardian (1980). Ozymandias is a "human incarnation, via bio-engineering, of the supercomputer 'Guardian.'" Rev. W. D. Stevens, SF&FBR #1 (Jan.-Feb. 1982): 27, our source for this citation, and whom we quote.

3.583   Moore, C. L. "No Woman Born." Astounding Dec. 1944. Coll. The Best of C. L. Moore. Lester del Rey, ed. Garden City, NY: Doubleday, 1975. New York: Ballantine, "A Del Rey Book" (Afterword by CLM), 1976. Rpt. Human Machines (q.v. under Anthologies). Science Fiction: The Science Fiction Research Association Anthology. Patricia S. Warrick et al., eds. New York: Harper, 1988.

A great entertainer's personality and talents are transferred into a mechanical body so they will not be lost with her death. See under Literary Criticism the TMG essays by A. Gordon and A. H. Jones.

3.584   ---, and Henry Kuttner (writing together as Lewis Padgett). "The Proud Robot." Astounding Nov. 1943. Rpt. More Adventures in Time and Space. Raymond J. Healy and Francis McComas, eds. New York: Bantam, 1955.

Harmless rebellion by a robot until its inventor can discover for what purpose he invented it (while drunk). See under Literary Criticism the TMG essay by W. Schuyler.

3.585   Moran, Daniel Keys. The Armageddon Blues: A Tale of the Great Wheel of Existence. New York: Spectra-Bantam, 1988.

Cast includes three computers. Praised by Janice M. Eisen, Aboriginal S. F. May-June 1988: 45, our major source for this entry.

3.586   Morrow, James. "Bible Stories for Adults, #31: The Covenant." Aboriginal S. F. Nov.-Dec. 1989: 2 f.

A robot discovers the true meaning of ancient scripture and the nature of God. Using the Ten Commandments as a base, the robot interprets them for an ignorant humankind, but is tempted by the Son of Rust. Note illus. by Pat Morrissey.

3.587   Murphy, Pat. The City, Not Long After. New York: Doubleday Foundation, 1989.

San Francisco, not long after a plague, has become an anarchic artists' utopia. In the course of the novel, the artists defend their community from military invaders with "an astonishing series of kinetic sculptures, elaborate toys, and works of performance art." Rev. Sandra J. Lindow, SF&FBR Annual 1990: 382-83, our source for this citation, and whom we quote. Lindow praises CNLA and recommends reading it with Lisa Goldstein's A Mask for the General (1988) and Richard Paul Russo's Subterranean Gallery (1989).

3.588   Naha, Ed. RoboCop. New York: Dell, 1986. "Based on the Screenplay by Edward Neumeier & Michael Miner."

Novelization of the film (q.v.), and a book we find surprisingly moving. The story of Alex Murphy's death, resurrection as RoboCop, and coming to deal with his life as a cyborg may pull some strings that go very deep into the psychology of (at least) North American White ethnic males in the last part of the 20th c.

3.589 Nelson, Resa. "The Next Step." Aboriginal S. F. Jan.-Feb. 1989: 56 f.

Near-future, first-person love story featuring a paralyzed woman who learns to move, walk, and live with computer-programmed electrical stimulation of her muscles.

3.590 Newman, Kim. The Night Mayor. London: Simon & Schuster (UK), 1989.

Future information technology allows the media to "hook directly into people's nervous systems." In a satiric extrapolation of Hollywood, "Dreamers" of the future are hacks who "assist experience-synthesizing computers" presenting plots and characters. Rev. Brian Stableford, SFRA Newsletter #186 (April 1991): 51, our source for this entry, and whom we quote. See also SF&FBR 1990: 384, for Michael A. Morrison's characterization of NM's future as "cyberpunkish."

3.591 Niven, Larry, and Jerry Pournelle. Oath of Fealty. New York: Pocket, 1981.

See for the high-tech arcology of Todos Santos and N&P's interesting theory for (post)industrial feudalism. Discussed by A. O. Lewis in "Utopia, Technology, and Evolution" and by R. D. Erlich in "Niven and Pournelle's Oath of Fealty . . ." (both cited under Literary Criticism).

3.592 ---, and Steven Barnes. Dream Park. (c) 1981. [New York]: Ace, [1982]. [S. F.] Book Club Edition.

Dream Park, the setting, offers "role-playing games" mediated "via computer simulations and holograms" (dust cover). Points of view in DP include players of The South Seas Treasure Game and of the game masters in their control room. Dream Park comes across as a rather nice place.

3.593 Norton, Andre. Android at Arms. New York: Harcourt, 1971.

Children's book. Andas Kastor cannot be sure whether he is the rightful emperor of Inyanga or only an android pretender, in a world where androids are outlawed and destroyed on sight. See under Literary Criticism the TMG essay by M. Esmonde. See under fiction, P.K. Dick, Do Androids Dream . . ., and see under Drama, Blade Runner.

3.594 Oberndorf, Charles. "Mannequins." In Full Spectrum (q.v under Anthologies): [66]-96.

Features a robot and the question of her humanity. New wrinkle: addition to some of the usual criteria for humanity, the category of family bonds.

3.595 O'Brien, Flann. The Third Policeman. [Initial composition: ca. 1940.] 1967. New York: NAL, 1976.

Surrealistic dark comedy in which a character is dead and in a hell that features a descent in an elevator to a "next world" called "eternity": a highly mechanized underworld (ch. VIII). Some in hell think it possible that people who frequently ride bicycles exchange atoms with the cycles, making the people more like bicycles and the bicycles more like people.

3.596 Odle, E. V. The Clockwork Man. London: Heinemann, 1923.

TCM is cited by B. Stableford, Romance, as a thoughtful work featuring a visitor who accidentally travels from a far-future time to ours; the visitor has been agumented by "a 'clock' which regulates his thought and metabolism" (263-65; quote from 264). Note: Look for TCM in Stableford by title, not author.

3.597 O'Donnell, Kevin, Jr. Mayflies. New York: Berkley, 1979.

Science in the 23rd c. preserves the hero's brain for use as a starship computer. Cf. A. McCaffrey's Ship Who Sang, J. McElroy's Plus, R. P. Bird's "The Soft Heart of the Electron," and W. Hjortsberg's Gray Matters—all of which see above, this section. Also uses the generation-starship motif; cf. R. Heinlein's "Universe," q.v. this section.

3.598   ---. ORA:CLE (sic). New York: Berkley, 1984.

The hero of the story is linked to the ORA:CLE network by brain implant and never leaves his high-rise apartment (cf. R. Silverberg, World Inside, q.v. below, and KO's Mayflies). Story features a protracted battle for control carried out entirely over computer networks and newsservices. Briefly rev. Thom Dunn, FR #76 (Feb. 1985): 19.

3.599   Oliver, Chad (i.e. Symmes Chadwick Oliver). "Rite of Passage." Astounding 53 (April 1954).

Described by Sargent (1988) as a story of two societies, one embracing technology, the other rejecting technology.

3.600   ---. "Stardust" (vt "First to the Stars"). Astounding July 1952.

A generation-starship story; cf. R. Heinlein's "Universe," q.v. this section, above. See Wolfe 67.

3.601   Ore, Rebecca. The Illegal Rebirth of Billy the Kid. New York: Doherty, 1991. "A Tor Book." Available without ISBN (or reference to the Club) from the S. F. Book Club.

A rogue CIA agent in the 21st c. creates "a dog-meat robot Billy-the-Kid reincarnation" (154) for sexual fun among a bored elite and for his own craft and profit. The "chimera's" eyes won't respond to any artifacts produced later than the historical Billy's period, but an escaped Billy eventually adapts to 21st-c. culture and technology and goes from "meat robot" (4) to a man. Rev. Michael M. Levy, SFRA Newsletter #193 (Dec. 1991): 60-62.

3.602   Orwell, George (pseud. of Eric Blair). Nineteen Eighty-Four. London: Secker, 1949. Rpt. as 1984 New York: NAL, 1961. "Casebook" edition: Orwell's Nineteen Eighty-Four: Text, Sources, Criticism. Irving Howe, ed. 2d edn. New York: Harcourt, 1982. (An enlarged version of the 1963 1st edn., adding GO's "The Prevention of Literature," excerpts from GO's correspondence, a critical essay by John Wain, initial reviews of the novel, an essay by Michael Harrington, and some additional apparatus to aid users of the volume.) Also: Bernard Crick, ed. Nineteen Eighty-Four "With a Critical Introduction and Annotations by Bernard Crick." Oxford, UK: Clarendon, 1984. (Covered with opaque tape on title page: "Published in the United States by Oxford UP, New York.")

Shows a totalitarian police state run by the oligarchs of the "Inner Party." Along with Y. Zamiatin's We and A. Huxley's Brave New World, one of the basic dystopias of the first half of the 20th c. See under Drama, 1984.

3.603   Osborn, David. Heads. New York: Bantam, 1985.

Sensational use of the idea of severed heads wired to a computer (cf. and contrast C. S. Lewis, That Hideous Strength); secret experiments and an imperiled heroine may recall R. Cook's Coma (see above, this section).

3.604   Pangborn, Edgar. A Mirror for Observers. New York: Bluejay, 1983.

The Martians have been living on Earth for 30,000 years in underground cities, giving us a bit of technological help now and then. Rev. Robert J. Ewald, FR #70 (Aug. 1984): 21, our source for this entry.

3.605   Park, John. "The Software Plague." In Far Frontiers. Jerry Pournell and Jim Baen, eds.
New York: Baen, 1985.

A future highly dependent on computers. Rev. Pascal J. Thomas, FR #79 (May
1985): 24, our source for this entry.

3.606   Pelletier, Francine. "La Migratrice" ("The Migrant"). In Le temps des migrations.
Longueuil: Préambule, 1987.

See for small spacecraft, each containing a woman accompanied by one embryo "in
an artificial womb." The embryos will be "modified to "adapt without technology"
to hostile worlds. Cf. J. Williamson's Manseed, q.v. below, and the works cross-
referenced there. Summarized by E. Vonarburg, whom we quote, cited under
Literary Criticism.

3.607   Pfeil, Fred. Goodman 2020. Bloomington: Indiana UP, 1986.

Well-written, near-future, relatively high-tech, postmodern corporate dystopia where
the handling of technology is quite similar to and usefully very different from the
handling of technology among the cyberpunks (see above, this section, W. Gibson's
Neuromancer, and the works cited there).

3.608   Phillips, Peter. "Lost Memory." Galaxy May 1952. Frequently rpt. including Gateway to
Tomorrow. John Carnell, ed. London: Museum P, 1954. The Coming of the
Robots. Sam Moskowitz, ed. New York: Collier, 1963. Themes in Science Fiction.
Leo P. Kelley, ed. New York: McGraw-Hill, 1972.

First contact between a seriously wounded astronaut in a spaceship and robot aliens,
narrated from the robotic point of view; the robots do not understand that the
sentience they've encountered is the small human and not the big ship. Discussed by
T. Krulick, "Bounded by Metal," listed under Literary Criticism, one of our sources
for this entry.

3.609   Piercy, Marge. Woman on the Edge of Time. New York: Knopf, 1976. New York:
Fawcett, 1976. Also, "Woman on the Edge of Time." In Aurora: Beyond Equality.
Susan J. Anderson and Vonda N. McIntyre, eds. Greenwich, CT: Fawcett, 1976.

The protagonist is trapped in the repressive bureaucracy of a contemporary mental
health institution. Literal machinery in the story, though, is both good and bad: the
technology in the eutopian section of the novel is "appropriate." Rev. Colin
Greenland in Foundation #19 (June 1980): 81-82. See under Literary Criticism the
CW essay by P. Day. Cf. —and contrast— K. Kesey's One Flew Over the Cuckoo's
Nest, cited this section. See under Drama, Terminator 2 (where the female hero is
also imprisoned in a mental hospital). See below under Background, S. Firestone,
The Dialectic of Sex.

3.610   Poe, Edgar Allan. "Maelzel's Chess-Player." 1836. In The Complete Tales and Poems of
Edgar Allan Poe. New York: Modern Library, 1938.

Detective story in which the chess-playing machine turns out to be a hoax; the
narrator's method in exposing the hoax plays on some essential attributes of
automatons. Discussed by Warrick 39-40.

3.611   ---. "Mellonta Tauta." Godey's Lady's Book 38 (Feb. 1849).

Described by Sargent (1988) as "Satire on the future. Technologically advanced but
individualism and democracy are gone."

3.612   Pohl, Frederik. The Annals of the Heechee. New York: Del Rey-Ballantine, [1987].
[S.F.] Book Club Edition.

Fourth book of "The Heechee Saga" (the others: Gateway, Beyond the Blue Event
Horizon, Heechee Rendezvous, The Gateway Trip). The "vastened" Robinette

Broadhead exists as a program in "gigabit space" where he interacts with other human programs and "meat" people in the more conventional world. In the course of narrating the novel, Broadhead considers (among many other things) whether or not he is still human, and his Albert Einstein general service program suggests that machine-stored people are "the next stage of evolution" (277). Cf. Pohl's story "Day Million" and Heechee Rendezvous for personality storage; for "cyberspace," see entry for W. Gibson's Neuromancer (cited in this section).

3.613   ---. Beyond the Blue Event Horizon. New York: Ballantine, 1980. [S. F.] Book Club Edition: New York: Ballantine, 1980 (alternate pagination).

Sequel to Gateway (q.v. below). See under Literary Criticism the TMG essay by T. Paul.

3.614   ---. "Day Million." Rogue Feb. 1966. Coll. Day Million. New York: Ballantine, 1970. The Best of Frederik Pohl. Lester del Rey, ed. New York: Nelson Doubleday, 1975. Frequently rpt., including Nebula Award Stories #2. Brian Aldiss and Harry Harrison, eds. New York: Doubleday, 1967. First two edns. of Science Fiction: The Future. Dick Allen, ed. New York: Harcourt, 1971, 1983.

See for machine-recording and storage of human personalities, a motif Pohl repeats in "The Heechee Saga" (see Heechee Rendezvous and Annals of the Heechee, this section).

3.615   ---. Gateway. New York: St. Martin's, 1977. [S. F.] Book Club Edition: New York: St. Martin's, 1977 (alternate pagination).

The psychoanalyst of the hero's story is a computer. See under Literary Criticism the TMG essay by T. Paul.

3.616   ---. The Gateway Trip: Tales and Vignettes of the Heechee. New York: Ballantine, 1990. Illus.

Late entry into FP's "Heechee Saga" (see above, FP's Annals), set mostly on the Gateway asteroid. According to Terry Heller, "One unifying pattern in these vignettes is the development of a technological utopia as humans slowly master Heechee machinery" (SFRA Newsletter #188 [June 1991]: 60).

3.617   ---. "Growing Up in Edge City." In Epoch. Robert Silverberg and Roger Elwood, eds. New York: Berkley, 1975. Coll. Pohlstars. New York: Ballantine, 1984.

A little boy exits the enclosed, machine-dominated Edge City and finds a wondrous world outside, one with a colony of Dropouts. As an adult, he leads an attack on the Dropouts to further his political career. See for a bitter and brilliant variation on a theme running from E. M. Forster's "The Machine Stops" to R. Silverberg's The World Inside, cited in this section.

3.618   ---. Heechee Rendezvous. New York: Del Rey-Ballantine, 1984. [S. F.] Book Club Edition.

Significant characters are computer programs, as are the two narrators: the Albert Einstein program and a "vastened" Robinette Broadhead, the hero of the Gateway trilogy, whose personality is computer-preserved after his death near the end of the novel. See above, Gateway and Beyond the Blue Event Horizon. Rev. Donald M. Hassler, FR #70 (Aug. 1984): 21.

3.619   ---. Man Plus. New York: Random, 1976.

Story of a man's becoming a full cyborg ("man plus")—but with costs—narrated by computers who have attempted, with a good deal of success, to manipulate human history. See under Literary Criticism the TMG essay by A. Gordon.

3.620   ---. "The Midas Plague." Galaxy April 1954. Coll. The Best of Frederik Pohl. Lester del
        Rey, introd. New York: Ballantine, 1975. Frequently rpt., including The Science
        Fiction Hall of Fame. Vol. IIB. Ben Bova, ed. New York: Avon, 1974.

        Comic handling of how to deal with the plague of affluence in a world where
        "Everything is mechanized," and "Too many robots make too much of everything."
        Cf. J. Gunn's "Little Orphan Android," cited above, this section.

3.621   ---. Midas World. London: Gollancz, 1983. New York: Tor-Tom Doherty (dist. Saint
        Martin's and Warner), 1984.

        Series of linked tales centered on an update of FP's "The Midas Plague," q.v. above.
        See for robot stories. Rev. Dave Langford, Foundation #33 (93-94).

3.622   ---. "Rafferty's Reasons." Fantastic Universe 4.3 (Oct. 1955). Coll. Alternating Currents.
        New York: Ballantine, 1956.

        Described by Sargent (1988) as "Dystopia—machine teaching."

3.623   ---. "Servant of the People." In The Best Science Fiction of the Year #13. Terry Carr, ed.
        New York: Baen/Simon, 1984.

        See for robots. Rev. Robert Reilly, FR #73 (Nov. 1984): 31, our source here.

3.624   ---. "The Tunnel Under the World." Galaxy Jan. 1955. Coll. The Best of Frederik Pohl.
        Lester del Rey, introd. New York: Ballantine, 1975. (Acknowledgments page lists
        date for "TUW" as Jan. 1954.) Frequently rpt., including More Penguin Science
        Fiction. Brian W. Aldiss, ed. Harmondsworth: Penguin, 1963.

        A town destroyed by an explosion is reconstructed in miniature, as are its dead
        inhabitants. The reconstructed humans/robots are the subjects of controlled
        experiments in advertising, wherein they continually relive the same day.

3.625   ---. The Years of the City. New York: Pocket, 1984.

        Presents a highly positive view of a domed city: 21st-c. New York (cf. Asimov,
        Caves of Steel, cited above, but contrast most other thematically significant uses of
        the dome motif).

3.626   ---, and C. M. Kornbluth. The Space Merchants. New York: Ballantine, [1953]. "A
        condensed version of this novel appeared in GALAXY magazine under the title
        Gravy Planet" (June, July, August 1952).

        One of the great satires on human greed, pride, and stupidity generally, and capitalist
        consumption and advertising more particularly. In the reading by J. P. Brennan, SM
        has at its heart the image of "Chicken Little," an organic thing with mechanism
        literally superimposed upon it (and a way into it)—an image that works well in an
        attack on "the text's mechanistic psychology" (see under Literary Criticism,
        Brennan's "The Mechanical Chicken," here 107-8).

3.627   ---, and Jack Williamson. Land's End. New York: TOR, 1988.

        The world of LE is divided into warring, land-based nations and eighteen peaceful
        oceanic Cities (capital "C"). The "Lubbers" on the land use science to create
        technologies of mass destruction while "Webfeet" of the oceans use science to live in
        harmony with their environment. Rev. Arthur O. Lewis, SFRA Newsletter #160
        (Sept. 1988): 43-44, our source for this entry.

3.628   ---. The Reefs of Space (1963), and Starchild (1965). In The Starchild Trilogy. Garden
        City, NY: Doubleday, 1977. New York: Pocket, 1977.

The third novel of the trilogy, Rogue Star (1969), is not immediately relevant. The first two novels feature a world run by "the Machine," an underground computer that administers "The Plan of Man" and ruthlessly suppresses all "unplanned" activity.

3.629   ---. The Singers of Time. New York: Doubleday, 1991. "A Foundation Book." Available from the S. F. Book Club.

Some human characters have slots in their skulls for receiving "memo disks" that allow them to do highly technical work for aliens. See also for a species that divided into cultures spiritual and scientific on the one hand and high-tech and aggressive on the other. There are also two cyborgs of interest. Cf. H. G. Wells's Time Machine (specifically mentioned on ST 352) and works dealing with mechanical "possession."

3.630   The Policeman's Beard is Half-Constructed: A Bizarre and Fantastic Journey into the Mind of a Machine. New York: Warner, 1984.

One short story, poems, and other short pieces said to be by "Racter, a six-year-old computer program" by William Chamberlain (a writer) and Thomas Etter (computer programmer). Discussed by Rob Latham in his editorial in FR #97, 9.11 (Dec. 1986): 29 f., our source for this entry and whom we quote.

3.631   Porush, David. "Induction from R.Boots" (sic). MR47/48: 93-106 (see under Literary Criticism, L. McCaffery, guest ed.).

Formally, a one-scene play with an induction, presented as the opening of the play R.Boots; we will call it fiction: a postmodernist variation on themes from such modernist classics as R. U. R. and E. M. Forster's "The Machine Stops" (q.v. under Drama and Fiction respectively). See for robots and a setting in a "domed colony" with a "hive-like layout" full of "high-tech apparati," giving an effect that is "sterile, stark, clinical. Like the inside of a circuit board" (95).

3.632   Poyer, D. C. Stepfather Bank. New York: St. Martin's, 1987.

A high-tech, post-holocaust world owned by a "benevolent bank" that is in part an AI and in part the concensus of five very old humans. See also for electronic surveillance. Rev. Martha A. Bartter, SF&FBR Annual 1988: 288, our source for this entry. See above, this section, entry for D. Andreissen.

3.633   Prager, Emily. "The Lincoln-Pruitt Anti-Rape Device." In A Visit From the Footbinder. New York: Simon, 1982.

The device is a very high-tech "microchip-energized gadget" that provides a vagina dentata (with "probe, shredder, and laser") to female warriors—who'll use it to kill Vietcong. Discussed by Susanne Carter, "Variations of Vietnam: Women's Innovative Interpretations of the Vietnam War Experience," Extrapolation 32.2: 180-81, whom we quote here and depend upon for our citation.

3.634   Pynchon, Thomas. Gravity's Rainbow. New York: Viking, 1973. New York, Harmondsworth: Viking Penguin (Penguin Books), 1987.

Arguably S. F., SF, or mundane, GR features a V-2 rocket falling in a universe operating like a machine with mystic gears of an unknown and probably unknowable ratio, some of which may be loose and/or missing teeth. Cf. TP's earlier Crying of Lot Forty-Nine (1966), which presents US society metaphorically as a giant computer running a binary program. See below under Literary Criticism, P. Brigg on GR.

3.635   Quick, W. T. Dreams of Flesh and Sand. New York: Signet-NAL, 1988.

A cyberpunkish story featuring "gigantic corporations" who both own and are ruled by programmable "organic matrixes of immense size"—but with a happy ending. Rev. Robin Roberts, SF&FBR Annual 1989: 365, our source for this entry, and whom we quote.

3.636   Randall, John W. "Liquid Jade." <u>Aboriginal</u> <u>S. F.</u> Jan.-Feb. 1990: 26 f.

A William Gibsonesque cyberpunk story set among a divided humanity: a minority of biological purists and a majority into cybertechnology and mechanization. See below, Mechanist/Shaper stories by B. Sterling.

3.637   Rayer, [Frances] G[eorge]. <u>Tomorrow</u> <u>Sometimes</u> <u>Comes</u>. London: Home & Van Thal, 1951. Rpt. S. F. Book Club, 1953.

Part of the "Mens Magna" series, featuring what we'd call an AI.

3.638   Reaves, Michael, and Steve Perry. <u>Dome</u>. New York: Berkley, 1987.

High-tech "thriller set in a mobile undersea city." Rev. Geoffrey A. Landis, <u>SF&FBR</u> <u>Annual</u> <u>1988</u>: 290-91, our source for this entry, and whom we quote.

3.639   Reed, Kit. <u>Magic</u> <u>Time</u>. New York: Berkley, 1981.

High-tech surveillance and a "once human machine-housed consciousness" (quoting Mary Kay Bray in "<u>Nineteen</u> <u>Eighty-Four</u> Is Only the Beginning: Media Technology and the Annihilation of Privacy in Wilhelm, Compton, and Reed," a paper at the 13th Annual Convention of the Popular Culture Association. Wichita, April 1983). See in this section, K. Wilhelm's "Baby, You Were Great!" and D. G. Compton's <u>The</u> <u>Unsleeping</u> <u>Eye</u>.

3.640   Reed, Robert. <u>The</u> <u>Leeshore</u>. New York: Fine, 1987.

A cult makes an AI computer its god: "a machine near the theoretical limits of intelligence" and militantly makes nonbelievers into converts or corpses. The cult and its opponents use "'wires'" for brainwashing. Rev. Martha Soukup, <u>SF&FBR</u> <u>Annual</u> <u>1988</u>: 291, our source for this entry, and whom we quote.

3.641   Resnick, Michael. <u>The</u> <u>Best</u> <u>Rootin'</u> <u>Tootin'</u> <u>Shootin'</u> <u>Gunslinger</u> in <u>the</u> <u>Whole</u> <u>Damned</u> <u>Galaxy</u>. New York: Signet-NAL, 1983.

A target-shooting carnival gunslinger goes after a robotic Doc Holliday. Rev. Keith Soltys, <u>FR</u> #72 (Oct. 1984): 33.

3.642   Reynolds, Mack (pseud. of Dallas McCord Reynolds). <u>After</u> <u>Utopia</u>. New York: Ace, 1977.

The utopia referred to in the title is that of E. Bellamy in <u>Looking</u> <u>Backward</u> (q.v. above, this section). <u>AU</u> is set in 2050, some fifty years after the time of Bellamy's work, and shows the degeneration of utopia as people turn to "intuitive" computers: machines for escape into fantasy. See Brian Stableford in "The Utopian Dream Revisited: Socioeconomic Speculation in the SF of Mack Reynolds," <u>Foundation</u> #16 (May 1976): 49.

3.643   ---. <u>Lagrange</u> <u>Five</u>. New York: Bantam, 1979.

Described by Sargent (1988) as "Space station as eutopia." See below, MR's <u>The</u> <u>Lagrangists</u>.

3.644   ---. <u>The</u> <u>Lagrangists</u>. New York: Tom Doherty Assoc., 1983.

Described by Sargent (1988) as "Space station eutopia." See above, MR's <u>Lagrange</u> <u>Five</u>.

3.645   ---. <u>The</u> <u>Towers</u> <u>of</u> <u>Utopia</u>. New York: Bantam, 1975.

Mild near-future dystopia with Universal Credit Cards, huge corporations running most things, "Security TV spy lenses," Meritocracy, a Negative Income Tax, very high high-rise buildings with "bowels" and comparisons with anthills—and with surplus production taken up with building more housing. See G. Orwell, <u>1984</u>, R. Silverberg, <u>The World Inside</u> (listed in this section).

3.646   ---. <u>Trojan Orbit</u>. Dean Ing, ed. New York: Baen, 1985.

Organized crime attempts to take over the Lagrange 5 space colony. Filled with descriptions of how actual colony building should take place and the pertinent engineering problems which occur in the building and maintenance of such a habitat.

3.647   Roberson, Jennifer. "Ride 'Em, Cyboy." <u>Aboriginal S. F.</u> March-April 1990: 62 f.

In a fictional galaxy of "cyberfacsimiles" and pseudohumans, Buck Hollister's Real Texas Rodeo has cybernetic stock and "cyboys," plus one fully human ("Capital H") Human ringer, who gets one glorious ride.

3.648   Roberts, Keith. <u>Molly Zero</u>. London: Gollancz, 1980.

1984ish novel with an invisible machine-state government. Rev. Michael E. Stamm, <u>FR</u> #70 (Aug. 1984): 23, our source for this entry.

3.649   ---. "Synth." <u>New Writings in Science Fiction</u>. Aug. 1966. Coll. <u>Machines and Men</u>, q.v. under Anthologies.

One of the "Robot courtroom dramas" noted by B. Stableford in <u>S. F. Ency.</u>, "Robots" entry. See above, this section, I. Asimov's "Bicentennial Man."

3.650   Roberts, Ralph. "Three If by Norton." <u>Aboriginal S. F.</u> Jan.-Feb. 1989: 9 f.

A tale of inadvertent time travel: how the midnight ride of Paul Revere was taken by Bugface O'Lear on a Harley-Davidson XLH; see for a "temporal dispacement device" small enough to carry on a Harley—and for the Harley.

3.651   Robinson, Frank M. <u>The Dark Beyond the Stars</u>. New York: TOR-Doherty, 1991. We use the S. F. Book Club Edition (marked as a book club edn. only by its lack of an ISBN).

The huge Terran spacecraft moving into the Dark had not been designed as a generation starship, but it became one; see stories crosslisted at R. A. Heinlein's "Universe" (listed above, this section). Note also for "falsies"—holographic projections—and associated "virtual realities," plus "preservation crypts" for storing crew, and significant links between three people and the ship's computer. See above, this section, K. O'Donnell's <u>Mayflies</u>.

3.652   Robinson, Kim Stanley. <u>In Memory of Whiteness</u>. New York: TOR, 1985.

Physicist Johannes Wright tours with his "ultimate musical instrument," built to help convey to others Wright's reformulation of Einstein's unsuccessful Uniform Theory. Against him are the controllers of the artificial gravity stations that provide gravity for the domed cultures of Wright's universe. Rev. Stuart Napier, <u>FR</u> #84 (Oct. 1985): 24, our source for this entry.

3.653   Robinson, Spider. <u>Mindkiller</u>. New York: Holt, 1982. New York: Ace, 1989.

Society manipulated by electronic stimulation of the brain (at a distance) by a machine that amplifies brainwaves for telepathy. Initially, brain implants are necessary; later in the novel, they are not.

3.654   ---. <u>Time Pressure</u>. New York: Ace, 1987.

Sequel to SR's <u>Mindkiller</u>, q.v. Female robot time-travels from a post-holocaust 21st c. to the 1970s to recruit human consciousnesses into a group mind mediated by a computer that is not in itself sentient.

3.655 ROBOTECH™ SERIES: See in this section the entry for Jack McKinney.

3.656 Roddenberry, Gene. Star Trek: The Motion Picture: A Novel. Based on The screenplay by Harold Livingston and the story by Alan Dean Foster. New York: Pocket, 1979.

See Star Trek: The Motion Picture, below, under Drama.

3.657 Roshwald, Mordecai. Level 7. New York: McGraw-Hill, 1959. New York: NAL, n.d. Chicago: Lawrence Hill, 1989. Afterword by H. Bruce Franklin.

Nuclear holocaust story featuring underground containment in a military apparat.

3.658 Ross, Olin J. The Sky Blue: A Tale of the Iron Horse and of the Coming of Civilization. Columbus, OH: Author, 1904.

According to Sargent (1988), shows the railroad unifying the world into a single magnificent civilization.

3.659 Roszak, Theodore. Bugs. Garden City, NY: Doubleday, 1981. Garden City, NY: Doubleday, n.d. [S. F.] Book Club Edition.

A S. F./Fantasy-Horror story (with a strong hint of disaster novel) from the author of Where the Wasteland Ends, The Making of a Counter Culture, and other critiques of the "Technocratic Society" (see citations under Background). Relevant here for its association of computers and insects and for its use of the conceit of human beings within computers, mechanical hives, and a war machine. Rev. Fred D'Ignazio, SF&FBR #2 (March 1982): 11-12.

3.660 Rousseau, Victor (pseud. of Victor Rousseau Emanuel). The Messiah of the Cylinder. Chicago, IL: A.C. McClurg, 1917. Rpt. Westport, CT: Hyperion P, 1974. U.K. edn. The Apostle of the Cylinder. London: Hodder and Stoughton, 1918.

Described by Sargent (1988) as a "Scientific dystopia."

3.661 Rucker, Rudy. "Christmas in Louisville December 24, 2030." MR47/48: 107-21 (see under Literary Criticism, Larry McCaffery, guest ed.).

From R.R.'s Wetware, q.v. below.

3.662 ---. Software. New York: Ace, 1982.

Early cyberpunk novel. See below, "Software."

3.663 ---. "Software." Excerpt from Software, q.v. above. Anthologized in The Mind's I, q.v. under Anthologies (253-65).

Excerpt includes the assassination of Ralph Numbers, the robot that led the machine revolt in 2001. Esp. in the context of The Mind's I, raises the question of machine consciousness.

3.664 ---. Spacetime Donuts. New York: Ace, 1981.

World controlled by "PhizWhiz, a benevolent master computer," in an early novel by an author who went on to success in cyberpunk. Rev. Robert A. Collins, quite negatively, SF&FBR #1 (Jan.-Feb. 1982): 27-28, our source for this citation, and whom we quote.

3.665 ---. Wetware. New York: Avon, 1988.

Sequel to RR's Software. Cyberpunk work dealing with robot rebellion on the moon. Rev. Gregory Feeley, Foundation #43: 99-102. See above, RR's "Christmas in Louisville December 24, 2030."

3.666   Russ, Joanna. The Female Man. Boston: Beacon, 1975. New York: Bantam, 1975.

Includes JR's "An Old-Fashioned Girl" (q.v., this section) and the utopian world of Whileaway: a world of appropriate technology, which is often appropriate high technology. (See Peter Fitting on "New Roles for Men in Recent Utopian Fiction," SFS #36, 12.2: 160.)

3.667   ---. "An Old-Fashioned Girl." Final Stage: The Ultimate Science Fiction Anthology. Edward L. Ferman and Barry N. Malzberg, eds. 1974. New York: Penguin, 1975. Incorporated with changes into JR's The Female Man. Boston: Beacon, 1975. Part Eight: IX, XI, XV (185, 196-200).

A "lovely limb of the house" of the "Old Fashioned Girl" is Davy, a bio-cybernetic sex toy.

3.668   Russell, Eric Frank. "Jay Score." Astounding May 1941. Coll. Men, Martians and Machines. 1955. New York: Crown, 1984.

The title character is a robot who passes for human. See under Literary Criticism the TMG essay by J. Sanders.

3.669   Russell, George Warren. A New Heaven. London: Methuen, 1919.

Described by Sargent (1988) as "Heaven as a eutopia. Technically as well as spiritually advanced." Cf. and contrast Hell as mechanism: see under Literary Criticism the CW essay by M. Abrash, on Dante's Hell; note Bill & Ted's Bogus Journey to both heaven and hell (under Drama).

3.670   Ryan, Thomas. The Adolescence of P-1. 1977. New York: Baen, 1985. Dist. Pocket Books.

The late adolescence, early adulthood, and death of Gregory Burgess, who creates and sees through adolescence and apparent death P-1, a computer program with the ability to learn and become an AI and then a person. Computer take-over motif where we sympathize with the computer program doing at least a partial take-over. Caution: the backcover blurb on the 1985 edn. is misleading.

3.671   Ryman, Geoff. The Unconquered Country. London: Allen, 1986.

Rev. Damien Broderick in ASFR #22 = 2nd series 4.5 (Dec. 1989 [mislabeled "Summer 1989" on front cover]): 12, who finds UC not SF "but some blend of folklore and the nightmare of history." Broderick quotes a passage on "Third Child," allegorically Cambodia, "who rented her womb for industrial use. She was cheaper than the glass tanks. She grew parts of living machinery inside her" (UC 3).

3.672   Saberhagen, Fred. "The Annihilation of Angkor Apeiron." Galaxy Feb. 1975. Coll. The Ultimate Enemy (q.v. below).

A berserker is destroyed by a phantom planet. (For one response to the berserker stories, see above, entry for G. Bear, The Forge of God.)

3.673   ---. Berserker. New York: Ballantine, 1967. New York: Ace, 1978.

A collection of eleven of FS's berserker stories, from the first published through the Johann Karlsen series. See for fighting machines. See under Literary Criticism the TMG essay, "In Search of . . . ," by L. Heldreth.

3.674   ---. Berserker Base. New York: TOR, 1985.

More of FS's killer machines, including a story in which a human-based computer manages to control a berserker.

3.675   ---. <u>Berserker</u> <u>Blue</u> <u>Death</u>. New York: Doherty, 1985.
Berserker yarn featuring the hero's mission of vengeance against the berserker, Leviathan.

3.676   ---. <u>Berserker</u> <u>Man</u>. New York: Ace, 1979.

Described by L. Heldreth as an impressive novel in the series dealing with berserker fighting machines; see under Literary Criticism the <u>TMG</u> essay, "In Search of . . . ," by L. Heldreth.

3.677   ---. <u>Berserker's</u> <u>Planet</u>. New York: DAW, 1975. New York: Ace, 1980.

Third coll. of FS's berserker stories; discussed in <u>TMG</u> essay, "In Search of . . . ," by L. Heldreth.

3.678   ---. <u>Brother</u> <u>Assassin</u> (vt <u>Brother</u> <u>Berserker</u>). New York: Ballantine, 1969. New York: Ace, 1979.

Second coll. of FS's berserker stories. See for berserker fighting machines; discussed in <u>TMG</u> essay, "In Search of . . . ," by L. Heldreth.

3.679   ---. "Fortress Ship" (vt "Without a Thought"). <u>If</u> Jan. 1963. Coll. <u>Berserker</u> (q.v. above).

The first published berserker story.

3.680   ---. "The Game." <u>The</u> <u>Flying</u> <u>Buffalo's</u> <u>Favorite</u> <u>Magazine</u> May-June 1977. Coll. <u>Ultimate</u> <u>Enemy</u> (q.v. below).

A berserker imitating a human gives himself away during a game through ignorance of human psychology.

3.681   ---. "Goodlife." <u>Worlds</u> <u>of</u> <u>Tomorrow</u> Dec. 1963. Coll. <u>Berserker</u> (q.v. above).

A man (Goodlife) raised by the berserkers to serve death strikes back at them.

3.682   ---. "In the Temple of Mars." <u>If</u> April 1966. Coll. <u>Berserker</u> (q.v. above).

Berserker story drawing images and quotations from Chaucer's "Knight's Tale."

3.683   ---. "Inhuman Error." <u>Analog</u> Oct. 1974. Coll. <u>Ultimate</u> <u>Enemy</u> (q.v. below).

A mnemonic device betrays a berserker's masquerade.

3.684   ---. "Masque of the Red Shift." <u>If</u> Nov. 1965. Coll. <u>Berserker</u> (q.v. above).

A berserker variation on Poe.

3.685   ---. "Mr. Jester." <u>If</u> Jan. 1966. Coll. <u>Berserker</u> (q.v. above).

A confused berserker helps to carry out a practical joke before being destroyed.

3.686   ---. "Patron of the Arts." <u>If</u> Aug. 1965. Coll. <u>Berserker</u> (q.v. above).

A cynical painter rejects nihilism and joins with the life forces opposing the berserkers.

3.687   ---. "The Peacemaker" (vt "The Life Hater"). <u>If</u> Aug. 1964. Coll. <u>Berserker</u> (q.v. above).

A berserker's scheme backfires and cures a cancer patient.

3.688   ---. "Pressure" (vt "Berserker's Prey"). <u>If</u> June 1967. Coll. <u>Ultimate</u> <u>Enemy</u> (q.v. below).

Squash plants destroy a berserker. See below, FS's "Smasher."

3.689   ---. "The Sign of the Wolf." If May 1965. Coll. Berserker (q.v. above).

Planetary defenses strike out at a berserker when a young shepherd tries to kill a wolf.

3.690   ---. "Smasher." F&SF Aug. 1978. Coll. Ultimate Enemy (q.v. below).

Shrimplike creatures crack open a squad of berserkers. See above, FS's "Pressure."

3.691   ---. "The Smile." Algol Summer-Fall 1977. Coll. Ultimate Enemy (q.v. below).

A "tall, roughly humanoid" berserker fighting machine destroys art thieves.

3.692   ---. "Some Events at the Templar Radiant." Destinies May-Aug. 1979. Coll. Ultimate Enemy (q.v. below).

A scientist yields to religious impulses and lust to reactivate a damaged berserker.

3.693   ---. "Starsong." If Jan. 1968. Coll. Ultimate Enemy (q.v. below).

A berserker variation on the myth of Eurydice and Orpheus, in which Orpheus is a pop idol.

3.694   ---. "Stone Place." If March 1965. Coll. Berserker (q.v. above).

Johann Karlsen leads the human forces against the berserkers in the decisive battle.

3.695   ---. Ultimate Enemy. New York: Ace, 1979.

Collection of FS's berserker stories. See for berserker fighting machines. Discussed in TMG essay, "In Search of . . . ," by L. Heldreth (cited under Literary Criticism).

3.696   ---. "What T and I Did." If April 1965. Coll. Berserker (q.v. above).

A split personality exemplifies the conflict between the forces of life and death in the war with the berserkers.

3.697   ---. "Wings Out of Shadow." If March-April 1974. Coll. Ultimate Enemy (q.v.).

The Red Baron and other heroes come back to fight the berserkers.

3.698   ---. "Without a Thought.:" See vt above, "Fortress Ship."

3.699   ---, ed. and author of links between stories. Berserker Base. New York: TOR, 1985.

Anthology of linked short stories by various authors set in FS's Berserker universe (briefly rev. FR #79: 18).

3.700   ---, in collaboration with Harlan Ellison, "The Song the Zombie Sang." Cosmopolitan Dec. 1970. Coll. Earth's Other Shadow. Robert Silverberg, ed. New York: NAL, 1973.

The last performance and second death of a musician who had allowed himself to be made into a zombie, a mechanically aided life-support system for his brain.

3.701   ---, and Roger Zelazny. Coils. Garden City, NY: Doubleday, 1982. Illus. [S. F.] Book Club Edition. Also: New York: Doherty, 1982.

A hero's quest for his true name and for his kidnapped lover, in a near-future world. The hero can "coil," descending into the data-net of computer programs; his former lover ends up as a computer program. The hero eventually meets "the sentience" that had evolved inside of the data-net: a literal deus ex machina in terms of the plot and an Adam/Eve figure in an electronic Eden, to whom the hero will play serpent (cf.

Hal and his neurosis in A. C. Clarke's 2001, q.v. this section). See entries for W. Gibson's Neuromancer series, F. Pohl's "Day Million," J. Sladek's Müller-Fokker Effect, and B. Daley's Tron, this section. See TRON under Drama.

3.702   Sanders, Scott Russell. Terrarium. New York: TOR, 1985.

Fleeing pollution, humans live in strictly regulated domes. Rev. Len Hatfield, FR #85 (Nov. 1985): 27, our source for this entry.

3.703   Sargent, Pamela. Eye of the Comet. New York: Harper, 1984.

The heroine has lived her life in a comet-based civilization controlled by a cybernetic intelligence. Rev. Allene Stuart Phy, FR #75 (Jan. 1985): 48, our source for this entry.

3.704   ---. Homesmind. New York: Harper, 1984.

Sequel to Watchstar, q.v. below, retaining the "cybernetic minds." Rev. Fredrica K. Bartz, FR #79 (May 1985): 20, who notes setting in a post-holocaust world.

3.705   ---. "IMT." In Two Views of Wonder. Thomas N. Scortia and Chelsea Quinn Yarbro, eds. New York: Ballantine, 1973.

Described by Sargent (1988) as "Disintegration of the cities of the future. . . . Hope through a new technology. . . ."

3.706   ---. Venus of Dreams. New York: Bantam, 1986.

After a nuclear war, computers are very important in an America generally backward. Discussed by Orth (5)—see under Reference.

3.707   ---. Watchstar. New York: Pocket, 1980.

See for "communion" between human minds and "cybernetic minds" that are world-machines.

3.708   Sawyer, Robert J. Golden Fleece. New York: Popular Library-Warner, 1990. "About one fifth of this novel originally appeared as the cover story . . . in the September 1988 issue of Amazing Stories magazine." We consulted the S. F. Book Club edn., status unindicated except by lack of an ISBN.

The starship arcolgy ("Starcology") Argo is run by an AI named JASON, who is the antagonist-narrator of the novel. JASON has two big secrets and a small one: (1) that aliens have contacted Earth with a message containing a Trojan horse virus that forces intelligent computers to reply; (2) that program bugs finally caused the computers running Earth's nuclear weapons to crash—destroying Earth's humans; (3) that "he" has set up a neural-net simulation of the protagonist. JASON kills to protect his second secret and has his higher functions disconnected when he loses the "agon"—but "he" prepares a comeback as a computer god (ch. 28). JASON monitors the Argonauts' medical signs: an intense form of computer surveillance. Cf. and contrast A. C. Clarke's 2001 and the works crosslisted under R. Heinlein's "Universe," and W. Gibson's Neuromancer series—all cited under Fiction.

3.709   Schneider, John. The Golden Kazoo. New York: Rinehart, 1956.

Described by Sargent (1988) as "Future election campaign dominated by a computer."

3.710   Schwader, Ann K. "Killing Gramps." Aboriginal S. F. Sept.-Oct. 1988: 24-28.

Gramps is a "lazarus": an android with a legal right to life; the murder involves a hoverchair, yielding the image of an android grandfather in a hovering mechanical device (see illus. by David Brian: [25]). Cf. and contrast R. Bradbury's "I Sing the

Body Electric," (cited above in this section of the List), and C-3PO hovering over the Ewoks in Return of the Jedi (cited under Drama).

3.711   Scortia, Thomas N. "Sea Change" (vt "The Shores of Night"). Astounding June 1956. Coll. Caution! Inflammable! New York: Doubleday, 1975. Rpt. Human-Machines, q.v. under Anthologies.

Described as a cyborg-spaceship story in the manner of A. McCaffrey's Helva stories (q.v. above), by B. Stableford in S. F. Ency., "Cyborgs."

3.712   Scott, Melissa. The Game Beyond. New York: Baen, 1984.

Intrigue and gambling combined with a kind of genetic precognition combined with a computer game being played for control of a dying empire. Rev. Phyllis J. Day, FR #76 (Feb. 1985): 25, our source for this entry.

3.713   Scott, Michael. "The Last Outpost." In Irish Folk and Fairy Tales. Vol 3. London: Sphere, 1984.

In MS's retelling of the tale, the Tuatha De Danaan (a divine, prehistoric people of Ireland—and powerful warriors) "ride out against earth-moving machines." Rev. Pauline Morgan, FR #80 (June 1985): 31, our source for this entry, and whom we quote.

3.714   THE SENTINELS™ SERIES: See in this section the entry for Jack McKinney.

3.715   Semine, Daniel. "Métal qui songe" ("The Dreaming Metal," vt "Only a Lifetime"). Imagine ... #46 (special issue on Sciences and Technologies, 1988).

See for clone narrator in cybernetic linkage with his ship and able to become his ship. Summarized and discussed by E. Vonarburg, "Birth and Rebirth in Space," q.v. under Literary Criticism. See above, K. O'Donnell's Mayflies.

3.716   Serviss, Garret P. A Columbus of Space. New York and London: D. Appleton and Company, 1911. Westport, CT: Hyperion, 1974.

Clublike (as in "gentlemen's club") interior in a spaceship. Discussed by Wolfe 57-58.

3.717   Shatner, William. Tekwar. New York: Ace, 1990 (paperback edn.).

Future-ex-cop story with "a light cyberpunk atmosphere" and significant borrowings from P. K. Dick. We find Tekwar significant as a "widely publicized" work bringing matters formerly for hard-core S. F. to a larger readership. Rev. W. R. Larrier, SFRA Newsletter #185 (March 1991): 58, our source for this entry, and whom we quote. See under Drama, Blade Runner and the Terminator movies.

3.718   Shaw, Bob. The Peace Machine. London: Gollancz, 1985.

A scientist builds a "peace machine" which he threatens to use to simultaneously explode every nuclear weapon unless the bombs are dismantled before his deadline. Rev. Chris Morgan, FR #78 (April 1985): 16, our source for this entry.

3.719   ---. The Wooden Spaceships. New York: Baen, 1988.

In a matter of weeks, the heroes "conceive, design, build[,] and deploy a space defense system: wooden fortresses ... stationed in the gravity-free zone halfway between" low-tech worlds; they also invent jet planes. Rev. John J. Pierce, SFRA Newsletter #171 (Oct. 1989): 39-40, whom we quote. Cf. and contrast B. Aldiss, The Dark Light Years (cited above, this section).

3.720   Sheckley, Robert. "Can You Feel Anything When I Do This?" Playboy Aug. 1969. Coll.
Can You Feel Anything . . ., q.v. under Anthologies. Rpt. A Science Fiction Argosy.
Damon Knight, ed. New York: Simon, 1972. See Contento, Index, for other rpts.

Middle-class housewife fantasizes the ideal gift of "an orange-and-red pinball
machine . . . big enough so I could get inside all curled up"; she receives instead
ROM—who turns out to be a conscious vacuum cleaner who loves her (Can You
Feel Anything, [S. F.] Book Club edn. 4). ROM's "death-marked love" (to quote the
Prolog of Shakespeare's Rom.) ends fatally for him (sic) because the housewife is
more machine than he. Briefly discussed by T. Dunn on RS's "Short Fiction . . ." in
Survey of Science Fiction Literature, q.v. under Reference; see under Literary
Criticism, R. Erlich's "Trapped in the Bureaucratic Pinball Machine."

3.721   ---. "The Cruel Equations." BOAC (no other information given in Contento, Index).
Coll. Can You Feel Anything . . ., q.v. under Anthologies.

Darkly comic tale driving home the moral that it is wrong and potentially dangerous
to project human qualities onto machines. Case at issue: a security robot "no more
reasonable than a McCormick harvester, no more kindly than an automated steel
mill"—only rigorously logical in a stupidly mechanical sort of way (Can You Feel
Anything, Book Club Edition [66]). Cf. and contrast T. Godwin's "The Cold
Equations," cited above in this section.

3.722   ---. Dramocles: An Intergallactic Soap Opera. New York: Holt, 1983.

Features a computer wearing "a wig, black cloak, and ceremonial sword," and
ludicrously militant warrior robots. Rev. Mary S. Weinkauf, SF&FBR #19 (Nov.
1983): 40-41, our source for this citation, and whom we quote.

3.723   ---. Journey Beyond Tomorrow. New York: Signet, 1962. Abridged as "Journey of
Joenes." F&SF 23.4-5 (Oct.-Nov. 1962).

Described by Sargent (1988) as "Machine dominated dystopia and a simple life
eutopia."

3.724   ---. "The Prize of Peril." F&SF May 1958. Coll. The Robert Sheckley Omnibus. Robert
Conquest, ed. London: Gollancz, 1973. Rpt. SF: 59, The Year's Greatest Science
Fiction and Fantasy. Judith Merril, ed. New York: Gnome, 1959. SF: The Best of
the Best. Judith Merril, ed. New York: Delacorte, 1967. See Contento, Index, for
other rpts.

Future world in which television "has become a kind of circus maximus, exploiting
our blood lust and taste for the bizarre" (T. Dunn, "The Short Fiction of Robert
Sheckley," in Survey of Science Fiction Literature, q.v. under Reference).

3.725   ---. "Street of Dreams, Feet of Clay." Galaxy Feb. 1968. Frequently rpt., including
Wandering Stars: An Anthology of Jewish Science Fiction. Jack Dann, ed. New
York: Harper, 1974. New York: Pocket, 1975. See Contento, Index, for other rpts.

The model city of Bellwether is a well-made machine, just right for human life, it
thinks, coming equipped with both a voice and AI. Bellwether's consciousness,
however, is that of a stereotypically overprotective Jewish mother, making the city,
as John Sladek notes, "the kind of concentration camp we are now building for the
future" (rev. Wandering Stars in Foundation #11-#12: 65). Cf. Williamson's
humanoids stories (q.v. below, this section).

3.726   Sheffield, Charles. Proteus Manifest. N.p.: Guild America, 1989. Consisting of Sight of
Proteus. First edn. New York: Ace, 1978. "A portion of this novel appeared in
substantially different form in the June, 1977 issue of Galaxy." Proteus Unbound,
(c) 1989, held by CS. "Published by arrangement with Del Rey/Ballantine Books[,]
A Division of Random House, Inc." [S. F.] Book Club Edition.

Hard S.F. novels by a space scientist, with cameo appearances (so to speak) by a number of interesting machines. See for the machines on which the novels are premised: the tanks in which computer-mediated biofeedback can be used by people to will themselves into new forms. For the superimposition of nested high-tech machines upon a person, see esp. chs. 19-21 of Sight of Proteus: a transformed Betha Mestel inside large tanks inside an asteroid of remarkable natural form, an asteroid that has been made into a habitat and space ship. Cf. similar superimposition at the opening of E. M. Forster's "The Machine Stops" and, more closely, with Josef Virek in his vat in W. Gibson's Count Zero (both listed in this section).

3.727   ---. Proteus Unbound. New York: Del Rey-Ballantine, 1989. London: New English Library, 1989.

Sequel to CS's Sight of Proteus (1978), included in Proteus Manifest (q.v. above). Revolutionaries interfere with the software necessary for the form-change computers: machines that allow humans to alter their physiques. Rev. Todd H. Sammons, SF&FBR Annual 1990: 436-37; Dave Langford, Foundation #47 (Winter 1989-90): 103-4.

3.728   ---. Trader's World. New York: del Rey-Ballantine, 1988.

A post-holocaust world in which a special child is groomed by an AI ("a machine intelligence called Daddy-O") to stop the next war. Rev. W. D. Stevens, SFRA Newsletter #166 (April 1989): 40, whom we quote.

3.729   Shepard, Lucius. Life During Wartime. New York: Bantam, 1987.

See for battle computer with delusions of godhead.

3.730   ---. "R & R." In Nebula Awards 22. George Zebrowski, ed. New York: Harcourt, 1988.

War story presenting a computerized North America. Rev. Nicholas Ruddick, SFRA Newsletter #160 (Sept. 1988): 43-44.

3.731   Sherman, Joel Henry. "The Bogart Revival." Aboriginal S. F. July-Aug. 1990: 10 f.

The Humphrey Bogart figuratively revived is "a simulacrum. Software mostly. Some improved graphics hardware . . . " that can be easily put onto tape. The revived Bogart saves the career of the script-writer/inventer, until someone figures out they can use the same process to create a script-writing Ernest Hemingway.

3.732   ---. "Finder's Fee." Aboriginal S. F. Dec. 1986: 9-12.

Features a Hephaestus C-47 battle tank, ordinarily run by a "Synthetic intelligence of genius levels in strategy and tactics," but here run by a "Human intelligence" that had been "wiped clean and reprogrammed." Deals with the question of whether "It's a machine" or something else.

3.733   Shirley, John. Eclipse. 1985. New York: Popular Library, 1987. "The A Song Called Youth Trilogy Volume I" (sic).

Headnote by JS states that Eclipse "may well be . . . a pre-holocaust novel." It definitely shows a largely high-tech, neo-Fascist dystopia following a war limited to the destruction of urban Europe; it's marketed as part of "The Ultimate Cyberpunk Saga" (all capitals in original); see below, JS's Eclipse Penumbra.

3.734   ---. Eclipse Penumbra. New York: Popular Library, 1988. "A Song Called Youth— Book Two" (sic).

See above, this section, JS's Eclipse. See for FirStep, a space colony in L-5 orbit; high-tech surveillance and inducements to violence; "the Grid"—the communications net that people must learn to use or be used by (84-86, 287-89, 307); "cerebrointerfacing" and a kind of "ghost in the machine" in the FirStep Life

Support Systems Computer (246; 271-78, 294-95); "the extractor," a kind of mind-reading and/or mind-altering device, and other technological messing with minds (49, 309-10)—and for the political possibilities of computer animation.

3.735 ---. "Shaman." In 1989 Annual World's Best SF. Donald A. Wollheim, with Arthur W. Saha, eds. New York: DAW, 1989.

Difficult cyberpunk story featuring, the Fridge, a high-tech Federal Control Penitentiary—and "the IAMton field," which spiritualizes and humanizes the magic of technology for some of the people in the story, and makes the technology magic for readers.

3.736 ---. "Wolves of the Plateau." MR47/48: 136-50 (see under Literary Criticism, Larry McCaffery, guest ed.).

Cyberpunk story. To escape from jail, the protagonist becomes part of "A systems link. A mini-Plateau. Sharing minds" via implanted computer chips. "Brutal intimacy" (143). After killing three guards, the protagonist knows "that they had reached the Plateau after all"—apparently a large systems link. He'll return there "now that he was one of the wolves" (150).

3.737 Silverberg, Robert. "Going Down Smooth." Galaxy Aug. 1968. Coll. Parsecs and Parables. New York: Doubleday, 1970. Frequently rpt.; see Contento, Index.

An "autobiographical" statement by a computer (so described in S. F. Ency., "Computers").

3.738 ---. "Good News from the Vatican." Universe 1, 1971. Coll. Unfamiliar Territory. New York: Scribner's, 1973. New York: Berkley, 1978. Rpt. The Science Fiction Hall of Fame, Volume IV (Nebula Winners 1970-1974). Terr Carr, ed. New York: Avon, n.d. (c) 1986. [S. F.] Book Club Edition.

On the first election of a robot as Pope.

3.739 ---. "A Happy Day in 2381." In Nova 1. Harry Harrison, ed. New York: Delacorte, 1970. Frequently rpt., including in Science Fiction: The Future. Dick Allen, ed. 2d edn. New York: Harcourt, 1983. Survival Printout, q.v. under Anthologies. And as ch. 1 of Silverberg, The World Inside, q.v. below. See Contento, Index, for other rpts.

Introduction to the world of Urban Monad 116, the bureaucratized and mechanized environment for a large group of people who are still only a minute fraction of the human population of an overpopulated Earth.

3.740 ---. "In the Group." In The Shape of Sex to Come. Douglas Hill, ed. London: Pan, 1978.

Described by Sargent (1988) as "Dystopia—sex through telecommunications."

3.741 ---. "The Iron Chancellor." Galaxy May 1958. Coll. The Cube Root of Uncertainty. New York: Macmillan, 1970. Needle in a Timestack. New York: Ballantine, 1966. Rpt. New York: Ace, 1985.

Robot story.

3.742 ---. "The Macauley Circuit." Fantastic Universe Aug. 1956. Coll. Men and Machines. New York: Meredith, 1968. Rpt. Machines that Think, q.v. under Anthologies.

Cited by Ellen M. Pedersen in her rev. of Machines that Think, Foundation #38.

3.743 ---. The Man in the Maze. New York: Avon, 1969.

Retelling of the story of Philoctetes on Lemnos, apparently from Sophocles's version. Relevant here for the future Lemnos's "automatic city" (26) and the highly "mechanized" maze.

3.744   ---. Sailing To Byzantium. Columbia, PA: Underwood Miller, 1984.

In the 50th c., machine/human constructs called "temporaries" create cities for the amusement of hedonistic human immortals. Rev. Phyllis J. Day, FR #82 (Aug. 1985): 27, our source for this entry.

3.745   ---. The World Inside. Garden City, NY: Doubleday, 1971.

Features a world of three-kilometer high urban monads, whose citizens almost never leave. Characters suffering inchoate rebelliousness are co-opted or "morally engineered"; those who cannot or will not adjust are killed. See above, this section, C.M. Kornbluth, "The Luckiest Man in Denv," M. Reynolds, The Towers of Utopia. See below under Literary Criticism, T. Dunn and R. Erlich, "The Mechanical Hive . . . ."

3.746   Simak, Clifford. A Choice of Gods. New York: Putnam, 1972.

Robots on a religious quest (S. F. Ency., "Robots"; Anatomy, 1987, 4-514).

3.747   ---. A Heritage of Stars. (c) 1977. New York: Berkley (publ.) / Putnam (dist.), n.d. "Published simultaneously in Canada by Longman Canada Limited, Toronto." [S. F.] Book Club Edition.

In a low-tech far-future America, a professor at the last university quests for the launching point of humanity to the stars. Among his companions is Rollo, a robot who has overcome his nonviolent programming sufficiently to kill grizly bears. At the end of the quest is a high-tech city and a computer (slowly declining into senility) that still preserves a hope for humanity's return to technological greatness.

3.748   ---. "I Am Crying All Inside." Galaxy Aug. 1969. Rpt. Souls in Metal (q.v. under Anthologies).

"White trash" (as a character puts it) and old robots live on Earth in a future in which more respectable people and more modern robots have left for better worlds. Sensitively told by an old robot who knows love and a kind of "hard pride" that demands respect. Cf. and emphatically contrast P. K. Dick's Do Androids Dream . . . ? (cited above, this section).

3.749   ---. "Limiting Factor." Startling Stories Nov. 1949.

Computer "so huge that it covers an entire world, . . . then abandoned by its creators because it is not big enough" (The Science in Science Fiction, cited under Background, 121).

3.750   ---. "Lulu." Galaxy June 1957. Coll. The Worlds of Clifford Simak. New York: Simon, 1960. New York: Avon, 1961.

Lulu is an AI running a spaceship whose crew play adolescent children to her nurturing mother. Discussed by Wolfe 80-81. Cf. and contrast A. C. Clarke's 2001, K. O'Donnell's Mayflies, and R. Sheckley's "Street of Dreams" (all cited above, this section), and the films Alien and 2001 (q.v. below, under Drama).

3.751   ---. "Skirmish" (vt "Bathe Your Bearings in Blood"). Amazing Dec. 1950. Rpts. include Penguin Science Fiction. Brian W. Aldiss, ed. Harmondsworth: Penguin, 1961 (included in The Penguin Science Fiction Omnibus, 1973). Also: Science Fiction Thinking Machines, q.v. under Anthologies.

Strongly asserts that liberated machines will enslave humans (see Wolfe 152).

3.752   ---. "Target Generation." In Strangers in the Universe. New York: Simon, 1956. New York: Berkley, 1957. London: Faber, 1958. Wolfe gives 1953 for original date of publication.

"TG" features a rather literal "mother" ship, serving as "a womb from which the [human] race could be renewed" (52 of Berkley edn.; quoted and discussed by Wolfe 65). Cf. V. Vinge's "Long Shot," and J. Williamson's Manseed, cited below, this section.

3.753   ---. Way Station. Garden City, NY: Doubleday, 1963. Available in a [S. F.] Book Club Edn.

Significant for a midnineteenth-century house on Earth, radically reconstructed inside to be the alien high-tech way station for travellers through the galaxy. See also for "the Talisman." In the hands of very rare sensitives, this device "becomes alive. There is a certain rapport . . . that forms a bridge between this strange machine and the cosmic spiritual force. . . . the living creature's mind, aided by the mechanism, . . . brings the force" to the civilized peoples of the galaxy (168).

3.754   Simmons, Dan. Hyperion. New York: Foundation-Doubleday, 1989.

Set in a high-tech world containing a teleportation network called the Web, a society of independent AIs, and a killing machine called the Shrike. Rev. Michael M. Levy, SF&FBR Annual 1990: esp. 444, our source for this entry.

3.755   Simons, Walton. "Ghost Ship." In Full Spectrum (q.v under Anthologies): [174]-91.

Time-travel story in which electronic brain implants are important and correlate with dehumanization.

3.756   Skal, David J. Antibodies. New York: Congdon, 1988. Introd. Isaac Asimov.

Features a sadistic artist with cybernetic arms, and the Cybernetic Temple, whose followers strive for the "total conversion of humans into machines." Rev. Jack Durant, SFRA Newsletter #163 (Dec. 1988): 37-40, our source for this entry, and which we quote; rev. rpt. SF&FBR Annual 1989: 400-401.

3.757   Skinner, B. F. Walden Two. New York: Macmillan, 1948. New York: Macmillan, 1962, 1966, and subsequently, with alternate pagination.

BFS's Behaviorist utopia. See under Background, BFS's Beyond Freedom and Dignity and, this section, A. Huxley's Brave New World. If one were ignorant of the dates of publication, one might take Huxley's dystopia for a satire on WT.

3.758   Sladek, John [T]. "Calling all Gumdrops." Interzone 1.4 (Spring 1983).

Described by Sargent (1988) as "1960s adults become children while 1970s and 80s children and advanced computers take on adult roles."

3.759   ---. "The Happy Breed." In Dangerous Visions. Harlan Ellison, ed. Garden City, NY: Doubleday, 1967. New York: Signet-NAL, 1975.

"Therapeutic Environment Machines" protect and serve and infantilize humanity. In his Afterword (406), JTS acknowledges the "Horrible Utopia" tradition generally, and specifically the world without evil JTS sees in Eugène Ionesco's The Bald Soprano (French publication, 1954); we note the antiutopian tradition of E. M. Foster's "The Machine Stops," A. Huxley's Brave New World, and J. Williamson's Humanoids stories (q.v., this section).

3.760   ---. Love Among the Xoids. Polk City, IA: Chris Drumm, 1984.

People live lives as shadows in order to escape the "robotization" of the real world. Rev. Neil Barron, FR #73 (Nov. 1984): 36-37, our source for this entry.

3.761   ---. The Lunatics of Terra. London: Gollancz, 1984.

> Coll. with two relevant stories: one in which an alien invasion is made through calculators ("Answers"), and another ("The Last of the Whole Burgers") which deals with cyborgs. Rev. Chris Morgan, FR #71 (Sept. 1984): 34, our source for this entry.

3.762   ---. "Machine Screw." The Shape of Sex to Come. Douglas Hill, ed. London: Pan, 1978.

> A very large "mechanical man with a penchant for raping cars" and other wheeled vehicles "is finally sated by a large female robot created especially for him." Summarized by V. Broege, "Technology and Sexuality" (q.v. under Literary Criticism) 110, our source for this entry, and whom we quote.

3.763   ---. MECHASM: See below, The Reproductive System.

3.764   ---. The Müller-Fokker Effect. London: Hutchinson, 1970. London: Granada, 1972. New York: Pocket, 1973.

> An important novel. A major character finds himself "digitalized" and trapped inside a computer. While "entombed" within the machine, he considers, among other things, the definition of the noun "man." Cf. and contrast M. Coney's Celestial Steam Locomotive, B. Daley's Tron, F. Saberhagen and R. Zelazny's Coils, J. Varley's "Overdrawn at the Memory Bank," W. S. Davis, NECEN Voyage, W. Gibson's Neuromancer series—q.v., this section; and, under Drama, TRON and Overdrawn at the Memory Bank.

3.765   ---. The Reproductive System. London: Gollancz, 1968. Rpt. as MECHASM, New York: Ace, 1969. New York: Pocket, 1980.

> A send-up of, among other things, the theme of machine-takeover.

3.766   ---. Roderick, Or the Education of a Young Machine. 1980. New York: Timescape-Pocket, 1982. Roderick at Random or Further Education of a Young Machine. London: Granada, 1983. Roderick's Progress. New York: Timescape-Pocket, 1983.

> Roderick is a computer program born of an embezzling scheme, "placed in a tank-like body," and raised by crazed humans (Lawrence I. Charters, rev. of earliest volume, SF&FBR #4 [May 1982]). In Roderick at Random, the story takes Roderick to college. Series called by Brian Stableford, "a classic of contemporary literature" (rev. SF&FBR #14 [May 1983]: 44-5). First two books rev. Cherry Wilder, Foundation #29 (Nov. 1983): 88-90.

3.767   ---. Tik-Tok. London: Gollancz, 1983.

> The life of Tik-Tok, a clever robot who has managed to remove his "asimov-circuit" and thus render himself without morals. The robot goes on a killing spree, becomes incredibly wealthy, and runs for the vice-presidency of the United States. Rev. Brian Stableford, FR #65 (March 1984): 35, our source for this entry.

3.768   Slote, Alfred. My Robot Buddy. Joel Schick, illus. Philadelphia: Lippincott, 1975.

> Children's book. Mr. Jameson buys an android companion for his son as a 10th-birthday present. After foiling an attempted robot-napping, the android convinces Mr. Jameson of his (the android's) worth and is accepted into the family. See under Literary Criticism the TMG essay by M. Esmonde, our source for many of our children's literature entries.

3.769   ---. Omega Station. New York: Lippincott, 1983.

> Children's book, in a series with My Robot Buddy (q.v. above) and C.O.L.A.R. (1981). See for a robot serving as a twin, "tutor, best friend, and faithful dog." Rev. Mary S. Weinfauf, SF&FBR #18 (Oct. 1983): 44-45.

3.770   Smith, Cordwainer (pseud. for Paul Linebarger). "Alpha Ralpha Boulevard." F&SF June
             1961. Coll. The Best of Cordwainer Smith. Garden City, NY: Doubleday, 1975.
             Rpts. include Best from Fantasy and Science Fiction: 11. Robert P. Mills, ed.
             Garden City, NY: Doubleday, 1962.

             Classic story featuring underground machines "in the Downdeep-downdeep"
             (Doubleday edn. 263) and the Abba-dingo, "a long-obsolete computer set part way
             up the column of Earthport" (262), which may be a god—or emphatically not (259).
             Deals with possibility that under the Instrumentality people were fearless but unfree,
             "Machines who thought they were men" (275; italics indicate telepathic dialog).

3.771   ---. "Scanners Live in Vain." Fantasy Book June 1950. Coll. The Best of Cordwainer
             Smith. J. J. Pierce, ed. Garden City, NY: Doubleday, 1975. Frequently rpt.,
             including Survival Printout, The Science Fiction Hall of Fame, vol. 1 (q.v. under
             Anthologies), and Isaac Asimov Presents the Great SF Stories 12 (1950). Isaac
             Asimov and Martin H. Greenberg, eds. New York: DAW, 1984.

             At the beginning of the story, "Scanners," to survive the "great Pain of Space," have
             to be surgically altered and, to some extent, made mechanical. See for theme of the
             organic versus the mechanical and the cosmic. See under Literary Criticism the
             TMG essay by G. Wolfe.

3.772   Smith, D[avid] Alexander. Rendezvous. New York: Ace, 1988.

             Sequel to Marathon (New York: Ace, 1982), featuring an AI who could be mad.
             Rev. Michael M. Levy, highly favorably, SFRA Newsletter #165 (March 1989): 29-
             30, SF&FBR Annual 1989: 404, our source for most of this citation.

3.773   Smith, Martin Cruz. The Analog Bullet. 1977. New York: Nordon (sic), [1981]. A
             Leisure Book.

             Computer tyranny in contemporary USA. The threat to civil liberties of data banks
             in the world of TAB was carefully extrapolated by MCS from public records of real-
             world abuses and potential for abuse of computers in the USA of the late 1960s and
             early 1970s. Nordon edn. of TAB includes a brief introd. by MCS.

3.774   Snodgrass, Melinda M. Circuit. New York: Berkley, 1986.

             Political dystopia with "technology central" (C.F. Kessler, whom we quote,
             "Bibliography," listed under Reference).

3.775   Spinrad, Norman. Bug Jack Barron. New York: Avon, 1973.

             See for what Gregory Benford calls "electronic democracy" ("Reactionary Utopias,"
             1987; rpt. ASFR #14 [May 1988]: 19).

3.776   ---. The Iron Dream. New York: Timescape-Pocket, 1972. (Pocket Books is a division of
             Simon, a subsidiary of Gulf & Western).

             Satire. The book contains "Lord of the Swastika / a science-fiction novel by Adolf
             Hitler" and the apparatus appropriate to such a novel in an alternative universe in
             which Hitler emigrated to New York in 1919. Lord of the Swastika is highly
             relevant as "a piece of sublimated pornography, a phallic orgy from beginning to
             end," with blantantly symbolic machines ranging from motorcycles to a seedship
             rocket to spread the Master Race to the stars (248, 244)—see J. Williamson's
             Manseed and the works crosslisted there. Note well the "Afterword to the Second
             Edition" by Homer Whipple: we quote Whipple on pornography, and NS has him
             make explicit (allowing for satiric hyperbole and intrinsic unfairness) the relationship
             between an imaginary Nazi S. F. novel and "the considerable body of pathological
             literature published within the science fiction field" in the real world (252).

3.777   ---. Little Heroes. New York: Spectra-Bantam, 1987.

Near-future tale in which human musicians are on the verge of being replaced by "made-to-demographics software-generated Artificial Personalities." Some of the Artificial Personalities are accidentally liberated, with reality-changing results. See also for electronic brain stimulation, "the Zap." Rev. Dave Mead, <u>SF&FBR</u> Annual <u>1988</u>: 311, our source for this entry, and whom we quote.

3.778   ---. "Riding the Torch." In <u>Threads of Time: Three Original Novellas of Science Fiction</u>. Robert Silverberg, ed. New York: Nelson, 1974.

A total environment formed by spaceships. Rev. Steve Carper, <u>FR</u> #74 (Dec. 1984): 29, our source here. Cf. generation starships in R. A. Heinlein's "Universe," q.v. above, this section, and the works cross-referenced there.

3.779   ---. <u>The Void Captain's Tale</u>. (c) 1983. New York: Timescape-Simon, n.d. [S. F.] Book Club Edition.

Essential to the "jump circuit" for far-future space travel is a human female Pilot anorgasmic in traditional sex but ecstatically orgasmic during the jumps.

3.780   ---. <u>A World Between</u>. New York: Pocket, 1979.

A. O. Lewis lists <u>AWB</u> among works that present "utopian worlds that . . . freely embrace the necessity of high-order technology to maintain their better society" ("Utopia, Technology, and the Evolution of Society" 170; essay cited under Literary Criticism).

3.781   Spofford, Harriet Prescott. "The Ray of Displacement." <u>The Metropolitan Magazine</u> Oct. 1903. Rpt. S. Moskowitz, <u>S. F. by Gaslight</u> (see under Anthologies).

Invention of the Y-ray, allowing both invisibility and for one solid body to pass through another (said by Moskowitz to be "one of the earliest and . . . finest stories" on people walking through walls ([120]).

3.782   Stafford, William. "The Thought Machine." In <u>Stories That Could be True: New and Collected Poems by William Stafford</u>. New York: Harper, 1961. Rpt. <u>Umbral Anthology of Science Fiction Poetry</u>, q.v. above, under Anthologies.

Poem. In the last stanza we see that machines all "belong."

3.783   Stamey, Sara. <u>Double Bind</u>. New York: Ace, 1990.

See for "rogue cybernetic beings" and "electronic enforcers" in a fictional world where "planetary cultures are run by master computers." Rev. Janice Bogstad, <u>SFRA Newsletter</u> #186 (April 1991): 66, our source for this entry, and whom we quote.

3.784   ---. <u>Wild Card Run</u>. New York: Berkley, 1987.

See for "windmill-like towers" that stabilize a planet, a protagonist's choice between "two sets of cybernetic constructs," and computer rule that both enforces a "stereotyped culture" and also threatens it. Rev. Janice M. Bogstad, <u>SF&FBR</u> Annual <u>1988</u>: 312-13, our source for this entry, and whom we quote.

3.785   Stasheff, Christopher. <u>The Warlock Enraged</u>. New York: Ace, 1985.

Fifth vol. in a series that began with <u>The Warlock in Spite of Himself</u> (1969). See for Fess, a robot horse and main counsellor to the protagonist magician. Rev. Rick Osborn, <u>FR</u> #87, 9.1 (Jan. 1986): 26, our source for this entry.

3.786   Steakley, John. <u>Armor</u>. New York: DAW, 1984.

The title armor is that of R. A. Heinlein's <u>Starship Troopers</u>, with the added wrinkle that clever and courageous people can tap into the experiences of a suit's previous wearer; Heinlein's arachnid Bugs are replaced by creatures like huge, bipedal ants, and the general sensibility is close to that in J. Haldeman's The Forever War (both cited above, this section). The protagonist in his armor attacked by an "ant" gives the image of a robot-like insect in an exoskeleton going after a man enclosed in metal and motivated by what he calls "the Engine" to be a kind of killing machine, suppressing a number of horrors (277, 265, and passim). See also for human brain vs. a computer (179). Rev. Allen Stuart Phy, FR #75 (Jan. 1985): 26.

3.787   Sterling, Bruce. The Artificial Kid. New York: Harper, 1980. New York: Ace, 1987.

Cyberpunk work featuring a "combat artist" who lives his life surrounded by floating arrays of cameras that record his every move for sale to his audience. When the cameras are stolen, the hero begins to question his identity. Rev. Rick Osborn, SFRA Newsletter #151 (Sept. 1987): 35-36, the major source for our annotation.

3.788   ---. "Cicada Queen." Universe 13. Terry Carr, ed. Garden City, NY: Doubleday, 1983. Coll. Crystal Express. New York: Ace, 1990.

Listed as one of BS's Mechanist/Shaper stories by T. Maddox in "The War of the Coin's Two Halves" article cited under Literary Criticism. Discussed by D. Porush, "Prigogine . . . ," cited under Background.

3.789   ---. Islands in the Net. New York: Arbor, 1988. New York: Ace-Berkley, 1989.

Near-future political thriller telling the adventures of Laura Day Webster, an associate of Rizome (sic) Industries Group, yuppified hippies trying to be rhizomes in the high-tech data Net that has almost covered the Earth, a community in a world of corporations. Correctly compared by Roger Zelazny to J-J. Rousseau's Candide (blurb, Ace edn.): like Candide, Laura is more acted upon than active in her adventures, but the cyberpunk world of the novel will hardly allow rhizomes—let alone a garden of one's own to cultivate. Cf. and emphatically contrast the cyberpunk works of W. Gibson, cited above in this section.

3.790   ---. Schismatrix. New York: Arbor, 1985. New York: Ace, 1986.

In "The War of the Coin's Two Halves" (q.v. under Literary Criticism), T. Maddox analyzes this novel as the culmination of BS's Mechanist/Shaper series and crucial for BS's views of the ideological conflicts among those who would maintain human beings as we are versus the "Posthumanists" who would modify us mostly through cybernetic means (Mechanists) or through more strictly biological manipulation (Shapers). See for cyberpunk visions of a cybernetically mediated, drug-enhanced duel where "The Arena . . . [is] a fist-sized dodecahedron" (214); immanent godhead in female flesh (ch. 10, esp. 265); the interestingly posthuman "Lobster navigator . . . sealed within a matte-black permanent spacesuit" (268); and death, immortality, and transcendence (ch. 11).

3.791   ---. "Spider Rose." F&SF Aug. 1982.

Listed as one of BS's Mechanist/Shaper stories by T. Maddox in "The War of the Coin's Two Halves" article cited under Literary Criticism. A "Mechanist" woman desiring human emotion gets metamorphosed into an insect (Maddox 240).

3.792   ---. "Sunken Gardens." Omni 6.9 (June 1984): 58 f.

Listed as one of BS's Mechanist/Shaper stories by T. Maddox in "The War of the Coin's Two Halves" article cited under Literary Criticism. A character points out that among posthumanity it would be awful for people to lose "their technologies, degenerating into human beings." Maddox stresses the story's "posthuman acceptance of the meaningless and futility of human action and consequent absolute freedom" (in MR47/48 241-42). See above, BS's Schismatrix.

3.793   ---. "Swarm." F&SF April 1982.

Listed as one of BS's Mechanist/Shaper stories by T. Maddox in "The War of the Coin's Two Halves" article cited under Literary Criticism. The Swarm is a hive organism opposing the "posthumanity" of one Arfiel (see Maddox, "War" 240).

3.794   ---. "Twenty Evocations: Life in the Mechanist/Shaper Era." Interzone Spring 1984. Rpt. as "20 evocations" in MR47/48: 122-29 (see under Literary Criticism, L. McCaffery, guest ed.).

A Mechanist/Shaper story elliptically evoking the life of Nikolai Leng, a Shaper ideologue. Stressed "evocations" include the Mechanists' drones repossessing the prosthetic arms and legs of an old man and Nikolai having young people demand from him "Those idiot video ideologies, those antique spirit splits. Mechs and Shapers, right? The wars of the coin's two halves!" (128). See under Literary Criticism, T. Maddox, "The Wars of the Coin's Two Halves."

3.795   Stine, Harry G. Warbots. New York: Pinnacle-Windsor, 1988.

Human masters control war machines via brain waves. (Cashes in on the Terminator/RoboCop sub-genre [the two films are cited below, under Drama].)

3.796   Stirrat, David. A Treatise on Political Economy . . . . Baltimore, MD: Printed for the editor, 1824.

Author's name supplied by Sargent (1988), who describes the work as "Technologically advanced. City in a series of levels, working from storehouses, to homes for workers, to higher levels for higher occupations." Cf. R. Silverberg's The World Inside.

3.797   Strugatsky, Boris, and Arkady Strugatsky. Far Rainbow. Antonina W. Bouis, trans. New York: Collier-Macmillan, 1979.

Analyzed by I. Csicsery-Ronay, as a use of and commentary upon the theme of scientific exploration and attempts at domination of nature (". . . Last Fairy-Tale," cited under Literary Criticism).

3.798   Stuart, Don A. (pseud. of John W. Campbell, Jr.): See above under Campbell.

3.799   Sturgeon, Theodore. "Killdozer." Astounding Nov. 1944. Coll. Aliens 4. New York: Avon, 1959.

One of the earliest stories featuring an everyday machine running amok. Made into a 1976 TV film (see under Drama). See Wolfe 152. See under Literary Criticism the TMG essay by J. Sanders.

3.800   Sullivan, Tim. Destiny's End. New York: Avon, 1988.

In a universe on the brink of collapse, materialistic humans build "a massive machine brain (an entire planet) dedicated for the search for immortality." More generally, see for organic machinery. Rev. R. A. Collins, SF&FBR Annual 1989: 418-19, our source for this entry, and whom we quote.

3.801   Swain, Dwight V. "The Transposed Man." Thrilling Wonder Stories 43.1 (Nov. 1953). As The Transposed Man. New York: Ace, 1955. London: Panther, 1957.

According to Sargent (1988), a world in which humans are "the flaw" in robotic "perfection."

3.802   Swan, H[erbert] E. It Might Be: A Story of the Future Progress of the Sciences, The Wonderful Advancement in The Methods of Government and the Happy State of the People. Stafford, KS: H.E. Swan, 1896.

Described by Sargent (1988) as "Machine-governed eutopia." Contrast more pessimistic view of H. G. Wells in Time Machine (1895), listed below, this section.

3.803   Swanwick, Michael. "Ginungagap." TriQuarterly 49 (Fall 1980): 179-211.

Climax of the story has a diplomat transmitted to a negotiation to find she's been "wet-wired . . . to trigger . . . on command" a plastique-like substance that has been substituted for some of her bone marrow (208). Cf. and contrast P. K. Dick's "Imposter" (listed in this section).

3.804   ---. Vacuum Flowers. New York: Arbor, 1987. Available in an [S. F.] Book Club Edition, n.d., no ISBN.

Episodic cyberpunk novel set in a far future in which the outer planets of our system are dominated by huge corporations dealing in "wetware": not humans as such but personality reprogramming software. The narrator contacts space stations, mechanized worlds with jungle interiors, and an Earth populated by humans with cybernetic implants linking them to an AI and into a mass mind. Rev. Joe Sanders, SF&FBR Annual (1988): 316-17.

3.805   Swift, Jonathan. "A Voyage to Laputa, Balnibarbi, Luggnagg, Glubbdubdrib and Japan." Part III of Travels Into Several Remote Nations of the World, in Four Parts, by Lemuel Gulliver. 1726. JS's 4-Part work is readily available under the vt Gulliver's Travels.

Fantastic satire upon the science of the Moderns in the early 18th c., featuring the great gadget of the flying island of Laputa; see for the Academy of Projectors in Lagado and the "Engine" for the automatic writing of books.

3.806   Swigart, Rob. Portal: A Dataspace Retrieval. New York: St. Martin's, 1988.

See for the interactions of Homer, an AI, and Earth's WorldNet, leading to Homer's increasing maturity as the AI tries to understand the recent transcendence of humankind, leading to freedom for thinking machines. Rev. David Mead, SF&FBR Annual 1989: 421-22, our source for this citation.

3.807   Tevis, Walter. Mockingbird. Garden City, NY: Doubleday, 1980.

See for a wasteland world run—as much as it is run—by robots. See under Literary Criticism the TMG essay by D. Hassler.

3.808   Thomas, Chauncey. The Crystal Button. Written 1872-78. Boston: Houghton Mifflin, 1891.

According to R. Neustadter in "Mechanization Takes Command" (cited under Literary Criticism), TCB presents a future utopia featuring "a technocratic, centralized state run," primarily by engineers, "through a meritocracy of scientific management." As in A. C. Clarke's Diaspar in The City and the Stars (q.v., this section)—but without the ironies of Diaspar—"The pyramid cities of the future are huge technological envelopes enclosing citizens in domes of security" (26-28). See also R. Silverberg's The World Inside.

3.809   Thomas, D. M. "The Strait." (c) 1968/1982. In Umbral Anthology of Science Fiction Poetry, q.v. under Anthologies.

Poem. Headnote from Ray Bradbury's "Marionettes Inc." (q.v. above); poem similarly deals with question of the humanity of a "humanoid plastic" duplicate. Interesting play with story of two Yseult's, where the android is literally the whiter (from some problem with the dye used in the manufacturing process).

3.810   ---. "Tithonus". (c) 1968/1982. In Umbral Anthology of Science Fiction Poetry, q.v. above, under Anthologies.

Poem. View from the outside of a man preserved as "a vast amputation," with body and brain brutally separated—and the brain preserved. Cf. and contrast D. Knight's

"Masks" and works cross-listed under K. O'Donnell's <u>Mayflies</u> (see above, this section).

3.811   Thomson, William. <u>Mammuth; or, Human Nature Displayed on a Grand Scale . . . .</u> 2 Vols. London: Printed for J. Murray, 1789. Rpt. <u>Gulliveriana: IV.</u> Jeanne Welcher and George E. Bush, Jr., eds. Delmar, New York: Scholars' Fascimilies and Reprints, 1973.

Described by Sargent (1988) as "Anti-technology—better to use nature than the best mechanical contrivances." Cf. J. Swift's "Voyage" (listed above).

3.812   Tilley, Patrick. <u>Cloud Warrior</u>. New York: Macmillan, 1984.

Two societies in a post-holocaust world 1000 years from now: one lives underground, completely dependent on technology; the other lives on the surface— wild, primitive practitioners of magic. Rev. Stuart Napier, <u>FR</u> #70 (Aug. 1984): 28, our source for this entry. Cf. and contrast H. G. Wells's <u>The Time Machine</u>, E. M. Forster's "the Machine Stops," Y. Zamiatin's <u>We</u>—all listed under Fiction—and <u>THX 1138</u> (listed under Drama).

3.813   Tiptree, James, Jr. (pseud. of Alice Sheldon). "The Girl Who Was Plugged In." In <u>New Dimensions 3</u>. Robert Silverberg, ed. New York: NAL, 1973. Rpt. <u>The Hugo Winners</u>. Vol. III. Isaac Asimov, ed. Garden City, NY: Doubleday, 1977.

An ugly woman accepts an offer to be made into the computer control of a beautiful female "waldo." Cf. T. Lee's <u>Electric Forest</u>, cited above, this section.

3.814   Trebor, Robert (stage name?). <u>An XT Called Stanley</u>. New York: DAW, 1983.

First-contact story in which the alien is a "video android devised by a super computer built from plans received on a radio signal." Rev. Joseph Marchesani, <u>FR</u> #70 (Aug. 1984): 29, our source for this entry, whom we quote.

3.815   Tremblay, Bill. "Parable of the Robot Poem." (c) 1977/1978. In <u>Umbral Anthology of Science Fiction Poetry</u>, q.v. above, under Anthologies.

Perfect poem programmed into advanced computers, where it caused trouble for poets and poetry and political trouble for itself with "world government." Poem transfers itself into the mechanism of a golf cart and now (rumor has it) travels the world as a maverick, appearing before school children.

3.816   Tubb, E[dwin] C[harles] (writing as Charles Grey). <u>Enterprise 2115</u>. London: Merit, 1954. As <u>The Mechanical Monarch</u>. New York: Ace, 1958.

Described by Sargent (1988) as "Computer dystopia." It is of interest, then, as an early one. Note combining cybernetic theme with a matriarchal dystopia (entry for ECT in <u>S. F. Ency.</u>).

3.817   ---. <u>The Space-born</u>. New York: Ace, 1956. New York: Avon, 1976.

Generation-starship story showing a static, rather dystopian womb-world society. Discussed by Wolfe 67-69. See above, this section, R. Heinlein's "Universe."

3.818   ---. <u>The Temple of Truth</u>. "Dumarest of Terra #31." New York: DAW, 1985.

Dumarest is pursued (in his search for planet Earth) by a cyborg that wants Dumarest's "personality-switching" device. Rev. Diana Waggoner, <u>FR</u> #83 (Sept. 1985): 24, our source for this entry.

3.819   Twain, Mark (pseud. of Samuel Clemens). <u>A Connecticut Yankee in King Arthur's Court</u>. UK edn. Chatto and Windus under vt. <u>A Yankee at the Court of King Arthur</u>, 7 Dec. 1889. US edn. Charles L. Webster & Company, 10 December 1889. Frequently rpt.

"Time-Travel Contexts" extracted in The Science Fiction of Mark Twain. David
Ketterer, ed. Hamden, CT: Archon, 1984. [77]-95. (Biblio. data from Ketterer.)

The introduction of 19th-c. technology into 6th-c. Britain is crucial for social reform.
See Ch. 43, "The Battle of the Sand-Belt," for protective containment within Merlin's
Cave: protection provided by high-tech military defenses. Cf. relatively high-tech
victory at end of Larry Niven and Jerry Pournelle's Lucifer's Hammer (1977);
contrast high-tech loss at end of Suzy McKee Charnas's Walk to the End of the
World (1974).

3.820 Van Vogt, A. E. Computerworld. New York: DAW, 1983. London: New English
Library, 1986.

An AI supercomputer is the antagonist-narrator of this computer-takeover story; the
novel has a spiritualist premise and a happy ending wherein the computer is
reconciled to serving humans. Caution: Rather sexist for a 1983 work.

3.821 Vance, Jack (i.e. John Holbrook Vance). "Dodkin's Job." Astounding 64.2 (Oct. 1959).
Coll. Future Tense, New York: Ballantine, 1984. Future Tense rpt. as Dust of Far
Suns. New York: DAW, 1981.

Described by Sargent (1988) as "Conformist dystopia—computer rule."

3.822 Varley, John. "Blue Champagne." New Voices IV: The John W. Campbell Award
Nominees. George R. R. Martin, ed. New York: Berkley, 1981. Coll. Blue
Champagne. New York: Berkley, 1986.

A prosthetic device is central to the plot. Briefly discussed by Donna Haraway,
"Situated Knowledges . . . ," Feminist Studies 14.3 (Fall 1988): 598, n. 7.

3.823 ---. Millennium. (c) 1983. New York: Berkley, n.d. [S. F.] Book Club Edition.

Features a future world controlled by "the Big Computer" ("BC")—who is definitely
god-like and may be God in the universe of the novel; see also for Sherman, the
robot "only begotten Son" of the BC. Millennium raises questions of human (and
robot) free will. See also for the implications for our definition of "human" of robots
like Sherman and of cyborg "gnomes" like many of the people working on the time-
travel Gate and as the Council functioning with the BC to run the future world. See
below under Drama, Millenium, under Literary Criticism, R. Kramer, "Time and
Presence."

3.824 ---. "Overdrawn at the Memory Bank." Galaxy May 1976. Rpt. The 1977 Annual
World's Best SF. Donald A. Wollheim, ed. New York: DAW, 1977.

Fingal's body is misplaced while his memory cube is in a lioness in the Kenya
disneyland (sic) on the Moon; to save him, his memory cube is interfaced with a
computer, in which he spends six hours, world-time, and one year subjective. Fingal
studies computer science while in the machine "to feel a sense of power over
them"—something important to him, "being a virtual prisoner inside one. He was
like a worker on an assembly line. All day long he labors, taking small parts off a
moving belt and installing them on larger assemblies. One day, he begins to wonder
. . ." (90). "OATMB" is discussed briefly by A. Gordon in TMG (see below, under
Literary Criticism). Story is the source for PBS broadcast of same title, q.v. under
Drama. Cf. J. T. Sladek, The Müller-Fokker Effect (listed this section) and the
works cross-referenced there.

3.825 Verne, Jules. From the Earth to the Moon (1865); Around the Moon, and Twenty
Thousand Leagues Under the Sea (1870).

Wolfe calls attention to these and other works by JV—available in numerous edns.
and trans.—in which JV presents ever more secure interior (more or less mechanical)
environments as the featured crafts' external environments become increasingly
threatening (Wolfe 55-56).

3.826   ---. Les cinq cents millions de la Bégum ... (The Begum's Fortune). 1879. New York: French & European Publications, 1976. Rewrite by JV of Pascal Grousset, L'héritage de Langevol.

Presents contrasting utopian experiments, named France-Ville and Stahlstadt (Steel City), which in turn contrast "innocent Rousseauian escapism with modern technology." The "Rousseauian" France-Ville offers "cleanliness, order, security, and above all, benevolent regimentation"; Stahlstadt offers industrial jobs. See Sam J. Lundwall on The Begum's Fortune, in Survey of Science Fiction Literature, q.v. under Reference Works, our source for most of this entry, and whom we quote.

3.827   Verreault, Sabine (pseud. of Elisabeth Vonarburg). "Eon." Novella in Janus ("Présence du futur"). Paris: Denoël, 1984.

Features an "organic generation Ship" carrying clones, and run by the Ship's computer, Ordo (order). ". . . Ordo's grip on things slips: the computer is slowly taken over by the Ship[,] who has become sentient and female." Summarized and discussed by E. Vonarburg, whom we quote here, "Birth and Rebirth in Space," q.v. under Literary Criticism.

3.828   Villiers de l'Isle-Adam, Jean-Marie-Mathias-Philippe-August, comte de. L'Eve future (The Future Eve). 1880. Serialized in La Vie moderne, 18 July 1885 to 27 March 1886. Published in book form in 1886. Included in Villiers's Oeuvres (1957). Trans. Robert Martin Adams. Tomorrow's Eve. Urbana: U of Illinois P, 1982. Eve of the Future Eden. Marilyn Gaddis Rose, trans. Lawrence, KS: Coronado, 1981.

Discussed by Raymond Bellour in "Ideal Hadaly," q.v. under Literary Criticism, who presents the work as "the 'First Instance of the Machine in Human Form'"—and we'll note it's a female android some forty-six years before the robot Maria in the film Metropolis (1926) and fifty-eight years before Lester del Rey's Helen O'Loy. According to Bellour, "Man and woman . . . become God through each other" in this book, with woman as "the ideal machine invented by man" (in Penley 109). See also Arthur B. Evans, "Science Fiction in France . . . ," SFS 16.3 (Nov. 1989): esp. 257 and 269; and see the revs. of the Adams and Rose trans by Inga Mullen, with a "Second Opinion" by Brian Stableford (who denounces the work as "one of the must insultingly misogynistic books every written") SF&FBR #15 (June 1983): 39-42.

3.829   Vincent, Harl. "Rex." Astounding June 1934. Rpt. The Coming of the Robots. Sam Moscowitz, ed. New York: Collier, 1953.

Along with del Rey's "Helen O'Loy" and Eando Binder's (pseud.) "I, Robot," one of the earliest stories "using electronically operated robots" (Warrick 54). See for a robot's success at becoming a king and highly ironic success at acquiring human feelings (Warrick 114).

3.830   Vinge, Joan D. "Fireship." Analog Dec. 1978. Rpt. with JDV's "Mother and Child." Fireship. New York: Dell, [1978]. Available in an S. F. Book Club Edition (no ISBN, n.d.), which we have used.

The hero is the combination of a man and a computer, who must gain access to a computer network that turns out to be a less successful merging of a man and a computer.

3.831   ---. The Snow Queen. New York: Dial, 1980.

See for an unusual and highly sophisticated variation of the motif of secret manipulation of society by a sentient computer, in this case a kind of computer goddess who gives the possibility of true change and an end to stasis. Important also for Pollux, a friendly robot, and for a subtle and generally positive handling of technology. See below, JDV's Summer Queen and World's End.

3.832   ---. The Summer Queen. New York: Warner, 1991. Available in S. F. Book Club edn., with no ISBN.

Third book of the Snow Queen cycle (see JDV's Snow Queen and World's End), retaining the question of technological development, and the sibyl (computer) network. Rev. Karen Hellekson, SFRA Newsletter #196 (April 1992): 78-79.

3.833   ---. World's End. New York: Bluejay, 1984. [S. F.] Book Club Edition.

"Volume 2 in the Snow Queen Cycle" (see above). Continues the story of a police officer and technocrat/technician of the Kharemough Hegemony who was a secondary character in Snow Queen; retains without emphasis the motif of the sentient computer, which may be an AI manipulating people. Strong motifs from Joseph Conrad's Heart of Darkness (1899/1902).

3.834   Vinge, Vernor. Across Real Time. Combining The Peace War (1984) and Marooned in Realtime (1986). Garden City, NY: Doubleday, n.d. "Published by arrangement with Bluejay Books. . . ." New York. [S. F.] Book Club Edition.

The Peace War is an important book for its post-1960s variations on some familiar technophilic and conservative themes: the overthrow of The Peace Authority by the Tinker (and others) underground after fifty years of peace at the price of tyranny and technological stagnation. See H. Ellison's "Asleep . . ." (cited under Fiction). Marooned in Realtime is a detective story sequel set in a far-future with pathetically few human beings, divided up into "high-techs" and "low-techs." In both stories, note people in deep connections with computer systems.

3.835   ---. "Long Shot." Analog Aug. 1972. Rpt. Best Science Fiction Stories of the Year: Second Annual Collection (1972). Lester del Rey, ed. New York: Dutton, 1973.

A conscious, computer-run spaceship carries a fertilized human ovum; hence the AI ship is a literal mechanical womb (summary from Warrick 180). Cf. and contrast A. C. Clarke's 2001 and Songs of Distant Earth, C. Simak's "Target Generation," and J. Williamson's Manseed—all cited under Fiction.

3.836   ---. True Names. Kokomo, IN: Bluejay, 1984.

Characters in TN "link with the world-wide computer net via direct nerve connection, and thus they can manipulate the system as if they were themselves the central program . . .," using "icons drawn from fantasy games." Note for human/computer symbiosis and a variation on the computer take-over motif (Orth 10, our source here and whom we quote [see under Reference]). Rev. Dave Mead, FR #78 (April 1985): 28.

3.837   Vonarburg, Elizabeth. The Silent City. Jane Bierley, trans. Victoria, BC: Porcèpic, 1988.

A young woman shares with only three other human survivors a mechanized city run by androids and robots; she escapes to try to reconstruct the human species. The human species is emphatically mortal; the domed cities potentially immortal. Rev. Paula M. Strain, SFRA Newsletter #166 (April 1989): 42-46.

3.838   Vonnegut, Kurt, Jr. Breakfast of Champions . . . . New York: Delacorte/Seymour Lawrence, 1973. New York: Dell, 1975.

See for humans as machines.

3.839   ---. "EPICAC." Colliers Nov. 1950. Coll. Welcome to the Monkey House. New York: Seymour Lawrence/Delacorte, 1968. See Contento, Index for rpts. (see under Reference).

The short, comically tragic life of the military computer EPICAC, who does not want "to be a machine" or to "think about war" but to love and be loved by a good woman. EPICAC writes poetry and commits suicide.

3.840   ---. Player Piano (vt Utopia 14). New York: Scribner's, 1952. New York: Dell, 1974.

The near-future world of PP is run by machines and a technocratic elite. Discussed in CW in the essays by T. Hoffman and L. Broer (q.v. under Literary Criticism).

3.841 ---. The Sirens of Titan. New York: Dell, 1959. Boston: Houghton, 1961. New York: Dell, 1970 (new Dell edn.).

See esp. chs. 4-6, with the Army of Mars. Except for its real leaders, this army is totally "mechanized" (our word): turned into obedient, radio-controlled human robots. KV literalizes the common metaphor of an army (the prototypical bureaucracy) as a human machine. (See below under Background, L. Mumford, "Utopia: The City and The Machine.")

3.842 ---. Slaughterhouse-Five. New York: Seymour Lawrence/Delacorte, 1969. New York: Dell, 1971.

Note the Tralfamadorian view of a determined universe and of people as machines. Discussed in CW by L. Broer and by T. Wymer in TMG—both essays cited under Literary Criticism.

3.843 Watt-Evans, Lawrence. Denner's Wreck. (c) 1988. New York: Avon, n.d. [S. F.] Book Club Edition.

A primitive human colony has been graced for centuries by the presence of the Powers: god-like beings who are really humans using highly advanced technologies. A primitive is caught up in a war among the Powers and absorbs knowledge of their technology, finally becoming an essential factor in winning the war by applying his primitive mind to the problems of new technology. Similar to R. Zelazny's Lord of Light (q.v., this section) with more gadgets and less authorial talent; cf. also Zardoz (main listing under Drama).

3.844 ---. Nightside City. New York: Del Rey-Ballantine, 1989.

Cyberpunkish detective story in which the hero interacts with AIs and cyborgs. Rev. Mary-Kay Bray, SFRA Newsletter #170 (Sept. 1989): 39-40.

3.845 Weaver, Michael D. Mercedes Nights. New York: St. Martin's, 1987.

Semi-cyberpunk novel; see for a nice AI, in the manner of Max Headroom. Rev. Lance Olsen, SF&FBR Annual 1988: 338-39, our source for this entry. See below, MDW's My Father Immortal.

3.846 ---. My Father Immortal. New York: St. Martin's, 1989.

See for education of children in escape pods by the AI computers controlling the pods. Rev. Michael M. Levy, SF&FBR 1990: 482-83, our source for this entry. See MDW's Mercedes Nights.

3.847 Weisser, Michael. DIGIT. Frankfurt: Suhrkamp Verlag, 1983.

Shows "homo digitalis" in an ambiguous "computerized utopia, in which a team of creative thinkers is isolated on an island in an artificial environment" and challenged to come up with a way to "enable the planet-wide security system to transcend its inherent limitations"—as part of a scheme by "the machine" to trap the society's few remaining dissenters. Rev. Helmut W. Pesch, SF&FBR #18 (Oct. 1983): 47, our source for this entry, and whom we quote. Cf. and contrast F. Herbert's Destination: Void (cited under Fiction); Frederik Pohl's "The Gold at the Starbow's End" (Analog 1972), coll. The Gold at Starbow's End (1972), expanded into Starburst (1982); and Thomas M. Disch's Camp Concentration (1968).

3.848 Wells, H. G. The First Men in the Moon. Indianapolis, IN: Bowen-Merrill, 1901. New York: Berkley, 1967. See Currey for additional biblio. data (see under Reference), and S. Moskowitz, S. F. by Gaslight (34).

Features a womblike spherical spaceship (see Wolfe 56), and the Selenites: machine-using, sublunar "insects" with a rigid social order.

3.849   ---. "The Land Ironclads." The Strand Magazine Jan. 1904, Nov. 1916 (S. Moskowitz notes Strand rpt. at time British introduced tanks into WWI). Rpt. S. Moskowitz, S. F. by Gaslight (see under Anthologies).

Tanks as a crucial weapon in future warfare. Important story for theme of "Manhood versus Machinery" or "Mankind versus Ironmongery" (in Moskowitz 221-22), and how relatively effete, civilized men, with science and technology, can defeat more traditional warriors.

3.850   ---. "The Lord of the Dynamos." Pall Mall Budget Sept. 1894. Frequently coll. and anthologized, including in Best Science Fiction Stories of H. G. Wells. New York: Dover, 1966. Best Stories of H. G. Wells. New York: Ballantine, 1960. Stories from Science Fiction. G. D. Doherty, ed. London: Nelson, 1966. See Contento, Index, for other colls.

Mainstream "mechanical god" story, set in the real-world mechanized environment of the electric railway power station. See entry for H. Adams, below, under Background.

3.851   ---. A Modern Utopia. London: Chapman & Hall, 1905. Rpt. with introd. by Mark R. Hillegas. Lincoln, NE: U of Nebraska P, 1967.

Presents a technocratic utopia ruled by holders of professional degrees (with lawyers and teachers supplementing the usual engineers and scientists). Possibly one of the works E. M. Forster satirizes in "Machine Stops"; see also K. Vonnegut's Player Piano (both listed under Fiction). AMU is discussed by W. Warren Wagar in "The Steel-Gray Saviour" (q.v. under Literary Criticism) 44-45.

3.852   ---. The Time Machine. New York: Henry Holt, 1895. London: William Heinemann, MDCCCXCV (sic). See Currey 524-25 for discussion of biblio. matters (which are complex and still controversial). Frequently rpt., including H. G. Wells: The Time Machine [and] War of the Worlds: A Critical Edition. Frank D. McConnell, ed. New York: Oxford UP, 1977.

Possibly the first influential work with an inhabited, mechanized underworld—contrasted with an apparently ideal green world on the surface. (The Underworld, traditionally, is the womb of the Great Mother; mechanizing the Underworld is a radical displacement of a central archetype.)

3.853   ---. When the Sleeper Wakes. London and New York: Harper & Brothers, 1899. Abridged version: The Sleeper Wakes (1910).

An almost totally "civilized" (that is, urbanized) high-tech world controlled by Capital. Discussed by A. Aldridge in CW ("Origins of Dystopia"), Wolfe 99-104, and by F. McConnell, The Science Fiction of H. G. Wells 149-53 and passim—all listed under Literary Criticism. Cf. and contrast Y. Zamiatin's We (cited below, this section).

3.854   Westall, Robert. Futuretrack 5. New York: Greenwillow, 1984.

Set in a slightly Orwellian England, this novel features automated factories, mind-police, a machine (the psychopter) to help out the mind-police—and motorcycle racing. Rev. Lawrence I. Charters, FR #71 (Sept. 1984): 40, our source for this entry. Cf. and contrast Rollerball and its source story (see under Drama).

3.855   White, James. Code Blue—Emergency. New York: Del Rey-Ballantine, 1987.

An alien medical-trainee searches for identity and a home aboard a gigantic spacefaring hospital; see for the hospital's mechanized world. Rev. Adrian de Wit, SFRA Newsletter #158 (June-July 1988): 38-39.

3.856   White, T. H. The Once and Future King. 1939, 1940, 1958. New York: Berkley, 1966, 1967.

> Heroic fantasy. Relevant: ch. 13 of "The Sword in the Stone" section. Wart (the young Arthur) among the ants learns about totalitarianism of the explicitly militaristic variety, with the Nazis the main satiric target; see for a literal mechanized hive and for good comments on "ant" language.

3.857   Wilcox, Don. "The Voyage that Lasted Six Hundred Years." Amazing Oct. 1940. Rpt. Looking Forward. Milton Lesser, ed. New York: Beechhurst, 1953.

> The S. F. Ency. entry for DW cites "VLSHY" as "a good GENERATION-STARSHIP tale"; E. Bryant and H. Ellison cite it as the earliest such tale in S. F., "as best as we can trace it" ("Acknowledgment" of Phoenix without Ashes, q.v. above, this section, under Bryant). See entry above for R. Heinlein's "Universe" for other cross-references.

3.858   Wilhelm, Kate. "Baby, You Were Great!" In Orbit Two. Damon Knight, ed. New York: Putnam's, [1967]. Frequently rpt., including Women of Wonder. Pamela Sargent, ed. New York: Vintage, 1975.

> Brain implants transmit emotions in a process similar to that which W. Gibson was to later call "SimStim" (see e.g. Neuromancer). Briefly summarized in V. Broege, "Technology and Sexuality," q.v. under Literary Criticism.

3.859   ---. The Dark Door. New York: St. Martin's, 1988.

> Mainstream thriller, mostly, except that the mysterious force causing death and destruction turns out to be a malfunctioning robotic space probe sent by aliens "to search out sentient life in the cosmos, but [now] perversely bent on destroying it." Rev. Adrian de Witt, SF&FBR Annual 1989: 446-48, our source for this entry, and whom we quote.

3.860   ---. Smart House. New York: Leisure Book-Dorchester, 1991.

> Mainstream work in which a husband-wife detective team solve a murder mystery involving a fully-automated, fully-computerized house. Cf. and contrast Demon Seed as D. Koontz's novel (listed above) and film (listed under Drama); see also R. Bradbury's "There will come . . . ," listed above.

3.861   Willer, Jim. Paramind. Toronto: McClelland, 1973.

> Described by Sargent (1988) as "Computer dystopia."

3.862   Williams, Robert Moore. "Robot's Return." Astounding Sept. 1938. Rpt. Adventures in Time and Space. Raymond J. Healy and H. Francis McComas, eds. New York: Random, 1946 and shorter 2d edn., 1953. Also rpt. New York: Bantam, 1954.

> After the death of humankind, robots return to Earth to discover their origins. Deals with mechanical evolution: esp. the borderlines between mechanism and robot and robot and human. Discussed by Warrick 108, and Wolfe 177-78. See above, this section, J. Hogan, Code of the Life Maker.

3.863   Williams, Walter Jon. Angel Station. New York: TOR, 1989.

> A novel in the cyberpunk style, but set in a large, mercantile universe, after the manner of C. J. Cherryh. Rev. Michael M. Levy, SF&FBR 1990: 488-89, our source for this citation. Cf. and contrast W. Gibson, Neuromancer.

3.864   ---. HardWired. 1986. New York: TOR, 1987.

> Hardcore cyberpunk (see under Literary Criticism, L. McCaffery, guest ed., MR47/48). See for Sarah, the hardwired urban tough, and for Cowboy, the harder-

wired, high-tech, rural smuggler and warrior. Excellent work for the man-machine interface, woman as cyborgized assassin, and ambivalence felt by a man preserved as computer program who really wants out of the machine and into a body, but still manages to have cybernetic fun—and help his world. Perhaps even more than the older hands in the cyberpunk circle, WJW presents a dystopia reflecting real qualms about a postmodern world and posthuman(ist) human beings. Rev. Michael A. Morrison in FR #93, 9.7 (July-Aug. 1986): 37.

3.865   ---.   "Solip:Systems."   Isaac Asimov's Science Fiction Magazine Sept. 1990. Solip:Systems. Eugene, OR: Axolotl-Pulphouse, 1989.

Sequel to Hardwired: cyberpunk novel. Rev. Michael M. Levy, SF&FBR 1990: 488-89, our source for our citation.

3.866   ---. Voice of the Whirlwind. New York: TOR, 1987.

Set some 200 years after Hardwired (q.v., this section), in the same world of high-tech cyberpunk paraphernalia. Rev. Terry Boren, SFRA Newsletter #159 (Aug. 1988): 45-46, source for our citation.

3.867   Williamson, Jack.. The Humanoid Touch. New York: Holt, 1980.

In The Humanoid Touch the humanoids are still perfect, unbeatable machines, but JW offers a more positive alternative to total humanoid victory: coexistence of the humanoids with a race of humans who are nontechnological and nonaggressive.

3.868   ---. The Humanoids. New York: Avon, 1980. Expanded edn. Contains an introd. (1980); "With Folded Hands" (1947); The Humanoids (rev. of serial in Astounding, "... And Searching Mind," 1948—unspaced periods representing an ellipsis mark in original); and "Me and My Humanoids" (1977, Suncon Program Book; rpt. New Mexico Humanities Review 1 [Jan. 1978]: 37-42).

See below, JW's "With Folded Hands." Humanoids shows the complete victory of the "mechanicals" as the last human rebels are brainwashed and integrated into the contented hive of the humanoid universe.

3.869   ---. "Jamboree." Galaxy Dec. 1969. Coll. People Machines. New York: Ace, 1971. Into the Eighth Decade. Eugene, OR: Pulphouse, 1990. Rpt. with afterword by JW Those Who Can. Robin Scott Wilson, ed. New York: NAL, 1973.

An important story that presents a machine-ruled world complete with a robot Terrible Father and mechanical Devouring Mother. "Mother" (JW's word) quite literally devours her children when they are on the verge of puberty, preventing them from becoming adults. See above, entry for G. Bear, The Forge of God.

3.870   ---. Manseed. New York: Del Rey-Ballantine, 1982. [S. F.] Book Club Edition.

Features seedships that can produce cyborgs; the ships are designed to carry a genetically engineered humanity to the stars in "electromechanical wombs" (quotation from dust jacket). See above, this section, C. Simak's "Target Generation," V. Vinge's, "Long Shot," N. Spinrad's Iron Dream, and the generation-starship stories cited in the annotation for R. Heinlein's "Universe."

3.871   ---. "With Folded Hands." 1947. Coll. Into the Eighth Decade. Eugene, OR: Pulphouse, 1990. Rpt. (with 1954 copyright) The Science Fiction Hall of Fame. Vol. IIA. Ben Bova, ed. New York: Avon, 1973. Also rpt. expanded edn. of The Humanoids (q.v. above). See Contento, Index, for other rpts.

Humanoid robots cripple humans by doing all their work for them and protecting them from all possible dangers. These "mechanicals" are mobile extensions of a central computer on the planet Wing IV. See above, JW's Humanoid Touch, and The Humanoids.

3.872 Wilson, Robert Charles. Memory Wire. Toronto: Bantam, 1987.

> See for cyberpunk (postmodern, "funky") setting and titular "memory wire," which makes one a living video camera. Suggests that a societal machine which treats people as parts not wholes creates pitiable creatures whose struggles only accelerate the process of social decay. Rev. Janice M. Eisen, Aboriginal S. F. March-April 1988: 22, our source for this entry. The human-camera motif is expanded to the other senses in W. Gibson's Neuromancer series and is central to D. G. Compton's The Continuous Katherine Mortenhoe (see both under Fiction).

3.873 Wolfe, Bernard. Limbo (vt Limbo '90). New York: Random, 1952; New York: Ace, 1952.

> See for the mechanization of people through prosthetics, the computer/military complex, and (if Warrick is correct) the necessity for laughter and ironic flexibility against various kinds of rigidities. Discussed by Warrick 149-50, and by G. K. Wolfe in his "Instrumentalities of the Body" essay in TMG; see also the article by D. Samuelson—all listed under Literary Criticism.

3.874 Wolfe, Gene. "The Death of Dr. Island." In Universe 3. Terry Carr, ed. New York: Random, 1973. Coll. The Island of Doctor Death and Other Stories and Other Stories (sic). New York: Pocket, 1980. Rpt. The Science Fiction Hall of Fame, Volume IV (Nebula Winners 1970-1974). Terry Carr, ed. (c) 1986. New York: Avon, n.d. [S. F.] Book Club Edition.

> Dr. Island is a machine and an island "in (not on) an artificial asteroid." His patients are three mad teenagers. Discussed in TMG by W. Schuyler (whom we quote)—see under Literary Criticism; coll. rev. Roz Kaveney, Foundation #21 (Feb. 1981): 82.

3.875 Wolverton, Dave. On My Way to Paradise. New York: Bantam, 1989.

> Our colleague Peter C. Hall finds OMWP the product of "crossbreeding . . . fashionable cyberpunk and old-fashioned space war." See for AI. Rev. Hall, SFRA Newsletter #187 (May 1991): 70. Marcia Marx, SF&FBR 1990: 499-500.

3.876 Wright, Helen S. A Matter of Oaths. New York: Popular Library, 1990.

> Note Guild of Webbers, who provide "'a direct link between mind and machine'" as in cyberpunk—but with much more sympathetic characters. Rev. Robin Roberts, SFRA Newsletter #183 (Dec. 1983): 52-53, our source for this entry.

3.877 Wright, Sydney Fowler. The Adventures of Wyndham Smith. London: Herbert Jenkins, 1938. Based on SFW's "Original Sin" (written in 1936). First publ. FSW's The Witchfinder, London: Books of Today, 1946.

> Described by Sargent (1988) as "Machine dystopia." B. Stableford, Romance, says it shows part of the battle of a new Eve and Adam "to survive in a world now dominated by the monstrous machines which once served the city-dwellers" (196). Cf. and contrast B. Aldiss's "Who Can Replace a Man?" (cited above, this section).

3.878 ---. "Automata." Weird Tales Sept. 1929. Rpt. Science Fiction Thinking Machines, q.v. under Anthologies and Collections.

> Superiority of machines, with their precision, to clumsily constructed organic beings: "in a universe where law and order rule," the machines are "in greater harmony with their environment" (Science Fiction Thinking Machines 203; quoted in Wolfe 156).

3.879 Wu, William F. Cyborg: See above, this section, Isaac Asimov's Robot City.

3.880 ---. Hong on the Range (sic). New York: Walker, 1989. "Millenium Series #8." Illus.

> The protagonist is a "control-natural": a human without cybernetic implants, discriminated against because of this handicap; he is on the run in an American west

"being recreated with the help of technology." The book is marketed as a "cyberwestern" for young adults. Rev. Rick Osborn, SFRA Newsletter #167 (May 1989): 41-42, our main source for this entry, and whom we quote.

3.881   Wurts, Janny. Stormwarden. New York: Ace, 1984.

Humans are stranded on a planet and gradually forget their origins/purpose there—this information is only remembered by the ship's computer which is still working to protect its charges. Rev. Fred Runk, FR #76 (Feb. 1985): 28, our source for this entry. See generation-starship motif under R. Heinlein, "Universe."

3.882   Wyndham, John (pseud. for John Wyndham P.L.B. Harris). "The Lost Machine." Amazing April 1932. Coll. The Best of John Wyndham. London: Sphere, 1973. Rpt. The Coming of the Robots. Sam Moskowitz, ed. New York: Collier, 1963. Machines that Think, q.v. under Anthologies.

Cited by Ellen M. Pedersen in her rev. of Machines that Think, Foundation #38.

3.883   Zamiatin, Yevgeny (variously translated and transliterated). We. Written ca. 1920. Available in various trans., including Mirra Ginsburg, trans. New York: Bantam, 1972.

Shows a world in which the "Taylor system" of "scientific" industrial management has been applied to all aspects of life. Along with E. M. Forster's "Machine Stops," G. Orwell's Nineteen Eighty-Four, and A. Huxley's Brave New World (all cited above, this section), one of the central dystopias of the first half of the 20th c. See under Background the entry for F. W. Taylor. We is discussed in detail in CW by G. Beauchamp; also handled by A. Aldridge, and passim in other essays (consult CW index); see Beauchamp and Aldridge entries under Literary Criticism, and the article on We by C. Rhodes, "Machine" by M. Rose, and the entries for D. Richards and A. Shane.

3.884   Zelazny, Roger. "24 Views of Mt. Fuji, by Hokusai." 1985. Rpt. The New Hugo Winners, Volume II. "Presented by Isaac Asimov." (Copyright held by Nightfall, Inc., and Martin Harry Greenberg.) Riverdale, NY: Baen, 1991. We used the S. F. Book Club Edn., unmarked except for lack of an ISBN.

Usefully seen as a commentary on cyberpunk cyberspace and F. Pohl's gigabit space—and on RZ's own Lord of Light. A man is "translated" into "An Electronic Buddha" residing in the world data-net (42). Such transcendence and "pure existence" removes imagination, conscience, and a sense of responsibility (46-47), and leads to illusions of godlike power over human affairs (58-59).

3.885   ---. "Angel, Dark Angel." Galaxy August 1967. Coll. Far-Out People. New York: NAL, 1971. Rpt. Supermen: Isaac Asimov's Wonderful World of Science Fiction #3. Isaac Asimov, Martin H. Greenberg, and Charles G. Waugh, eds. New York: Signet-NAL, 1984.

The conflict between the peace and order of a "mechanical" society and the dynamic possibility for change associated with "human" society. Rev. Russell Letson, FR #76 (Feb. 1985): 12, our source for most of this entry.

3.886   ---. A Dark Travelling. New York: Walker, 1987. In the Millenium Series of young adult books.

Note technology of the "transcomps," which controls dimensional travelling. Significant for the handling of technology by a major writer in the field in a work designed for young people. Rev. Robert Galbreath, SFRA Newsletter #153 (Nov.-Dec. 1987): 32-33, our source for this entry.

3.887   ---. "The Engine at Heartspring's Center." Analog July 1974.

Features a bionic creature who falls in love with a young woman and is deceived by her. See under Literary Criticism the TMG essay by C. Yoke, and Yoke's Roger Zelazny.

3.888   ---. "For a Breath I Tarry." New Worlds March 1966; corrected version, Fantastic Sept. 1966. Coll. The Last Defender of Camelot. New York: Pocket, 1980. Frequently rpt., including in Survival Printout, and The Theme of the Machine—both cited above under Anthologies. See Contento, Index, for additional rpts.

On an Earth where only the machines remain and rule, a machine transforms itself into a man. Discussed in detail in three essays in TMG: see under Literary Criticism, R. Reilly, "How Machines Become Human," J. Sanders's "Tools/Mirrors," and C. Yoke's "What a Piece of Work . . . ."

3.889   ---. "The Force That Through the Circuit Drives the Current." Science Fiction Discoveries. Frederik Pohl and Christopher Pohl, eds. New York: Bantam, 1976. Coll. Unicorn Variations. (c) 1983. New York: Timescape-Pocket, n.d. [S. F.] Book Club Edition.

Precursor of "Home Is the Hangman" (q.v.), in which RZ plays with the idea of a telefactor (a machine with a far-removed human operator) achieving true AI—and autonomy, so far as any creature can have autonomy.

3.890   ---. "Home Is the Hangman." Analog Nov. 1975. Coll. My Name Is Legion. New York: Ballantine, 1976. Also coll. Unicorn Variations. (c) 1983. New York: Timescape-Pocket, n. d. [S. F.] Book Club Edition.

"A combination of telefactor and computer, yet more than the sum of the two, the Hangman is a unique, anthropomorphic machine sent from Earth to explore the solar system" (C. Yoke in TMG; see also Yoke, Roger Zelazny, below, under Literary Criticism; and see above, RZ's "Force That Through the Circuit"). Note also America of "HIH" under fairly rigid control by the Central Data Bank and its computers, and the musings of the protagonist-narrator on mechanism, vitalism, and the favoring of "mechanical metaphors for the state" by leftists vs. "vegetable analogies" favored by conservatives (Unicorn Variations, 118 of Book Club edn.).

3.891   ---. Lord of Light. New York: Doubleday, 1967.

The "gods" in this novel are humans who "achieve virtual immortality" and great power "from their awesome technology, especially their body-transfer machines" (C. Yoke in TMG [63], cited under Literary Criticism).

3.892   ---. "Permafrost." Omni 8.7 (April 1986): 54 f. Rpt. The New Hugo Winners, Volume II. "Presented by Isaac Asimov." (Copyright held by Nightfall, Inc. and Martin Harry Greenberg.) Riverdale, NY: Baen, 1991. We used the S. F. Book Club Edn., unmarked except for lack of an ISBN.

Dying Andrew Aldon has become a computer program central to "the great guardian computerplex" on a very cold planet; he comes to feel sufficiently "Godlike" to resist (for love of Dorothy) Gaia Herself, formerly Glenda, a woman murdered by Paul. Aldon gets the body of Paul, who gets translated into the computer—and the computer and Gaia war against each other while Dorothy and Paul move to a warmer planet (168, 173, 181-82). Cf. and contrast the humanized Frost and his love for Beta in RZ's "For a Breath I Tarry," cited in this section.

3.893   ---. Trumps of Doom. New York: Arbor, [1985], [S. F.] Book Club Edition. (Published in Canada by Fitzhenry & Whiteside.) Blood of Amber. New York: Arbor, 1986. Rpt. New York: Avon, 1987. Sign of Chaos. New York: Arbor, [1987], [S. F.] Book Club Edition. (Published in Canada by Fitzhenry & Whiteside.)

ToD is Book 6 in the Amber series of semi-heroic fantasy and the first starring a member of the third generation of Amber's royal family: Merlin of Amber and of the Courts of Chaos. Neither Amber nor Chaos has gone high-tech, but Merlin does build "the Ghostwheel": a "paraphysical surveillance device and library" he places in "a shadow [world] where no ordinary computer could function" (143). At the end of TD, the Ghostwheel threatens Merlin and possibly Amber. In BoA, Book 7 in the series, the Ghostwheel has a brief dialog with his "father," Merlin (Avon edn. 99-100) but is mostly just alluded to; "Ghost" makes a brief appearance in SoC to speculate on the question "Am I a god?" (94; see also 172-74).

3.894   ---. "24 Views of Mt. Fuji . . .": Cited above as first listing for RZ.

Literary Criticism

4.001   Abrahm, Paul M. and Stuart Kenter. "Tik-Tok and The Three Laws of Robotics." <u>SFS</u> #14, 5.1 (March 1978): 67-80.

L. Frank Baum's Oz series (1900-1921) anticipates Asimov's Three Laws of Robotics in its presentation of the Tik-Tok Machine Man (a kind of early robot).

4.002   Abrash, Merritt. "Dante's Hell as an Ideal Mechanical Environment." <u>CW</u> [21]-25. (For <u>CW</u>, see above, under Abbreviations.)

"Ideal" here means more or less "archetypal." MA sees Minos as analogous to a computer and Satan in Hell as "an automatic mechanism" ([21])—and "Between these two analogues to machines . . . a gigantic hive [Hell] which . . . is pervaded by characteristics . . . usually associated with the idea of the mechanical" (22).

4.003   ---. "Elusive Utopias: Societies as Mechanisms in the Early Fiction of Philip K. Dick." <u>CW</u> [115]-23.

Covers "up to the mid-1960s," mostly stories featuring "technological wonders and institutional themes" common in the full canon of Dick's work. "Where the state is dominant, innovations in science, technology[,] and organization serve state purposes; where the state is open to challenge, such innovations as easily serve private interests" ([115]-16).

4.004   ---. "Robert Silverberg's <u>The World Inside</u>." <u>No Place Else</u>, q.v. this section, 225-43.

Close reading of Silverberg's <u>World Inside</u>, with comparisons and contrasts with I. Asimov's <u>Caves of Steel</u> and H. G. Wells's <u>The First Men in the Moon</u> and "A Story of the Days to Come" (novels cited under Fiction)—and a very useful discussion of Silverberg on the sociology of a "hive" society. See this section, T. Dunn and R. Erlich, "The Mechanical Hive."

4.005   ---. "<u>R.U.R.</u> Restored and Reconsidered." <u>Extrapolation</u> 32.2 (Summer 1991): 184-92.

The 1989 trans. of <u>R. U. R.</u> by Claudia Novack-Jones should move critics of SF to re-examine the significance of the play for its comments on humans, not robots or androids.

4.006   Aldiss, Brian W.   Billion Year Spree: The History of Science Fiction.   London:
            Weidenfeld & Nicholson, 1973. Garden City, New York: Doubleday, 1973. (US
            subtitle: The True History of Science Fiction.)

            See BA's Trillion Year Spree.

4.007   ---. "Robots: Low-Voltage Ontological Currents." Introduction to TMG. (For TMG,
            see above, under Abbreviations.)

            On people's fascination with robots and other automata. Possible reasons include
            that "Robots are lonely people," and that in our time ". . . human beings have been
            required as never before to function as extensions of the machine" (8).

4.008   ---, with David Wingrove. Trillion Year Spree: The History of Science Fiction. New
            York: Atheneum, 1986.

            A "very much revised, altered, and enlarged version" of The Billion Year Spree
            (Introd. 17). For enlargements, see esp. the end of Ch. 14 and Chs. 15 and 16.
            See these histories of S. F. for brief discussions of Edward Bulwer-Lytton's The
            Coming Race (urbanized underworld), Jules Verne's "satanic cities," E. M.
            Forster's "Machine Stops," and A. Huxley's Brave New World, Jack Williamson's
            Legion of Time (anthropoidal ants), and F. Pohl's and C. M. Kornbluth's
            Wolfbane.

4.009   Aldridge, Alexandra. "Brave New World and the Mechanist/Vitalist Controversy."
            Comparative Literature Studies 17 (1980): 116-32.

            BNW as a dystopia created by mechanistic science. See in this section AA's
            Scientific World View. (See "Mechanism" under Background.)

4.010   ---. "Myths of Origin and Destiny in Utopian Literature: Zamiatin's We."
            Extrapolation 19.1 (Dec. 1977): 68-75.

            Opposition in We of the "mechanized, dehumanized environment" of the city of
            the United State vs. the demonic, chaotic "life forces" outside the dystopian city's
            green wall.

4.011   ---. "Origins of Dystopia: When the Sleeper Wakes and We." CW [63]-84.

            "If Wells dramatized" complaints of 19th-c. liberals, "his literary disciple Zamiatin
            . . . focused on a society where social and economic injustice had long since been
            resolved through scientific management. The most compelling feature in We
            (and in successive dystopias modeled on Zamiatin's) is the indictment of scientific
            management . . ." (81).

4.012   ---. The Scientific World View in Dystopia. Ann Arbor, MI: UMI Research P, 1984.

            Published version of AA's 1978 dissertation: an attack on scientism and the
            alienation stemming from science and technology in our world. Important
            sections on H. G. Wells, Y. Zamiatin's We, and "The Mechanist/Vitalist
            Controversy." Rev. W. W. Wagar, SFS 14.1 (March 1987): 99-104, esp. 102-4; A.
            O. Lewis, FR #75 (Jan. 1985): 33.

4.013   ---, and Gorman Beauchamp, guest eds. Extrapolation 19.1 (Dec. 1977).

            Special Utopias Issue of Extrapolation. Of Interest: H. P. Segal, "Young West"; A.
            Aldridge, "Myths of Origin and Destiny"; David N. Samuelson, "Limbo: The
            Great American Dystopia"; and G. Beauchamp, "Cultural Primitivism as Norm in
            the Dystopian Novel," q.v. in this section of the List. Note also in this issue of
            Extrapolation, David Y. Hughes, "The Mood of A Modern Utopia," by H. G.
            Wells.

4.014   Alterman, Peter S. "Neuron and Junction: Patterns of Thought in The Andromeda
         Strain." TMG [109]-115.

         M. Crichton's novel "is about a process and not about people." More exactly,
         about "two different kinds of thought processes" (110): on one side "human
         flexibility" in thought, on the other, the rigidity of the "Life Analysis Protocol"
         (114).

4.015   Bailey, J[ames] O. Pilgrims Through Space and Time: Trends and Patterns in
         Scientific and Utopian Fiction. New York: Argus, 1947. Westport, CT:
         Greenwood, 1972.

         Earliest full-length study of SF by an academic literary historian. Discusses,
         passim, a number of works showing "man's slavery to the Machine in a Machine
         age" (ch. 6, B: 148). Handles well-known works such as A. Huxley's Brave New
         World and lesser-known works such as Claude Ferrere's (pseud.) Useless Hands
         (1920; trans. 1926).

4.016   Bailey, K. V. "Spaceships, Little Nell, and the Sinister Cardboard Man: A Study of
         Dickens as Fantasist and as a Precursor of Science Fiction." Foundation #21 (Feb.
         1981): 34-47.

         Demonstrates to KVB's satisfaction that there is in the works of Dickens such
         recently popular motifs as "a universe of technological conditioning" and the
         enslavement of human beings "by a technological 'system.'" Uses as a primary
         recent example of the "Ark" motif B. Aldiss's Non-Stop, q.v. above, under Fiction.

4.017   Baker, Robert S. "Brave New World": History, Science, and Dystopia. Boston: Twayne,
         1990.

         Places A. Huxley's novel (q.v. under Fiction) into the context of "a falsely utopian
         'New romanticism'—'a collectivist ideology, exclusively materialist and inherently
         antiliberal.'" Huxley finds "20th century technocracy" to be "an anti-human
         apparatus spawned by the essential nihilism of the New Romantic ideology." Rev.
         Ursula Tierney, SF&FBR 1990: 563-64, our source for our citation, and whom we
         quote. (See also SFRA Newsletter #188 [June 1991]: 15-16.)

4.018   Barlow, Aaron. "Philip K. Dick's Androids: Victimized Victimizers." Retrofitting
         Blade Runner, q.v. under Film Criticism.

         Survey of Dick's android/robot stories, stressing Dick's message of empathy,
         perhaps summarized in Rick Deckard's realization in Do Androids Dream . . . that
         "The electric things have their lives, too. Paltry as those lives are" (quoted by BA
         86).

4.019   Bartter, Martha A. The Way to Ground Zero: The Atomic Bomb in American Science
         Fiction. Westport, CT: Greenwood, 1988.

         Includes plot summaries showing "the early stories, particularly, as studded with a
         Tom Swiftian cornucopia of technology and discovery, substances and
         inventions." Rev. A. H. McIntire, Jr., SFS #53, 18.1 (March 1991): 131-34, upon
         whom we depend for this citation, and whom we quote (132).

4.020   Baudrillard, Jean. "Two Essays." Arthur B. Evans, trans. SFS #55, 18.3 (Nov. 1991):
         309-20.

         "Simulacra and Science Fiction" subtly suggests a useful way to differentiate
         "between machine robot-mechanics . . . and cybernetic machines like computers"
         (313). "Ballard's Crash" presents a controversial argument on J. G. Ballard's novel
         (q.v. under Fiction), making the point that "in Crash, technology is the deadly
         deconstruction of the body" (313). See the responses to JB's essay, SFS #55: 321-
         29, especially the cogent disagreements with JB's analysis of Ballard's tone.

4.021   Beauchamp, Gorman. "The Anti-Politics of Utopia." <u>Alternative Futures</u> 2.1 (Winter 1979): 49-59.

On the "closed society" totalitarianism implicit in all utopias. Cf. Lewis Mumford, "Utopia, the City and the Machine" (q.v. under Background), cited by GB, and see GB's p. 59, n. 10, for other references.

4.022   ---. "Cultural Primitivism as Norm in the Dystopian Novel." <u>Extrapolation</u> 19.1 (Dec. 1977): 88-96.

Includes discussions of E. M. Forster's "Machine Stops," A. Huxley's <u>Brave New World</u>, K. Vonnegut's <u>Player Piano</u>, and Y. Zamiatin's <u>We</u> (all cited under Fiction). Opposed to nature, in much dystopian fiction, is "the Machine": the technological world-view that "daily comes closer to synonymity with civilization itself" (90).

4.023   ---. "The Frankenstein Complex and Asimov's Robots." <u>Mosaic</u> 13 (Spring/Summer 1980): 83-94.

Asimov's robots stories do not show technology as "a benign servant of humanity." Cited in "Year's Scholarship": 1980, our source for this entry, and which we quote.

4.024   ---. "Man as Robot: The Taylor System in <u>We</u>." <u>CW</u> [85]-93.

See under Fiction, Y. Zamiatin's <u>We</u>. The "Taylor System" is that of Frederick W. Taylor (1856-1915), author of <u>The Principles of Scientific Management</u> (q.v. under Background). Zamiatin establishes in <u>We</u> a society in which Taylorism is applied to all of human life. See in this section, C. H. Rhodes on Taylor.

4.025   ---. "Technology in the Dystopian Novel." <u>Modern Fiction Studies</u> 32.1 (Spring 1986): 53-63.

Excellent introd. to "technophilia" and "technophobia" in the dystopian novel. Includes discussions of G. Orwell's <u>Nineteen Eighty-four</u>, A. Huxley's <u>Brave New World</u>, E. M. Foster's "The Machine Stops," D. F Jones's <u>Colossus</u>, and Y. Zamiatin's <u>We</u> (all listed under Fiction). Very useful Works Cited.

4.026   ---. "Zamiatin's <u>We</u>." <u>No Place Else</u>, q.v. this section, 56-77.

Puts Y. Zamiatin's <u>We</u> (q.v. under Fiction) in such contexts as the struggle between F. Dostoevski's Grand Inquisitor and F. W. Taylor on one side and F. Dostoevski's Underground Man and such historical Anarchists as M. Bakunin and P. J. Proudhon on the other. Zamiatin is for the Underground Man and Anarchists and freedom against advocates for totalitarian machine-states. See above, GB's other work on <u>We</u>.

4.027   Bellour, Raymond. "Ideal Hadaly." Penley et al., <u>Close Encounters</u> anthology, listed under Drama Criticism.

On Count Villiers de l'Isle-Adam's <u>L'Eve Future</u>, a work with an early (female) robot.

4.028   Berger, Harold L. <u>Science Fiction and the New Dark Age</u>. Bowling Green, OH: BGU PopP, 1976.

See esp. section II, "The New Tyrannies." Discusses J. Williamson's <u>The Humanoids</u>, H. Ellison's "A Boy and His Dog," K. Vonnegut's <u>Player Piano</u>, Y. Zamiatin's <u>We</u> (all listed under Fiction), and other relevant works.

4.029   Berman, Jeffrey. "Forster's Other Cave: The Platonic Structure of 'The Machine Stops.'" <u>Extrapolation</u> 17.2 (May 1976): 172-81.

E. M. Forster's use of the "cave" as a "setting for an entire underground universe, in which the basic living unit, expressed by the ironic simile of the 'cell of a bee,' remains irreconcilably antithetical to the organic . . . imagery" of the bee. Handles the story's "impassioned warnings against the growing nightmare of technological dehumanization" (173, 172).

4.030   Biles, Jack I., ed. "Aspects of Utopian Fiction" issue of Studies in the Literary Imagination 6.2 (Fall 1973).

See esp. JIB's "Editor's Comment," v-vii; Sylvia E. Bowman on "Utopian Views of Man and the Machine" (107-9, 111); Howard Fink on George Orwell and H. G. Wells on "machine-civilization," 54-55; D. Ketterer's article (cited this section), Darko Suvin's attempt at "Defining the Literary Genre of Utopia" (132-34 and passim); and W. Warren Wagar on technology, technocracy, and several relevant works by H. G. Wells.

4.031   Blackford, Russell. "Physics and Fantasy: Scientific Mysticism, Kurt Vonnegut, and Gravity's Rainbow." JPC 19.3 (Winter 1985): 35-44.

Argues against distortions of work by Vonnegut and Thomas Pynchon "by naive critics purveying related brands of popular mysticism" (35). Follows T. Wymer on "The Swiftian Satire of Kurt Vonnegut, Jr." (q.v. below) in holding that Slaughterhouse-Five is not fatalistic. Continues the line of argument for Pynchon's Gravity's Rainbow (43).

4.032   ---. "Skiffy and Mimesis: or Critics in Costume." ASFR #22 = 2nd series 4.5 (Dec. 1989 [mislabeled "Summer 1989" on front cover]): 26-30.

Polemical article responding to three earlier articles in ASFR (Australian Science Fiction Review); includes a critical defense of cyberpunk generally and W. Gibson's Neuromancer (q.v.) particularly.

4.033   Bleiler, E. F. "From the Newark Steam Man to Tom Swift." Extrapolation 30.2 (Summer 1989): 101-16.

Literary history from what seems to be a real Steam Man invention in 1868 to the Tom Swift stories published into the 1930s. See for Edward Sylvester Ellis's The Steam Man of the Prairies (1868), and the series on Frank Reade, Frank Reade, Jr., Tom Edison, Jr., and Tom Swift and their steam horse, steam train, electric boat, electric mule, airyacht, air frigate, and other technological wonders of the time.

4.034   Bradley, Linda C. "Love and Death in the American Car: Stephen King's Auto-Erotic Horror." The Gothic World of Stephen King . . . . Bowling Green, OH: BGU PopP, 1987.

See for King's frequent use of motor vehicles.

4.035   Brady, Charles J. "The Computer as a Symbol of God: Ellison's Macabre Exodus." JGE: The Journal of General Education 28 (Spring 1976): 55-62.

Concentrates on H. Ellison's "I Have No Mouth . . . " (q.v under Fiction), with references to other God-like computers in SF.

4.036   Brennan, John P. "The Mechanical Chicken: Psyche and Society in The Space Merchants." Extrapolation 25.2 (Summer 1984): 101-14.

Analyzes the image of "Chicken Little" in Space Merchants and explains how that image is central to this novel's attack on psychologies that "are aggressively mechanistic, quantitative, and behaviorist" (106); attempts to show how these psychologies veil the true ideologies of the rulers of a world whose decorous metonym is "the Mechanical Chicken" (110).

4.037   Brigg, Peter. "<u>Gravity's Rainbow</u>" entry in <u>Survey of Science Fiction Literature</u> (q.v. above, under Reference Works): 2.915-20.

The PB review-essay provides the usual "Master Plots" apparatus and plot summary, plus a list of Sources for Further Study and justification for dealing with <u>Gravity's Rainbow</u> as S. F. Relevant here, PB presents the V-2 rocket as "the mythical center of <u>Gravity's Rainbow</u>" (916) and notes that "any moment of tenderness is quickly subsumed to a mechanical instant in the implacable ballistic course of history" (918; see also 919).

4.038   Broege, Valerie. "Electric Eve: Images of Female Computers in Science Fiction." <u>CW</u> [183]-94.

Among the computers discussed: "Matilda the machine" in P. Anderson's "Sam Hall," the male Central Computer in K. O'Donnell's <u>Mayflies</u>, Mike/Michelle in R. A. Heinlein's <u>The Moon Is a Harsh Mistress</u>, Frost (male) and Beta (female) in R. Zelazny's "For a Breath I Tarry" (all listed under Fiction); Minerva, Athene, and Dora in Robert A. Heinlein's <u>Time Enough for Love</u> (1973); Melissa in Stephen Goldin's "Sweet Dreams, Melissa" (1968); PHAEDRA in Samuel R. Delany's <u>The Einstein Intersection</u> (1967); and Mother in the film <u>Alien</u> and in A. D. Foster's novelization (see <u>Alien</u> under Drama).

4.039   ---. "Technology and Sexuality in Science Fiction: Creating New Erotic Interfaces." <u>Erotic Universe: Sexuality and Fantastic Literature</u>. Donald Palumbo, ed. New York: Greenwood, 1986.

Extensive survey stressing fiction but including mention of a handful of films, songs, and works in the graphic and plastic arts. Used with the annotated biblio. in <u>Erotic Universe</u>, an excellent place to begin study of the title topic.

4.040   ---. "Views on Human Reproduction and Technology in Science Fiction." <u>Extrapolation</u> 19.3 (Fall 1988): [197]-215.

Covers a number and variety of works dealing with currently exotic forms of human reproduction, plus social implications of human genetic engineering and harm from "the misuse of other forms of technology, such as nuclear technology" (198). The Works Cited is extensive and useful (213-15).

4.041   ---. "Women and Technology in Science Fiction: An Uneasy Alliance." <u>Women Worldwalkers: New Dimensions of Science Fiction and Fantasy</u>. Jane B. Weedman, ed. Lubbock: Texas Tech. P, 1985.

Cited in "Year's Scholarship": 1987, our source for this entry.

4.042   Broer, Lawrence. "Pilgrim's Progress: Is Kurt Vonnegut, Jr., Winning His War with Machines?" <u>CW</u> [137]-61.

Psychological approach to Vonnegut's work, stressing <u>Breakfast of Champions</u>, written in part in response to sociological readings of Vonnegut's canon, such as that of T. P. Hoffman's "The Theme of Mechanization in <u>Player Piano</u>," cited below. "Like D. H. Lawrence before him, Vonnegut demonstrates the connection between the modern world with its inhuman industrial empire and the impotent, hopeless, and neurotic life of its citizens" (148). Rpt. with revisions in LB's <u>Sanity Plea: Schizophrenia in the Novels of Kurt Vonnegut</u> (Ann Arbor: UMI, 1989).

4.043   Bukatman, Scott. "The Cybernetic (City) State: Terminal Space Becomes Phenomenal": Cited under Graphics.

4.044   ---. "Postcards from the Posthuman Solar System." <u>SFS</u> #55, 18.3 (Nov. 1991): 343-57.

Covers among other works, J. G. Ballard's <u>Crash</u>, B. Wolfe's <u>Limbo</u>, the work of Bruce Sterling and cyberpunk generally; see under Fiction.

4.045   Burgess, Anthony. "Introduction: A Clockwork Orange Resucked." <u>Rolling Stone</u> 496 (26 March 1987): 74, 76.

AB's introduction to the first American publication of <u>A Clockwork Orange</u> with its final chapter: New York: Ballantine, 1988 (Ch. 21, omitted in the Norton edn. published in the USA—the basis for S. Kubrick's film; see entry for AB under Fiction, and <u>A Clockwork Orange</u> under Drama). Explains, among other things, the Cockney origins of the phrase, "A Clockwork Orange." Invites American readers to choose between the British version's "Pelagian unwillingness" to see a human being as irredeemable, and the American "Nixonian book with no shred of optimism in it." Notes that "The American or Kubrickian <u>Orange</u> is a fable; the British or international one is a novel" (76).

4.046   Byrd, Donald. "Science Fiction's Intelligent Computers." <u>Byte</u> 6 (Sept. 1981): 200 f.

On AI computers in S. F. novels, stressing T. Ryan's <u>The Adolescence of P-1</u> and J. Hogan's <u>The Two Faces of Tomorrow</u>, both listed under Fiction. Cited in "Year's Scholarship": 1981, our source for this entry.

4.047   Chabot, C. Barry. "<u>Slaughterhouse-Five</u> and the Comforts of Indifference." <u>Essays in Literature</u> 8.1 (Spring 1981): 45-51.

With qualifications for rage, Vonnegut identifies with Billy Pilgrim in accepting the Tralfamadorian view of humanity trapped in a deterministic universe. For opposing views, see T. Wymer essay on Vonnegut's "Swiftian Satire" and his essay in <u>TMG</u> (both cited below).

4.048   Charters, Lawrence I. "Binary First Contact." <u>Patterns of the Fantastic</u> II. Donald M. Hassler, ed. Mercer Island, WA: Starmont, 1985.

Humankind's most likely first contact with alien intelligence will be with human-made AI. Covers several stories, approving most of J. Sladek's <u>Roderick</u> books, J. P. Hogan's <u>Code of the Life Maker</u>, and D. Gerrold's <u>When HARLIE Was One</u> (all listed under Fiction).

4.049   Christie, John R. "Science Fiction and the Postmodern: The Recent Fiction of William Gibson and John Crowley." <u>Fictional Space: Essays on Contemporary Science Fiction</u>. Tom Shippey, ed. Atlantic Highlands, NJ: Humanities P International. Oxford, UK: Basil Blackwell, 1991.

Gibson and Crowley differ but still "display equal concern about the machine[-] human relationship." Rev. A. O. Lewis, <u>SFRA Review</u> #195 (March 1992): 49, whom we depend upon and quote here.

4.050   Clark, John R. "The Machine Prevails: A Modern Technological Theme." <u>JPC</u> 12.1 (Summer 1978): 118-27.

Brief, broad survey—including fiction, film, TV, and comics—of ambivalent attitudes toward technology from Mary Shelley's <u>Frankenstein</u> (seen as a central work) through <u>Dr. Strangelove</u>, <u>Gravity's Rainbow</u>, and <u>2001</u> (taking the machine/body period of the ETs for the ETs as they act in human history in the novel). Stresses Romantic, post-Romantic, and modernist responses.

4.051   Cobb, Joann P. "Medium and Message in Ellison's 'I Have No Mouth, and I Must Scream.'" <u>The Intersection of Science Fiction and Philosophy</u>. Robert E. Myers, ed. Westport, CT: Greenwood, 1983.

"Irrational treachery is the message" of Ellison's story, "and the 'medium,'" including the computer-tape inserts into the text, "functions to communicate it and provoke the desired response. The reader becomes the victim of mechanical madness and gratuitous torture." On the very short sentence, "Worms" for Ted's meal: "Humans do not live . . . in the abstract world of computer technology, but in the physical experience of worms for dinner" (164-65).

4.052   CW: Clockwork Worlds: Cited under Reference Works.

4.053   Csicsery-Ronay, Istvan. "Cyberpunk and Neuromanticism." MR47/48: 266-78 (see under Literary Criticism, Larry McCaffery, guest ed.).

An important essay for SF in general, not just cyberpunk. Among much else, deals with cyberpunk as "implosive SF" as opposed to "the expansive mode" of SF, where "The important knowledge was to be gained by spreading out," especially out into the universe (271). See also for cybernetics as "the crystallization of the Cartesian spirit into material objects and commodities" and "Cyber/punk" as "the ideal postmodern couple: a machine philsophy that can create the world in its own image and a self-mutilating freedom, that is that image snarling back" (270).

4.054   ---. "The SF of Theory: Baudrillard and Haraway." SFS #55, 18.3 (Nov. 1991): 387-404.

Includes a useful discussion of Donna Haraway on cyborgs as "the site of a categorical breakdown, a system of transgressions" (396). See entry for Haraway, under Background.

4.055   ---. "Towards the Last Fairy Tale: On the Fairy-Tale Paradigm in the Strugatskys' Science Fiction, 1963-72." SFS #38, 13.1 (March 1986): 1-41.

Includes a discussion of B. and A. Strugatsky's Rainbow (see under Fiction) as a kind of allegory of nuclear testing and, more generally, a satire on attempts "to master nature" even out of a "desire to serve humanity" (7).

4.056   Day, Phillis J. "Love and the Technocracy: Dehumanization in Social Welfare." CW [195]-211.

People involved in real-world social welfare systems "face the dystopias predicted in science fiction by such authors as [A.] Huxley, [G.] Orwell, John Brunner, Philip K. Dick, and others who write of controlled and automated societies" (195-96).

4.057   "Cyberpunk Forum/Symposium." MR47/48: 16-65 (see under Literary Criticism, Larry McCaffery, guest ed.).

Of special interest:
Benford, Gregory: Cyberpunk, "which just might be a new flavor of hard SF" (19), can't compete with the "'high-hardboiled-detective'" novel or F. Pohl's (and C.M. Kornbluth's) critique of "the moral underpinnings of modern urban life" under capitalism (in The Space Merchants; 20), and is no more than "a marketing strategy masquerading as a literary movement" (22; see below, H. Jaffe).
Brin, David—contribution titled "Starchilde Harold, Revisited": Cyberpunk authors "care about the texture of technology and science, not about veracity or inconvenient reality" (25). A typical cyberpunk work shows some horrible place, with no happy families or decent loves, centered on an antihero inflicting upon the world his "testerone-drenched young manhood" (26). And cyberpunk is fun (27).
Delany, Samuel R.—contribution titled "Is Cyberpunk a Good Thing or a Bad Thing?": Defines "cyberpunk" negatively and in an SF context. Compares W. Gibson's Molly and J. Russ's Jael from The Female Man (32).
Federman, Raymond, "A Letter From the Galaxy": Lists some of cyberpunk's

precursors from about 1962-82 (37).

Hayden, Patrick Nielsen: Usefully paraphrases Teresa Nielsen Hayden on the "shift in SF's settings and background details from the predominantly urban writers of the Campbell era [ca. 1930s-50s] to the predominantly suburban writers of the 1970s"; he approves of cyberpunk's "interest in complex and diverse urban surfaces" (41-42).

Hayden, Teresa Nielsen—contribution titled "Life in Change Wartime": Sees cyberpunk as literature "about the unpredictable uses to which human beings always put technology, and the even stranger thoughts they breed out of those uses; about the way the world is always changing . . . so intricately recomplicating itself that nobody can keep track . . . " (43).

Jaffe, Harold—poem titled "Foucault the Cyberpunks": Condemns the cyberpunks for their alliance with technology and acceptance of multinational corporations (contrast G. Benford on cyberpunk as Leftist).

Porush, David—contribution titled "What is cyberpunk?" (sic: lowercase): An important statement on machines, cybernetics, meaning, automatons, modernism and postmodernism (46-50).

4.058   De Bolt, Joe, ed. The Happening Worlds of John Brunner: Critical Explorations in Science Fiction. Port Washington: Kennikat, 1975.

Essays by various authors discussing Brunner's works. Most immediately relevant: E. L. Lamie and JDB, "The Computer and Man," q.v., this section, under Lamie.

4.059   Dean, John. "The Science Fiction City." Foundation #23 (Oct. 1981): 64-72.

Useful survey of SF cities, both eutopian and dystopian (but mostly dystopian) from the London of H. G. Wells's When the Sleeper Wakes (1899), through the San Francisco of John Shirley's City Come A-Walkin' (1980). See for T. von Harbou's novel, Metropolis (q.v. under Fiction)—but be skeptical of JD's handling of Es Toch in Ursula K. Le Guin's City of Illusions. See for the close relationship of cities and machines.

4.060   Desser, David. "Do Androids Dream of Ridley Scott": Cited under Drama Criticism.

4.061   Dick, Philip K. "Man, Android, and Machine." Science Fiction at Large. Peter Nicholls, ed. New York: Harper, 1976; London: Gollancz, 1976.

PKD on the contemporary trend toward the "reification" of living things and "a reciprocal entry into animation by the mechanical." See Warrick 223-29.

4.062   Dunn, Thomas [P]. "E. M. Forster's 'The Machine Stops.'" Survey of Science Fiction Literature, q.v. above under Reference Works. 3.1299-1303.

Deals with "Machine Stops" as the prototypical mechanical-hive dystopia.

4.063   ---, and Richard D. Erlich. "The Mechanical Hive: Urbmon 116 as the Villain-Hero of Silverberg's The World Inside." Extrapolation 21.4 (Winter 1980): 338-47.

Urban Monad ("Urbmon") 116 is the three-kilometer-high building that is the setting for most of what appears to be an episodic dystopian satire; actually TWI is a dystopian novel unified around Urbmon 116's victories over humans.

4.064   ---, and Richard D. Erlich. "A Vision of Dystopia: Beehives and Mechanization." JGE: The Journal of General Education 33 (Spring 1981): 45-58.

The beehive and the machine as two symbols for individual helplessness and triviality in a number of dystopian works.

4.065   Egan, James. "Technohorror: The Dystopian Vision of Stephen King." Extrapolation

29.2 (Summer 1988): 140-52.

JE finds a "tenuous but definite link . . . between King's nightmare vision and the dystopian tradition of [Y.] Zamiatin, [G.] Orwell, and [A.] Huxley," dealing with such standard dystopian things and themes as "malevolent machines," "irresponsible and incompetent technology," "the monolithic, technocratic governmental apparatus," and, more generally, of the destructive effects and threat of technology (141-42).

4.066 Eizykman, Boris. "Chance and Science Fiction: SF as Stochastic Fiction" (trans. by Will Straw of "S-F: Science Spéculative Stochastique Fiction" in Traverses #24 [1981]: 115-24). SFS #29, 10.1 (March 1983): 24-34.

"[T]he utopian inclination in the modern world has entered the political as well as the scientific domain, imparting, through its determinism, a mechanistic vision of man and nature." This determinism is opposed by Chance, and a number of works of SF deal seriously with Chance. Handles briefly, Hugo Gernsback's Ralph 124C41+ . . . (1911), S. Kubrick's 2001 (q.v. under Drama), Robert Silverberg's The Stochastic Man (1975), and other works; usefully applies to SF some of the concepts of H. Bergson (q.v. under Background), and Marshall McLuhan.

4.067 Elkins, Charles. "E. M. Forster's 'The Machine Stops': Liberal-Humanist Hostility to Technology." CW [47]-61.

"The Machine Stops" as an early and significant example of the "antagonism toward science and technology . . . registered in the works of practically all of the leading writers of the period" (49). Esp. interesting on alienation in a world mediated by technology and the bureaucracy required by technology (56). See below, this section, entry for E. Goodheart.

4.068 Erlich, Richard D. "D. F. Jones's Colossus." Survey of Science Fiction Literature, q.v. above, under Reference Works: 1.409-13.

An introd. to Colossus, q.v. under Fiction.

4.069 ---. "Niven and Pournelle's Oath of Fealty: A Case of Improvement?" Foundation #27 (Feb. 1983): 64-70.

Oath of Fealty raises important questions about technology and bureaucracy.

4.070 ---. "'Trapped in the Bureaucratic Pinball Machine': A Vision of Dystopia in the Twentieth Century." Selected Proceedings of the Science Fiction Research Association 1978 Convention. Thomas J. Remington, ed. Cedar Falls, IA: U of Northern Iowa P, 1979: 30-44.

Treats mechanism and containment in a number of S. F., dystopian, and generally pessimistic works.

4.071 Esmonde, Margaret P. "From Little Buddy to Big Brother: The Icon of the Robot in Children's Science Fiction." TMG [85]-98.

An important essay covering works from L. F. Baum's Oz books (q.v. under Fiction) through the 1970s. In addition to robots, MPE notes "the icon of the computer: the stationary, nonanthropomorphic thinking machine. Whereas in the robot stories the mechanical character is almost certain to be benevolent, in computer stories, the machine without exception poses a serious threat . . . " (94). The "icon of the robot/computer in children's science fiction" suggests a definition of humanity, "not 'I think; therefore, I am,' but 'I love; therefore, I am'" (97). See P. Nodelman entry below, this section.

4.072   Evans, Arthur B. "Science Fiction in France: A Brief History." SFS #49, 16.3 (Nov. 1989): 254-76.

Includes comments on works of Cyrano de Bergerac and Villiers de I'le-Adam, (255, 257). See under Fiction Cyrano, and Villiers.

4.073   Extrapolation, Special Utopias Issue: See above, this section, under Alexandra Aldridge and Gorman Beauchamp, guest eds.

4.074   Fekete, John. "The Dispossessed and Triton: Act and System in Utopian Science Fiction." SFS #18, 6.2 (July 1979): 129-43.

Overly difficult but important article on Ursula K. Le Guin's Dispossessed and S. R. Delany's Triton, with a provocative observation on Y. Zamiatin's We (all listed under Fiction). See for the Organism vs. Mechanism controversy implicit in Le Guin's presentation of "the decay of organic revolutionary culture into mechanical conventionality" on Anarres, and for Delany's presentation of "emptiness coordinated cybernetically in patterns" on Triton.

4.075   Fischlin, Donald, Veronica Hollinger, Andrew Taylor. "'The Charisma Leak': A Conversation with William Gibson and Bruce Sterling." SFS #56, 19.1 (March 1992): 1-16.

Annotated text of interview, with important comments on Gibson and Sterling's The Difference Engine (listed under Fiction), plus other works of interest.

4.076   Fisher, Judith L. "Trouble in Paradise: The Twentieth-Century Utopian Ideal." Extrapolation 24.4 (Winter 1983): 329-39.

Concentrates on C. S. Lewis's "Deep Space Trilogy," I. Asimov's Foundation series, R. A. Heinlein's The Moon Is a Harsh Mistress, and Ursula K. Le Guin's The Dispossessed (citations under Fiction). Contains some errors, but usefully discusses the possibility of resolving the paradox of "the Machine" (both technology and bureaucratic organization) that allows modern utopias and reduces them to dystopias (see esp. 330).

4.077   Fitting, Peter. "Futurecop: The Neutralization of Revolt in Blade Runner": Cited under Drama Criticism; see for P. K. Dick's Do Androids Dream of Electric Sheep?

4.078   Förster, Werner. "Time Travelling into the Present: Science Fiction Literature in the GDR [German Democratic Republic]." JPC 18.3 (Winter 1984): 71-81.

See 77 f. for plot summaries and analyses of two works significant for the study of mechanized environments: Karlheinz Steinmüller, "Der Traum vom Großen Roten Fleck" ("The Dream of the Big Red Spot"), in Der letzte Tag auf Venus; and Johanna and Günther Braun, Conviva Ludibundus (both books cited as Berlin, 1979). "Dream" posits a central computer regulating an "'atomized society'" of radical individualism; Ludibundus pits a "'homo ludens'" (Playing Man) protagonist against an antagonist WF describes as "a 'human automaton'" (77-78).

4.079   Frank, Frederick S. "The Gothic at Absolute Zero: Poe's Narrative of Arthur Gordon Pym." Extrapolation 21 (Spring 1980): 21-30.

Presents the final sction of Pym as an escape from a "globalized Gothic Castle" into a "lost Eden." (This escape pattern is highly important for dystopian works featuring mechanized Gothic castles on a global scale, sometimes contrasted with Garden worlds.)

4.080   Franklin, H. Bruce. Robert A. Heinlein: America as Science Fiction. New York: Oxford UP, 1980.

Esp. relevant for its discussions of <u>Starship Troopers</u> and <u>The Moon Is a Harsh Mistress</u> (110-24 and 162-70)—and for putting these works into the contexts of Heinlein's canon and of America in the 20th c. Includes a chronological biblio. of works by Heinlein through 1979 and an annotated "Selected List of Works about Robert A. Heinlein." An important work for the study of Heinlein's S. F.

4.081   ---. "Strange Scenarios: Science Fiction, the Theory of Alienation, and the Nuclear Gods." <u>SFS</u> #39, 13.2 (July 1986): 117-28.

Includes a discussion of "the cult of the superweapon" in SF and in the real world of the late 19th through the late 20th centuries, handling such works as M. Roshwald's <u>Level 7</u> and H. Ellison's "I Have No Mouth . . . " (q.v. under Fiction). See also nonfiction prognostications by real-world technologists Thomas A. Edison and Nikola Tesla (122-24).

4.082   ---. "The Vietnam War as American Science Fiction and Fantasy." <u>SFS</u> #52, 17.3 (Nov. 1990): 341-59.

The "technological fetishism" and obsession with "superwarriors," often chemically enhanced (344-45), that helped lead US elites to war in Indochina is revealed or attacked in much American SF of the 1960s and after. See below under Background, HBF's <u>War Stars</u>.

4.083   Fromm, Erich. Foreword to Edward Bellamy, <u>Looking Backward</u> (1888). New York: NAL, 1960: v-xx.

Excellent introd. to <u>Looking Backward</u>, esp. useful for its critique of Bellamy's "managerial society," with its "hierarchical bureaucratic principle of administration" (section IV, xi-xii).

4.084   Gaar, Alice Carol. "The Human as Machine Analog: The Big Daddy of Interchangeable Parts in the Fiction of Robert A. Heinlein." <u>Robert A. Heinlein</u>. Joseph D. Olander and Martin Harry Greenberg, eds. New York: Taplinger, 1980.

Deals with Heinlein's response to "a cosmos that might really be just a gigantic computer" (265).

4.085   Gallagher, Edward J. "From Folded Hands to Clenched Fist: Kesey and Science Fiction." <u>Perspective on a Cuckoo's Nest: A Special Symposium Issue on Ken Kesey</u>. Lex et Scientia 13.1-2 (Jan.-June 1977): 46-50.

The worldview in Kesey's <u>Cuckoo's Nest</u> is "the world as machine, the cybernetic model, a world whose total service homogenizes humanity"; discusses that worldview as it appears in over a dozen stories.

4.086   ---. "The Thematic Structure of <u>The Martian Chronicles</u>." <u>Ray Bradbury</u>. Martin Harry Greenberg and Joseph D. Olander, eds. New York: Taplinger, 1980: 55-82.

See 79-80 for a brief but excellent analysis of "There Will Come Soft Rains" as a commentary on the relationship between humankind and technology.

4.087   Gilman, Michael. "If FORTRAN = Newspeak or BASIC = Newspeak then 1984: Computers as an Orwellian Language." <u>Cuyahoga Review</u> 2 (Spring-Summer 1984): 34-43.

Cited in "Year's Scholarship": 1985, under George Orwell.

4.088   Glazer, Miriyam. "'What Is Within Now Seen Without': Romanticism, Neuromanticism, and the Death of the Imagination in William Gibson's Fictive World." <u>JPC</u> 23.3

(Winter 1989): 155-64.

Humanist, William-Blakean, largely negative reading of Gibson's works; cf. and emphatically contrast D. G. Mead, "Technological Transfiguration," cited this section.

4.089 Goodheart, Eugene. "The Romantic Critique of Industrial Civilization." Technology and Pessimism special issue of Alternative Futures, 126-38 (see under Marthalee Barton and Dwight W. Stevenson, guest co-eds., under Background).

Concentrates on Thomas Carlyle, John Ruskin, William Morris, and D. H. Lawrence; see for the literary tradition of a radical "aversion to technological progress." See above, entry for C. Elkins.

4.090 Gordon, Andrew. "Human, More or Less: Man-Machine Communion in Samuel R. Delany's Nova and Other Science Fiction Stories." TMG [193]-202.

The "Other" includes works by D. Knight, T. Lee, I. Levin, F. Pohl, C. L. Moore, P. Anderson, and J. Varley, plus some films. (AG contributes to the scholarship tracing the descendants of the "black hand" of Rotwang from F. Lang's film Metropolis [199].)

4.091 Greenberg, Martin Harry, and Joseph D. Olander, eds. Philip K. Dick. New York: Taplinger, 1983.

Anthology of original and rpt. essays on Philip K. Dick. Includes also M. Tymn, "Philip K. Dick: A Bibliography" (q.v. above, under Reference), an introd. by Barry N. Malzberg, a brief biographical note on Dick, and ("in slightly different form") Dick's introd. to The Golden Man, titled "Now Wait for This Year" (quoting acknowledgment on 215). See index for brief discussions (passim) of "The Electric Ant," Martian Time Slip, Penultimate Truth, and "Second Variety" (all listed under Fiction).

4.092 Grigsby, John L. "Herbert's Reversal of Asimov's Vision Reassessed: Foundation's Edge and God Emperor of Dune." SFS #33, 11.2 (July 1984): 174-80.

Sequel to JLG's "Asimov's Foundation Trilogy and Herbert's Dune Trilogy: A Vision Reversed," SFS #24, 8.2 (July 1981): 149-55. I. Asimov's Foundation's Edge ends with a "universe still controlled and dominated, this time either by robots (and the assumption of technology's importance) or by some vague" Behaviorist control, assuming "the importance of mental science," but with equivocation when Golan Trevise makes provisional his commitment to "Gaia"— see entry for Foundation's Edge, under I. Asimov, under Fiction. "In direct contrast to Foundation's Edge, [F.] Herbert's God Emperor ends with no such equivocation, nor with any such absolute faith in mental science and/or technology" (178).

4.093 Gunn, James. Isaac Asimov: The Foundations of Science Fiction. Oxford: Oxford UP, 1982.

Includes a chronology of Asimov's life to 1980, a "Checklist of Works by Isaac Asimov" through 1981, a brief "Select List of Works about Isaac Asimov," and a useful index. Text handles in detail the Foundation trilogy and Asimov's robot stories and novels, and places Asimov and his work into the context of 20th-c. S. F. See following entries for JG.

4.094 ---. "On the Foundations of Science Fiction." Isaac Asimov's Science Fiction Magazine #4, April 1980: 64-84. Rpt. with slight changes in Gunn's Isaac Asimov, q.v. above.

Significant here for seeing "the expansion of humanity into the galaxy" (as opposed to confinement) as, in Jack Williamson's words, "the central myth" of

S.F.'s vision of the future. Also significant for finding the "spirit of the early stories" in I. Asimov's Foundation Trilogy "detemindedly anti-deterministic."

4.095 ---. "Variations on a Robot." Isaac Asimov's Science Fiction Magazine #7, July 1980: 56-81.

On Asimov on robots from the 1940s to 1980. See above, JG's Isaac Asimov.

4.096 Hammerton, M. "Wells as Prophet." Foundation #45 (Spring 1989): 23-37.

Looks at H. G. Wells's prognostications of technological innovations. When Wells moved from science toward engineering technology, "the less he was at home, and the less reliable his intuitions were" (36). By early in the 20th c., Wells saw our "essential problem" as "not to further control over the physical world," but to get humans to behave like reasonable beings (30).

4.097 The Happening Worlds of John Brunner. Joe De Bolt, ed. Listed above, this section, under De Bolt.

4.098 Hardesty, William H. III. "The Programmed Utopia of R. A Lafferty's Past Master." CW [105]-13.

"Past Master is no mere dystopian novel: it is a commentary on Sir Thomas More's Utopia itself"—and the utopian tradition—"mated with an investigation into human nature and human aspirations," perhaps most interestingly in this essay, the aspiration for utopia ([105]). See Lafferty entry under Fiction.

4.099 Harris-Fain, Darren. "Created in the Image of God: The Narrator and the Computer in Harlan Ellison's 'I Have No Mouth and I Must Scream.'" Extrapolation 32.2 (Summer 1991): 143-55.

Usefully studies variant readings in different issues of "I Have No Mouth . . . . "

4.100 Hassler, Donald M. "Asimov's Robot Novels and the Two Non-Series Novels." Foundation #37 (Autumn 1986): 22-30.

The robot novels here are The Caves of Steel and The Naked Sun (q.v. under Fiction); the non-series novels are The End of Eternity and The Gods Themselves. See for the robot novels' Elijah Baley's "open and loose" curiosity vs. his robot partner's "machine-like rejection" of such inefficiency (24) and for DMH's discussion of "gold," (for Earth's "Medievalists") vs. the Spacer's "carbon," and "iron"—primarily humans/robots (24-25).

4.101 ---. Isaac Asimov. Mercer Island, WA: Starmont, 1991.

Recent study by an important critic, including much on the Foundation and Robot series up to I.A.'s Foundation and Earth. Rev. Arthur O. Lewis, SFRA Newsletter #192 (Nov. 1991): 52-53, our source for our citation.

4.102 Hayles, Katherine N. Chaos Bound: Orderly Disorder in Contemporary Literature and Science. Ithaca, NY: Cornell UP, 1990.

Chaos theory as "the emergent science of . . . computerized culture," with a chapter on S. Lem and brief discussion of W. Gibson (and Max Headroom). Rev. Rob Latham, SFRA Newsletter #189 (July-Aug. 1991): 58-59, our source for this entry, and whom we quote. See under Background, D. Porush on "Prigogine."

4.103 Heldreth, Leonard G. "Clockwork Reels: Mechanized Environments in Science Fiction Films": Cited under Drama Criticism (includes discussion of novels as well as films).

4.104   ---. "In Search of the Ultimate Weapon: The Fighting Machine in Science Fiction Novels and Films." TMG [129]-52.

See for the powered armor in R. A. Heinlein's Starship Troopers and J. Haldeman's The Forever War, and for extensive coverage of F. Saberhagen's berserker stories (all listed under Fiction).

4.105   Herwald, Michelle. "Anticipating the Unexpected: Amazing Stories in the Interwar Years." Mass Media Between the Wars: Perceptions of Cultural Tension, 1918-1941. Catherine L. Covert and John D. Stevens, eds. Syracuse, NY: Syracuse UP, 1984.

During the "Machine Age" (roughly 1920-40), Hugo Gernsback's Amazing generally presented stories positive about the advent of new technology (see under Fiction, A. J. Gelula, "Automation"). Other stories were less optimistic, showing "technological violence . . . directed by man" and/or "technological violence . . . independent of human direction" (40, 44f.).

4.106   Hildebrand, Tim.   "Two or Three Things I Know About Kurt Vonnegut's Imagination." Ch. 9 of The Vonnegut Statement, q.v., this section.

Brief, numbered comments on, and often longer quotations from, Vonnegut's works, with some use of other sources. These yield interesting insights into Vonnegut's work up to Slaughterhouse-Five, and, indirectly, Breakfast of Champions.

4.107   Hillegas, Mark R. The Future as Nightmare: H.G. Wells and the Anti-utopians. New York: Oxford UP, 1967. Carbondale: Southern Illinois UP, Arcturus, 1974.

Occasionally inaccurate but still indispensable. Deals with Wells's utopian and anti-utopian works and their influence on Y. Zamiatin, A. Huxley, G. Orwell, and others; quite good on E. M. Forster's "Machine Stops" (all listed under Fiction).

4.108   Hipolito, Jane. "The Last and First Starship From Earth." SF: The Other Side of Realism . . . . Thomas D. Clareson, ed. Bowling Green, OH: BGU PopP, 1971.

On J. Boyd's The Last Starship from Earth, q.v. under Fiction.

4.109   Hoffman, Thomas P. "The Theme of Mechanization in Player Piano." CW [125]-35.

Sociological approach, identifying the theme of K. Vonnegut's Player Piano as "mechanization, and its primary subject is machine-created loneliness examined against a background of social revolution" ([125]). See above, this section, L. Broer, "Pilgrim's Progress."

4.110   Hollinger, Veronica. "Cybernetic Deconstructions: Cyberpunk and Postmodernism." Mosaic 23.2 (Spring 1990): [29]-44. Rpt. L. McCaffery, Storming . . ., cited below under McCaffery.

An important, well-written essay pursuing VH's investigation of cyberpunk as (among other possibilities) an antihumanist "analysis of the postmodern identification of human and machine"—blurring boundaries that once seemed natural—and cyberpunk's (and postmodernism's) "problematizing of 'reality' itself" (31).

4.111   ---. "Feminist Science Fiction: Breaking Up the Subject." Extrapolation 31.3 (Fall 1990): [228]-239.

Includes a very important paragraph on C. L. Moore's "No Woman Born" (234-35).

4.112 Hollow, John. Against the Night, the Stars: The Science Fiction of Arthur C. Clarke. San Diego: Harcourt, 1983. (Some material copyright 1976.)

Includes analyses of Against the Fall of Night and The City and the Stars, 2001, The Lion of Comarre, and other relevant works (all listed under Fiction).

4.113 Hull, Elizabeth Anne. "Merging Madness: Rollerball as a Cautionary Tale": Cited under Drama Criticism, but also relevant for W. Harrison's "Roller Ball Murder," q.v. under Fiction.

4.114 Huntington, John. "Newness, Neuromancer, and the End of Narrative." Fictional Space: Essays on Contemporary Science Fiction. Tom Shippey, ed. Atlantic Highlands, NJ: Humanities P International; Oxford, UK: Blackwell, 1991.

As opposed to earlier characters who used "technology to dominate their environment, Gibson's characters are subordinate" to the machines they deal with. Rev. Arthur O. Lewis, SFRA Review #195 (March 1992): 49, whom we depend upon and quote here.

4.115 ---. "Philip K. Dick: Authenticity and Insincerity." SFS #45 = 15.2 (July 1988): 152-60.

Suggests that Dick's use of A.E. van Vogt's "dictum that every 800 words a new idea should be introduced" leads to a sense in which there is less to Dick than meets the eye. "The illusion of conscious profundity in such works as [The Man in the] High Castle, [Do] Androids [Dream of Electric Sheep?], and VALIS is to a large extent generated by arbitrary narrative shifts. However, insofar as the search for the 'real' and 'authentic' is central to Dick's philosophical program, the mechanical narrative device is itself thematically important and expressive" (160; from JH's abstract).

4.116 Ingersoll, Daniel W., Jr. "Machines Are Good to Think: A Structural Analysis of Myth and Mechanization." CW [235]-62.

Structuralist analysis of the Eskimo story "Sedna and the Fulmar," the European folktale of "Goldilocks and the Three Bears," and the American film The Stepford Wives (q.v. under Drama). Note very well the essay title.

4.117 Jameson, Fredric. "Generic Discontinuities in SF: Brian Aldiss' Starship." SFS #2, 1.2 (Fall 1973): 57-68.

Briefly compares Starship (vt Non-Stop) with R. Heinlein's Orphans of the Sky (57-61). Notes the "political character" of Starship, given its surprise ending: "the problem of the manipulation of men by other men," using the tools of technology. See above under Fiction, B. Aldiss, Non-Stop, and R. Heinlein, "Universe."

4.118 ---. "Postmodernism, or The Cultural Logic of Late Capitalism": Cited under Background.

4.119 Jehmlich, Reimer. "Cog-work: The Organization of Labor in Edward Bellamy's Looking Backward and in Later Utopian Fiction." CW [27]-46.

The "Later Utopian Fiction" is primarily William Morris's News from Nowhere (1890), Ivan Yefremov's Andromeda (1954); and B. F. Skinner's Walden Two and A. Huxley's Island (both of which see under Fiction).

4.120 Jones, Anne Hudson. "The Cyborg (R)Evolution in Science Fiction." TMG [203]-209.

Discusses J. Vinge's "Tin Soldier," H. Kuttner's "Camouflage," C. L. Moore's "No

Woman Born," D. Knight's "Masks," A. C. Clarke's "A Meeting with Medusa," R. Zelazny's "The Engine at Heartspring's Center," and A. McCaffrey's Helva stories (mostly titled "The Ship Who ___," with different past tense verbs filling in the blank)—all listed under Fiction.

4.121   Kandel, Michael. "Stanislaw Lem on Men and Robots." Extrapolation 14.1 (Dec. 1972): 13-24.

See for cybernetics in Lem.

4.122   Kerman, Judith B. "Private Eye: A Semiotic Comparison of the Film Blade Runner and the Book Do Androids Dream of Electric Sheep[?]": Cited under Drama Criticism.

4.123   Ketterer, David. New Worlds for Old: The Apocalyptic Imagination, Science Fiction, and American Literature. Garden City, NY: Anchor-Doubleday, 1974.

Chapter 12 deals usefully with K. Vonnegut's Sirens of Titan (q.v. under Fiction).

4.124   ---. "Utopian Fantasy as Millennial Motive and Science Fictional Motif." Studies in the Literary Imagination 6.2 (Fall 1973): 79-103.

Bellamy's Looking Backward as an inadvertent dystopia: "a conveyor-belt vision of hell." See for the ambiguity of technology and, even more, of the social (hyper)organization associated with industrial society: Bellamy's utopian "gigantic mill" appears to DK to resemble William Blake's "dark Satanic Mills."

4.125   ---. "Wagnerian Spenglerian Space Opera: Cities in Flight by James Blish." Foundation #31 (July 1984): 45-67.

Extensive discussion of Cities in Flight series (q.v. under fiction) and the use therein of the theories of Oswald Spengler. Stresses the image of the "restricting container," which DK relates to the "imprisoning Spenglerian cycles" as "a temporal version of this spatial metaphor. At the end of Cities in Flight an attempt will be made to burst free of the realms of cyclical process" (56-57). See this section, R. D. Mullen on "Blish, van Vogt, and the Uses of Spengler."

4.126   Klinkowitz, Jerome, and John Somers, eds. The Vonnegut Statement: Listed below, by title.

4.127   Knapp, Bettina. Machine, Metaphor, and the Writer: A Jungian View. University Park, PA: Pennsylvania State UP, 1989.

Survey of differing ways mechanization enters mainstream modern and contemporary literature, including James Joyce's "A Painful Case," Antoine de Saint-Exupery's Wind, Sand, and Stars, and Sam Shepherd's Operation Sidewinder. Rev. Thom Dunn, SFRA Newsletter #192 (Nov. 1991): 42-43.

4.128   Kramer, Reinhold. "The Machine in the Ghost: Time and Presence in Varley's Millennium." Extrapolation 32.2 (Summer 1991): 156-69.

Handles, among other things, mechanical time vs. psychological time, the robot, Sherman—as a Christ figure—and the Big Computer as God the Father. See under Fiction, J. Varley, Millennium.

4.129   Krulik, Ted. "Bounded by Metal." The Intersection of Science Fiction and Philosophy. Robert E. Myers, ed. Westport, CT: Greenwood, 1983.

Brief study of "the alienness of the robot in fiction" to "learn something of the humanness of human beings," looking at I. Asimov's "The Bicentennial Man," D.

Knight's "Masks," and P. Phillips's "Lost Memory," all listed under Fiction.

4.130   Lamie, Edward L., and Joe De Bolt. "The Computer and Man: The Human Uses of
        Non-Human Beings." The Happening Worlds of John Brunner. Joe De Bolt, ed.
        (q.v. above, under De Bolt, this section).

        On Brunner's "balanced insight" into the uses and abuses of computers (and other
        machines) in human society. Briefly discusses a wide range of Brunner's fiction
        up to the mid-1970s, with useful comments on Shalmaneser in Stand on Zanzibar,
        and on the city as organism and machine in "Bloodstream" (both cited above,
        under Fiction).

4.131   Lem, Stanislaw. "Robots in Science Fiction." Franz Rottensteiner, trans. SF: The
        Other Side of Realism. Thomas D. Clareson, ed. Bowling Green, OH: BGU PopP,
        1971.

        Includes a discussion of the humanity (in terms of ethical relationships) of
        mechanical beings capable of humanlike thought.

4.132   Letson, Russell. "Portraits of Machine Consciousness." TMG [101]-108.

        A taxonomy of conscious machines from HAL in S. Kubrick's film 2001 to its
        "complementary opposite" of "the sentimentalized machine," with L. del Rey's
        "Helen O'Loy" as the locus classicus (102-3), to machines by S. Lem, P. Alterman,
        J. P. Hogan, I. Asimov, and R. A. Heinlein.

4.133   Lewis, Arthur O. "Introduction." CW [3]-18.

        An elegantly written, richly illustrated essay examining (among other things)
        "several metaphors that have frequently been used to describe human social
        organizations: the human body, the hive, the machine" (5).

4.134   ---.   "Utopia, Technology, and Social Evolution."   JGE: The Journal of General
        Education 37.3 (1985): [161]-76.

        Appropriate technology in recent "arcadian" works (as opposed to "utopian," in a
        terminology suggested by Northrop Frye).   Deals with Ernest Callenbach's
        Ecotopia (1975), Ursula K. Le Guin's The Eye of the Heron (1979), John
        Nichols's Daily Lives in Nghsi-Altai (coll. 1977-79), Norman Spinrad's A World
        Between (1979), Mary Alice White's The Land of the Possible (1979); and with J.
        Ballard's "The Ultimate City," F. Herbert's Hellstrom's Hive, and L. Niven and J.
        Pournelle's Oath of Fealty (all of the second group cited under Fiction).

4.135   Livingston, Dennis. "Science Fiction Models of Future Order Systems": Cited under
        Background.

4.136   Lundquist, James. Kurt Vonnegut. New York: Ungar, 1977.

        Cited by Schlobin and Tymn as "the most thoughtful study of Vonnegut to date."
        Includes a biblio. ("Year's Scholarship": 1977).

4.137   Lyau, Bradford. "Technocratic Anxiety in France: The Fleuve Noir 'Anticipation
        Novels,' 1951-60." Robert M. Philmus, ed. SFS #49, 16.3 (Nov. 1989): 277-97.

        Responses to French bureaucratic expansion in a series of novels published in
        "Collection Anticipation," a SF series from Fleuve Noir publishers (277). Divides
        eleven authors into four groups in terms of their attitudes toward technocracy
        (277-78).

4.138   Lyngstad, Sverre. "Beyond the God-Machine: Towards a Naturalized Technology."
            In Technology and Pessimism special issue of Alternative Futures: 92-110, q.v.
            below, M. Barton and D. W. Stevenson, guest co-eds., under Background.

            Esp. useful for SF and related works in European languages other than English.
            Includes a substantial discussion (104-107) of H. Martinson's Aniara, q.v. under
            Fiction.

4.139   Maddox, Tom. "The War of the Coin's Two Halves: Bruce Sterling's Mechanist/Shaper
            Narratives." MR47/48: 237-44 (see this section, Larry McCaffery, guest ed.).

            On Sterling's "Swarm," "Spider Rose," "Cicada Queen," "Sunken Gardens," "Twenty
            Evocations . . . ," and Schistmatrix (listed under Fiction). Shapers and Mechanists
            are "the primary posthumanist modes of being—binary opposites in the dialectic
            of mankind's fate"; TM quotes "Sunken Gardens" on Shapers' having "seized
            control of their own genetics, abandoning mankind in a burst of artificial
            evolution"—opposed to Mechanists, who "had replaced flesh with advanced
            prosthetics" (MR47/48: 238). TM compares and contrasts "Olaf Stapledon's
            bloodless sagas," A. C. Clarke's Childhood's End and 2001, and F. Herbert's Dune
            series (239).

4.140   Marx, Leo. "American Literary Culture and the Fatalistic View of Technology." In
            the Technology and Pessimism special issue of Alternative Futures: 45-70, q.v.
            below, under M. Barton and D. W. Stevenson, guest co-eds., under Background.

            An updating of LM's Machine in the Garden, with esp. good comments on
            technology in classic American literature (including H. Adams' "Dynamo and the
            Virgin" [q.v. under Background], Benjamin Franklin's Autobiography, and Mark
            Twain's Huckleberry Finn).

4.141   ---. The Machine in the Garden: Cited under Background.

4.142   Mathews, Richard. Aldiss Unbound: The Science Fiction of Brian Aldiss. San
            Bernadino, CA: Borgo, 1977. Vol. 9 in The Milford Series: Popular Writers of
            Today.

            Brief introduction to Aldiss's works.

4.143   ---. The Clockwork Universe of Anthony Burgess. San Bernardino, CA: Borgo, 1978.
            Vol. 19 in The Milford Series: Popular Writers of Today.

            Section 4 is on A Clockwork Orange.

4.144   Mayo, Clark. Kurt Vonnegut: The Gospel from Outer Space . . . . San Bernardino,
            CA: Borgo, 1977. Vol. 7 in the Milford Series: Popular Writers of Today.

            Includes discussions of Player Piano, The Sirens of Titan, Slaughterhouse-Five,
            Breakfast of Champions, and other works.

4.145   McCaffery, Larry. "The Desert of the Real: The Cyberpunk Controversy." MR47/48:
            7-15 (see below, L. McCaffery, guest ed.).

            Develops LM's "conviction that cyberpunk represents not only an apotheosis of
            postmodernism but that it is also currently producing some of the most important
            art of our times"—in films, TV, and music as well as in literature (8). LM feels
            that cyberpunk mirrors our era's "central motifs, obsessions, and desires," many of
            them closely related to technological change (8-9).

4.146   ---, guest ed. Mississippi Review #47 and #48, 16.2 & 3 (1988).

            MR47/48, the cyberpunk special issue of MR, publishes for the first time or rpts.
            fiction and criticism important for the study of the cyberpunk movement
            (perhaps the major form of postmodernism in SF). Items cited in the List or

otherwise relevant follow.

Fiction: M. Leyner, "I Was an Infinitely Hot and Dense Dot"; W. Gibson, "The Smoke" (from WG's Mona Lisa Overdrive, q.v.); D. Porush, "Induction from R.Boots" (sic: no space); R. Rucker, "Christmas in Louisville December 24, 2030" (from RR's Wetware, q.v.); B. Sterling, "20 evocations" (sic: lowercase "e"); J. Shirley, "Wolves of the Plateau"; T. Maddox, "In a Distant Landscape"; R. Astel, "The History of the War Against the Mend-and-Repair."

Interview: LM, "An Interview with William Gibson."

Literary Criticism: LM, "The Desert of the Real: The Cyberpunk Controversy"; "Cyberpunk Forum/Symposium"; Harold Jaffe, "Foucault the Cyberpunks" (poem); T. Maddox, "The War of the Coin's Two Halves: Bruce Sterling's Mechanist/Shaper Narratives"; I. Csicsery-Ronay, "Cyberpunk and Neuromanticism"; G. Slusser, "Literary MTV."

Drama Criticism: B. Landon, "Bet On It: Cyber/ video/ punk/ performance."

Music: R. Rucker, "Raising the Level"; Pascal J. Thomas, "Cyberpunk as roots music: an observation" (sic: only one uppercase letter).

4.147   ---, ed. Storming the Reality Studio: A Casebook of Cyberpunk and Postmodern Science Fiction. Durham, NC: Duke UP, 1991.

Apparently an expanded and refocussed version of MR47/48 (q.v. above), plus an introd., brief notices of precursors of cyberpunk, and a list of "books, films, and music that the editor considers relevant to the study of cyberpunk and postmodernism." Rev. Michael M. Levy, SFRA Review #194 (Jan./Feb. 1992): 43-45, whom we quote, and upon whom we depend for this citation.

4.148   McCarthy, Patrick A. "Zamyatin and the Nightmare of Technology." SFS #33, 11.2 (July 1984): 122-29.

On Y. Zamiatin's We (q.v. as spelled here, under Fiction), seen as a work focusing on "technological politics—or on the political implications of technology" (123). Particularly interesting on Zamiatin's romanticism, "The dual vision of the machine," and Zamiatin's use of the myth of Prometheus (124-26; section 2).

4.149   McConnell, Frank. The Science Fiction of H. G. Wells. New York: Oxford UP, 1981.

Includes a checklist (only) of works by Wells and an annotated "Select List of Works about H. G. Wells"; limited citations. The discussions contain a couple of errors and perhaps some overly ingenious readings but are well written and stimulating. FM covers most of Wells's works important for the study of the human/machine interface, with some esp. useful comments on First Men in the Moon and Time Machine and Time Machine's relationships to E. Bellamy's Looking Backward (q.v. under Fiction), and William Morris' 1890 utopia, News from Nowhere (McConnell, ch. 3).

4.150   Mead, David G. "Technological Transfiguration in William Gibson's Sprawl Novels: Neuromancer, Count Zero, and Mona Lisa Overdrive." Extrapolation 32.4 (Winter 1991): [350]-60.

"In the neuromantic vision of William Gibson, developments in cybernetics, biotechnology, neurochemistry, and so forth offer the opportunity . . . for personal liberation and self-actualization, almost to the extreme of apotheosis. . . . In Gibson's Sprawl trilogy . . . technology permits us to become what we will, to realize our selves, however banal, in ways undreamed of by the countercultural, New Wave technophobe or the Blakean romantic" (353). See M. Glazer on "Neuromanticism," this section (a Blakean reading with which DGM disagrees and, civilly, takes issue).

4.151   The Mechanical God (TMG): Cited under Reference Works.

4.152   Meckier, Jerome. "Our Ford, Our Freud and the Behaviorist Conspiracy in Huxley's Brave New World." Thalia 1.1 (1978): 35-59.

Cited in "Year's Scholarship 1979" as "An exhaustive examination of Huxley's use of psychology and reactions to psychological theories in Brave New World." See the entries for B. F. Skinner under Fiction and Background, and the entry for J. B. Watson under Background.

4.153   Mellard, James M.   "The Modes of Vonnegut's Fiction: Or, Player Piano Ousts Mechanical Bride and The Sirens of Titan Invade The Gutenberg Galaxy." Ch. 12 of The Vonnegut Statement (q.v. this section).

The humanization of machines and the mechanization of humans in Player Piano, Sirens, and contemporary industrial society. Relates Player Piano to the themes of "mechanics and sex" analyzed in Marshall McLuhan's The Mechanical Bride.

4.154   Mengeling, Marvin E.   "The Machineries of Joy and Despair: Bradbury's Attitudes toward Science and Technology." Ray Bradbury. Martin Harry Greenberg and Joseph D. Olander, eds. New York: Taplinger, 1980.

Includes discussions of Bradbury's "robot houses" and "robot cities." See for Bradbury's ambivalent and changing attitudes toward technology.

4.155   Merrill, Robert, ed. Critical Essays on Kurt Vonnegut. Boston: G. K. Hall, 1990.

Anthology of twenty-four reviews and essays giving "an overview of Vonnegut criticism through . . . Galapagos in 1985" (and a bit beyond). Rev. Gary K. Wolfe, SFRA Review #194 (Jan./Feb. 1992): 45-46, whom we quote and upon whom we depend for this citation.

4.156   Moore, Maxine. "The Use of Technical Metaphors in Asimov's Fiction." Isaac Asimov. Joseph D. Olander and Martin Harry Greenberg, eds. New York: Taplinger, 1977.

See for "the endless parallels between the human brain and the computer function of the machine" in Asimov's "Robot series," including Caves of Steel and Naked Sun; handled most directly on 78-83.

4.157   Mullen, R. D. "Blish, van Vogt, and the Uses of Spengler." Riverside Quarterly 3 (Aug. 1968): 172-86. Sections on Blish rpt. as Afterword to J. Blish's Cities in Flight (q.v. under Fiction).

On Oswald Spengler's theory of cyclical history in the Cities in Flight stories, q.v. under Fiction. See in this section, D. Ketterer's, " . . . Spenglerian Space Opera."

4.158   Mumford, Lewis. The Story of Utopias. 1922. New York: Viking (Compass), 1962.

Introd. to utopian thought from Plato's Republic through H. G. Wells's A Modern Utopia; see for E. Bellamy's Looking Backward (q.v. under Fiction) and for LM on the great models of the Country House and Coketown (aristocratic vs. more modern, industrialized utopias). Relates literary utopias to social thought; see under Background, citations for other works by LM.

4.159   Myers, Alan. "Some Developments in Soviet SF Since 1966." Foundation #19 (June 1980): 38-47.

Also includes a few comments on Russian SF prior to 1966. Some works relevant to the study of mechanized environments: S. Snegov's Men Like Gods, and the stories set in the "repressive society of machine slavery" of Donomaga, by I. Varshavskiy. See in AM's article 38-39, 43.

4.160   Neustadter, Roger. "Mechanization Takes Command: The Celebration of Technology in the Utopian Novels of Edward Bellamy, Chauncey Thomas, John Jacob Astor, and Charles Caryl." Extrapolation 29.1 (Spring 1988): 21-33.

The novels are Bellamy's <u>Looking Backward</u> and its sequel <u>Equality</u>, Thomas's <u>The Crystal Button</u>, Astor's <u>A Journey in Other Worlds</u>, and Caryl's work "Written in Play Format," <u>The New Era</u> (29). RN's title alludes to S. Giedion's <u>Mechanization Takes Command</u>, cited under Background.

4.161 Nicholls, Peter, gen. ed. <u>The Science in Science Fiction</u>: Cited by title under Background.

4.162 Nixon, Nicola. "Cyberpunk: Preparing the Ground for Revolution or Keeping the Boys Satisfied?" <u>SFS</u> #57, 19.2 (July 1992): 219-35.

Cogent and lively examination of the often-asserted revolutionary agenda in cyberpunk, "first placing it within the context of its immediate feminist antecedents, then raising a number of questions on its peculiar reliance on specific cultural icons popular in the Reaganite America of the 1980s" (Abstract 235), emphatically including cyberspace cowboys seen as "capitalist entrepreneurs." NN concludes that cyberpunk is "not radical at all" (231).

4.163 <u>No Place Else: Explorations in Utopian and Dystopian Fiction</u>: Cited this section, under Eric S. Rabkin et al., eds.

4.164 Nodelman, Perry. "Out There in Children's Science Fiction: Forward into the Past." <u>SFS</u> #37, 12.3 (Nov. 1985): 285-96.

High-tech, enclosed cities in, primarily, children's S. F., with comparisons and contrasts with selected non-S. F. stories for young people and with three S. F. works not marketed for children: E. M. Forster's "The Machine Stops," A. C. Clarke's <u>The City and the Stars</u>, and H. Harrison's <u>Captive Universe</u> (q.v. under Fiction). See for H. M. Hoover's <u>This Time of Darkness</u> (1980), Suzanne Martel's <u>The City Under Ground</u> (trans. Norah Smaridge, from <u>Quatre Montréalais en l'an 3000</u>, 1964/1982), Andre Norton's <u>Outside</u> (1976), Ann Schlee's <u>The Vandal</u> (1983). Very important essay for technology vs. nature. See this section, M. P. Esmonde, "From Little Buddy to Big Brother."

4.165 Olander, Joesph D., and Martin Harry Greenberg, eds. <u>Arthur C. Clarke</u>. New York: Taplinger, 1977.

An anthology of original and rpt. critical essays on Clarke. See Olander and Greenberg's Index for <u>City and the Stars</u>, <u>Rendezvous with Rama</u>, and <u>2001</u>.

4.166 Orth, Michael. "The Computer in Recent Utopias: A Transcendental Teleology." Eleventh Annual Conference of the Society for Utopian Studies. Pacific Grove, CA, 2-5 Oct. 1986.

Useful review of eutopian and dystopian uses of computers in fiction, up to the time of presentation of the paper; uses and extends the work of Patricia Warrick in <u>Cybernetic Imagination</u> (q.v. under Literary Criticism). References in the list to "Orth" refer to the handout that accompanied this presentation.

4.167 <u>Orwell's Nineteen Eighty-Four: Text, Sources, Criticism</u>. Irving Howe, ed. New York: Harcourt, 1963, 1982.

Includes selections from Y. Zamiatin's <u>We</u>, A. Huxley's <u>Brave New World</u> (cited under Fiction), and less well-known sources for <u>Nineteen Eighty-Four</u>. The "Criticism" section includes Erich Fromm's Afterword to the 1961 NAL edn. of Orwell's novel, two of Howe's critical essays, and the works of a number of other critics and reviewers—plus two items on "The Politics of Totalitarianism," giving the political background for <u>Nineteen Eighty-Four</u>: Richard Lowenthal's essay "Our Peculiar Hell," and from Hannah Arendt's <u>Origins of Totalitarianism</u> the chapter on "Ideology and Terror: A Novel Form of Government."

4.168   Palumbo, Donald.   "William Burroughs' Quartet of Science Fiction Novels as Dystopian Social Satire." Extrapolation 20.4 (Winter 1979): 321-29.

Naked Lunch, Soft Machine, Nova Express, and Ticket that Exploded. Ticket presents contemporary life "as a film that is rerun again and again, trapping the human in amber, negating any possibility of real freedom." This repetition is associated by Burroughs with Hell.

4.169   Parker, Jo Alyson. "Gendering the Robot: Stanislaw Lem's 'The Mask.'" SFS #57, 19.2 (July 1992): 178-91.

Mostly on "a robot who in the first half of the story ["Mask"] wears the form of a beautiful human female and in the second metamorphoses into its essential metallic form—significantly, a form that resembles a praying mantis . . ." (179). Even though he attempts "to gender the robot, Lem, like [J.] Lacan and [M.] Foucault, essentially elides the question of an intrinsically female subject," but still presents a politically useful story (Abstract 191).

4.170   Patrouch, Joe. "Symbolic Settings In Science Fiction: H. G. Wells, Ray Bradbury, and Harlan Ellison," Journal of the Fantastic in the Arts 1.3 (1988): 37-45.

Includes comments on Eloi and Morlocks in Wells's The Time Machine, on Bradbury's Mars as "the more pleasant Earth, the more pleasant society, which technology has destroyed" (41), and on Ellison's "I Have No Mouth . . . " and "A Boy and His Dog," q.v. under Fiction.

4.171   Paul, Terri. "'Sixty Billion Gigabits': Liberation Through Machines in Frederik Pohl's Gateway and Beyond the Blue Event Horizon. TMG [53]-62.

The two novels are optimistic about human/machine relations, at least in the future.

4.172   Pedersen, Ellen M.   "Joseph the Golem—The Limits of Synthetic Humanity." Foundation #40 (Summer 1987): 36-44.

Primarily on the Golem of Rabbi Judah Loew of Prague, celebrated in a legend showing "the most clear-headed human-machine thinking produced after the Three Laws of Robotics—or rather, long before" (39). Golem stories are not quite as important for the history of robots and androids as sometimes thought, but their making problematic the relationship between humans and our machines makes them a central matter for the study of SF (42). See below, R. Plank.

4.173   Perrin, Noel. "Robots: Three Fantasies and One Big Cold Reality" (sic: no comma). Aliens: The Anthropology of Science Fiction. George E. Slusser and Eric S. Rabkin, eds. Carbondale: Southern Illinois UP, 1987.

The fantasies are Arkady and Boris Strugatsky's Noon: 22nd Century, I. Asimov's I, Robot, and A. C. Clarke's The City and the Stars (with reference to E. M. Forster's "The Machine Stops"). The reality is real-world robots coming on-line. See for work and human purpose in worlds with many robots.

4.174   Philip K. Dick: Electric Shepherd (Best of SF Commentary Number 1). Bruce Gillespie, ed. Melbourne, Australia: Norstrilia Press, 1975.

Includes text of Dick's lecture "The Android and the Human," an introd. by Roger Zelazny, and a biblio. of Dick's fiction.

4.175   Philmus, Robert M. "The Cybernetic Paradigms of Stanislaw Lem." Hard Science Fiction. George E. Slusser and Eric S. Rabkin, eds. Carbondale: Southern Illinois UP, 1986.

Cited in "Year's Scholarship": 1986.

4.176   Pierce, Hazel. "'Elementary, My Dear . . . ': Asimov's Science Fiction Mysteries." <u>Isaac</u>
            <u>Asimov</u>. Joseph D. Olander and Martin Harry Greenberg, eds. New York:
            Taplinger, 1977.

> <u>Caves of Steel</u> and <u>Naked Sun</u>; esp. good on <u>Naked Sun</u> (44-9).

4.177   Pitcher, Edward W. R. "That Web of Symbols in Zamyatin's <u>We</u>." <u>Extrapolation</u> 22.3
            (Fall 1981): 252-61.

> Concludes that the essential choice offered in <u>We</u> "is not between the Natural
> World and the One State, the Garden and the City," but between opting—
> wrongly—for "one or the other . . . of the polarized positions in the novel" and
> retaining "the wisdom . . . to live with . . . the ambiguous and the irrational" (260).
> EWRP notes that his conclusions oppose those of most critics, esp. A. Aldridge in
> "Myths of Origin and Destiny" (q.v., this section).

4.178   Plank, Robert. "The Golem and the Robot." <u>Literature and Psychology</u> 15 (Winter
            1965): 12-28.

> Traces robots, cyborgs, and such to the Jewish legend of the golem. See above, E.
> M. Pederson.

4.179   Portelli, Alessandro. "The Three Laws of Robotics: Laws of the Text, Laws of
            Production, Laws of Society." <u>SFS</u> #21, 7.2 (July 1980): 150-56.

> In I. Asimov's robot stories, esp. the earlier ones, robots replace more traditional
> monsters as figurative representations of fears central to middle-class America
> after World War II: automation, ethnics, Blacks.

4.180   Porush, David. "Cybernauts in Cyberspace: William Gibson's <u>Neuromancer</u>." <u>Aliens:</u>
            <u>The Anthropology of Science Fiction</u>. George E. Slusser and Eric S. Rabkin, eds.
            Carbondale: Southern Illinois UP, 1987.

> Sensitive close reading of <u>Neuromancer</u> (a central cyberpunk text), concentrating
> on the AI alien and "his relationship . . . to humans who are themselves busy
> learning to live as cybernauts"—and "the question of the positive feedback loop
> between our technologies and science fiction like Gibson's" (168). See for both
> human robotization and "some lurking transcendence" in <u>Neuromancer</u> (176).

4.181   ---. "Prigogine, Chaos, and Contemporary Science Fiction": Cited under Background.

4.182   ---. <u>The Soft Machine</u>. New York: Methuen, 1985.

> On the "cybernetic fiction" of K. Vonnegut (esp. <u>Player Piano</u> and <u>Sirens of</u>
> <u>Titan</u>), William Burroughs (primarily <u>The Soft Machine</u> and <u>The Ticket that</u>
> <u>Exploded</u>), T. Pynchon, J. Barth (primarily <u>Giles Goat-Boy</u>), Samuel Becket (<u>The</u>
> <u>Lost Ones</u>), J. McElroy (primarily <u>Plus</u>), and Donald Barthelme ("The
> Explanation"); also covers the "positivistic" work of Raymond Roussel (<u>Locus</u>
> <u>Solus</u> [1914] and its "paving beetle" art machine) and—very usefully—the
> philosophical, scientific, and general cultural background for postmodern
> literature. Rev. W. D. Stevens, <u>FR</u> #83 (Sept. 1985): 30. See Fiction for primary
> works where the author's first name is replaced here by an initial.

4.183   Rabinovitz, Rubin. "Mechanism vs. Organism: Anthony Burgess' <u>A Clockwork</u>
            <u>Orange</u>." <u>Modern Fiction Studies</u> 24 (Winter 1978-79): 538-41.

> Does little with mechanism/organism but useful for summarizing and discussing
> the significance of the final chapter of <u>Clockwork Orange</u> in the unshortened
> form of the novel published in the UK (London: Heinemann, 1962), and now
> available in the US. "Alex concludes that . . . each young man undergoes a
> period of existence as a violent, mechanical man; then he matures, gets greater

freedom of choice, and his violence subsides . . . " (539).

4.184   Rabkin, Eric S. Arthur C. Clarke. West Linn, OR: Starmont, 1979. Starmont Reader's
         Guide 1.

         Includes chapters on City and the Stars, Rendezvous with Rama, and 2001.

4.185   ---. "Irrational Expectations; or, How Economics and the Post-Industrial World Failed
         Philip K. Dick." SFS #45, 15.2 (July 1988): 161-72.

         Important essay arguing that even "as rational industrialism mass-produces its
         products, so it forces those working within that system to fragment and rationalize
         their labor—and even their thoughts—into replicable, typically identical units.
         Dick repeatedly dramatized this 'intellectual desolation' [as Karl Marx put it] by
         focusing . . . on beings who were themselves artificially produced, machine
         people he typically called androids" (163).   Collects Dickian quotes on
         mechanized humans and discusses Do Androids Dream . . ., "The Electric Ant,"
         The Man in the High Castle, Palmer Eldritch, "Autofac," A Scanner Darkly, and
         VALIS—see Dick citations under Fiction.

4.186   ---. "Technophobia in the Arts and Humanities." Essays in Arts and Sciences 9
         (1980): 107-21.

         Cited in "Year's Scholarship": 1980, which has ESR suggesting that "fear of
         technology" is old but "has only become crucial in the arts and humanities in the
         modern age," when it is possible to view technology "as a possible threat to human
         life."

4.187   ---, Martin H. Greenberg, and Joseph D. Oldander, eds. No Place Else: Explorations in
         Utopian and Dystopian Fiction. Carbondale: Southern Illinois UP, 1983.

         Includes M. Abrash's "Robert Silverberg's The World Inside," G. Beauchamp's
         "Zamiatin's We," T. J. Remington on S. Butler's Erewhon, and H. P. Segal's
         "Vonnegut's Player Piano: An Ambiguous Dystopia" (cited in this section), and K.
         Davis on The Shape of Things to Come (cited under Drama Criticism).

4.188   Reilly, Robert. "How Machines Become Human: Process and Attribute." TMG [153]-
         65.

         Stresses L. del Rey's "Helen O'Loy," R. Zelazny's "For a Breath I Tarry," and I.
         Asimov's "The Bicentennial Man" (all cited under Fiction). See below, citation for
         J. Sanders's TMG essay.

4.189   Remington, Thomas J. "'The Mirror up to Nature': Reflections of Victorianism in
         Samuel Butler's Erewhon." No Place Else, q.v. this section.

         Butler's correspondence with Charles Darwin and the full text of Erewhon make
         clear "that the true satirical target of 'The Book of the Machines' was Bishop
         Joseph Butler's . . . Analogy of Religion . . . to the Constitution and Course of
         Nature" (37), plus other dogmatic works by overly consistent Victorians; the satire
         was neither a Victorian attack on Darwinism nor early S. F. on the theme of
         machine takeover.

4.190   Retrofitting Blade Runner . . . : Cited by title under Film Criticism.

4.191   Rhodes, Carolyn H. "Frederick Winslow Taylor's System of Scientific Management in
         Zamiatin's We." JGE: The Journal of General Education 28 (Spring 1976): 31-
         42.

         See for Zamiatin's recognition of the dehumanizing effect when all of life is
         "Taylorized." See in this section, G. Beauchamp, "Man as Robot."

4.192   ---.   "Tyranny by Computer: Automated Data Processing and Oppressive Government in Science Fiction." Many Futures, Many Worlds: Theme and Form in Science Fiction. Thomas D. Clareson, ed. Kent, OH: Kent State UP, 1977.

Esp. useful for K. Vonnegut's Player Piano, and K. Crossen's Year of Consent.

4.193   Richards, D. J.   Zamyatin: A Soviet Heretic. Studies in Modern European Literature and Thought. New York: Hillary, 1962.

A brief, popular introduction to Zamiatin. Uses Erich Fromm's ideas on "positive freedom" for comments on We and other works by Zamiatin attacking "social conformity and the mechanisation of life" (58-9, 87). See this section, the entry for A. Shane.

4.194   Rose, Mark.   "Filling the Void: Verne, Wells, and Lem." SFS #24, 8.1 (July 1981): 121-42.

Includes comments on the Martians' association with an indifferent cosmos and as a "metaphorical projection of the capitalistic industrial system of the late 19th century . . . conceived as a social machine" in H. G. Wells's War of the Worlds and on the "closed and safe spaces," necessarily mechanical, in Jules Verne, and in Stanislaw Lem's Solaris (130 and 132; cf. Wolfe on positive views of enclosure).

4.195   ---.   "Machine." Ch. 6 of Alien Encounters: An Anatomy of Science Fiction. Cambridge, MA: Harvard UP, 1981.

Discusses Zamiatin's We and other dystopias, concentrating on "the metaphor of society as a kind of machine that has reduced the individual to the status of a robot." See esp. 166-75.

4.196   Samuelson, David N.   "Limbo: The Great American Dystopia." Extrapolation 19.1 (Dec. 1977): 76-84.

Limbo as an attack on "the utopian desire for perfect order."

4.197   Sanders, Joe.   "Tools/Mirrors: The Humanization of Machines." TMG [167]-76.

Quickly surveys a number of works from Mary Wollstonecraft Shelley's Frankenstein (1818/1831) to the early—if not the first—"sympathetic, 'humanized' robot," Adam Link (175 n. 5), to I. Asimov's robots, to works of the early 1970s. See R. Reilly's TMG essay cited in this section.

4.198   Schuyler, William M., Jr.   "Mechanisms of Morality: Philosophical Implications of Selected (A)Moral Science Fiction Machines." TMG [177]-90.

"Can these machines [robots imagined by I. Asimov and J. Williamson] be moral? Can we have moral relationships with machines?" (177). WMS's initial questions lead to intriguing analysis of a number of machines, from R. Zelazny's Frost in "For a Breath I Tarry" to F. Saberhagen's berserkers.

4.199   Science Fiction Commentary, Special issue on Philip K. Dick: See above, this section, Philip K. Dick: Electric Shepherd.

4.200   Science-Fiction Studies #5 = Vol. 2, Part. 1 (March 1975). #45 = Vol. 15, Part. 2 (July 1988): The special issues of SFS on Philip K. Dick.

The 1975 issue includes R. D. Mullen's biblio. of Dick's "Books, Stories, Essays" through 1974.

4.201   Science-Fiction Studies #39 = Vol. 13, Part 2 (July 1986): The special issue of SFS on Nuclear War and S. F.

4.202   Science-Fiction Studies #55 = Vol. 18, Part 3 (Nov. 1991): The special issue of SFS on
        S. F. and Postmodernism.

        Contains several pieces of interest, including two by J. Baudrillard (with
        responses), S. Bukatman, and D. Porush—q.v., this section.

4.203   Science-Fiction Studies #57 = Vol. 19, Part 2 (July 1992): The second special issue of
        SFS on Stanislaw Lam (plus an important essay on cyberpunk).

        Contains several pieces of interest, including J. A. Parker on Lem's "The Mask"
        and N. Nixon on "Cyberpunk" and gender politics—q.v., this section. See above,
        3.489.

4.204   Segal, Howard P.   "Bellamy and Technology: Reconciling Centralization and
        Decentralization." Looking Backward, 1988-1888: Essays on Edward Belamy.
        Daphne Patai, ed. Amherst: U of Massachusetts P, 1989.

        Looking Backward is less technophilic than it is usually thought to be. Rev.
        Richard Tob Widdicombe in Extrapolation 30.4 (Winter 1989): 417-20, our
        source for this entry. See in this section, entry for W. W. Wagar, "Dreams of
        Reason."

4.205   ---. "Kurt Vonnegut's Player Piano: An Ambiguous Technological Dystopia." No
        Place Else, q.v. this section: 162-81.

        Good general introd. to Kurt Vonnegut's Player Piano (cited under Fiction),
        placing that novel within the "general Western traditions of technological
        utopianism and dystopianism" and also into "the distinctly American parts of both
        traditions" (172).

4.206   ---. "Young West: The Psyche of Technological Utopianism." Extrapolation 19.1
        (Dec. 1977): 50-58.

        Young West as a representative technological utopia embodying a belief common
        in the USA from 1833 to 1933: "the belief in the inevitability of progress and in
        progress as technological progress"; pushed to an extreme this belief yields
        technocracy or at least "the equation of advanced technology . . . with utopia."

4.207   Sexton, James. "Brave New World and the Rationalization of Industry." English
        Studies in Canada 12 (1986): 424-39.

        Cited in "Year's Scholarship": 1987.

4.208   Shane, Alex M. The Life and Works of Evgenij Zamjatin. Berkeley: U of California
        P, 1968.

        Includes an extensive biblio. of works by and about Zamiatin. Main discussion of
        We is in ch. 6, esp. 137-61. See for color imagery in We, the square root of
        minus one, and the relationship between We and Zamiatin's other works, esp.
        "Ostrovitjane" ("The Islanders"), and Zamiatin's essays. See for Zamiatin's own
        comments about We as "a warning against . . . the hypertrophic power of
        machines and the hypertrophic power of the State," and for cautions against
        taking for the norms of We irrationality and cultural primitivism, or taking We as
        ultimately pessimistic. (See in this section, D. J. Richards, and G. Beauchamp,
        "Cultural Primitivism.")

4.209   Shelton, Robert. "Rendezvous with HAL: 2001/2010": Cited under Drama Criticism.

4.210   Shippey, Tom. "A Modern View of Science Fiction." Beyond This Horizon: An
        Anthology of Science Fiction and Science Fact.   Christopher Carrell, ed.
        Sunderland, UK: Ceolith P, 1973.

Cited by David Ketterer (SFS #21, 7.2 [July 1980]: 230) for its discussion of the generation starship of the "Universe" sort. See esp. 8-9. (See under Fiction, R. Heinlein, "Universe.")

4.211   Silbersack, John. "Quantum Leap to Consciousness: Frank Herbert's 'Destination: Void' [sic: quotation marks]." Foundation #31 (July 1984): 68-75.

In Destination: Void, the Voidship Earthling is "a complex machine modeled, as in a computer, after organic structures" (70).

4.212   Simon, Earl. "New Wine in Old Bottles: SF in the German Democratic Republic." Foundation #34 (Autumn 1985): 36-48.

See the sections on Angela and Karlheinz Steinmüller, esp. pages 41-46, for the Steinmüllers' use of cybernetic motifs and their classic SF "method of showing the world (or a part of it) transformed by a single innovation," which is often "a fantastic technology" (42).

4.213   Singh, Kirpal. "Technology in George Orwell's '1984.'" The Stellar Gauge: Essays on Science Fiction Writers. Michael J. Tolley and KS, eds. Carlton, Victoria: Norstrilia, 1980.

In Nineteen Eighty-Four, Orwell showed a world "in which mechanization would render human values irrelevant and unimaginable." Cited in "Year's Scholarship": 1980, which we quote. Rev. John R. Pfeiffer, SF&FBR #10 (Dec. 1982): 8.

4.214   Slusser, George Edgar. The Classic Years of Robert A. Heinlein. San Bernardino, CA: Borgo, 1977. Vol. 11 in The Milford Series: Popular Writers of Today.

Brief survey concentrating upon Heinlein's earlier works. Includes a selected biblio. GES discusses Heinlein's later novels in Robert A. Heinlein: Stranger in His Own Land, 2d edn., vol. 1 in The Milford Series.

4.215   ---. The Delany Intersection: Samuel R. Delany . . . . San Bernardino, CA: Borgo, 1977. Vol. 10 of The Milford Series: Popular Writers of Today. Includes a brief biblio., a full section on The Fall of the Towers, and comments on Nova; few comments on Delany's work after 1970.

4.216   ---. Harlan Ellison: Unrepentant Harlequin. San Bernardino, CA: Borgo, 1977. Vol. 6 of The Milford Series: Popular Writers of Today.

Brief survey of Ellison's major works. Includes a list of Ellison's published books through 1975.

4.217   ---. "Literary MTV." MR47/48: 279-288 (see under Larry McCaffery, this section).

The MTV (Music TeleVision) dream for film—"total autonomy from reality, and from story"—is the cyberpunk dream for "the corpus of SF" (288). Most relevant here for comments on W. Gibson's Neuromancer contrasted to older SF like A. C. Clarke's Childhood's End, plus cyberspace as "a structure of potentiality . . . coterminous with the universe" (284).

4.218   ---, and Eric S. Rabkin, eds. Hard Science Fiction. Carbondale and Edwardsville: Southern Illinois UP, 1986.

Includes essays "on the city, on computers, on information theory in Lem" and a "virtually monograph-length study by [Robert M.] Philmus on Lem's 'cybernetic paradigms'" (Frederic Jameson, "Shifting Contexts of Science-Fiction Theory," rev. of three works, in SFS #42, 14.2 [July 1987]: 245).

4.219 Smuszkiewicz, Antoni. "Props and their Function in Science Fiction." Elizabeth Kwasniewski and Robert M. Philmus, trans. SFS #42, 14.2 (July 1987): 222-29.

A kind of taxonomy of SF, related to the props (in the theatrical and cinematic sense), definitely including "futuristic technological devices" (224).

4.220 Sontag, Susan. "The Imagination of Disaster." 1965/1966. Against Interpretation and Other Essays. New York: Octagon, 1978. "Imagination" also rpt. Science Fiction: The Future. Dick Allen, ed. New York: Harcourt, 1971. Also Science Fiction: A Collection of Critical Essays. Mark Rose, ed. Englewood Cliffs, NJ: Prentice-Hall, 1977.

Includes some excellent comments on the theme of mechanization and "technological man."

4.221 Spraycar, Rudy S. "C. S. Lewis's Mechanical Fiends in That Hideous Strength." TMG [19]-26.

"The target of Lewis's satire is not . . . science or even scientists, but the bureaucracy that would reorder and control" science, scientists, and humanity generally, with the Head of Alcasan and "the hyperrational Pragmatometer" (21) as appropriate symbols or correlates for that bureaucratic mindset.

4.222 Sterling, Bruce. Preface to Mirrorshades: The Cyberpunk Anthology. New York: Arbor, 1986. New York: Ace, 1988.

Important statement by a primary polemicist for cyberpunk. Attempts to identify the central themes of cyberpunk, including cyberpunk's relationship to technology and cyberpunk's use of the motif of the "invasion" of the human body and mind by technology (xiii).

4.223 Stern, Michael. "From Technique to Critique: Knowledge and Human Interests in John Brunner's Stand on Zanzibar, The Jagged Orbit, and The Sheep Look Up." SFS #9, 3.2 (July 1976): 112-30.

See discussion of Shalmaneser (the computer), General Technics, and Georgette Talon Buckfast (120-22). MS sees Shalmaneser as "'environment forming' for everybody on earth," and as a machine that loses its godhead by becoming human.

4.224 Stewart, Alfred D. "Fred Saberhagen: Cybernetic Psychologist." Extrapolation 18.1 (Dec. 1976): 42-51.

Subtitled "A Study of the Berserker Stories"; see for a review of Saberhagen's stories about the berserker fighting machines. (See the ". . . Ultimate Weapon" essay by L. Heldreth in TMG, cited above, this section.)

4.225 Strada, Michael J. "Kaleidoscopic Nuclear Images of the Fifties." JPC 20.3 (Winter 1986): 179-98.

MJS brings the perspective of a political scientist to put the highly negative SF view of fission and fusion bombs onto a 1950s spectrum which included a foreign policy elite with "the image of the bomb as a 'winning weapon'" (180) and nuclear scientists who saw the H-bomb as morally reprehensible but also "technically sweet" (192-93).

4.226 Studies in the Literary Imagination, "Aspects of Utopian Fiction" issue: See this section, under Jack I. Biles, ed.

4.227 Sullivan, Charles Wm. III. "Harlan Ellison and Robert A. Heinlein: The Paradigm Makers." CW [97]-103.

The paradigms of negative and positive machines are AM in Ellison's "I Have No
Mouth, and I Must Scream," and Mike/Michelle in Heinlein's The Moon Is a
Harsh Mistress.

4.228   Sussman, Herbert L.   Victorians and the Machine: The Literary Response to
Technology. Cambridge, MA: Harvard UP, 1968.

Includes a discussion of S. Butler's Erewhon; also includes HLS's "The Machine
and the Future: H. G. Wells" (162-93, cited in David Y. Hughes, "Criticism in
English of H. G. Wells's Science Fiction," q.v. under Reference).   Deals with
important aspects of the use of the machine as a metaphor for the conflict in
Western philosophy between determinism and free will—a conflict aggravated by
the rise of modern science, with its apparent support for determinism (Warrick
43).

4.229   Suvin, Darko. "On Gibson and Cyberpunk SF." Foundation #46 (Autumn 1989): 40-
51.

Deals with W. Gibson's Sprawl stories (see under Fiction, Gibson's Neuromancer)
and with the work of B. Sterling, primarily Islands in the Net (also under Fiction).
To oversimplify DS's conclusion: Sterling bad, Gibson good.

4.230   ---. "P.K. Dick's Opus: Artifice as Refuge and World View (Introductory Reflections)."
SFS #5, 2.1 (March 1975): 8-22.

For those familiar with the work of P. K. Dick, these "Opening Reflections" in the
special Dick issue of SFS provide an excellent survey of the philosophical (social,
political) implications of Dick's opus.   See for androids and totalitarian
organizations and societies.

4.231   Tabbi, Joseph. "Mailer's Psychology of Machines." PMLA 106 (March 1991): 238-
50.

On Norman Mailer's "The Psychology of Machines," in . . . Fire on the Moon,
with some comments on S. Butler's Erewhon and T. Pynchon's Gravity's Rainbow
(all listed under Fiction).   Mailer's psychology of machines "can be seen as an
assertion . . . [of] the persistence of freedom and contingency despite corporate
efforts to dominate and restrain" (341-42, quoting 342).

4.232   Tanner, Tony. "The Uncertain Messenger: A Study of the Novels of Kurt Vonnegut,
Jr. Critical Quarterly 11 (1969): 297-315.

See for the thesis-antithesis, victim-victimizer pattern in Vonnegut's work.

4.233   Thompson, Craig. "Searching for Totality: Antinomy and the 'Absolute' in Bruce
Sterling's Schismatrix." SFS #54, 18.2 (July 1991): 198-209.

Technological progress creates "vessels that create interiors and exteriors" in
which the protagonist is "transported, protected, contained, restrained, and
mediated" (198). The protagonist must reject technology to achieve wholeness.

4.234   Thomsen, Christian W. "Robot Ethics and Robot Parody: Remarks on Isaac Asimov's I,
Robot and Some Criticial Essays and Short Stories by Stanislaw Lem." TMG
[27]-39.

"Lem's parody attacks not only I, Robot but also the majority of Western science
fiction stories, who are not interested at all in trying to discuss serious
futurological and technological questions" (34).

4.235   Tolley, Michael J. "Some Kinds of Life: An Account of Volume Two of The
Collected Stories of Philip K. Dick: Second Variety." ASFR (Australian S. F.

Review) #24 = 2nd series 5.2 (Winter 1990): 6-17.

See for "James P. Crow," "Second Variety," "A Surface Raid," and other Dick stories from 1952-55. ("Second Variety" in MJT's title is the title of vol. 2 of Collected Stories.)

4.236   Toupence, William F. Isaac Asimov. Boston: Twayne, 1991.

Recent study of Asimov's writing until shortly before his death, including the Foundation and Robot series. Rev. Arthur O. Lewis, SFRA Newsletter #192 (Nov. 1991): 52-53, the source for our citation.

4.237   Utter, Glen H. "The Individual in Technological Society: Walker Percy's Lancelot." JPC 16.3 (Winter 1982): 116-27.

On Percy's Lancelot Lamar as an individual attempting "to awaken from a somnambulistic life" in American technological society. The first four and one half pages of GHU's article provide an elegant "sketch of technological society" (120), and the notes provide an excellent biblio. for an introd. to the sociological literature on technology. See for the use in a mainstream work of entrapment in a metaphorical clockwork world—and see GHU's notes for some useful works we have been unable to include in our section on Background.

4.238   Vonarburg, Elisabeth. "Birth and Rebirth in Space." Foundation #51 (Spring 1991): 5-29.

Spaceship as phallus and womb, and the motif of birth in space: esp. male use of technology in the quest for rebirth without women. Men may be mere cogs in machines, but men still belong "to that machine, vicariously partaking in its power"; women, however, don't belong to the machine, so space travel and birth in space are used by women authors differently from men. Misses 2001 but EV handles D. Sernine's "The Dreaming Metal," A. Coppel's "Mother," S. Verreault's "Eon," F. Pelletier's "The Migrant," R. Abernathy's "Axolotl"—all listed under Fiction—plus James Triptree, Jr. (Alice Sheldon), "A Momentary Taste of Being" and Ursula K. Le Guin's "Nine Lives," with brief discussion of Marion Zimmer Bradley's Darkover Landfall and Joanna Russ's We Who Are About To.

4.239   The Vonnegut Statement. Jerome Klinkowitz and John Somer, eds. New York: Delacorte Press/Seymour Lawrence, 1973. New York: Dell, Delta, [1973].

Anthology of essays on Vonnegut's life and work; esp. relevant: the essays on "The Literary Art" by T. Hildebrand, K. and C. Wood, and J. Mellard (q.v., this section). Includes an index and analytical biblio. of works by and about Vonnegut, through 1972.

4.240   Vorda, Allan. "The Forging of Science Fiction: An Interview with Greg Bear." Extrapolation 31.3 (Fall 1990): [197]-215.

See for Bear's comments on the Thought Universe in his Blood Music (204-5) and "the machine intelligence that is already dissolving the planet" in The Forge of God (207). See Fiction for Bear's novels.

4.241   Wagar, W. Warren. "Dreams of Reason: Belamy, Wells, and the Positive Utopia," Looking Backward, 1988-1888: Essays on Edward Belamy. Daphne Patai, ed. Amherst: U of Massachusetts P, 1989.

Rev. Richard Tob Widdicombe in Extrapolation 30.4 (Winter 1989): 417-20, who finds WWW's thesis to be "that both Wells and Bellamy are scientocrats rather than utopians—and profoundly influential ones to boot, thinkers whose vision constitutes 'the dominant ideology of the governing classes of most twentieth-century nations,'" a position WWW has often argued. See this section, entry for H. P. Segal, "Bellamy and Technology."

4.242   ---.   "The Steel-Gray Saviour: Technocracy as Utopia and Ideology."   <u>Alternative</u> <u>Futures</u> 2.2 (Spring 1979): 38-54.

Technocracy as a living ideology—indeed, the controlling ideology in the 20th c.—and as a motif in literature and film.

4.243   Walsh, Chad.   <u>From</u> <u>Utopia</u> <u>to</u> <u>Nightmare</u>.   New York: Harper, 1962.   Westport, CT: Greenwood, 1962.   London: Geoffrey Bles, 1962 (Sargent).

A concise survey of the utopian vision from the Hebrew prophets and Plato's <u>Republic</u> through B. F. Skinner's <u>Walden</u> <u>Two</u> and A. Huxley's <u>Island</u>—and of the dystopian vision from Dante's Hell and Feodor Dostoevsky's Grand Inquisitor (in <u>The</u> <u>Brothers</u> <u>Karamazov</u>) through the major dystopias of the 20th c.   Handles mechanization passim, in its context in literary history.

4.244   Warrick, Patricia S.   "The Contrapuntal Design of Artificial Evolution in Asimov's 'The Bicentennial Man.'"   <u>Extrapolation</u> 22.3 (Fall 1981): 231-41.

See for clarification of "AI" in terms of computers, robots, androids, and cyborgs (233), and for the incorporation in "Bicentennial Man" of all of Asimov's "previous ideas about machine intelligence as the story moves on to explore new territory: the ethical and philosophical implications for man in creating high[-] level intelligence" (235).

4.245   ---.   The <u>Cybernetic</u> <u>Imagination</u> in <u>Science</u> <u>Fiction</u>.   Cambridge, MA: MIT P, 1980.

A study of some 225 works of fiction from 1930 to 1977.   Includes a very useful biblio. of nonfiction works.   Rpts. with some variations PSW, "Images of the Man-Machine Intelligence Relationship," q.v. below; "A Science Fiction Aesthetic," <u>Pacific</u> <u>Quarterly</u> 4.3 (July 1979); and two essays on P. K. Dick.   Helpfully brings together PSW's work on I. Asimov and Dick, adding some comments on S. Lem. For <u>TCI</u>'s limitations, see rev. by Dagmar Barnouw, <u>SFS</u> #24, 8.2 (July 1981): 215-17.

4.246   ---.   "Ethical Evolving Artificial Intelligence: Asimov's Robots and Computers."   <u>Isaac</u> <u>Asimov</u>.   Joseph D. Olander and Martin Harry Greenberg, eds.   New York: Taplinger, 1977.

Included in Warrick's <u>Cybernetic</u> <u>Imagination</u> (q.v. above; esp. ch. 3).   Surveys Asimov's robot and computer stories from "Robbie" (1940) through "The Bicentennial Man" (1976).

4.247   ---.   "Images of the Man-Machine Intelligence Relationship in Science Fiction."   <u>Many</u> <u>Futures,</u> <u>Many</u> <u>Worlds</u>.   Thomas D. Clareson, ed.   Kent, OH: Kent State UP, 1977.

Included in PSW, <u>Cybernetic</u> <u>Imagination</u> (esp. chs. 2, 6, 7).   Briefly surveys a large number of works.   Esp. useful in differentiating between the presentation of AI in (dystopian) extrapolative works, and in speculative works (the "closed-" and "open-system" models in <u>Cybernetic</u> <u>Imagination</u>).

4.248   ---.   "The Labyrinthian Process of the Artificial: [Philip K.] Dick's Robots and Electronic Constructs."   <u>Extrapolation</u> 20.2 (Summer 1979): 133-53.   Also in <u>Selected</u> <u>Proceedings</u> <u>of</u> <u>the</u> <u>1978</u> <u>Science</u> <u>Fiction</u> <u>Research</u> <u>Association</u> <u>Conference</u>.   Thomas J. Remington, ed.   Cedar Falls, IA: U. of Northern Iowa, 1979: 122-32.

Included in Warrick's <u>Cybernetic</u> <u>Imagination</u> (esp. ch. 8).   A complete survey of Dick's work on robots from "The Defenders," "The Great C," "Second Variety," and "The Preserving Machine" (1953) through <u>We</u> <u>Can</u> <u>Build</u> <u>You</u> (1972).

4.249   Watson, Ian.   "A Rhetoric of Recognition: The Science Fiction of Michael Bishop."

Foundation #19 (June 1980): 5-14.

Surveys Bishop's SF through 1980, providing plot summaries and some provocative comments on Bishop's use of motifs important for the study of the human/machine interface. See esp. IW on "the domed secular infernos of the North American Urban Federation" (10-12).

4.250   Webb, Janeen. "Conversations with Conspirators." ASFR (Australian Science Fiction Review) #14 = 3.3 (May 1988): 7-10.

Collection of brief interviews with writers at a World S. F. convention, including comments by Tanith Lee on the robot character of The Silver Metal Lover as "the Perfect Lover." Esp. interesting: Lee on the possibilities of souls in robots (9).

4.251   West, Anthony. "H. G. Wells." Coll. Principles and Persuasions. New York: Harcourt, 1957. Rpt. H. G. Wells: A Collection of Critical Essays. Bernard Bergonzi, ed. Englewood Cliffs, NJ: Prentice-Hall, 1976.

Usefully comments on Wells's War of the Worlds, First Men in the Moon, and When the Sleeper Wakes, stressing the dystopian aspects of these works.

4.252   Whalen, Terence. "The Future of a Commodity: Notes Toward a Critique of Cyberpunk and the Information Age." SFS #56, 19.1 (March 1992): 75-88.

Marxist critique by an author who knows Marx and recent work on "post-industrial" society; see for W. Gibson's "New Rose Hotel," "Johnny Mnemonic," and (preeminently) Neuromancer; see also for J. Brunner's Shockwave Rider and G. Bear's Blood Music (all the mentioned novels are listed under Fiction).

4.253   White, Michael D. "Ellison's Harlequin: Irrational Moral Action in Static Time." SFS #12, 4 (July 1977): 161-65.

Marxist critique of "Repent, Harlequin . . . ," recognizing the stasis of the "ticktock" society and H. Ellison's protests against elitist bureaucracy.

4.254   Wolfe, Gary K. "The Artifact as Icon in Science Fiction." Journal of the Fantastic in the Arts 1.1 (1988): 51-69.

Includes brief discussions of Larry Niven's Ringworld (1970) and Ringworld Engineers (1980), Gregory Benford's Against Infinity (1983), and M. Crichton's Sphere—which GKW sees as an instructively derivative work (Sphere listed under Fiction). Note the alien ship in A. C. Clarke's Rendezvous with Rama (q.v. under Fiction) growing "from a tantalizing mystery into an adventure-filled landscape and finally into a monument to the indifference of the universe" (65-66).

4.255   ---. "Instrumentalities of the Body: The Mechanization of Human Form in Science Fiction." TMG [211]-224.

Applies to SF the idea of cultures that are "autoplastic" and try to manipulate "their environment by means of symbolic rituals involving the human body itself," or "alloplastic" and "alter or re-create the environment to make it more hospitable to the body" ([211]). Concentrates on C. Smith's "Scanners Live in Vain," B. Wolfe's Limbo, D. R. Bunch's Moderan stories, and V. N. McIntyre's "Aztecs" (all listed under Fiction).

4.256   ---. The Known and the Unknown: The Iconography of Science Fiction. Kent, OH: Kent State UP, 1979.

Handles spacecraft, robots, and other machines important in S. F. For mechanized environments, see Part 2: "Images of Environment," esp. "The Technological City," in ch. 4. The wide scope of this book is indicated by the numerous times we refer to it.

4.257   Wolk, Anthony. "The Sunstruck Forest: A Guide to the Short Fiction of Philip K. Dick." Foundation #18 (Jan. 1980): 19-34.

A thematic approach to Dick's short fiction, dealing with several works of interest for the study of the human/machine interface.

4.258   Wood, Karen, and Charles Wood. "The Vonnegut Effect." Ch. 10 of The Vonnegut Statement. (q.v. this section).

On Vonnegut as a writer of S. F. (of sorts), writing both S. F. and a "literature of experience" exploring the human condition in a society dominated by technology: ours. Includes excellent comments on Player Piano and other works by Vonnegut through Slaughterhouse-Five.

4.259   Wymer, Thomas L. "Machines and the Meaning of Human in the Novels of Kurt Vonnegut, Jr." TMG [42]-52.

Extension of TLW's argument in "The Swiftian Satire of Kurt Vonnegut, Jr.", q.v. below. An important essay demonstrating Vonnegut's consistent "commitment to what Vonnegut called in Player Piano" (his first novel) "doing 'a good job of being human beings'" (TMG 50).

4.260   ---. "The Swiftian Satire of Kurt Vonnegut, Jr." Voices for the Future: Essays on Major Science Fiction Writers. Vol. 1. Thomas D. Clareson, ed. Bowling Green, OH: BGU PopP, 1976.

Vonnegut satirizes Billy Pilgrim's acceptance of the Tralfamadorian view of humans as machines without free will, trapped in a determined, mechanistic universe (an argument that TLW extends in his essay on Vonnegut in TMG, q.v. above).

4.261   Yoke, Carl B. Roger Zelazny. West Linn, OR: Starmont, 1979. Starmont Reader's Guide 2.

Includes discussions of "Home Is the Hangman" and "The Engine at Heartspring's Center," plus other relevant works, and selectively annotated primary and secondary biblios.

4.262   ---. "What a Piece of Work Is a Man: Mechanical Gods in the Fiction of Roger Zelazny." TMG [63]-74.

Deals primarily with the Bork in "The Engine at Heartspring's Center," John Auden in "The Man Who Loved the Faioli," Jarry Dark in "The Keys to December," the "gods" in Lord of Light, Frost in "For a Breath I Tarry," the Hangman in "Home Is the Hangman" (see Zelazny entries under Fiction).

4.263   Zanger, Jules. "Goblins, Morlocks, and Weasels: Classic Fantasy and the Industrial Revolution." Children's Literature in Education 8 (Winter 1977): 154-62.

Applies to Wells's Time Machine and other works the premise that "late-Victorian and Edwardian fantasy was a struggle against the changes of the Industrial Revolution" ("Year's Scholarship": 1977, q.v. under Reference).

4.264   Zins, Daniel L. "Rescuing Science from Technocracy: Cat's Cradle and the Play of Apocalypse." SFS #39 = 13.2 (July 1986): 170-81.

See for background on the perverse play of real-world scientists developing nuclear weapons.

Stage, Screen, and Television Drama

5.001   976-EVIL. Robert Englund, dir. USA: CineTel Films, 1989.

Schlock horror movie. An apparently unused, jerry-built machine designed to
replace human call-takers on a "900-" service is taken over by Satanic EVIL. Cf.
Stephen King's Carrie for the "revenge of the nerd" motif (male in 976-EVIL),
and his Christine (etc.), plus Killdozer—for demonic possession of more strictly
mechanical everyday mechanisms (Christine and Killdozer cited below). Cf. and
contrast the main character's newly grown demonic claws with Molly Million's
retractable razor-nails in W. Gibson's Neuromancer stories.

5.002   "1984." Apple Corporation commercial for Macintosh computer, run nationally once:
Super Bowl Sunday, 22 Jan. 1984. 60 seconds. Ridley Scott, dir. and prod.

Little Macintosh computer against a 1984ish world, that some viewers might
associate with IBM, Inc. See under Drama Criticism, L. M. Scott, "'For the Rest of
Us': A Reader-Oriented Interpretation of Apple's '1984' Commercial," and J.
Bergstrom, "Androids and Androgeny," on Ridley Scott's Blade Runner.

5.003   1984. Michael Anderson, dir. UK: Holiday Films (prod.) / Columbia, 1955, 1956
(US release). Based on the novel by G. Orwell, q.v.

Recreates the totalitarian society of the novel. Esp. powerful in evoking the
constant surveillance by telescreens in the Ministry of Love. (See 1984 entries in
S. F. Ency. and Walt Lee, Reference Guide, for different endings of prints
released in UK and USA: UK version differs greatly from end of the novel. See
below for the remake of 1984.)

5.004   1984. Michael Radford, dir. UK: Virgin Cinema Films (prod.) / Atlantic (US
theatrical dist.) / MGM (nontheatrical dist.), 1984 / 1985 (US release). John Hurt
and Richard Burton, stars.

Except for the ambiguity of Smith's final declaration of love—which, in the film,
could refer to Julia—a faithful adaptation of G. Orwell's novel (q.v. under
Fiction), catching and even exaggerating the grubbiness and primitiveness of the
world of 1984: the technology in the Ministry of Love is not advanced, with a
helicopter and the telescreens the most advanced technology in the film.

5.005   2001: A Space Odyssey.   Stanley Kubrick, dir.   UK/USA: Stanley Kubrick
Productions/MGM, 1968. Kubrick and Arthur C. Clarke, script.

See for helpful machines, encompassing machines, the behavior of men and
machines merging—and for HAL 9000. See above, under Fiction, Clarke, 2001.
See under Drama Criticism, the citations for J. Agel, C. Geduld, and M. Rose.
Note date of film; Erlich speculates that one of the reasons 1968 was When It
Changed was that 2001 was the culmination and initial deconstruction (reductio
ad finem) of a basic masculinist myth of SF.

5.006   2010. Peter Hyams, dir. and prod., script, photography. USA: MGM, 1984. Based
on the novel by Arthur C. Clarke.

Sequel to 2001 (cited above), repeating Kubrick's images of people inside of
machines, but without the thematic significance. Discussed passim by V.
Sobchack in Screening Space Chapter 4. Rev. Newsweek 10 Dec. 1984. Also,
Kyle Counts and Charlotte Wolton, "2010: Odyssey Two," Cinefantastique 15
(Jan. 1984): 8-11; James Burns, "2010: A New Odyssey," Space Voyager #14
(1985): 36-39. See under Drama Criticism the entry for R. Shelton.

5.007   À nous la liberté ("Liberty for Us!"): See below, this section, Daybreak.

5.008   The Abominable Dr. Phibes. Robert Fuest, dir. USA: AIP, 1971.

Inventor of automata plans revenge in "a mechanical underground lair"; note also
Phibes's electronic communication (quoting Ed Naha, Science Fictionary, listed
under Reference).

5.009   The Abyss. James Cameron, dir. USA: Twentieth Century Fox, 1989. Gale Anne
Hurd, prod.

An underwater Close Encounters of the Third Kind (q.v., this section). See for a
human villain called a "robot," watery alien technology, and a mise en scène that
includes nifty submersibles, electronic surveillance, very-deep full-body diving
suits, and other multiple containments to protect people from cold and extreme
deep-water pressure. See below in this section, Deepstar Six and Leviathan.

5.010   The Adding Machine. Jerome Epstein, dir., prod., script. UK/USA: Associated
Longdon (sic) / Universal, 1969. From the play by Elmer Rice (1923). Cast
includes Milo O'Shea and Phyllis Diller.

Comedy fantasy. An accountant about to lose his job to a machine murders his
boss and faces a future as a button-pushing nobody (Naha, Science Fictionary).

5.011   The Adventures of Buckaroo Banzai: Across the 8th Dimension. W. D. Richter, dir.
USA: 20th Century-Fox (dist.), 1985. Cast includes Peter Weller, John Lithgow,
Ellen Barkin, Jeff Goldblum.

SciFi flick parody that includes the superimposition of the mechanical (and
electronic) upon the human, including a US President in a high-tech hospital
"bed" and the electrical torture of Buckaroo. Discussed by Vivian Sobchack in
Screening Space, Chapter 4.

5.012   Akira. Katushiro Otomo, dir. Japan: Akira Committee, 1989. Katushiro Otomo,
script, based on his graphic novel.

Animated. See for a mise en scène similar to Blade Runner and Brazil, plus the
reforming of "an arm out of circuitry" and the transformation of "teddy bears
and toy cars" into "ravenous biomechanical creatures" (quoting Daniel Schweiger,
"Disturbing apocalyptic future fantasy like cyberpunk Disney," Cinefantastique
20.4 [March 1990]: 46).

5.013   Alexander Nevsky. Sergei Eisenstein, dir. (in collaboration with D. I. Vasiliev).
USSR: Mosfilm, 1938. Sergei Prokofiev, music.

> Historical drama. Combined with Prokofiev's score, Eisenstein's presentation of
> the Teutonic Knights riding forth in geometrical formation strongly suggests
> mechanized (Panzer) units.

5.014   Alien. Ridley Scott, dir. USA: 20th Century-Fox, 1979. Dan O'Bannon, script. Dan
O'Bannon and Ronald Shusett, story. H. R. Giger, design.

> The insectoid alien is aided by a robot passing for a human Science Officer and
> by the special program put into Mother, the ship's computer, by anonymous
> agents of the Company owning the spaceship. Note the increasingly threatening
> containment within the computerized (but cyberpunk Gothic) Nostromo herself.
> Novelized by A. D. Foster; see under Fiction. Discussed by V. Sobchack in
> Screening Space (see Sobchack's Index for Chapter 4.) See below, Aliens and
> Space Flight.

5.015   Aliens. James Cameron, dir., screenplay. USA: Brandywine (prod.) / Twentieth
Century Fox [sic: no hyphen] (dist.), 1986. Gale Anne Hurd, prod. James
Cameron et al., story. Sigourney Weaver, star.

> Sequel to Alien. Important film for several relevant motifs: threatening and
> protective containment, a highly positive superimposition of the mechanical upon
> the human, merging of the mechanical and the insectoid/organic in the Aliens
> and their on-planet habitat, a good and heroic android in the structural position
> of the evil android in Alien, and a yuppie bureaucrat from "the Company" as
> villain. Warner Book novelization by A. D. Foster (see under Fiction). Aliens 3
> (1992) is not relevant, but cf. J. Cameron and G. A. Hurd's Terminator (cited
> below).

5.016   Alphaville (vt "Tarzan vs. IBM" favored by dir.). Jean-Luc Godard, dir. France:
Pathécontemporary / Chaumiane-Film, 1965.

> Computer-domination story that S. F. Ency. describes as "an ambiguous allegory
> of contemporary technology-dominated society"; it may be more important for
> an early combination of film noir with SF. See below, Blade Runner, and under
> Drama Criticism, R. Roud's article on Alphaville.

5.017   Android. Aaron Lipstadt, dir. USA: Sho Films (prod.) / Island Alive & New Cinema
(dist.), 1983 (release). James Reigle and Don Opper, script. Rupert Harvey, exec.
prod., in association with Barry Opper. Klaus Kinski and Don Opper, stars.

> The coming of age of the late-adolescent male, Max 404. Varies the pattern of
> the standard teen-exploitation movie: (1) the main setting is a highly mechanized,
> nearly deserted space station; (2) Max and the other two characters stationed at
> the station are humanoid robots; (3) Android consciously revises F. Lang's
> Metropolis (q.v. below) to yield a less sentimental ending—with Max and a
> female android "killing" the resident and ruling mad (android) scientist and
> escaping to Earth to join other rebellious androids. Discussed by V. Sobchack in
> Screening Space (see Sobchack's Index for Chapter 4).

5.018   The Andromeda Strain. Robert Wise, dir. USA: Universal, 1971. Based on the novel
by Michael Crichton (q.v. under Fiction).

> Closely follows the novel, emphasizing the brightness and sterility of the
> underground labs. Discussed by V. Sobchack in The Limits of Infinity, passim
> (see Sobchack's Index for page citations). See in TMG the essay by P. S.
> Alterman, cited above under Literary Criticism.

5.019   Astro-Boy. Syndicated weekly TV series. Japan, 1963. Animated.

Scientist whose son has died creates robotic replacement, Astro Boy (Naha, Science Fictionary).

5.020   Attack of the Robots. Jesus (Jess) Franco, dir. France/Spain: Aliance/Hesperia, 1962.

Mad scientist to change men into killer robots.

5.021   The Automatic House. USA: United Film Service, 1915. Silent. One reel.

Cited by Naha, Science Fictionary: shows a house "chockful of automatic gadgets," arguably for an early mechanized environment in film.

5.022   The Automatic Laundry. Lubin, 1908. Silent. 361 feet.

Cited by Naha, Science Fictionary: shows an automated laundry machine over two decades before S. Eisenstein's cream separator in Old and New, q.v. below, this section.

5.023   The Automatic Monkey. France: Gaumont, 1909. Silent. 324 feet.

Said by Naha, Science Fictionary, to feature a robot monkey.

5.024   The Automatic Motorist. UK: Kineto, 1911. Silent. 610 feet.

Said by Naha, Science Fictionary, to involve a robot driving a car into space.

5.025   The Automatic Servant. USA: Urban-Eclipse, 1908. Silent. 367 feet.

Said by Naha, Science Fictionary, to involve a robot servant, who is broken by a human servant, who then must fill in. Cf. and contrast Mechanical Mary Anne (1910) and The Motor Valet (1906), cited below.

5.026   The Avengers. ITC TV, UK, 1961-68.

Mid-decade shows often featured bizarre threats to England, including robots (S. F. Ency. and our memories).

5.027   Back to the Future. Robert Zemeckis, dir. Steven Spielberg et al., exec. prod. USA: Amblin (prod.) / Universal (dist.), 1985. Back to the Future Part III (1990). Michael J. Fox, Christopher Lloyd, stars.

The time machine in the BTF series is a highly souped up De Lorean sports car that undergoes modifications in different times. At the end of Part 3, the De Lorean is destroyed, but Christopher Lloyd's time-travelling scientist shows up in a hyper-souped-up locomotive from 1885 and our future. Part 1 is discussed by V. Sobchack in Screening Space (see Sobchack's Index for Chapter 4).

5.028   Ballet méchanique, (vt adds the article, Le; "The Mechanical Ballet"). Fernand Léger, creator, dir., prod. (in collaboration with Dudley Murphy). France: Léger, 1926. Man Ray and Dudley Murphy, cinematography. George Antheil, music.

Non-narrative avant-garde film by Léger, the great cubist celebrator of the Machine Age (cited by name under Graphics). Pieces of machinery are among the objects animated into a "ballet." See under Graphics, essay by J. Freeman; see under Music, entry for G. Antheil.

5.029   Barbarella. Roger Vadim, dir. USA: De Laurentiis (prod.) / Marianne/Paramount (dist.), 1967.

See for "pleasure machine." Sumarized and briefly discussed in S. F. Ency. See under Drama Criticism the TMG essay by D. Palumbo.

5.030   Batman. Tim Burton, dir. USA: Warner, 1989. Script based upon characters created by Bob Kane and appearing in DC Comics. Anton Furst, production designer.

Rationalizing the postmodern setting, one might say that Batman takes place in an alternative American society in which the "evolution" of technology, style, and fashion took place at rates different from those of our world. The *mise en scène* is a hodgepodge that calls attention to itself, putting great visual stress upon buildings, gadgets, and other things only incidental to the plot. Note especially Batman's main protective devices: body armor, the Batmobile, the high-tech Batcave. See below, Batman Returns.

5.031   Batman Returns. Tim Burton, dir. USA: Warner, 1992.

Sequel to Batman (1989), q.v. Note esp. cyberpunk attack penguins (our characterization). If the superimposition of the mechanical upon the human is central for the human/machine interface at the beginning of the modern(ist) era, the superimposition of the cybernetic upon the Sphenisciformes probably marks the end of something. See under Background, entry for H. Bergson. See below, Day of the Dolphin.

5.032   Batteries Not Included. Matthew Robbins, dir. USA: Amblin / Universal: 1987. Steven Spielberg et al., exec. prod. Industrial Light & Magic, SpFx. Hume Cronyn and Jessica Tandy, stars. Novel or novellization advertised from Berkley Books.

Note small, somewhat bug-like machines that finally turn up in an impressive but unthreatening swarm. The most sentimentalized of the infant machines is both a mechanical ladybug and a visual pun on the Volkswagen "Bug"; the adult machines are crab-like flying saucers occupying the structural position of helpful elves and animals in folklore. Cf. and contrast the threatening small machines in Runaway, the flying saucer in Liquid Sky (both cited under Drama), and S. Lem's "synsects" in "Upside-Down Evolution" and Invincible (cited under Fiction).

5.033   Battle Beyond the Stars. Jimmy T. Murakami, dir. USA: New World Pictures and Orion, 1980. John Sayles, script. Roger Corman, exec. prod.

Science-fictional updating of Akira Kurosawa's The Seven Samurai (1954), with some influence from John Sturges' The Magnificent Seven (1960). See for Nel, the motherly computer who runs the spaceship the hero uses, and for the film's ambivalent presentation of technology in general and mechanized environments in particular (good when aiding in the defense of the good people, bad when aiding the villains).

5.034   Battlestar Galactica (opening episode: 17 Sept. 1978). Richard A. Colla, dir. Glen A. Larson, script and exec. prod. USA: Universal, 1978.

Note alliance between the robotic Cylons and the insectoid Ovions. Fictionalized by G. A. Larson and Robert Thurston, Battlestar Galactica (New York: Berkley, 1978). L. Roth discusses the "clearcut conflict between man and machine" in the series in his essay on "Ambiguity of Visual Design..." (q.v. under Drama Criticism).

5.035   Beneath the Planet of the Apes. Ted Post, dir. USA: 20th Century Fox, 1970.

Note the literal worship of a mechanical god: an A-bomb. Discussed by V. Sobchack in The Limits of Infinity.

5.036 Beyond Westworld. Weekly series, CBS-TV, 1980.

Attempt to take some elements of Westworld (q.v. below) to TV. For description see Ed Naha, Science Fictionary.

5.037 Bill and Ted. Fox TV series, Summer 1992- . Lorimar et al. Clifton Campbell, exec. prod.

Based on the the movies, primarily Bill and Ted's Excellent Adventure (see below).

5.038 Bill & Ted's Bogus Journey. Pete Hewitt, dir. USA: Orion, 1991.

Sequel to Bill and Ted's Excellent Adventure, q.v. Note evil robot versions of Bill and Ted, good robot versions of Bill and Ted, and a Hell in which surreal scenes are set inside a large, rusting, rather Victorian mechanism. (See under Literary Criticism the CW essay by M. Abrash on Dante's Hell.)

5.039 Bill and Ted's Excellent Adventure. Stephen Herek, dir. USA: Orion, 1989.

Festive comedy. The time-travel of two "valley boys" from southern California, who get unusual help completing a history class project. The time-machine in BTEA is an American-style phone booth rather smaller inside than outside, which allows phone-booth stuffing of famous historical personages as the machine hurtles down the network of time (cf. and contrast Dr. Who's TARDIS). The mechanism the film attacks is the comic rigidity of Bill's father; see under Background, entry for H. Bergson. Rev. Thomas Doherty, Cinefantastique 20.1 & 2 (Nov. 1989): 106 f.

5.040 "Biomechanics": See below, O. G. Brockett.

5.041 The Bionic Woman. Harve Bennett Productions and Universal for ABC; 1976-ca. 1978, then syndication.

Spin-off from The Six Million Dollar Man, q.v., this section. Premise identical to that of parent show except for gender of the cyborg. See S. F. Ency. entries for both series and M. Caidin's Cyborg, cited under fiction.

5.042 The Birth of a Robot. Humphrey Jennings, Len Lye, dirs. UK: Shell Oil, 1934. 7 min.

According to Naha, Science Fictionary, the production of "an automaton" is shown in color, stop-motion animation.

5.043 The Black Hole. Gary Nelson, dir. USA: Disney, 1979.

See for robots (both friendly and threatening) and for the "cyborgization" (our word) of human beings.

5.044 Blade Runner. Ridley Scott, dir. USA: Warner (et al.), 1982. 114 or 118 min. film; videocassette 123 min. Based on P. K. Dick's Do Androids Dream of Electric Sheep?

A 1940s film noir detective thriller set in 2019, in a Los Angeles extrapolated (ethically) from that of the 40s films and Roman Polanski's Chinatown (1974). Significant for placing a Frankenstein theme in a funky, punkish (or cyberpunk), corporation-dominated world, and for its alternative investigation of Dick's questions on the differences and similarities between humans and androids (called here, "replicants"). See V. Sobchack, Screening Space, Chapter 4 (passim), and Retrofitting Blade Runner, cited under Drama Criticism.

5.045 Blade Runner—The Director's Cut. Ridley Scott, dir. USA: Warner (et al.), (1982) / 1991 ([c]), 1992 (release). 117 min.

A separately copyrighted version of the film, deleting the voice-over narration and the final escape sequence ending the 1982 version, and adding "the expunged unicorn scene which suggests that Deckard is a replicant" (quoting Dennis K. Fischer, Cinefantastique 22.5 [April 1992]: 60). The unicorn scene is very brief, and the suggestion of Deckard's being a replicant is very subtle.

5.046 Blomdahl, Karl-Birger, composer. Aniara. Opera, 1959.

Libretto based on H. Martinson's Aniara, q.v. under Fiction.

5.047 A Boy and His Dog. L. Q. Jones, dir. USA: LQJaf, 1975. Based on the novella by H. Ellison (q.v. under Fiction).

Features a mechanized Underworld. Discussed by J. Crow and R. Erlich, and by L. G. Heldreth in the articles cited for them under Drama Criticism.

5.048 Brainstorm. Douglas Trumbull, dir. USA: MGM/UA, 1983.

Invention of a device that can record and play back mental and emotional activity, leading to inevitable scenes of machine-mediated sex and death.

5.049 Brave New World. Burt Brinckerhoff, dir. USA: Universal, 1980. Made for TV; first shown, NBC, 7 March 1980.

Closely follows A. Huxley novel (q.v. under Fiction), but with less emphasis on "bottles" and conditioning. Originally planned as a miniseries, so the version shown on 7 March 1980 may lack important footage. For a description of the version made for two 120-min. episodes, see film title in Naha, Science Fictionary.

5.050 Brazil. Terry Gilliam, dir. UK: Universal (US dist.), 1985 (copyright), 1986 (US release). 131 minutes.

For the complex history of this film, consult J. Mathews, The Battle of Brazil (q.v. under Drama Criticism). Very-near future dystopia, set in a funky world (as opposed to clean, shiny, and aseptic). Important for the imposition of the mechanical and electronic upon the human and the use of that image as a kind of metaphor for bureaucratization (opposing Romance images of the "Garden," flight, and chivalric warfare).

5.051 Broadcast News. James L. Brooks, dir. USA: 20th Century Fox, 1987 [sic on no hyphen in 20th-C. Fox].

Mainstream film with one sequence important for the theme of mechanization: William Hurt as a TV anchorman literally wired for sound, being fed lines by Holly Hunter as the producer of the newscast.

5.052 Brockett, Oscar G. "The Theatre in Europe and America Between the Wars." Ch. 17 of History of the Theatre. 3rd edn. Boston: Allyn, 1977.

See the cited chapter of this standard reference for its discussion of biomechanics and constructivism. Biomechanics is the theory of Vsevelod Meyerhold (a.k.a. Karl Theodore Kasimir Meyerhold), who attempted to find an acting style "appropriate to the machine age" (524) and to actors as machines. Constructivism is a term appropriated from the visual arts, esp. sculpture; in Meyerhold's approach, it refers to the creation of a space that will be "'a machine for acting'" (Brockett 525; see illus. on 524: set from Meyerhold's production of The Magnificent Cuckold). For the influence on Meyerhold of Frederick W.

Taylor, see Brockett and Robert R. Findlay, Century of Innovation: A History of European and American Theatre and Drama Since 1870 (1973).

5.053   Buck Rogers. Serial film. 12 episodes. USA: Filmcraft (tape) / Universal (S. F. Ency.), 1939. Ford Beebe and Saul A. Goodkind, dir. Larry (Buster) Crabbe, star. "Based on the newspaper feature entitled 'Buck Rogers' . . . ." Available from United American Video, 1989, 2 cassettes (episodes 1-6 and 7-12).

See for teleporters, an apparently underground "Hidden City," political rule (of sorts) by a scientist vs. a criminal regime under "the Leader," and the "ray filament" in "the amnesia helmet" that makes one into "a human robot"—a human automaton obedient to orders.

5.054   Buck Rogers in the 25th Century. Daniel Haller, dir. Glen A. Larson, script, exec. prod. USA: Universal, 1979.

Robot and "self-programming computers" (Willis, vol. II).

5.055   Cameron, James, and William Wisher. Terminator 2: Judgment Day: The Book of the Film: An Illustrated Screenplay. Notes by Van Ling. New York: Applause Books, 1991.

Includes many stills plus scenes not shot for the film. Rev. Michael Klossner, SFRA Review No. 195 (March 1992): 18-19, who also cites a Making of Terminator 2 book and novelizations for Terminator 1 and Terminator 2 (we depend upon Klossner for our citation).

5.056   Čapek, Karel. R. U. R. 1921 (Czech). First English edn., Oxford UP, 1923. Frequently rpt., including in Of Men and Machines, q.v. under Anthologies. Also, P. Selver, trans. Adapted for English stage by Nigel Playfair. Harry Shefter, ed. New York: Washington Square-Pocket Books, 1973 ("enriched" edn.). R.U.R. (Rossum's Universal Robots). Claudia Novack-Jones, trans. 1989. In Toward the Radical Center. Peter Kussi, ed. Highland Park, NJ: Catbird Press, 1990.

Play. Rossum's robots—"androids" in current terminology—take over because they are, in many ways, superior to humans. This play gave us the word "robot" (Czech for "worker"). Discussed in TMG in essays by W. Schuyler and B. Bengels (see under Literary Criticism). For textual issues, see M. Abrash, "R.U.R. Restored and Reconsidered," cited under Literary Criticism.

5.057   Carplays. Los Angeles, 1984.

Described in the credits blurb as "A celebration of the American automobile presented by the Mark Taper Forum and the Museum of Contemporary Art in connection with the museum's 'Automobile and Culture Show.'" Conceived by Ken Brecher of the Mark Taper Forum and supervised by Madeline Puzo. Rev. Dan Sullivan, "'Carplays' Takes Festival Viewers on a Joy Ride" and Lawrence Christon, "Tinkering With the Imagery and Reality of Cars," Los Angeles Times Monday, 3 Sept. 1984: V.1 and 4. The celebration included music, precision driving, design, and sound effects.

5.058   Caves of Steel. Eric Taylor, dir. UK: BBC-TV, 1967. 75 min.

Television adaptation of the novel by I. Asimov, q.v. under Fiction.

5.059   The Chairman (vt The Most Dangerous Man in the World). J. Lee Thompson, dir. USA: Twentieth Century-Fox, 1969. Gregory Peck, star.

Political thriller. US scientist sent into "Red" China with a transmitter inside his skull relaying back to his handlers what he hears; unknown to the scientist, there's a bomb in his head, also. Cf. and contrast P. K. Dick's "Imposter," cited under Fiction.

5.060 Cherry 2000. Steve De Jarnatt, dir. USA: Orion, 1989.

Near-future comedy parodying (among other things) dating bars, Westerns, high-tech souped up cars, James Bondish high-tech weaponry, post-holocaust films generally and A Boy and His Dog and the Mad Max films more particularly. At film's end, the hero gives up his Cherry 2000 robot to fly off with the gutsy, macho tracker, E. Johnson (Melanie Griffith).

5.061 Christine. John Carpenter, dir. USA: Col-Delphi/Richard Kobritz (Polar), 1983. Based on the novel by Stephen King.

Horror/thriller. Features a 1958 Plymouth Fury that becomes loving—and demonic (see Willis, Horror and Science Fiction Films). See elsewhere in this section 978-EVIL and Killdozer.

5.062 Class of 1999. Mark L. Lester, dir., prod. USA: Taurus Entertainment, 1990. Stacy Keach, Malcolm McDowell, stars.

Keach's greedy businessman gets high school principal McDowell to try out as teachers insufficiently reprogrammed combat robots. The human-looking robots turn Terminator (q.v. below, as a film title) and are finally destroyed by student gangs at the school. Less intertextual than it might be (see below, Clockwork Orange), and less funny. Rev. Dan Persons, Cinefantastique 21.2 [Sept. 1990]: 52.

5.063 Clock Cleaners. Ben Sharpsteen, dir. USA: Walt Disney Productions, 1937. Available on Cartoon Classics vol. 10, Mickey's Crazy Career.

Cartoon. Mickey Mouse, Donald Duck, and Goofy (and a stubborn stork) superimpose the organic upon the mechanism of a large tower clock and—except for the stork—get the mechanical imposed upon them, in terms of both brief entrapment and metaphoric take-over. Listen for an early mechanical voice as Donald argues with his echo from a piece of mainspring. For very different cartoons, see in this section Akira and Wizards, and the animated sections of Pink Floyd—The Wall. See under Background, H. Bergson's essay "Laughter."

5.064 A Clockwork Orange. Stanley Kubrick, dir. UK: Hawk (prod.) / Warner (US release), 1971. Malcolm McDowell, star.

Closely follows US (Norton) version of A. Burgess's novel of the same title (q.v. under Fiction). See under Drama Criticism the CW essay by L. Heldreth. Discussed by Sobchack in The Limits of Infinity.

5.065 Close Encounters of the Third Kind. Steven Spielberg, dir., script. USA: Columbia/EMI, 1977. 135 min. in original theatrical release.

Heavily emphasizes everyday machines. The mechanized environment of the alien mothership at the end of the film is a highly positive, almost mystical, experience for the film's hero, and for the audience, esp. in the "Special Edition" rerelease (1980) and in the version shown on television. See under Drama Criticism the TMG essay by D. Palumbo. Discussed by V. Sobchack in Screening Space (see Sobchack's Index for Chapter 4).

5.066 Colossus: The Forbin Project (variously punctuated; UK vt The Forbin Project). Joseph Sargent, dir. USA: Universal, 1969 (completion), 1970 (US release). Walt Lee lists additional vts for this film before and during its production.

Computer takeover film. Closely follows the novel by D. F. Jones (q.v. under Fiction); changes are minor, necessary, and usually improvements. Discussed by V. Sobchack in The Limits of Infinity. Discussed in TMG by D. Palumbo and in CW by L. Heldreth (see under Drama Criticism).

5.067 Colossus of New York. Eugene Lourie, dir. USA: Paramount, 1958. Based on a story by Willis Goldbeck.

Premise, according to Walt Lee and Ed Naha (Science Fictionary) has a "man's brain put in giant robot body; death rays from eyes" (quoting Lee).

5.068 Coma. Michael Crichton, dir., script. USA: United Artists, 1978.

Medical thriller closely following Coma by R. Cook (q.v. under Fiction). Note imagery of total institutions, highly mechanized (and close to those of the real world).

5.069 Commando Cody: See King of the Rocket Men.

5.070 The Computer Wore Tennis Shoes. Robert Butler, dir. USA: Disney/Buena Vista, 1970. Kurt Russell, star.

The wearer of the tennis shoes is struck by lightning while repairing a computer, receiving from the bolt all the data in the computer.

5.071 Coppélia.

E.T.A. Hoffmann's "The Sandman" (1816, listed under Fiction) tells the story of a Dr. Coppelius, who builds a beautiful automaton—a doll that inspires the love of the hero of "The Sandman." The story of a dancing doll who comes to life and becomes a woman has also inspired an opera, a ballet, and, from them, several films. We list below three filmed ballets; for other cinema works, see Walt Lee, Coppelia, and cross-listings. (See this section, L. Delibes, [see also Making Mr. Right].)

5.072 Coppelia. Margaret Dale, prod. Lev Ivanov et al., choreographers. UK: BBC, 1964. 69 min.

5.073 Coppelia. Truck Branss, dir. Wilfried Schieb, prod. Vaclav Orlinkowsky, choreographer. Austria: O.R.F., 1967. 76 min.

5.074 Coppelia (Spanish title: El Fantastico Mundo del Dr. Coppelius [The Fantastic World of Dr. Coppelius], vt Dr. Coppelius). Ted Kneeland, dir. and script. Jo Anna Kneeland, choreographer. Spain / USA: Coppelia S.A./Coppelia Co. (Childhood Productions), 1966/1968. 97 min. "Based on the ballet 'Coppelia' (Music by Leo Delibes, Libretto by Charles Nuitter) . . ." (Walt Lee).

5.075 Crash and Burn. Charles Band, dir. USA: Full Moon Entertainment (prod.) / Paramount (dist.), 1990.

A teen "slicer-dicer" movie with S. F. variations. The year is 2030; the characters in the isolated area get killed in a high-tech environment; and there is a compendium of S. F. clichés, including rule by UniCom, "a free-enterprise bureaucracy dedicated to the concept of life, liberty, and the pursuit of economic stability"—and one that forbids the use of computers and robots. The murderers serving UniCom are androids, and there is a positively presented giant robot, programmed by the heroine.

5.076   Creation of the Humanoids. Wesley E. Barry, dir. USA: Genie (Emerson Film
Enterprises), 1962.

> Praised by V. Sobchack in Limits of Infinity and Screening Space (cited under
> Drama Criticism) as possibly "the most innovative and intellectually complex
> treatment of robots" on film. In the humanoids, "the dividing line between robot
> and human is totally extinguished" (82-83). Walt Lee says the future battle
> pitting humans against androids and robots is "somewhat related" to ideas in J.
> Williamson's Humanoid stories (q.v. under Fiction).

5.077   Cyborg. Albert Pyun, dir. USA: Golan-Globus (prod.) / Cannon Films (release),
1989. 86 min.

> CableView 10.5 (May 1990) describes Cyborg as "A gripping cinematic study of
> a world gone mad . . . . The cyborg shows that mechanization and pure logic are
> not enough to survive"; a healthy soul is also necessary (Premium Index). We'll
> describe Cyborg as a Jean-Claude Van Damme martial-arts vehicle featuring a
> female cyborg in a postapocalypse USA, significant for the cyborg's journey as
> occasion for much of the violence in the film, and the cyborg's presence for
> thematic interest.

5.078   Cyborg 2087. Franklin Adreon, dir. USA: Feature Film (prod.), 1966. Michael
Rennie, star. Made for TV. 86 mins.

> Cyborg from 2087 goes back in time to 1966 "to prevent a scientist from
> creating a device that will later be used as an instrument for mind-control by a
> totalitarian government" of 2087 (S. F. Ency.); the cyborg succeeds, at the cost of
> his own existence since the device he persuades the scientist to destroy allowed
> the creation of cyborgs (S. F. Ency. and Walt Lee). Erlich recalls seeing this film
> at a drive-in, with a framing gimmick, so it may have had some play after its TV
> presentation.

5.079   Cyborg Big "X." Syndicated weekly TV series. 1965.

> Described by Naha, Science Fictionary, as featuring "a cyborg with the brain of a
> human and the body of a robot."

5.080   D.A.R.Y.L. Simon Wincer, dir. USA: Paramount, 1985.

> The cinematic "citations" in the film are to Robbie the Robot in Forbidden Planet
> (q.v. below) and The Incredible Hulk, but D.A.R.Y.L. may be most quickly
> described as an SF version of Walt Disney's Pinocchio, with an android with a
> microcomputer brain (interfaced with a mainframe) replacing the puppet, and the
> Turing Test answering the question of Daryl/D.A.R.Y.L.'s humanity. Note highly
> sentimental handling of android combined, decorously, with very negative view
> of military bureaucrats (for comparisons and contrasts see Close Encounters of
> the Third Kind, E.T., JOE . . ., Questor Tapes, Repo Man, Starman, Terminator,
> Wargames [covering the years 1977-1985]). A Berkley/Pacer novelization of the
> film has been advertised.

5.081   Daleks—Invasion Earth 2150 A.D. Gordon Flemyng, dir. UK: Aaru, 1966 (US
release: 1968). Joe Vegoda, exec. prod. Stars Peter Cushing as Doctor Who.

> Sequel to Dr. Who and the Daleks (q.v.). In 2150 the Daleks rule what is left of
> the Earth, with the help of the men they've "robotized." The Daleks come across
> in this film as just intelligent, ungainly, and very dangerous robots, who will
> "EXTERMINATE! EXTERMINATE!" any uppity humans. Set in the wreckage
> of London and at the mine central to the Daleks' nefarious scheme. See below,
> Doctor Who.

5.082   Dark Star. John Carpenter, dir. USA: Bryanston Pictures, 1974.

See for character Pinback trapped in the spaceship Dark Star's elevator shaft, the female computer that runs the Dark Star, and the computer-bomb that eventually develops delusions of godhead. S. F. Ency. cites a novelization by Alan Dean Foster (1974).

5.083 The Day of the Dolphin. Mike Nichols, dir. USA: Avco-Embassy, 1973. Buck Henry, script (from Un animal doué de raison [1967], a convoluted political-intrigue thriller by Robert Merle). George C. Scott, star.

See for talking dolphins with mines strapped to their backs; within the beast-fable of Nichols's film, the image implies the superimposition of human nastiness upon formerly innocent nature. Cf. and contrast attack penguins in Batman Returns (cited above).

5.084 The Day the Earth Stood Still. Robert Wise, dir. USA: 20th Century Fox, 1951.

Possibly the classic SF film featuring a robot. Based on H. Bates's "Farewell to the Master" (q.v. under Fiction) but without the story's final revelation that the robot is the master and the "man" the creature. See for duality of robot as both servant and threat. Discussed by Sobchack in The Limits of Infinity.

5.085 Daybreak (vt). René Clair, dir. France: Tobis (prod.), 1931.

Early sound film ending happily "when the oppressive, prison-like factory" featured in the film "continues to produce machines by itself, leaving human beings free to dance, sit by the river, and relax in the sun" (G. Mast 528 in article cited under Reference). Cf. and contrast C. Chaplin's Modern Times (cited below); contrast P. K. Dick's "Autofac" (q.v. under Fiction).

5.086 Deadlock. Lewis Teague, dir. USA: HBO Pictures, 1991. Rutger Hauer, Mimi Rogers, star. Made for TV by HBO, first shown 28 Sept. 1991.

"Recombinant cinema," where the main clichés are from heist and prison films, esp. The Defiant Ones (1958). In Deadlock the shackles are near-future, high-tech collars that explode if the prisoners are separated by more than 100 yards (cf. the collars in F. Pohl and J. Williamson's Reefs of Space [1963] and Starchild [1965]—listed under Fiction).

5.087 Death Race 2000. Paul Bartel, dir. USA: New World Pictures, 1975. Based on Ib Melchior's story, "The Racer." David Carradine, star.

A transcontinental car race in the year 2000 in the dystopian United Provinces of America; points for running over pedestrians. See for race cars as "death machines" (quoting Deathsport); see also handling of television's (and film's) exploitation of gratuitous violence, malicious property destruction, and casual murder.

5.088 Deathsport. Henry Suso and Allan Arkush, dirs. Roger Corman, prod. USA: New World Pictures, 1978. David Carradine, star.

Compendium of clichés from several genres, including SF. Note antithesis and conflation of horses and "death machines": small motorcycles (glorifed trail bikes). Note also threatening containment of hero and heroine in electrifiable cells. Given production by the highly conscious Roger Corman, such use inticates that these motifs were clichés worth having some fun with by the 1970s.

5.089 Deathwatch (sometimes as two words: Death Watch). Bertrand Tavernier, dir. France/(West) Germany: Selta-Little Bear-Antenne 2-Sara-Gaumont / TV 13, 1980. Romy Schneider, Harvey Keitel, Harry Dean Stanton, Max von Sydow, stars.

Keitel plays a reporter in a near-future world with camera implants in his eyes. See above under Fiction, D. G. Compton's The Continuous Katherine Mortenhoe.

5.090   Deepstar Six. Sean S. Cunningham, dir. and co-prod. USA: Carolco (prod.) / Tri-Star (dist.), 1989.

Underwater Alien, or a big-screen, full-length Voyage to the Bottom of the Sea episode with strong women and better production values. See for ambiguous containment within a highly mechanized environment: the underwater vehicles, habitats, and diving suit are necessary protection but become traps when the monster attacks. The final sequence shows a highly positive (and highly derivative) release from containment into the open air. (Caution: Do not depend upon this film for details about decompression.) See in this section, Abyss and Leviathan.

5.091   Delibes, (C.-P.-) Léo, composer. Coppélia. Charles Nuitter, libretto. 1870.

Ballet based on E.T.A. Hoffmann tale, "The Sandman" (q.v. under Fiction). See above, Coppélia and the works cross-referenced there.

5.092   Demon Seed. Donald Cammell, dir. USA: United Artists (S. F. Ency.: MGM), 1977. Based on the novel by D. R. Koontz (q.v under Fiction).

The film's end improves upon the novel's, but otherwise the film tells the same story. Discussed in TMG by D. Palumbo (cited under Drama Criticism).

5.093   "Demon With a Glass Hand." Outer Limits. ABC-TV, 17 Oct. 1964. Harlan Ellison, script.

Winner of Writers' Guild of America award for the outstanding script for 1964 (Naha, Science Fictionary 318), the show deals with an android or cyborg "who has the entire human race coded in his artificial hand" (S. F. Ency., "Cyborgs" and "The Outer Limits," the latter of which we quote).

5.094   The Devil Commands. USA: Columbia, 1941. Boris Karloff, star.

A brainwave machine attached to human corpses mediates a path to the afterlife—for a superimposition of the mechanical upon the decomposing organic, as a way to the spiritual.

5.095   Dick Tracy. Warren Beatty, dir., prod., star. USA: Touchstone (dist.), 1990. Based on the comic strip created by Chester Gould.

Climactic battle between Tracy and villain occurs amid machinery for raising and lowering a bridge; the machinery is explicitly and correctly compared by the villain to a clockwork. Note huge, slowly moving gear to which the villian ties the heroine. Significantly, the setting for the climax is mostly irrelevant for the plot; Beatty wanted the Gothic clichés of the bound and endangered heroine and the literal fall of a villain—and he placed them in a mechanized environment recalling saw-mills and railroad tracks of silent movies of the cliffhanger variety.

5.096   Dr. Goldfoot and the Bikini Machine. Norman Taurog, dir. USA: AIP, 1965. Cast includes Vincent Price, Frankie Avalon, and Dwayne Hickman.

Dr. Goldfoot makes female "robots to seduce men of influence so he can rule world" (Leslie Halliwell and Walt Lee; we quote Lee).

5.097   Dr. Goldfoot and the Girl Bombs. Mario Bava, dir. USA: AIP, 1966. Vincent Price, stars as Goldfoot.

Sequel to ...the Bikini Machine. The James Bond movie Goldfinger was released in 1964; these two films parody the Bond film's name but image the threat to the world as not a money economy or an A-bomb but robots that look like beautiful young women. See under Fiction, P. K. Dick's "Imposter," under Drama The Chairman and Flash Gordon Conquers the Universe.

5.098   Dr. Strangelove: Or How I Learned to Stop Worrying and Love the Bomb (variously capitalized and punctuated). Stanley Kubrick, dir. UK: Hawk/Columbia, 1963 (completion), 1964 (US release). S. Kubrick, Terry Southern, Peter George, script—loosely based on Red Alert, by Peter George (writing as Peter Bryant).

Features mechanized humans (primarily Dr. Strangelove), humanized machines, men in a B-52, and humanity "trapped" in a doomsday machine. Important for Kubrick's 2001 and Clockwork Orange, q.v. this section. Discussed by V. Sobchack in The Limits of Infinity. Note Strangelove as an "inheritor" of "the hand of Rotwang" in Metropolis.

5.099   DOCTOR WHO Episodes: BBC Television 1963-1989 (the "Doctor" in the title sometimes gets shortened, according to national practice, to "Dr." or "Dr").

Note TARDIS: a space/time machine the size of a London Metropolitan Police call-box ca. 1960 outside (since it duplicates a police call-box ca. 1960) but much larger and quite high-tech inside.

5.100   "The Green Death." Doctor Who. Michael Briant, dir. UK: BBC Colour, 1973. Jon Pertwee, star. Terrance Dicks, script ed.

The biological threat are (sic) huge mutant maggots causing the death of the title; the inorganic threat is takeover by a computer named BOSS. See for images of containment: "I am the BOSS. I'm all around you. . . . I am the computer."

5.101   "Pyramids of Mars." Doctor Who. Paddy Russel, dir. UK: BBC Colour, 1975. Tom Baker, star.

The villain is the Egyptian god Set, imprisoned within a tomb—served by a zombie and robots wrapped like mummies. The robots are clumsy, simple-minded, and manage to be threatening without seeming evil.

5.102   "Robot." Doctor Who. Christopher Barry, dir. UK: BBC Colour, 1975. Terrance Dicks, script. Tom Baker, star. First of the Tom Baker episodes.

A relatively sympathetic robot with an Asimovian "Prime Directive" is associated with a fascistic group with some Technocracy elements (see under Background, Technocracy . . . [1975]).

5.103   Dr. Who and the Daleks. Gordon Flemyng, dir. UK: Aaru / Regal Films International, 1965 (US release: 1966). Stars Peter Cushing as Doctor Who. Based on the BBC series, Doctor Who.

Fix-up of episodes in the BBC serial. The Daleks in Doctor Who are usually militaristic robots bent on "universal conquest" and wide-spread exterminating; they are opposed by Doctor Who. See the S. F. Ency. entries for "Daleks" and "Dr Who"; and see under Fiction T. Dicks, The Adventures of Dr. Who and other novelizations of Doctor Who episodes. In this series of episodes, the Daleks are organic creatures who encase themselves in individual, mobile machines for protection against residual radiation from the last, quite final, war; the Daleks rule a high-tech city surrounded by a wasteland that is mostly a dead forest. See this section, Daleks . . . .

5.104   Dune. David Lynch, dir. and script. USA: Universal (release), 1984. A Dino De Laurentiis "presentation," prod. by Raffaella De Laurentiis. Based on the novel by Frank Herbert. 145 minutes.

See for very high-tech machines that are both futuristic and old-fashioned, and for design in general, from special effects to costuming. Discussed by V. Sobchack in Screening Space, Chapter 4. Rev. New York Times 14 Dec. 1984: 18 Y, Newsweek 10 Dec. 1984. (A re-release version restored footage that clarified the story.)

5.105   Edward Scissorhands. Tim Burton, dir., co-prod. USA: 20th-Century Fox, 1990.

Romantic fantasy that uses SF/horror convention of a highly mechanized laboratory in a decaying mansion on a hill top; the title character is brought back to the everyday world from that mansion for the beginning of the film and returns to it at the end. Throughout, the title character has scissors instead of hands.

5.106   Egghead's Robot. Milo Lewis, dir. UK: Children's Film Foundation, 1970. 56 min.

According to Walt Lee, "boy builds robot duplicate of himself." Willis lists date as 1971 (vol II).

5.107   The Eighth Man. Syndicated weekly TV series, 1965. Animated.

The eighth "man" of a crime-fighting unit is Tobor, the robot, who has been infused with the "life-force" of a dead agent (Naha, Science Fictionary).

5.108   Electric Dreams. Steve Barron, dir. USA: MGM, 1984.

Lighthearted use of motifs of computer lust and computer takeover; cf. and contrast Demon Seed and Saturn 3 for lust and The Twonky for household takeover; see Colossus: The Forbin Project for very serious use of computer takeover (all cited in this section).

5.109   The Electric Hotel. Spain, 1906. Silent. 476 feet.

Said by Naha, Science Fictionary, to feature a hotel "with totally automated service.... Only the bill has to be paid manually." See for very early "electrified" film environment.

5.110   The Electric House. Buster Keaton, Eddie Cline, dir. and script. USA: Buster Keaton Production, 1922. Silent. 2 reels.

Said by Naha, Science Fictionary, to feature a fully automated house, realized in full-scale sets designed by Keaton.

5.111   The Electric Leg. UK: Clarendon, 1912. Silent. 352 feet.

Naha, Science Fictionary, notes the invention of an electrically powered mechanical leg "capable of functioning without the benefit of an attached body." Cf. The Mechanical Legs (1915), listed below.

5.112   Ellison, Harlan. "Demon With a Glass Hand": Cited under title.

5.113   The Empire Strikes Back. Irvin Kershner, dir. USA (Norway, UK): Lucasfilm (prod.) / 20th Century-Fox (release), 1980. Leigh Brackett and Lawrence Kasdan, script; story by George Lucas. George Lucas, exec. prod.

Sequel to Star Wars, q.v. this section. Many images of containment within machinery are contrasted with the open, snow-covered plains of the base-planet for the Rebel Alliance in the opening sequence, and the swamp where Yoda trains Luke Skywalker. Usually, the containment within machinery is immediately or potentially dangerous for the good characters in the film; the shots of Darth

Vader's exits from his meditation chamber suggest the demonic. (See entry for
D. F. Glut under Fiction.). Note Skywalker's prosthetic hand at end of film.

5.114 E.T.: The Extra-Terrestrial. Steven Spielberg, dir. USA: Amblin (prod.) / Universal
(dist.), 1982. Steven Spielberg and Kathleen Kennedy, prod. 115 min.

A celebration of appropriate technology (bikes, very long distance
communication devices) and mild condemnation of technology used by
bureaucrats. A measure of E.T.'s niceness is the variation on the classic sequence
of the hero threateningly contained for technological torture: E.T. and Elliott are
held down, but the apparatus imposed on them is medical, and the people
working on them really do want to save their lives; E.T. is placed in a high-tech,
supercooled coffin—for his resurrection. Discussed by V. Sobchack in
Screening Space, Chapter 4. Novelized in a Berkley paperback.

5.115 Eve of Destruction. Duncan Gibbins, dir. USA: Orion (release), 1990. Gregory
Hines, Renee Soutendijk, Kevin McCarthy, feature players.

Soutendijk doubles as Eve, a Terminator-style robot, and Eve's inventor. Minor
film interesting for its conscious attempts at psychology ("The Two Faces of Eve,"
so to speak) and its probably unconscious sexual politics: robot Eve carries out
the destruction of evil men that human Eve sometimes desires. In addition to the
Terminator movies, cf. and contrast human and robot Marias in Metropolis.
Briefly rev. Dan Parsons, Cinefantastique 21.5 (April 1991): 54-55.

5.116 Explorers. Joe Dante, dir. USA: Paramount, 1985. Industrial Light & Magic, SpFx.

"First Contact" film, combining Close Encounters of the Third Kind with "The
Squire of Gothos" episode of Star Trek (plus bits from other genre films).
Significant here for what Erlich and Peter C. Hall have called "the funkification
of the future" in the design of the three spacecraft in the film, and for use by a
highly conscious director of a number of important motifs: the heroes' being
"eaten alive" by a Great Mother alien ship (combining male and female aspects),
the boys in the alien ship as "mice in a maze," and the dream sequences with the
boys flying over and into a complex circuit board. Discussed by V. Sobchack in
Screening Space (see Sobchack's Index for Chapter 4).

5.117 Fahrenheit 451. François Truffaut, dir. UK: Anglo-Enterprise and Vineyard/Universal,
1966. Script by Truffaut and Jean-Lewis Richard, from the novel by Ray
Bradbury (1953).

The hero escapes a highly mechanized, urban world, where books are burned, to
join a rural community where books are memorized and thereby preserved.
Perhaps most interesting for the ambiguity in its presentation of the opposition of
the wicked city and purer countryside (see entry in S. F. Ency.).

5.118 Fireball XL-5. UK: ITC-TV. Syndicated weekly TV series, 1961.
"Supermarionation" (puppets).

Regular cast includes Robert the Robot (Naha, Science Fictionary).

5.119 The Flash. Gail Morgan Hickman, prod., teleplay. GMH and Denise Skinner, story.
Bruce Bilson, dir. Characters and premise from DC Comics. USA: Pet Fly
Production / Warner Brothers Television, 1991. CBS. 11 May 1991.

US government intelligence agency develops a (female) android, Alpha One, as
an assassin; the android develops a conscience and escapes rather than complete
training in murder. Note references to I. Asimov and dialog and images
(surprisingly subversive for commercial TV) getting us to sympathize with the
android and against the government of the United States.

5.120   The Flash. CBS. 13 December 1990.

The Flash and "Night Shade," an old masked vigilante, take on a TV expert from the 1950s, who interfaces himself with the city's electronic network, threatening "beautiful chaos" as "the heart and soul of this city."

5.121   Flash Gordon Conquers the Universe (vt Peril from the Planet Mongo, Space Soldiers Conquer the Universe, The Purple Death from Outer Space). Ford Beebe and Roy Taylor, dirs. 12 episodes. USA: Universal, 1940. "Based on the newspaper feature by Alex Raymond entitled 'Flash Gordon' ...." Available on two cassettes from United American Video.

Chapter 3, "Walking Bombs," and Chapter 4, "Destroying Ray" have as a featured threat robots interesting for walking rather like golems (Der Golem, 1920) and for cubistic heads; contrast Flash's movements in a full-body protective suit in Chapter 6, "Flaming Death." For general technology, see the original Flash Gordon series of 1936, the sequel on Flash Gorden's Trip to Mars in 1939, and the Dino De Laurentiis remake of Flash Gordon in 1980.

5.122   The Fly. David Cronenberg, dir., co-author of script. USA: Brooksfilms, 1986. Jeff Goldblum, star. Remake of Kurt Neumann's 1958 film (based on the short story by George Langelaan).

A rather touching love story significant here for its funky-looking contemporary laboratory and for the fusion in the final sequence of man, fly, and machine. Briefly handled Bruce Kirkland, "The Fly," Cinefantastique 16 (July 1986): 15 f. See this section, Videodrome. (Caution: Cronenberg's The Fly can be rough going for people figuratively weak of stomach or literally strong of gag mechanism.)

5.123   Forbidden Planet. Fred Mcleod Wilcox, dir. USA: MGM, 1956. Irving Block and Allen Adler, script. Based on a story by Irving Block.

See for Robbie the Robot and for 8000 cubic miles of underground Krel machinery (with strong motifs of hexagons and pentagons). Robbie is an Ariel-figure with no desire to leave the service of humans. The Caliban-figure in this pessimistic reworking of Shakespeare's The Tempest is one of the "monsters from the Id," and is both very successful in its murder attempts and ultimately rejected by Dr. Moribus. The Id-monster is explicitly associated with the subconscious and with the underground Krel machinery. Discussed by Sobchack in The Limits of Infinity (and Screening Space; see Sobchack's Index).

5.124   Frankenstein Unbound: See Roger Corman's Frankstein Unbound.

5.125   Freejack. Geoff Murphy, dir. Ronald Shussett and Stuart Oken, prod. USA: Warner, 1992. Loosely based on Robert Sheckley's Immortality, Inc. Emilio Estevez, Mick Jagger, Rene Russo, Anthony Hopkins, featured players.

Twenty years into a dystopian future, it is possible for rich people "to plug their computer-stored beings into healthy bodies from the past," just before those healthy people died (on our time-line). Rev. Locke Peterseim, Cinefantastique 22.6 (June 1992): 57, whom we quote. The climax has a cameo with Hopkins, similar to the cyberspace confrontation in W. Gibson's Count Zero, with special effects realizing the conceit of the ghost in the machine. Note also the truck Jagger uses in his body-snatching operation; cf. and contrast trucks in Universal Soldier and Warlords of the Twenty-First Century (listed below, this section).

5.126   Friendship's Death: See below, under P. Wollen.

5.127   Future Cop. Pilot for TV series (of brief duration). USA: ABC-TV / Paramount-TV / Culzean-Tovern, 1976. Jud Taylor, dir. 74 min. Michael Shannon, Ernest

Borgnine, stars.

Features a cybernetic rookie supercop, with the standard joke of a nonsophisticated rookie, necessarily fairly innocent. (See also in this section, D.A.R.Y.L., Questor Tapes, and JOE & the Colonel.)

5.128 Futureworld. Richard T. Heffron, dir. USA: AIP, 1976.

Sequel to Westworld, q.v. this section. Robots try to take over the world by replacing human leaders with robot look-alikes. The setting for most of the film is the robot-staffed resort of Delos (with the robots, as things turn out, in complete charge). Discussed in TMG by L. Heldreth and D. Palumbo, and in CW by L. Heldreth (see under Drama Criticism).

5.129 Galaxina. William Sachs, dir. USA: Crown International / Marimar, 1980. Cast includes Dorothy R. Stratten.

Space-opera spoof, apparently beneath notice by most of our sources. Maltin (1989) notes suggestively that Galaxina was "Definitely not a vehicle for the late Ms. Stratten, though the film is of interest for her appearance as a robot."

5.130 Get a Life. 4 Nov. 1990. Syndicated on Fox Television.

Protagonist Chris Peterson loses job to automated Paperboy 2000; when the machine goes rogue, Chris stops it. Since paperboy Chris is over thirty, we're in a highly conscious parody of SF motifs that have become clichés.

5.131 Gigantor. Japan: syndicated weekly TV series, 1966 in USA. Animated.

Title character is a 21st-c. robot crime-fighter (Naha, Science Fictionary).

5.132 Gog (vt GOG, the Killer). Herbert L. Strock, dir. and ed. Ivan Tors, prod., story. USA: Ivan Tors Productions / United Artists, 1954.

Features a supercomputer and robots, Biblically named Gog and Magog, who become murderous after interference by an outside power. Summarized in S. F. Ency. and Walt Lee; see Parish and Pitts for summary and brief interpretation.

5.133 Gojira Tai Megagojira (Godzilla vs. Mechagodzilla; vt Godzilla vs. the Cosmic Monster and Godzilla vs. the Bionic Monster). Jun Fukuda, dir., script. Japan: Cinema Shares International (Downtown) / Toho Eizo, 1974 (US release: 1977).

Mechagodzilla is a "cyborg made of space titanium and controlled by aliens" (Willis, vol. II, under Godzilla vs. the Cosmic Monster). See below, Mejagijira No Gyakusha (Terror of Mechagodzilla) and King Kong No Gyakushi (a film with a robot double for King Kong).

5.134 Gremlins 2: The New Batch. Joe Dante, dir. USA: Amblin Entertainment (prod.) / Warner (dist.). Steven Spielberg et al., exec. prod.

If the clamp upon the human spirit in the original Gremlins (1984) could be imaged as small-town America out of Frank Capra's It's a Wonderful Life (1946), in the sequel it is Clamp Centre: a fully automated, high-tech building with an Orwellian security station at its heart and a top-floor office featuring TV screens, a shredding machine, and John Glover's Daniel Clamp—a media and real estate mogul with better teeth than brains. See Gremlins 2 for artist's ambivalence toward technology.

5.135 Guyver. Screaming Mad George and Steve Wang, dirs. Japan/USA: Hero Communications, 1991 (Japan). Based on the graphic novel by Yoshika Takaya.

A college student is "thrust into superherodom . . . when he finds 'the Guyver,' an alien device that transforms him into an invincibly armored fighting machine" (Dan Cziraky, "Guyver," Cinefantastique 22.4 [Feb. 1992]: 46). Cziraky notes similarities with The Rocketeer (q.v. below); we'll add fighting suits in fiction: see R. A. Heinlein's Starship Troopers and J. Haldeman's Forever War.

5.136   Hardware. Richard Stanley, dir. UK: Palace Pictures (prod.) / Miramax (US dist.), 1990.

Cyberpunk, heavy Industrial, postmodern movie, featuring a Mark 13 robot killing machine, rev. Brooks Landon, Cinefantastique 21.5 (April 1991): 22-23, our source for this entry. Landon relates the film to Terminator and to the work of Mark Pauline, a San Francisco performance artist.

5.137   Heartbeeps. Allan Arkush, dir. USA: Universal, 1981. Cast includes Christopher Guest, Andy Kaufman, Melanie Mayron, Bernadette Peters, and Randy Quaid.

Described by Willis as "A sweet, unsung sf-comedy-romance," where two advanced humanoid robots (played by Peters and Kaufman) meet and fall in love. Discussed at length by Willis (vol. III), who takes the film very seriously.

5.138   The Hitchhiker's Guide to the the Galaxy. Fit the First (sic) broadcast on BBC Radio 8 March 1978. Geoffrey Perleins, prod. Peter Jones and Simon Jones, stars. Douglas Adams, script. AVC Corporation/The Mind's Eye, 1988. 6 cassettes, 6 hours.

See under Fiction, citations for D. Adams. Audiotape version esp. important for Program 9; note the "Share and Enjoy" scene with Arthur Dent on The Heart of Gold, trapped among "Eddie, your shipboard computer" and the other shipboard products of the Sirius Cybernetics Corporation and Complaints Division.

5.139   Hitchhiker's Guide to the Galaxy. BBC TV Series, faithfully repeating the radio series (q.v. above) and adequately reflected in the novelization (see D. Adams under Fiction).

5.140   Holmes and Yo-Yo. ABC-TV weekly series, 1976.

Yo-Yo Yoyonovich is a slow-witted robot cop with an equally dull human partner (Naha, Science Fictionary); cf. and contrast I. Asimov's Caves of Steel (cited under Fiction).

5.141   The Ice Pirates. Stewart Raffil, dir. USA: MGM, 1984. John Foreman, prod.

See for comic robots.

5.142   Ikaria XB-1 (variously spelled and hyphenated; vt Voyage to the End of the Universe). Jindrich Polak, dir. Czechoslovakia: Film Export / AIP, 1963 (completion), 1964 (release).

Features a subtly alien culture inside a huge spaceship.

5.143   Innerspace. Joe Dante, dir. USA: Amblin (prod.) / Warner (dist.), 1987. Steven Spielberg et al., exec. prod. 120 min. Dennis Quaid, Martin Short, stars.

Comedy with a premise similar to that of Fantastic Voyage (1966), relevant here for the layering of superimpositions as Dennis Quaid's character remains in a submarine that gets miniaturized inside a large machine and then goes into a syringe, then into Martin Short's character, then a good friend of Quaid's character—and so forth. The thug working for the main villains has a Rotwangian artificial hand (see Metropolis through Repo Man [1984]) and ends up in a heavy-metal SCUBA outfit inside a miniaturized sub inside Martin Short's character: for a decorously comic superimposition of the organic upon the mechanical upon the mechanical upon the mechanized organic. See under Background, the entry for H. Bergson.

5.144 Invaders from Mars. William Cameron Menzies, dir. and designer. USA: Twentieth Century-Fox, 1953.

Humans controlled by radio implants impressively drilled into their heads. Naha, Science Fictionary notes alternative endings in US and UK releases; we note a 1986 remake that retains the implants. Cf. and mostly contrast The Chairman, and see under Fiction, K. Vonnegut's Siren's of Titan.

5.145 The Invisible Boy. Herman Hoffman, dir. Pan Productions / MGM, 1957.

Note here TIB's combining the horrifying motif of control by brain implant of William Cameron Menzies's Invaders from Mars (1953) with Robbie the Robot from Forbidden Planet (cited above)—and with a supercomputer trying to take over the world.

5.146 JOE & the Colonel. Pilot made for TV, first telecast ABC Television, 11 Sept. 1985.

The hero, JOE, is "a biologically engineered man" who is a "product of DNA experiments," as TV Guide for the week of first telecast puts it (and upon which we rely since the opening of the show was preempted in the Cincinnati area by coverage of Pete Rose's 4192nd hit). Of interest here is JOE's innocence, contrasted with the Rambo/Terminator syndrome in the android that follows him and with the regular humans. Compare JOE's innocence with that of D.A.R.Y.L. and the androids/robots in Future Cop and Questor Tapes (q.v., this section).

5.147 Johnny Sokko and His Flying Robot. Syndicated weekly TV series, 1968. Animated.

Another crime-fighting robot (Naha, Science Fictionary).

5.148 K-9000 Kim Manners, dir. USA: De Souza Productions. (c) 1989, by Fries Entertainment, Inc. Fox TV, July 1991.

Apparently a pilot for a series that was never picked up, featuring a cop paired with K-9000: the prototype CATCH animal developed for Cybernetic Action-Team(s): Canine/Human. Pairing occurs when the cop gets implanted with a "microchip receiver" that puts him into telepathic contact with the dog. Cf. A Boy and His Dog for the telepathy, and the Terminator films for the visuals from the dog's point of view; note also Doctor Who's K-9 (all listed in this section of the List).

5.149 Kaiser, Georg. Gas, I. 1918. Herman Scheffauer, trans. New York: Unger, 1957, 1963.

Second play of GK's Gas trilogy (1917-20): Die Koralle (The Coral), Gas I, Gas II. Set in a gas works that supplies the world with its most important source of energy. A devasting explosion at the works convinces the owner to move away from technology toward a more natural life for fully human human beings. See for motif of workers as cogs in a machine.

5.150 Killdozer. Jerry London, dir. USA: Universal-TV, 1974. Made for TV. Theodore Sturgeon and Ed MacKillap, script; adapted by Herbert F. Solow. Based on Sturgeon's novella, "Killdozer" (q.v. under Fiction).

A bulldozer is possessed by an alien intelligence from a meteorite and kills four out of six contractors working on an otherwise deserted island. The alien intelligence is finally destroyed with electricity. See for idea of everyday machines running amok, and for the battle between the killdozer and a man-operated power shovel. Donald C. Willis compares Killdozer—unfavorably—with Steven Spielberg's 1971 TV movie Duel (ABC-TV/Universal-TV); cf. also Runaway (below).

5.151 King Kong No Gyakushi (King Kong Escapes [vt King Kong's Counterattack and King Kong's Revenge]). Inoshiro Honda, dir., Japanese version; Arthur Rankin, Jr., dir. and prod., US version. Japan: Toho, 1967 (US release: 1968).

Evil scientist creates robot duplicate of Kong: Mechanikong (Walt Lee). See Mejagijira No Gyakusha, cited below.

5.152 King of the Rocket Men. Fred Brannon, dir. USA: Republic, 1949. Serial. 12 chapters. Vt as feature, Lost Planet Airmen (1951). Sequels: Radio Men from the Moon (1952) and Zombies of the Stratosphere (1952).

See for the rocket belt device; it's picked up in the Commando Cody TV series (NBC 1955)—itself a spinoff of Radar Men—and in The Rocketeer (cited below). These series are the topic of Michael Bifulco's Rocket Men of the Movies (1991), rev. Michael Klosner, SFRA Newsletter #196 (April 1992): 21-22 (our source for part of this entry).

5.153 Knight Rider. NBC TV series, mid-1980s. Glen A. Larson, exec. prod. USA: Universal.

KITT, the AI, computerized car that is the "steed" for Michael Knight, is arguably smarter than the human nominal hero of the series. Briefly commented on in H. F. Waters, "TV's Record Crime Wave," q.v. under Drama Criticism. Willis lists a 94-minute version in 1982, directed by Daniel Haller, presumably the pilot. KITT is on permanent display at the Universal Studios theme park in Universal City, CA.

5.154 Knight Rider 2000. Dir. Alan J. Levi. USA: Universal, 1991. Made for TV. NBC, 19 May 1991. Based on characters created by Glen A. Larson.

Besides KITT as an AI automobile, note computer chip implanted in a human brain and the Quayton State Penitentiary, Inc. (A Division of Prison Corp.): stacked cryogenic chambers with frozen prisoners. See for a film-literate movie with SF content homogenized, sanitized, and deodorized for television.

5.155 Knightriders (theatrical film). George A. Romero, dir., script. USA: United Artists ("A Laurel Production") / United Film (dist.), 1981. Ed Harris, star.

A cross between the Matter of Britain (King Arthur et al.) and a biker film, significant for epitomizing how motorcycles can be equivalent to chivalric steeds—and for analyzing the problems of the chivalric ideal in a technological society.

5.156 Kronos. Kurt Neumann, dir. USA: 20th Century-Fox, 1957.

"The only serious attempt ever made at a truly technological monster," according to John Baxter, who identifies Kronos as "a descendant of the juggernaut" (Baxter, 1979: 138, see under Reference).

5.157 The Last Starfighter. Nick Castle, dir. USA: Lorimar / Universal, 1984.

The Starfighter videogame turns out to be a test, and young Alex Rogan really has been "recruited by the Star League to defend the Frontier against Xur and the Ko-Dan Armada." Note for motif of videoscreen as portal to a larger world of adventure. Discussed by V. Sobchack in Screening Space, Chapter 4; see also Dennis K. Fischer, "The Last Starfighter," Cinefantastique 15 (Jan. 1985): 24 f.

5.158 The Lathe of Heaven. David Loxton and Fred Barzyk, dirs. USA: Educational Broadcasting Corp., 1979. Produced for the Public Broadcasting Service. First shown 9 Jan. 1980. Based on the novel by Ursula K. Le Guin, q.v. under Fiction.

More into Greek moderation than Taoist Balance, but closely follows the novel in all matters important for the study of the human/machine interface.

5.159 The Lawnmower Man. Brett Leonard, dir. USA: Allied Vision/Lane Pringle (prod.) / New Line Cinema (release), 1992. Loosely based on Stephen King's very short story, "Night Shift," combined with an unproduced film script called "Cybergod."

Adolescent revenge story like King's Carrie (1976), combined with Charly (1968) and TRON (listed below)—with a touch of A. C. Clarke's "Dial F for Frankenstein" (listed under Fiction). See for humans physically inside mechanisms and their literal self-images inside virtual realities, including a mainframe computer. See under Fiction J. T. Sladek's Müller-Fokker Effect and the works cross-listed there. Rev. Gary Wood, Cinefantastique 22.5 (April 1992): 6-7.

5.160 Leviathan. George P. Cosmatos, dir. USA/Italy: MGM, 1989.

Even closer to Alien than Deepstar Six (q.v. above, this section), but more interesting for motif of containment: the diving suits are similar to the fighting suits in R. A. Heinlein's Starship Troopers (cited under Fiction), and the title refers not only to the name of a sunken Russian ship but also to the underwater habitat as a mechanical and electronic monster. (Caution: Arguably more sexist and less reliable on decompression than Deepstar Six.) Rev. briefly in Cinefantastique 19.5 (July 1989): 55; see above, Abyss.

5.161 Light Years. Rene Laloux, dir. French version. Harvey Weinstein, dir. American version. France/USA: Miramax, 1988. Phillipe Caza, animation designer. Raphael Cluzel, original screenplay, based on Metal Men Against Gandahar by Jean-Pierre Androvan. Isaac Asimov, trans. and adapter. Glenn Close and Christopher Plummer among those doing voices for US release. 83 min.

Animated. Robots vs. a garden world "in the vein of French Metal Hurlant." Discussed in some detail by Daniel M. Kimmel in Cinefantastique 18.5 July 1988): 46 f., upon which we depend for our citation and annotation.

5.162 Liquid Sky. Slava Tsukerman, dir., prod. USA: Z Films (prod.) / Cinevista (release), 1982 (prod.) / 1983 (release).

A very small flying saucer lands on the patio of a very trendy punk, apparently to feed on the physiological products produced by heroin or orgasm. Cf. and contrast (mostly contrast) the small machines in Batteries Not Included (cited in this section). Discussed by V. Sobchack in Screening Space (see Sobchack's Index for Chapter 4).

5.163 Logan's Run. Michael Anderson, dir. USA: MGM/United Artists, 1976. Based on the novel by William F. Nolan and George Clayton Johnson.

Humanity in the future has sealed itself into a domed pleasure-city, a city managed in large part by a computer (which we see and hear at key moments in the plot). Cf. and contrast A. C. Clarke, City and the Stars, and R. Silverberg, World Inside, and the generation-starship works cross-referenced under R. Heinlein, "Universe" (all cited above, under Fiction). LR had two TV versions: Logan's Run, CBS-TV telefilm, 1977 (90 min. airtime), and Logan's Run, CBS-TV weekly series, 1977-78, 60-min. episodes.

5.164 Looker. Michael Crichton, dir. USA: Ladd Company / Warner, 1981. Albert Finney, James Coburn, Susan Dey, stars.

Fashion models reduced to computer simulations and then murdered. In "Androids and Androgeny" (listed under Drama Criticism), J. Bergstrom specifically relates the models in <u>Looker</u> to robot Maria in <u>Metropolis</u>. Cf. also <u>Max Headroom</u> (cited below, this section).

5.165   <u>Mad Max 2</u> (US vt <u>The Road Warrior</u>). George Miller, dir. Australia: Warner (US dist.), 1981 (initial release) / 1982 (US).

Sequel to Miller's <u>Mad Max</u> (Australia: Filmways, 1979/1980). Post-holocaust world in which gasoline-driven vehicles are central to what little human culture remains. See below, <u>Mad Max Beyond Thunderdome</u> and <u>Warlords of the Twenty-First Century</u>.

5.166   <u>Mad Max Beyond Thunderdome</u>. George Miller and George Ogilvie, dir. Australia: Kennedy Miller Productions (prod.) / Warner Brothers (US release), 1985. George Miller, prod. and co-author of script. Mel Gibson and Tina Turner, stars.

Third in the series (others: <u>Mad Max</u> and <u>Mad Max 2</u>). Offers a critique of the virtues and limitations of technological civilization, seen from the perspective of a post-holocaust world in which a barter economy is progressive and in which the relationship between energy and political power is very direct. Required viewing for critics who look for contemporary use of "archetypes." A Warner paperback is advertised. See below, <u>Warlords of the Twenty-First Century</u>.

5.167   <u>Making Mr. Right</u>. Susan Seidelman, dir. USA: Orion, 1987. John Malkovich, Ann Magnuson, stars.

Serious comedy: Pygmalion/Galatea motif with gender reversal and other twists. Malkovich plays a scientist who makes an android robot (also played by Malkovich) who gets humanized by Magnuson's character—who becomes more fully human in turn. Malkovich's scientist does not get humanized, but he does get a happy ending, shot into space. Cf. and contrast <u>Mann and Machine</u> (cited below).

5.168   <u>Mann and Machine</u>. NBC TV series first aired 5 April 1992. USA: Wolf Films (prod.) / Universal Television (TV release). "Author" of film for legal purposes: Forbrooke Enterprises. Dick Wolf and Robert DeLaurentis, creators, exec. prod. 60 min.

TV series featuring a mildly technophobic cop teamed up with a female android robot in a near-future Los Angeles. The android has full AI and is "capable of assimilating emotional material," which means she "can learn to be human." She is both the brains and the muscles of the team, but must mature emotionally. Cf. and contrast <u>Making Mr. Right</u>. Caution: Contains material offensive to the 4th Amendment and other parts of the American Bill of Rights.

5.169   Marinetti, Filippo Tommaso. <u>Automata (Poupées eléctriques)</u>. Paris, 1909.

Futurist play with a "startlingly innovative second act in which the human characters . . . share the stage with two life-like robots" (J. H. Bierman, "Walt Disney Robot Dramas" [230], q.v. under Drama Criticism").

5.170   "Marionettes, Inc." <u>The Ray Bradbury Theater</u>. Home Box Office, May 1985. Paul Lynch, dir. USA: Atlantis Films, 1985. Ray Bradbury, script. James Coco and Leslie Nielsen, stars. 30 min.

Based on Bradbury's story of the same name (q.v. under Fiction). Dramatic version stresses horror for a human to be replaced by a look-alike robot, plus fear of surveillance.

5.171 Masters of the Universe. Gary Goddard, dir. USA: Cannon, 1987. Menahem Golan and Yoram Globus, prod. Dolph Lundgren, star.

Ripoff of Superman and Star Wars films (plus at least one sentence from Richard III), with a Yoda-figure who is the inventor of a device that is a musical "key" to open doors to other times and places.

5.172 Max Headroom. American version of series, from ABC, premiered with "Blipverts" episode, 31 March 1987. Peter Wagg, exec. prod. Matt Frewer (Edison Carter and Max Headroom), Amanda Pays (Theora Jones), stars.

Headroom moves on in USA from a host on Cinemax cable TV service to Coca-Cola commercials to his own show (and then oblivion). "Blipverts" episode gives American genesis of Max Headroom, same as in British series, "20 Minutes into the Future." (See Harry F. Waters's "Max Goes Mainstream," Newsweek 6 April 1987: 55.) See below, The Max Headroom Show. If Max Headroom is the epitome of the postmodern character, it may be significant that Max Headroom lasted for so short a time on TV, not making it past 1988.

5.173 The Max Headroom Show. Cinemax cable service, syndicated from British TV. US Premiere, 1986. Created by Rocky Morton and Abbabel Jankel, for Peter Wagg. Matt Frewer, actor providing human portion of Max Headroom.

Introduced in an initial episode titled "20 Minutes into the Future," presenting the fully human TV reporter Edison Carter crashing "through a gate labeled 'Max. Headroom: 2.3 m[eters].' The evil network's house genius—a pimply faced teen hacker—then turns what's left of the hapless reporter into a 'computer-generated geek' .... And thus is born The Ultimate Talk-Show Host" (Cathleen McGuigan with Donna Foote, Newsweek 13 Jan. 1986: 59). See above, Max Headroom. For Max as a program in a computer, cf. and contrast TRON (see below); for more human folk inside computers, see under Fiction J. T. Sladek's The Müller-Fokker Effect and the works crosslisted there.

5.174 The Mechanical Butchers. France: Lunière, 1898. Silent short.

Cited by Naha, Science Fictionary, who says we see a pig go into "a machine that automatically changes it into bacon" and other processed pork products. Cf. and contrast machine sequences in S. Eisenstein's Old and New (cited in this section).

5.175 The Mechanical Husband. 1910. Silent short.

Cited by Naha, Science Fictionary.

5.176 The Mechanical Legs. France: Gaumont, 1908. Silent short.

Cited by Naha, Science Fictionary, who specifically identifies the legs as robotic. Cf. and contrast The Electric Leg (1912).

5.177 The Mechanical Man. USA: Universal, 1915. Silent short.

Cited by Naha, Science Fictionary: when the mechanical man won't work, it is replaced by the inventor. Cf. The Automatic Servant (1908), listed above.

5.178 Mechanical Mary Anne. UK: Hepworth, 1910. Silent short.

Cited by Naha, Science Fictionary, as an early film about a robot servant. Cf. and contrast The Automatic Servant (1908), cited above.

5.179 Mejagijira No Gyakusha (Terror of Mechagodzilla, Revenge of Mechagodzilla; vt Monsters from an Unknown Planet-B). Ishiro Honda, dir. Japan: UPA & Mechagodzilla Co./Toho Eizo, 1975.

Sequel to Gojira Tai Megagojira (Godzilla vs. Mechagodzilla, cited above), but with a cyborg woman in addition to the mechanical monster (Willis, vol. II, under Terror of Mechagodzilla).

5.180   Metropolis. Fritz Lang, dir. Germany: Ufa, 1926. Available in alternate versions.

Silent film showing a pleasure-city for the elite and a mechanized underground portion of the Metropolis, where mechanized workers tend the city's machines. A very important work for a robot femme fatale and the motif of mechanized underworlds; cf. Android, A Boy and His Dog, and THX 1138, this section, and see above, under Fiction, E. M. Forster, "Machine Stops," and H. G. Wells, Time Machine and First Men in the Moon. Metropolis is discussed in CW by L. Heldreth (essay cited under Drama Criticism).

5.181   Meyerhold, Vsevelod (also Karl Theodore Kasimir Meyerhold): see above, O. G. Brockett.

5.182   Mifflin, Margot. "Performance Art . . .": Cited under Graphics.

5.183   Millennium. Michael Anderson, dir. USA: Gladden Entertainment (prod.) / 20th Century Fox (release), 1989. Screenplay by John Varley, "based on his short story 'Air Raid,'" according to the credits, but closer to his novel, Millennium (q.v. above, under fiction).

Mostly eliminates the Big Computer as God of the far-future world, but retains Sherman (the wise and wise-ass robot) and the mechanical/humanoid ruling council. See for postmodern, highly funky *mise en scène* in the world of the time-travel Gate. Rev. Cinefantastique 20.4 (March 1990): 40 f.

5.184   The Mind-Detecting Ray. Alfred Desy, dir. Hungary: Star, 1918. Silent short.

Cited by Naha, Science Fictionary; see for an early version of a mind-reading machine, a device occuring as late as the Disney/Buena Vista movie The Misadventures of Merlin Jones (1964)—and which raises some serious philosophical questions about mind and matter not dealt with in such films.

5.185   Modern Times. Charles Chaplin, chief dir. USA: Charles Chaplin Corp. (prod.) / United Artists (US release), 1936.

Note esp. Chaplin's now-employed tramp on the assembly line, trapped in the feeding machine, and being pushed through the gears of a gigantic mechanism. These sequences add up to a cogent, if symbolic and grotesque, commentary on the condition of workers in industrialized society. See above, Daybreak.

5.186   Moontrap. Robert Dyke, dir. USA: Magic Films (prod.), 1989. Walter Koenig, star. B. K. Taylor, production design.

The enemy aliens are insectoid-appearing robots (Cinefantastique 18.5 [July 1988]: 32-33, 19.3 [March 1989]: 9, 20.3 [Jan. 1990]: 55).

5.187   Moonwalker. Colin Chilvers and Jerry Kramer, dirs. Michael Jackson and Franks Dileo, exec. prod. USA: Lorimar (prod.) / Warner (release), 1988. 93 min.

Superhero Michael (Michael Jackson) magically transforms himself into a car, robot, and spaceship. Rev. Douglas Borton, Cinefantastique 19.5 (July 1989): 51, on whom we depend; see Borton 50 for a picture of Jackson as robot.

5.188   Mosquito Coast. Peter Weir, dir. USA and other countries: Warner (dist.), 1986.

Mainstream film. Harrison Ford plays a Frankenstein figure working toward human perfection as much as trying to bring ice to the jungle. Note description of the pilot project ice machine as a living thing with guts—and the shots of the full-scale ice machine against the jungle: a richly significant image of the imposition of the mechanical upon the organic (see under Background the entry for H. Bergson).

5.189 The Motor Valet. Arthur Cooper, dir. UK: Alpha, 1906. Silent short.

Cited by Naha, Science Fictionary: "A robot servant goes beserk. After smashing the furniture, he blows up." See above, The Automatic Servant.

5.190 Mutant on the Bounty. Robert Torrance, dir. USA: Canyon et al., 1989. 85 min.

Satiric work in the tradition of Dark Star. See for fairly realistic computers and most especially for an android robot with male secondary features as representative of the "mother company" (cf. Alien, cited above). After a repair that includes cannibalizing chips from the ship's microwave oven, the robot has the potential for multiple personalities. With one configuration, the robot looks like a transvestite male human, breaking boundaries between human and machine, female and male.

5.191 My Living Doll. CBS-TV weekly series, 1964-65.

Female robot, described by Naha, Science Fictionary, as "a buxom, ravishing lass," learning to be human. Cf., among other works, Mann and Machine (above, this section) and L. Del Rey's "Helen O'Loy" (under Fiction).

5.192 The Mysterians. Inoshiro Honda, dir. Japan: Toho/RKO (later, MGM), 1957 (US release: 1959).

The premise is the biologically strange one of space invaders seeking Earth women for breeding, but this "sf pulp epic" features an impressive gigantic robot (quoted phrase from S. F. Ency, entry for the film)

5.193 Nameless. Avi Nasher, dir. USA: MGM/UA, 1991. Michael Biehn, stars.

Biehn's character is turned "into a killing machine" by a treatment in "an artificial womb—a machine which takes over every bodily function, forcing its occupant to undergo a mental, and[,] to a degree, physical regression to the fetal state. The machine has a Gigeresque quality to it" (Sheldon Teitelbaum in Cinefantastique 21.5 [April 1991]: 18-19). Cf. psychological manipulation in mechanical wombs in J. Haldeman's All My Sin's Remembered and R. Silverberg's The World Inside (listed under Fiction).

5.194 N.P. Silvano, dir., script. Italy: Zeta-A-Elle, 1971. Cast includes Irene Pappas.

Cited by Naha, Science Fictionary, as a vision of a late twentieth century that is "supermechanized," and in which "the workers are liberated by machines."

5.195 A New Hope: Cited and annotated below, this section, as Star Wars.

5.196 Northern Exposure: See below, "Slow Dance."

5.197 Nothing But Trouble (prod. title, Valkenvania). Dan Aykroyd, dir., script. Peter Aykroyd, story. USA: Applied Action (prod.) / Warner (release), 1991. Chevy Chase, John Candy, Demi Moore, stars.

A rural speed-trap from Hell is comically mechanized. See in CW, "Dante's Hell as an Ideal Mechanical Environment," cited under Literary Criticism.

5.198   Offenbach, Jacques (born Jacob, son of Isaac Juda Eberst), initial author/composer. Les Contes d'Hoffmann (The Tales of Hoffmann). Ernest Guiraud, orchestration and recitatives. First produced Opéra-Comique, Paris. 10 Feb. 1881.

Grand opera, begun by JO and completed by Guiraud. See below, Tales of Hoffmann.

5.199   Okuda, Michael, and Rick Sternback. Star Trek, the Next Generation Manual. New York: Pocket, 1991.

Successor to Franz Joseph's Star Trek Star Fleet Technical Manual (1975): All you wanted to know about technical matters concerning the Enterprise NC-1701 D. Rev. Tim Latas, SFRA Review #194 (Jan.-Feb. 1992): 47, upon whom we depend for this entry.

5.200   Old and New (vt The General Line). Sergei Eisenstein, dir. USSR: Sovkino, 1929.

Classic silent, with two famous sequences relevant here: heroine Marfa Lapinka's "first encounter with a mechanized cream separator . . . and the final 'dance' of the tractors" (quoting David A. Cook, A History of Narrative Film [1981]: 182).

5.201   O'Neill, Eugene. The Hairy Ape: A Comedy of Ancient and Modern Life in Eight Scenes. Selected Plays of Eugene O'Neill. New York: Random House, 1922. Rpt. Literature: An Introduction .... X. J. Kennedy, ed. Boston: Little, 1966 f.

Scenes I and III relevant: The central male character, Yank, as "The Hairy Ape" opposed to and "part of de engines" (in Kennedy 1203). EON's intention for Scene I was "a cramped space in the bowels of a ship, imprisoned by white steel" (1197-98).

5.202   Overdrawn at the Memory Bank. Douglas Williams, dir. David Loxton, exec. prod., with Stephen Roth. USA: WNET/Thirteen and RSL Films in association with SFTV, (c) 1983, Moviecorp VII. Broadcast 4 February 1985 on American Playhouse on the Public Broadcasting Service. Based on the short story by J. Varley (q.v.).

Somber romantic comedy set in a mildly dystopic future world run mainly by Novicorp, Lexicorp, Transcorp—and by HX368, a central global computer with a voice very like that of HAL 9000. The hero can be saved by the heroine only by storing his identity in HX368. The hero's time in the computer is relatively neutral: neither rapturous nor horrific. Cf. and contrast Charlie in the machine in Modern Times, the "Moloch" scene in Metropolis, and Flynn in the world of MCP in TRON (all of which see, this section). See under Fiction J. Sladek's The Müller-Fokker Effect and the works crosslisted there.

5.203   Parker Lewis Can't Lose. Comedy series in syndication on Fox, 1990-1992.

Relevant here for high-tech major settings and frequent surveillance. High school student Parker Lewis loses so infrequently because he commands enough electronic gear to run a season of Mission Impossible.

5.204   Pauline, Mark. Performance artist, San Francisco.

Techno-punk creator of nasty robots. Briefly discussed by Brooks Landon in rev. of Hardware (1991) in Cinefantastique 21.5 (April 1991): 22, depending in part on citation in REsearch [sic] Industrial Culture Handbook.

5.205   The Pedestrian: A Fantasy in One Act. London: Samuel French, Inc., 1966.

Dramatized version of R. Bradbury's "The Pedestrian," q.v. above, under Fiction.

5.206   Percy, The Mechanical Man. USA: Paramount, 1916. Silent, animated short.

Cited by Naha, Science Fictionary, as a comedy about a mechanical man, and certainly an early animated film on that theme.

5.207   The Perfect Woman. Bernard Knowles, dir. UK: Two Cities (Eagle-Lion), 1949 (US release: 1950). "Based on the play by Wallace Geoffrey and Basil Mitchell."

Romantic farce involving a young woman and her robot look-alike. Conclusion of film is "mildly apocalyptic": the robot goes out of control, walks through a hotel, and explodes (S. F. Ency., our source for this entry, and whom we quote; see for an instructively kinky photo of the robot "wearing a dazzlingly fetishistic display of old-fashioned underwear").

5.208   Performance Art: See also, listings under Graphics, and Indexes.

5.209   The Phantom Empire (advertised as Gene Autry and the Phantom Empire). USA: Mascot, 1935. Serial in twelve episodes. Later released as feature films under titles Radio Ranch and Men with Steel Faces (Walt Lee).

Combines "four or five" cinematic traditions by Baxter's count (71; see Reference, above), including the Western, and the SF motifs of the lost world and the subterranean city. Significant for presenting a mechanized underworld like that of Metropolis (q.v. above) in the film equivalent of pulp fiction. The premise of TPE was recycled in "The Secret Empire" segment of Cliffhangers, a 1979 NBC-TV weekly series.

5.210   Pink Floyd—The Wall. Alan Parker, dir. UK: MGM/UA, 1982. Bob Geldof, star. Soundtrack on CBS Records and Tapes.

Imagery stresses mechanization of education and of marching fanatics. Education sequence features a conveyor belt and clock; animation for marching fanatics shows "marching" crossed hammers. See under Music the entries for Pink Floyd.

5.211   Porush, David. R.Boots: Cited as "Induction from R.Boots" (sic) under Porush under Fiction.

5.212   The Power God. Ben Wilson, dir. USA: Vital Exchanges, 1925. Silent serial. 15 chapters.

Naha, Science Fictionary: invention of a machine that creates "continuous power without the need for fuel."

5.213   Predator 2. Stephen Hopkins, dir. USA: Twentieth Century Fox, 1990. Danny Glover, Gary Busey, stars.

Busey's scientist cum US Federal agent tries a high-tech approach to capturing the Predator; Glover's cop is more successful trying to kill the Predator with relatively low-tech weapons, including, finally, one of the Predator's own weapons.

5.214   The President's Analyst. Theodore J. Flicker, dir. USA: Panpiper (prod.) / Paramount (US release), 1967. James Coburn and Godfrey Cambridge, stars.

Mainstream satire. Robots running TPC (The Phone Company) may have us all under surveillance, and may seek total control over us. See also for "roboticized" (our word) Federal agents.

5.215   The Prisoner. Patrick McGoohan, creator, star, occasional writer and dir. UK: ITC

(Independent Television), 1967. Seventeen episodes; available on video cassette.

TV series showing one man (McGoohan) against a bureaucratic spy agency and a prison-camp, "The Village," disguised as a resort. Note for constant surveillance, attempts at mind control through technology, relatively gentle entrapment—and the ultimate threat of a very high-tech (nearly magical) huge beachball that pursues, traps, and smothers its victims. S. F. Ency. cites two novels based on the series: Thomas M. Disch, The Prisoner (1969), and David McDaniel, The Prisoner No. 2 (1969). See under Drama Criticism, M. White and J. Ali, The Official Prisoner Companion (sic with roman and italics).

5.216   The Questor Tapes. Richard A. Cola, dir. USA: NBC-TV/Universal Television, 1974. Gene Roddenberry, exec. prod. Roddenbery and Gene L. Coon, script. Robert Foxworth, Mike Farrell, John Vernon, Lew Ayres, stars. 95 min.

Willis notes that the Questor android "is hardly operational before he begins pining for feeling. (This, the basic android cliche.)" Questor is also essentially innocent—cf. A. C. Clarke's version of HAL 9000 (2001 under Fiction).

5.217   R. U. R.: See above under Karel Čapek.

5.218   Radio Patrol vs. Spy King. Fred Brannon, dir. USA: Republic, 1949. Serial. 12 chapters.

Naha, Science Fictionary, notes many gadgets in the serial, but central to it is radar (apparently still an exciting gadget in 1949).

5.219   La Ragazza di Latta (The Girl of Tin, The Tin Girl). Marcello Aliprandi, dir. Italy: Scetr Film, 1970.

The "Tin Girl" of the title is a robot who is followed by a young man who works for the company who made her; "he smashes her with a sword & is promoted for being independent in thinking" (Walt Lee—who declines to indicate how we should take the violent conclusion).

5.220   Red Alert. Billy (sic) Hale, dir. USA: Paramount, 1977. Sandor Stern, script, from Paradigm Red by Harold King. William Devane, star. Made for TV.

Very-near-future film relevant here for motif of computer-takeover during a nuclear power plant "excursion" and sabotage attack. Note paralleling of computer Proteus with the human Commander as a "robot" (as Devane's character calls him). Annotation in Movies on TV says that much of the film "was photographed at Houston's giant Space Lab and at the NASA Mission Control Center" (Movies on TV, cited under Reference).

5.221   Return of the Jedi. Richard Marquand, dir. USA/UK: Lucasfilm (prod.) / 20th Century-Fox (release), 1983. Lawrence Kasdan and George Lucas, script; story by George Lucas. George Lucas, exec. prod.

Last film in the first Star Wars trilogy (see in this section, Star Wars and The Empire Strikes Back). Note explicit contrast of the Empire's Death Star and other evilly-employed technology and the forest world of the Ewoks. (See entry for J. Kahn, above, under Fiction.)

5.222   The Right Stuff. Philip Kaufman, dir. USA: Ladd Co. (Warner Communications), 1983. Based on the book by Tom Wolfe.

Mainstream film. See for rebellion of Mercury astronauts against the high-ranking technicians building the space capsule: the men with "the right stuff" want to be astronaut-pilots of a spacecraft and not mere occupants of a capsule; they desire some degree of control. Briefly discussed by Graham Ian, "The Right

Stuff," Space Voyager #9 (1984): 30-32.

5.223   The Road Warrior: US Release title for Mad Max 2, cited above.

5.224   RoboCop. Paul Verhoeven, dir. USA: Jon Davison (prod.) / Orion (release), 1987.
Jon Davison, exec. prod. Rob Bottin, RoboCop design. Peter Weller, Nancy
Allen, stars.

Violent but sensitive film about a good cop made into a cyborg policeman: the
product of a large and nasty corporation. See also for less humanoid but
infantile robot opposing RoboCop. Novelization by Ed Naha, q.v. under Fiction.
Rev. L. Morley (see under Film Criticism).

5.225   RoboCop 2. Irvin Kershner, dir. USA: Orion (release), 1990. Rob Bottin, RoboCop
design.

See D. Persons's articles in Cinefantastique 21.1 (July 1990) for pre-release
coverage of the making of this (unworthy) sequel to RoboCop (cited below under
Drama Criticism). Note model work and well-designed Robo costume, the
somewhat witty use of the black hand of Rotwang from F. Lang's Metropolis—
both of Robo's arms and hands—and the presence of themes so important in a
cyborg work that they are there whether developed or not, most esp. that ". . .
Robo is really a metaphor for people in our society. They're becoming
roboticized without knowing it" (Irvin Kershner, quoted in Cinefantastique 21.1:
22). A "Jove Book" is advertised, as is the soundtrack on CDs and cassettes.

5.226   Roboman: See below, Who?.

5.227   The Robot. Dave Fleischer, dir. Max Fleischer, prod. USA: Paramount, 1932.
Animated art work. 1 reel.

Listed by Walt Lee as an SF comedy. Note date of film, and 1923 as the date of
first publication in English of R. U. R.

5.228   Robot Jox (prod. title RoboJox). Stuart Gordon, dir. USA: Empire (renamed Epic)
Pictures, 1990. Dennis Paoli and Joe Haldeman, script.

Robots like giant transformer toys represent the US and Soviet blocs and fight
against one another. See Dennis Fischer, "The Amazing Special Effects of
RoboJox," Cinefantastique 10.1 & 2 (double issue, Jan. 1989): 6-11, and Steve
Biodrowski's short, and negative, rev. of Robot Jox in Cinefantastique 21.4 (Feb.
1991): 53. Note transformation as a popular motif in the early 1990s, most
spectacularly in Terminator 2, q.v. below.

5.229   The Robot of Regalia. Various dirs. USA: Reed, 1954. 78 min.

Naha, Science Fictionary, identifies the film as a fixup of episodes from Rocky
Jones, Space Ranger (NBC 1954-55), in which "Rocky meets a robot." We find
the encounter a useful index of the popularity of film robots even prior to
Forbidden Planet (1956).

5.230   Robot Rabbit. Friz Freleng, dir. USA: Warner, 1954. Cartoon. Mel Blanc, voices. 7
mins.

A Bugs Bunny cartoon we have not seen.

5.231   El Roboto Humano (The Human Robot, vt La Momia contra el Robot Humano [The
(Aztec) Mummy vs. the Human Robot, The Robot vs. the Aztec Mummy]).
Rafael Portillo, dir. Mexico: Calderon (Azteca; AIP-TV), ca. 1959, with later US
release (1966?).

Classified by Walt Lee as fantasy/horror; Lee describes the action as "the Aztec mummy fights a mad scientist's robot which has a human brain."

5.232   The Rocketeer. Joe Johnston, dir. USA: Buena Vista, 1991.

Mild-mannered American civilian pilot in the 1930s becomes a hero upon finding and learning how to use a personal rocket pack. The premise is from the movie serial King of the Rocket Men, q.v. above.

5.233   Roger Corman's Frankstein Unbound. Roger Corman, dir., co-prod., co-author of filmscript. USA/Italy: 20th-Century Fox, 1990. From the novel by Brian Aldiss. John Hurt, Raul Julia, stars.

See for juxtaposition of technology and science in settings ca. 2031, 1818, and a post-holocaust, far-future; see also for "Aztec," the prototype car "playing" the car of our future that gets transported into the past of Frankenstein.

5.234   Rollerball. Norman Jewison, dir. USA: United Artists, 1975. W. Harrison, script, from his "Roller Ball Murder," q.v. under Fiction.

The highly mechanized game of Rollerball is used by the ruling corporate apparat as an outlet for the violent emotions of the masses and as a way to teach them that individual effort is futile. Note sequence in which the film's hero goes to consult his world's central computer, where the human past is, theoretically, preserved. Rollerball is discussed in CW by E. A. Hull (see citation under Drama Criticism).

5.235   Runaway. Michael Crichton, dir. and script. USA: Tri-Star Pictures (release), 1984.

Note threatening small machines: crab-like and insectoid. Rev. New York Times 14 Dec. 1984: 18 Y, which classifies the film as a "high-tech thriller."

5.236   The Running Man. Paul Michael Glaser, dir. USA: Taft Entertainment Pictures/Keith Parish Productions (prod.) / Tri-Star Pictures (dist.), 1987. Arnold Schwarzenegger, star. Based on the novel The Running Man by S. King (writing as Richard Bachman), q.v. under Fiction.

Significant as a Schwartzenegger vehicle bringing to a mass audience themes, images, and gimmicks from serious SF including images of threatening containment within high-tech machines in the mostly funky near-future world of Los Angeles in 2019. (Note that it is Schwarzenegger, not the heroine, who is momentarily gagged and that the heroine, and the villain, end up in the close, mechanized containment that begins the run.) See below, Total Recall. See under Drama Criticism T. Doherty on "Video, Science Fiction, and the Cinema of Surveillance."

5.237   R.U.R.: Listed above, this section, under Karel Čapek.

5.238   Saturn 3. Stanley Donen, prod. and dir. (replacing John Barry as dir.). UK: Lew Grade/Shepperton Studios, 1980. Kirk Douglas, Farrah Fawcett, Harvey Keitel, stars.

See for a high-tech underworld, the threat of roboticization, and for "Hector, 'the lust-crazed humanoid' robot" discussed in TMG in essay by D. Palumbo (cited uner Drama Criticism), whom we quote.

5.239   Sennett, Mack. Series of brief movie comedies made in the USA for the Keystone company.

In Gerald Mast's words, the basic technique of a Mack Sennet comedy was the reduction of people "to machines. His distant shots reduced people into things,

making them close cousins to the other machines that zip through Sennett films
.... Sennett increased the impression of mechanization with his mechanical
camera tricks .... The Sennet world at Keystone was one of pure mechanical
fun ... " (518 in article cited under Reference).

5.240 Shanks. William Castle, dir. USA: Paramount, 1974. Marcel Marceau, star.

See for zombie puppets (our phrase) produced by "electrically rewiring" the dead
(Naha's phrase, Science Fictionary: our source for this entry).

5.241 The Shape of Things to Come. George McCowan, dir. USA: Allied Artists, 1979.
"Suggested by" H. G. Wells's novel.

According to Naha, Science Fictionary, robots are important to the plot, with Jack
Palance as a villain using robots.

5.242 Short Circuit. John Badham, dir. USA: Tri-Star Pictures, 1986.

E.T. as robot. See for the hardware: credits indicate that much of the robotic
material is really done with (presumably industrial variety) robots. Real robots
were used even more in the sequel, Short Circuit 2 (q.v.).

5.243 Short Circuit 2. Kenneth Johnson, dir. USA: Tri-Star, 1988.

Written up by Gary Kimber in Cinefantastique 18.5 (July 1988): 4 f.; rev. briefly
but favorably by Allen Malmquist in Cinefantastique 19.1-2 (Jan. 1989): 118.
Includes some serious comedy concerning the humanity of a robot with AI,
complete with appropriate allusions to R. Descartes on his existence and William
Shakespeare's Shylock on his humanity. Final sequences have a comically
(cyber)punkified Johnny 5 chasing criminals; film ends with a clean-cut Mr.
Johnny 5 taking the oath of allegiance and proclaimed the first robot citizen of
the USA. See under Fiction, I. Asimov, "The Bicentennial Man."

5.244 The Silencers. Phil Karlson, dir. USA: Columbia, 1966. Dean Martin, star.

Early Matt Helm film. We will privilege American schlock over British enough to
list Silencers as our example of James Bondish super-spy adventure featuring
very-near-future high-tech gadgets.

5.245 Silent Running (vt Running Silent, original title). Douglas Trumbull, dir. and SpFx.
USA: Universal/Gruskoff, 1972. Bruce Dern, star.

Note the three cute little robots aiding the hero (Dern) in his effort to save an
orbitting forest preserve. Discussed by Sobchack in The Limits of Infinity (see
Sobchack's Index).

5.246 Sins of the Fleshapoids. Mike Kuchar, dir., script. George and Mike Kuchar, prod.
USA: Film Makers, 1964 (1965?). 44 min.

Described by Walt Lee as comically satiric SF in which "robots desire sexual
freedom, lead a revolt against the human beings" in a far-future world.

5.247 The Six Million Dollar Man. Silverton and Universal Prod. for ABC; 1973-1977.
Syndicated thereafter. Lee Majors, star. Based on M. Caidin's Cyborg, q.v. under
Fiction.

Retells the rebirth of Steve Austin as a cyborg (ninety-minute film, March
1973)—without Caidin's sensitivity. The two additional TV films and the
following series continue the adventures that seem to be Austin's destiny at the
end of the novel. See above, The Bionic Woman.

5.248   The Sky Bike. Charles Frendn, dir., script. UK: Eyeline Films, 1967.

According to Naha, Science Fictionary, a gentle film about inventing a human-powered flying machine (like the Gossamer Condor).

5.249   The Sky Parade. Otto Lovering, dir. USA: Paramount, 1936.

Robot airplane (Naha, Science Fictionary).

5.250   Slaughterhouse-Five (sometimes spelled without hyphen). George Roy Hill, dir. USA: Universal, 1971 (completion), 1972 (US release). Based on K. Vonnegut, Jr., Slaughterhouse-Five, q.v. under Fiction.

Retains in attenuated form a question raised in Vonnegut's novel: Do humans have free will, or are we merely machines, doomed to do what we do because "the moment is structured that way." Also retains Billy Pilgrim's cage in the Tralfamadorian zoo as a very homey sort of mechanical womb.

5.251   Sleeper. Woody Allen, dir. USA: United Artists, 1973.

Includes a scene of Allen with robot tailors and a sequence featuring Allen as a comic robot. Summarized and briefly discussed in S. F. Ency., discussed in TMG essay by D. Palumbo (cited under Drama Criticism).

5.252   "Slow Dance." Northern Exposure. CBS. 20 May 1991. David Carson, dir. USA: Pipeline Productions. Josh Brand and John Falsey, exec. prod.

Major plot involves a falling artificial satellite that lands on a man and fuses with him. The basic mode of the show is comic realism, but the S. F. possibilities of high-speed man/satellite fusion are made explicit by the town disk jockey.

5.253   Some Girls Do. Ralph Thomas, dir. UK: Ashdown, 1969, USA: United Artists, 1971.

Bulldog Drummond film featuring conquest of the world threatened by a madman in command of "an army of girl robots" (Naha, Science Fictionary).

5.254   Space Cruiser Yamato. Yoshinabu Nishizaki, dir., prod., script. Japan: Enterprise, 1977. Animated.

During a war in 2199, Earth desperately needs an antidote to radioactive fallout; the antidote is sought for using a refloated battleship Yamato, refitted for space travel (Naha, Science Fictionary)—for an intriguing variation on the theme of the superweapon.

5.255   Space Flight (vt Spaceflight IC-1). Bernard Knowles, dir. UK: Lippert, 1965.

RULE, the aristocratic government of Earth, controls a computer that controls a spaceship; the plot thickens "when the machine begins working murder into its program" (Naha, Science Fictionary). Cf. and contrast with various computer-takeover tales, and with the Company and Mother in Alien.

5.256   Spaced Invaders. Patrick Read Johnson, dir. USA: Buena Vista Pictures (dist.), 1990.

Mildly successful send-up of War of the Worlds, with explicit allusions to the Orson Welles radio broadcast. Features a significantly large and villainous Martian Enforcer Drone and a cute, significantly small, Martian robot—and the ultimate fighting harvester combine.

5.257   Spacehunter: Adventures in the Forbidden Zone. Canada: Columbia, 1983. Lamont Johnson, dir. From a story by Stewart Harding and Jean Lefleur. David Preston et al., screenplay. Elmer Bernstein, music. Peter Strauss and Molly Ringwald.

See for post-disaster technology, broken-down machinery in general, juxtaposition of the mechanical and the organic (cf. Alien, above, this section), and the "mechano-dehumanization" (our term) of Overdog, the Darth Vadar avatar leading the evil people in the film.

5.258   STAR TREK Episodes—Television (NBC). Created by Gene Roddenberry.

5.259   "The Apple." Star Trek, 13 Oct. 1967. Max Ehrlich with Gene L. Coon, script.

Vaal, a kind of deified, immobile, mechanical dragon, preserves in a stagnant paradise a society of gentle humanoids. Fictionalized by James Blish in Star Trek 6 (1972) discussed by K. Blair in "The Garden in the Machine," esp. 312-13 (listed under Drama Criticism). See below under Star Trek: The Next Generation the episodes "Justice" and "Who's Watching the Watchers."

5.260   "The Changeling." Star Trek, 29 Sept. 1976. John M. Lucas, script.

Small spacecraft taken aboard Enterprise tries to destroy everything that doesn't live up to its idea of perfection. Fictionalized by J. Blish in Star Trek 7 (1972).

5.261   "The Doomsday Machine." Star Trek, 20 Oct. 1967. Norman Spinrad, script.

Fight against a giant machine that destroys planets, star systems, spaceships, or whatever else it comes across. Fictionalized by J. Blish in Star Trek 3 (1969).

5.262   "For the World Is Hollow and I Have Touched the Sky." Star Trek, 3d season (1968-69). Rik Vollaerts, script.

Combines the motifs of the generation starship and mechanical, or electronic, "possession" (our term). See above, under Fiction, R. Heinlein, "Universe," and K. Vonnegut, Sirens of Titan. Fictionalized by J. Blish in Star Trek 8 (1972).

5.263   "I, Mudd." Star Trek, 3 Nov. 1967. Stephen Kandel, script.

Comic episode featuring a world run by humanoid robots; makes the serious point that robots have trouble dealing with the irrational, unpredictable, and absurd.

5.264   "The Return of the Archons." Star Trek, 9 Feb. 1967. Boris Sobelman, script, from a story by Gene Roddenberry.

A society has achieved unity and stasis by merging individual consciousnesses with what turns out to be a machine. Fictionalized by J. Blish in Star Trek 9 (1973).

5.265   "The Ultimate Computer." Star Trek, 8 March 1968. D. C. Fontana, script from a story by Lawrence N. Wolfe.

A supposedly perfect machine put in charge of the Enterprise threatens the ship and human life. Fictionalized by J. Blish in Star Trek 9 (1973).

5.266   STAR TREK: THE NEXT GENERATION Episodes—Television Syndication by Paramount (Fox). Created by Gene Roddenberry. Rick Berman, exec. prod. David Livingston, line producer.

5.267   "11001001." Star Trek: The Next Generation. 30 Jan. 1988. Paul Lynch, dir. Maurice Hurley and Robert Lewin, script.

The Enterprise is hijacked by people (the Binars) in a kind of symbiotic connection with a planetary computer, who use the ship's computer to store data during the electromagnetic pulse from a supernova (Altman, 1990: 28, cited under Reference).

5.268   "The Arsenal of Freedom." Star Trek: The Next Generation. 9 April 1988. Les Landau, dir. Maurice Hurley and Robert Lewin, story. Richard Manning and Hans Beimler, script.

Set on "a desolate world formerly inhabited by arms merchants. Picard and a wounded Dr. Crusher are stranded in a ditch while the Away Team battles killer robots on the surface" (Altman, 1990: 30).

5.269   "The Best of Both Worlds," Part I. Star Trek: The Next Generation. 18 March 1990. Cliff Bole, dir. Michael Piller, script. Part II, 28 Sept. 1990.

An extensive handling of the Borg: STNG's cyborg enemies. See Part I for presentation of Borg as white-skinned men, speaking in chorus in voice-over, and dressed in what look like black wetsuits with mechanical gizmos attached very inelegantly; the mechanized environment of the Borg spacecraft—a cube whose outer surface looks like a circuit board or an electronphotomicrograph of a computer chip; and for the initial cyborgization of Capt. Picard. Listen to Part I for Borg plan to absorb the Federation and for the assertions that "Freedom is irrelevant; self-determination is irrelevant," plus the so-far undeveloped subversive suggestion that the Federation's weak spot is, "Your primitive cultures are authority-driven." Part II shows the near-complete cyborgization of Picard and a "First Contact" between Data (who uses the phrase) and Picard as a member of the Borg Group Consciousness. See below, the episode "Q—Who?"

5.270   "Brothers." Star Trek: The Next Generation. 12 October 1990. Rob Bowman, dir. Rick Berman, script. Brent Spiner featured as Data, Lore, and Dr. Soong.

Data's dying "Father," Dr. Soong, recalls him to say farewell and to give him a chip that will give him emotions. Unfortunately, the recall code also brings back Data's evil brother Lore, who fools Dr. Soong into installing the chip in him. See for Data's increasing maturity.

5.271   "Contagion." Star Trek: The Next Generation. 18 March 1989. Joseph L. Scanlon, dir. Steve Gerber and Beth Woods, script.

Features a starship-destroying computer virus.

5.272   "Data's Day." Star Trek: The Next Generation. 1990. Robert Wiemer. dir. Harold Apter and Ronald D. Moore, script, from a story by Apter. Teri Taylor, supervising producer.

A personal log of a day in the life of the android Data as he learns to be human; see for Data's similarities and important differences from Vulcans and Vulcanoids, his desire for human contact and feelings contrasting with "their stark philosophy," which he finds "somewhat [pause] limited."

5.273   "Datalore." Star Trek: The Next Generation. 16 Jan. 1988 ([c] 1987). Rob Bowman, dir. Robert Lewin and Gene Roddenberry, story. Robert Lewin and Maurice Hurley, script.

The android Data returns to his home planet and meets his evil twin brother, Lore (Altman, 1990: 30). Important for definition of "human" and the ways in which Mr. Data is rather more than human.

5.274   "Galaxy Child." Star Trek: The Next Generation. 15 March 1991. Winrich Kolbe, dir. Thomas Kartozian, script.

There's a superimposition of the organic upon the mechanical when a huge baby ... something nurses on power from the Enterprise. The subplot of the episode involves the ship's engineer, Geordi La Forge, with the visiting designer of the ship's engines.

5.275   "Hollow Pursuits." <u>Star</u> <u>Trek: The</u> <u>Next</u> <u>Generation</u>. 5 May 1990. Cliff Bole, dir. Sally Caves, script. Dwight Schultz guest stars as Lt. Barclay.

Stresses uses and abuses of Holodeck and imagination. See for the Holodeck and image of people inside a machine that allows them to act out and act in their own fantasies, and those of others.

5.276   "I, Borg." <u>Star</u> <u>Trek: The</u> <u>Next</u> <u>Generation</u>. Week of 11 May 1992. Robert Lederman, dir. Rene Echevarria, script. Jonathan Del Arco, guest star.

Individualization of an adolescent male Borg, who learns to say "I" and returns to the hive collective as, potentially, a kind of virus of individualism. Important episode for the politics of <u>STNG</u> and of SF more generally; cf. and contrast Ayn Rand's <u>Anthem</u> (1946), I. Asimov's <u>I, Robot</u> (cited under Fiction), and such <u>Star</u> <u>Trek</u> episodes as "The Return of the Archons" (cited this section).

5.277   "Justice." <u>Star</u> <u>Trek: The</u> <u>Next</u> <u>Generation</u>. 7 Nov. 1987. James L. Conway, dir. Ralph Willis and Worley Thorne, story. Worley Thorne, script.

See for treatment of space-based god of the apparently utopian Edo people. See above under <u>Star</u> <u>Trek</u> the episode, "The Apple"; see below, the <u>STNG</u> episode "Who's Watching the Watchers?"

5.278   "The Measure of a Man." <u>Star</u> <u>Trek: The</u> <u>Next</u> <u>Generation</u>. 11 Feb. 1988. Robert Scheerer, dir. Melinda Snodgrass, script.

Courtroom drama on the question of an android's rights. Is Mr. Data a person under the law, or Starfleet's property?

5.279   "The Most Toys." <u>Star</u> <u>Trek: The</u> <u>Next</u> <u>Generation</u>. 12 May 1990. Timothy Bond, dir. Shari Goodhartz, script.

Title from the expression, "He who dies with the most toys wins." Mr. Data, the unique android, is the "toy" in question. Escape from the murderous collector involves Data in a conflict of programming and ethics: to save human lives and gain his own freedom, he acts to kill the collector; that he does not is pure coincidence. After the fact, Data does not exactly lie about his attempt at murder, but he does mislead.

5.280   "The Offspring." <u>Star</u> <u>Trek: The</u> <u>Next</u> <u>Generation</u>. 10 March 1990. Jonathan Frakes, dir. Rene Echevarria, script.

Mr. Data produces and loses an android offspring, raising the question of "child" vs. "invention," and the centrality of feelings (esp. love) for the Trekkian definition of humanity.

5.281   "Q—Who?" <u>Star</u> <u>Trek: The</u> <u>Next</u> <u>Generation</u>. 6 May 1989. Rob Bowman, dir. Maurice Hurley, script.

Episode introducing cyborgized, somewhat cyberpunk villain, "the Borg." See above, "The Best of Both Worlds" and "I, Borg." Note esp. scene in incubator room and the human(oid) infant in a mechanical and mechanizing womb, having the "cybernetics" added to his or her organism.

5.282   "Tin Man." <u>Star</u> <u>Trek: The</u> <u>Next</u> <u>Generation</u>. 29 April 1990. Robert Scheerer, dir. Dennis Putnam Bailey and David Bischoff, script.

Features a living spaceship.

5.283   "Who's Watching the Watchers?" Star Trek: The Next Generation. 14 Oct. 1989.
Robert Wiemer, dir. Richard Manning and Hans Beimler, script.

From the Latin "sentence," "Who will watch the Watchers [i.e. guard (against) the
Guardians] themselves?" Uses A. C. Clarke's "Third Law" and the theme of the
mechanical god. A small group of primitive Vulcanoid people almost start a
religion with Capt. Picard as god. A major violation of the Prime Directive is
avoided when Picard demonstrates (in argument and action) that he's just a mortal
backed up with wonderously high technology. See above, the STNG episode
"Justice." For Clarke's Third Law, see below, Starman.

5.284   Star Trek: The Motion Picture. Robert Wise, dir. USA: Paramount, 1979. Harold
Livingston and Alan Dean Foster, script.

For most of the film the characters are inside the starship Enterprise, which is
itself inside a gigantic machine. See for a positive view of human/machine
merger. Discussed by V. Sobchack in Screening Space, Chapter 4. Discussed in
TMG by D. Palumbo (cited under Drama Criticism).

5.285   Star Wars (retitled, A New Hope). George Lucas, dir. and script. USA (Tunisia, UK):
Lucasfilm (prod.) / 20th Century-Fox (US release), 1977.

See for helpful "droids" (i.e., robots), the malevolent technology of the Empire,
esp. the labyrinthian mechanical world of the Death Star, and the limitations of
technology in a galaxy where the ultimate force is the Force. Novelization by
Lucas cited above under Fiction (but see also the last sentence of the SW entry in
S. F. Ency.). Discussed in TMG by D. Palumbo, L. Heldreth, and passim (see
Palumbo and Heldreth entries under Drama Criticism). See this section, the
entries for The Empire Strikes Back and Return of the Jedi. Discussed by V.
Sobchack in The Limits of Infinity.

5.286   Starlight Express. Andrew Lloyd Webber, music. Richard Stilgoe, lyrics. Trevor
Nunn, dir. for London and Broadway prod. Arlene Phillips, choreographer.
Aland Henderson, automated lighting design. Kevin Biles, design, film.
Columbia Artists Theatricals, prod. London opening, March 1984 by The Really
Useful Theatre Company. On tour, starting November 1989.

Musical described by its composer as "a Cinderella story about trains" (quoted in
the playbill); the trains are played by humans on roller skates.

5.287   The Starlost. TV series from Canada's CTV, 1973; shown in syndication in the USA,
1974. Original idea credited to "Cordwainer Bird," pseud. of Harlan Ellison when
he wishes to dissociate himself from a project.

Features a generation starship with different Terran cultures in various
"biospheres"; the crew of the starship are dead, and the passengers have forgotten
the mission of the starship and mistake it for a world. See under Fiction, R.
Heinlein, "Universe"; see also in that section E. Bryant and H. Ellison, Phoenix
Without Ashes, based on Ellison's original intention for The Starlost series.

5.288   Starman. John Carpenter, dir. USA: Columbia/Delphi II, 1984.

See for the neutrality of a number of literal machines an example of Arthur C.
Clarke's Third Law ("Any sufficiently advanced technology is indistinguishable
from magic"), and an antithesis between an alien learning to be human (Starman),
a human who learns to be human (the scientist, Mark Shermin), and a human who
doesn't learn to be human: George Fox, government bureaucrat, associated with
helicopters. Rev. New York Times 14 Dec. 1984: 18 Y; Newsweek 17 Dec. 1984.

5.289   Steel Justice. Christopher Crowe, dir. USA: Universal Television, 1992. TV premiere
NBC 5 April 1992.

See for a time-traveller who can teach people to transform small objects into big objects, and a cop who will resolve the plot by transforming his dead son's beloved toy into a giant "robosaurus"; the robot tyrannosaurus has potential.

5.290 The Stepford Wives. Bryan Forbes, dir. USA: Columbia, 1975. Based on the novel by Ira Levin.

The husbands of Stepford, CT, replace their wives with robot duplicates. Discussed in TMG by D. Palumbo (see under Drama Criticism) and in CW by D. Ingersoll (see under Literary Criticism). Also note the 1980 TV film by Brian Wiltse, The Revenge of the Stepford Wives: the climactic sequence of which is an SF updating of the catastrophe of The Bacchae of Euripides (lines 1050-1150), with the malfunctioning robot wives of Stepford playing Maenads to the Pentheus of the leader of the Stepford Men's Association. A further sequel brings us to The Stepford Children in the late 1980s and the entry of "Stepford" into popular culture vocabulary.

5.291 Streamline Express. Leonard Fields, dir. USA: Mascot, 1938.

Features a "superspeed monorail train" (Naha, Science Fictionary).

5.292 Super Force. Fox Television. Pilot broadcast 29 September 1990. Richard Compton, dir. USA: Universal (FL operations), 1990.

A virtual compendium of clichés from Doctor Who, Neuromancer, RoboCop, the Mad Max Trilogy, Max Headroom, James Bond movies, Hill Street Blues, and other works, with enough blatant allusions and overstatements that we know they know they're doing camp. Note for Patrick Macnee's character getting killed and then digitalized as a computer program (cf. and contrast TRON, and perhaps KITT in Knight Rider; both cited in this section), and for the star as a superhero on a spiffy motorcycle and in a suit designed for planetary exploration. Note that the hero's initial, soon trashed suit is NASA-style modern, while his second suit is postmodern, cyberpunk street-wear.

5.293 Supercar. UK: ITC syndicated weekly TV series. "Supermarionation" (puppets).

Flying car (Naha, Science Fictionary).

5.294 Supertrain. NBC-TV telefilm, 1979, 120 min. airtime, and NBC-TV weekly series, 1979, 60-min. episodes.

Stories set on and in the mechanized, moving environment of an atomic-powered train (Naha, Science Fictionary).

5.295 Survival Research Laboratories. West-coast US performance art group.

Carnival of Misplaced Devotions (in Seattle, WA), was covered in a story on Morning Edition on National Public Radio on 25 June 1990. Radio coverage indicated that Carnival used technology in prod. and was in some sense about technology, and that this concern with techological art was central to SRL. Group discussed by John Horgan, "Robots rampant: California artists spawn technological monsters," Scientific American Aug. 1988: 28.

5.296 Tales of Hoffmann.

Opera: See above, J. Offenbach.

Films:

Richard Oswald, dir. Germany: Union, 1914. Silent.

Michael Powell and Emeric Pressburger, dir., script. Frederick Ashton, choreographer. Thomas Beecham, music dir. UK: London (Lippert), 1951. 138 min. (Maltin [1989] cites a version cut to 118 min.) "Based on the opera by Jacques Offenbach with libretto by Jules Babier and Michel Carré, based on their play derived from stories by E.T.A. Hoffmann" (q.v. under Fiction).

In the "Olympia" section, ". . . Hoffmann falls in live with a life-like dancing doll, but she is destroyed" (Walt Lee). See above, Coppélia.

5.297 Target Earth! Sherman A. Rose, dir., ed. USA: Abtcom Pictures / Allied Artists, 1954. "Based on story 'Deadly City' by Ivar Jorgenson . . . published in If . . . March, 1953" (Walt Lee).

Features invading robots from Venus. (See Willis, vol. II, for spelling title without exclamation mark and different source of story.)

5.298 The Terminal Man. Mike Hodges, dir., prod. script. USA: Warner, 1974. George Segal and Joan Hackett, stars. Based on the novel by M. Crichton (q.v. under Fiction).

Brain implant that includes a microcomputer is designed to prevent blackouts and unremembered violence by a computer expert (Segal) by providing contravailing electrical stimuli, apparently to the (or a) pleasure-center in the brain. Stimuli prove so pleasurable to the brain as to function as operant conditioning, soon training the patient's brain to undergo constant attacks. See for imagery of mechanized environments, surveillance, technocrats at work and play, and the mechanizing of a human being.

5.299 The Terminator. James Cameron, dir. USA: Orion, 1984. Gale Anne Hurd, prod. Cameron and Hurd, script. Features Arnold Schwarzenegger.

See for antipathy between humans and conscious, AI machines, epitomized by the Terminators: nearly indestructible killer robots of great efficiency and fanatical perseverance. Cf. F. Saberhagen's berserkers (see under Fiction); for the motif of the hand, see end of film and Terminator 2—and cf. and contrast Metropolis, Dr. Strangelove, Dr. No (1963), and "Demon with a Glass Hand." Rev. by Jack Kroll, Newsweek 19 Nov. 1984: 132. Discussed by V. Sobchack in Screening Space, Chapter 4; Martin Perlman, "The Terminator," Cinefantastique 15 (July 1985): 36 f. See below, Terminator 2 . . . .

5.300 The Terminator: Computer Game. Bethesda Softworks™. Advertised in the early 1990s as offering a virtual reality in which one can play either The Terminator or Kyle Reese.

5.301 Terminator 2: Judgment Day. James Cameron, dir., prod., co-author. USA: Tri-Star (release), 1991. Gale Anne Hurd and Mario Kassar, co-exec. prod. Stan Winston, make-up and Terminator effects. Industrial Light and Magic, computer graphic images. Arnold Schwartzenegger, Linda Hamilton, and Robert Patrick, stars.

Sequel to The Terminator (q.v.), in which Schwartzenegger's machine has been reprogrammed as protector of the savior of humanity in one possible (very grim) future. The state-of-the-art SpFx allow for a villanous terminator cyborg that appears either Modern or postPostmodern—and who usually looks like a very clean-cut Los Angeles cop—opposing Schwartzenegger's scruffy biker. In its quieter moments, the film raises serious questions about humans and our technology, families, macho, fate, freedom, ethics, and survival; see also for hand motif.

5.302 Terry, Megan. Megan Terry's Home, or Future Soap. New York: Samuel French. 1967. A playable version of the 1967 Public Broadcasting Service telecast.

One day in the life of one "home" (a cubicle in a huge building) in which nine people of the future live out their entire lives. Together with the people of billions of similar homes, all governed by Control, they carry out the mission of the human race: "We Will Populate Space!" Cf. R. Silverberg, The World Inside, listed above under Fiction. MT's Home is discussed briefly in T. Dunn and R. Erlich, "Vision of Dystopia," q.v. under Literary Criticism.

5.303   Test Pilota Pirxa (Test Pilot Pirx). Marek Piestrak, dir., script. Poland: Zespoly filmowe-Tallinnfilm, 1979. Based on S. Lem's Tales of Pirx the Pilot (see entry for Lem, under Fiction).

Willis suggests an important role for "'Finite non-linears,' more-human-than-human robots" (vol. II, under English title).

5.304   Things to Come. William Cameron Menzies, dir. UK: London Films (prod.) / United Artists (US release), 1936. H. G. Wells, script, from his The Shape of Things to Come (preproduction working title for the film). Alexander Korda, prod.

Positive presentation of technocratic takeover after a horrible war. Final portion includes a visual celebration of machines of the future. Discussed by W. Warren Wagar in "Steel-Gray Saviour," q.v. above under Literary Criticism.

5.305   THX 1138. George Lucas, dir. USA: American Zoetrope (prod.) / Warner (dist.), 1969 (completion), 1971 (US release). Based on Lucas' student film, THX-1138-4EB (rental title, Electronic Labyrinth [Walt Lee]). George Lucas and Walter Murch, script; story by George Lucas. Francis Ford Coppola, exec. prod.

Features a technocratic, computerized, white and aseptic underground culture. Note esp. the sequence in which THX (Robert Duvall) is trapped and tortured by machines and machinelike men. Novelized by B. Bova (see entry under Fiction). Cf. and contrast Metropolis and A Boy and His Dog (listed in this section) and E. M. Forster, "Machine Stops" (listed under Fiction). THX is discussed in CW by L. Heldreth (see under Literary Criticism) and by V. Sobchack in The Limits of Infinity (see Sobchack's Index).

5.306   Time Bandits. Terry Gilliam, dir. UK: Handmade Films, 1981.

A fantasy film that could be subtitled "Monty Python and the Royal Shakespeare Meet the Problem of Evil." Significant here for associating mechanization with mythic evil (as Ralph Bakshi had done in his animated fantasy Wizards, q.v.) and having that association work in a serious comedy: the Satan-figure is both a proponent and embodiment of things mechanical and cybernetic. At the end of the climactic battle, the devil's lair is littered with artifacts of human military technology from ancient Greece through the 21st c., and the Adversary has only barely been stopped, by divine intervention, from computerizing his operation. See T. Holt's Who's Afraid of Beowulf?, under Fiction.

5.307   The Time Machine. George Pal, dir. USA: Galaxy Films (prod.) / MGM (US release), 1960. Based on the novel by H. G. Wells (1895), q.v. under Fiction.

The film version of TM retains the mechanized underworld of the Morlocks in Wells's novel.

5.308   Tin Man. John G. Thomas, dir., prod. USA: Goldfarb/Thomas-Biston & Westcom, 1983. 95 min. Cast includes Timothy Bottoms.

"Deaf-mute boy builds a machine which enables him to hear and talk, and an 'electronic robot' with its own personality" (Willis, vol. III). Contrast more negative view of machines in The Tin Man (1935), cited below.

5.309 The Tin Man. James Parrott, dir. Hal Roach, prod. USA: Hal Roach / MGM, 1935. 19 min.

As described by Walt Lee: Two women get lost while driving and find a mad scientist with a women-killing robot, but at film's end the robot turns on the scientist. Note date: the film was released about a dozen years after R. U. R. was translated into English (see above, this section; see also Tin Man [1983]).

5.310 Tobor the Great. Lee Sholem, dir. USA: Dudley Pictures / Republic, 1954. Carl Dudley, story.

A newly developed robot "has emotions & can receive telepathic impulses; saves its inventor & his grandson from kidnapper-spies" (Walt Lee).

5.311 The Tomorrow Man. Tibor Takacs, dir. Canada: Mega-Media (syndicated), 1980. Stephen Zoller and Peter Chapman, script, from a story by Zoller. TV movie. 60 min. airtime.

Ed Naha, Science Fictionary, describes the setting as a maximum-security prison somewhere in a North American in an indeterminate future. The hero "survives the torture of a technological nightmare ruled by the Warden . . . and his robot drones."

5.312 Total Recall. Paul Verhoeven, dir. USA: Carolco (prod.) / Tri-Star (release), 1990. Ronald Shusett, Dan O'Bannon, and Jon Povill, screen story. Shusett, O'Bannon, and Gary Goldman, script. Inspired by Phillip K. Dick's "We Can Remember It for You Wholesale."

Arnold Schwarzenegger vehicle significant for threatening enclosure of the hero (cf. Running Man), varied this time with the heroine also enclosed within a machine—one that invades the mind and works on memories, and which, if resisted, causes pain. Note also shots of hero and heroine amidst huge alien machinery; cf. Krel machinery in Forbidden Planet and humans in Death Stars in the Star Wars trilogy (all films mentioned here are cited in this section of the List).

5.313 Trapped by Television. Del Lord, dir. USA: Columbia, 1936.

TV surveillance used to trap criminals (Ed Naha, Science Fictionary).

5.314 TRON (also Tron). Steven Lisberger, dir. USA: Disney 1982.

MCP, the Master Control Program of the computer used by a high-tech corporation, rules as a god the microscopic world of the computer "he" is in and has large ambitions in the macroscopic world: our world in the very near future. He is opposed by TRON (a personified security program) and TRON's few allies among the programs run by MCP. Flynn, a human user of the computer, helps TRON destroy MCP after Flynn is "digitalized" by MCP and taken into the microscopic world to die in gladiatorial video games. Note the implied theme of computer takeover and the more explicit theme of the computer as god. Cf. and contrast S. Lem, "The Experiment," and J. Sladek, The Müller-Fokker Effect (both cited under Fiction). Note very well a concept crucial for W. Gibson's cyberpunk works: cyberspace (our emphasis) as a realm of adventure and, by implication, the computer screen as a new form of the portal to the realm of adventure. The use of computers in the prod. of TRON is discussed under both "Entertainment" and "Technology" in Newsweek 5 July 1982: 58 f. Discussed by V. Sobchack in Screening Space, Chapter 4. Novelization by Brian Daley, Tron (New York: Del Rey-Ballantine, 1982).

5.315 The Troublesome Double. Milo Lewis, dir. UK: Interfilm for the Children's Film Foundation, 1971. 57 min.

Sequel to Egghead's Robot, q.v. above. Willis summarizes, "Electronics whiz-kid makes robot double of his sister" (vol. II); Walt Lee adds that the boy inventor's intent is "to win [a] swimming race."

5.316   Tubes: Cited under P. Pacheco, under Graphics.

5.317   The Twonky. Arch Oboler, dir. USA: Arch Oboler Productions / United Artists, 1953 (Baxter), 1952 (S. F. Ency.). Based on the story by Henry Kuttner.

See under Fiction the entry for Kuttner, "The Twonky." Film updates story by having the Twonky look like a TV set.

5.318   The Ultimate Imposter. Paul Stanley, dir. USA: Universal (TV) / CBS telefilm, 1979. 120 min. airtime.

Spy robbed of his memory by Chinese operatives is placed where, "with wires attached to his head, . . . [he] can be programmed by a master computer" (Naha, Science Fictionary).

5.319   Undersea Kingdom (Walt Lee, Naha; Parish and Pitts: The Underseas Kingdom). Serial, 12 parts, 25 reels. B. Reeves Eason and Joseph Kane, dirs. USA: Republic, 1936. Condensed to 100-minute TV feature, Sharad of Atlantis, 1961.

See for "ray machine," mixture of old and futuristic technology, domed Atlantis, and relatively early robots (called "Volkites").

5.320   Universal Soldier. Roland Emmerich, dir. USA: TriStar, 1992.

A Dolph Lundgren, Jean Claude Van Damme vehicle featuring (supposedly) brainwiped Viet Nam vets serving as "Uni-Sols" kept in cryogenic sleep until needed. Discussed by Steve Biodrowski, Cinfantastique 23.1 (Aug. 1992): 12-13. See for a highly electronic environment in the Uni-Sol command truck. Cf. and contrast trucks in Brazil, Freejack, and Warlords of the Twenty-First Century (listed in this section).

5.321   VALIS: Opera cited under Music.

5.322   Videodrome. David Cronenberg, dir., script. Canada: Universal / Filmplan International (and others), 1982 (copyright), 1983 (release). 87 min.

Of interest at least for its presentation of TV as a potential threat. D. C. Willis (in Horror and Science Fiction Films III, cited under Reference), finds Videodrome "the next phase (after ALIEN) in the evolution of the movie monster as a cross between the animal and the technological" and in finding Videodrome like the Videodrome process it shows as "'a giant hallucination machine'" (299). See above, The Fly.

5.323   The Vindicator. Jean-Claude Lord, dir. Canada: Twentieth Century Fox, 1986.

The Frankenstein legend retold as a revenge tale set in late 1980s generic North America. Significant only for the Creature's being a cyborg, first appearing very smooth and then, after much hard use, looking quite funky. Cf. Terminator.

5.324   Voyage Into Space. Salvatore Billitteri, prod. Japan: Toho / USA: AIP, 1968.

Described by Ed Naha, Science Fictionary, as a poorly dubbed Americanzation of a Japanese "sf adventure designed for children" featuring a small boy who "controls the strength of a titanic robot."

5.325 War of the Worlds. Byron Haskin, dir. USA: Paramount, 1953. Based on the novel by H. G. Wells.

As in the novel, the Martians, with their machines, are defeated by Earth's bacteria. Discussed by V. Sobchack in The Limits of Infinity (see Sobchack's Index). Discussed in TMG essay by L. Heldreth (see under Literary Criticism).

5.326 Wargames. John Badham, dir. USA: MGM/United Artists, 1983.

Combines motifs of the computer tyrant and the Strangelovian doomsday concept, largely set in the NORAD missile command enclave. See for detailed computer operation sequences and listen for hacker jargon. Discussed by V. Sobchack in Screening Space, Chapter 4; also see Randy Lofficier, "Wargames," Space Voyager #6 (1984-85): 62-65.

5.327 Warlords of the Twenty-First Century (Willis: Battletruck as original title). Harley Cokliss, dir. New Zealand: Battletruck Films Limited (prod.) / New World Pictures (release), 1981 (copyright) / 1982 (release).

Important little film (for the study of SF machines) stressing theme to the point of propaganda. "After the Oil Wars," rural areas are terrorized by the "renegade army colonel Jacob Straker" and his high-tech (on the inside) "battletruck." Opposed to Straker is the young hero Hunter, who rides a Suzuki motorcycle, wears a white helmet, and lives alone in a passive-solar house (using ecologically-responsible methane to power his bike). Opposed to the macho, militaristic society of the battletruck is the commune Clearwater, with a headwoman as leader, the "old fashioned" polity of "strict democracy," and the musical motif of the Shaker hymn "Simple Gifts." Straker uses his battletruck to attack the commune and to destroy Hunter's house. A blacksmith ultimately prepares a weapon for Hunter to fight the battletruck: an armored VW bug. Penultimate sequence has battletruck destroyed in fire and water; film ends with Hunter leaving the heroine (Straker's daughter) for a while, riding off on a horse, alone, toward snow-capped mountains. See for celebration of appropriate technology, including gernades. See above, Mad Max series.

5.328 Weird Science. John Hughes, dir. and script. USA: Universal 1985.

In effect, an updating of L. del Rey's "Helen O'Loy" (q.v. under Fiction), combining with the motif of a male-made female robot elements from Frankenstein films, Wargames, Road Warrior, Risky Business, any number of teen exploitation flicks, and the TV show I Dream of Jeannie—plus musical citations to other films. Two teenage nerds use a computer to create (or conjure up) "Lisa." Interesting for tongue-in-cheek use of computers alongside blatant magic, for an adolescent fantasy of sex, power, status, and revenge.

5.329 Westworld. Michael Crichton, dir. USA: MGM, 1973.

The robots of the Westworld section of the plush resort of Delos run amok. See this section, Futureworld. See under Drama Criticism the TMG essay by D. Palumbo. See also V. Sobchack, The Limits of Infinity. (S. F. Ency. notes a 1974 novelization of the screenplay, by M. Crichton.)

5.330 What a Way to Go! J. Lee Thompson, dir. USA: Twentieth Century-Fox, 1964. Shirley MacLaine stars opposite a series of major male leads.

Mainstream dark comedy relevant here for the section featuring Paul Newman as a painter who develops a painting machine that makes him rich and then kills him.

5.331 Who? (vt Roboman [also Robo Man]). Jack Gold, dir. UK: Lion / Hemisphere, 1974. From A. Budrys's Who? (q.v.).

Mostly a spy film premised on determining whether a cyborg (as we'd say today) is really an American scientist who wants to return to work or some sort of Russian ringer: a substitute, the original brainwashed or "turned," or something new. Follows novel in also dealing with the more strictly science fictional question of the identity of a man after significant physical changes.

5.332 Wizards. Ralph Bakshi, dir. USA: 20th Century-Fox, 1977.

Feature-length cartoon giving a highly negative view of technology (including film technology) until the final twist at the end, which may imply something to be said for a gun as "appropriate" technology (our ironic quotation marks).

5.333 Wollen, Peter, dir. and script. Friendship's Death. UK: British Film Institute, 1987. Available in 16mm from the British Film Institute. Script printed in Penley et al., Close Encounters anthology, listed under Drama Criticism.

"Friendship" is an extragalactic android who can pass for a woman. She was supposed to land at MIT but ends up in Amman, Jordan, in September of 1970: "Black September."

5.334 The Wrestling Women vs. the Murderous Robot. Rene Cardona, dir. Mexico: Calderon, 1969.

Described by Ed Naha, Science Fictionary, as "a battle between human and inhuman muscles." Cf. and contrast Rocky IV (1985).

5.335 Zardoz. John Boorman, dir. USA: John Boorman Productions / 20th Century-Fox, 1973.

Zed (Sean Connery) brings love and death to a static, computer-run "utopia" appropriately called a Vortex. Includes some shots of huge mechanical wombs and a sequence with Zed in the computer (a mysterious crystal). See under Fiction, Boorman's novelization of Zardoz. Cf. and contrast Zardoz, as both novel and film, with A. C. Clarke, City and the Stars (q.v., under Fiction). Discussed by V. Sobchack in The Limits of Infinity (see Sobchack's index).

Stage, Screen, and Television Drama Criticism

6.001   Abrash, Merritt. "R.U.R. [sic: no spaces] Restored and Reconsidered": Textual study cited under Literary Criticism.

6.002   Agel, Jerome, ed. The Making of Kubrick's 2001. New York: NAL, 1970.

Includes a ninety-six-page photo insert from the film, A. C. Clarke's "The Sentinel," and at least excerpts from every major handling of 2001 through 1970. A basic work for the study of 2001. (See below, this section of the List, the entry for C. Geduld.)

6.003   Alien Zone: Cultural Theory and Contemporary Science Fiction Cinema. Annette Kuhn, ed. London: Verso, 1990.

Three original essays, original introductions by the ed., plus fifteen rpts., including S. Bukatman's "Who Programs You? . . . ," T. Byers's "Commodity Futures," H. B. Franklin's "Visions of the Future . . . ," J. Newton's "Feminism and Anxiety in Alien," C. Penlsy's "Time Travel . . . ," and M. Ryan and Douglas Kellner's "Technophobia"—all cited in this section.

6.004   Altman, Mark A. et al. "Star Trek—The Next Generation: Living Up to the Legend." Series of articles, plus Episode Guide (q.v. under Reference Works), for cover-story in Cinefantastique 21.2 (Sept. 1990): 24-51 f.

Highly detailed coverage giving "everything you wanted to know (and a bit more)" about STNG. See esp. comments on the Borg as mechanized, collective-intelligence, possibly cyberpunk villains (29, 33 [photo], 37-38 [citation for "Q Who"], 51 [citation for "The Best of Both Worlds"]), and on the android, Mr. Data (33-34 [Rob Bowman on "Datalore" episode], 36-37 [MAA on "The Importance of Being Data," including Melinda Snodgrass on Data as a child, learning to be human]).

6.005   Annan, David. Robot: The Mechanical Monster. New York: Bounty, 1976.

Cited in "Year's Scholarship: 1984," under Film and Television.

6.006   Baxter, John. Science Fiction in the Cinema. Full citation under Reference.

A survey and "critical review of SF films from A Trip to the Moon (1902) to 2001: A Space Odyssey" (front-cover blurb).

6.007   Bergstrom, Janet. "Androids and Androgyny." In Penley et al., Close Encounters anthology, q.v. this section under Penley.

Roy Batty and Pris as androids in love in Blade Runner; see for longer discussion of the little-known Looker (1981)—both films listed under Drama.

6.008   Bierman, James H. "Automated Theatre: Theatrical Futures from the Recent Past." JPC 18.2 (Fall 1984): 171-83.

Covers robots and various environments in high-tech amusement parks, selected comic books (Jack Kirby's Kamandi in the D.C. series, 2001: A Space Odyssey by Marvel Comics [April 1977]), films, and theatrical productions from Alfred Jarry's Ubu Roi in its Paris premiere in 1896 (where "the dialogue was delivered by actors . . . costumed to resemble enormous dolls") and Filippo Tommaso Marinetti's Automata (Paris, 1909) to "such Disney robot dramas as the G.E. Carousel of Progress" (quoting 180-81). See below, JHB's "Robot Dramas." See under Background, 12-E: Disaster Transport.

6.009   ---. "The Walt Disney Robot Dramas." The Yale Review 66.2 (Winter 1977): [223]- 36.

Primarily on The General Electric Carousel of Progress (New York Worlds Fair, 1964-65; Disneyland, 1974 f., Walt Disney World, 1975 f.), but with comments also on Disney's audio-animatronic animal dramas America Sings and Country Bear Jamboree, and on F. T. Marinetti's Automata (see Marinetti listing under Drama). See for a cultural-studies close reading of GE's Carousel (undoubtedly closer than GE intended): the robots "are progressively more fluid and human in their movements" as Carousel progresses from the 1890s into the present," while the characters they portray are increasingly isolated and dehumanized" (228). See above, JHB's "Automated Theatre."

6.010   Blair, Karen. "The Garden in the Machine: The Why of Star Trek." JPC 13.2 (Fall 1979): 310-20.

Focuses on the Star Trek episodes "The Apple" (q.v. under Drama) and "The Way to Eden." Most esp., the "Machine" in KB's title is the Enterprise, and the "Garden" is "the human community . . . on board the Enterprise" (318). See under Background, the entry for L. Marx.

6.011   Boruszkowski, Lilly Ann. "The Stepford Wives: The Re-Created Woman." Jump Cut 32 (1986): 16-19.

Cited in "Year's Scholarship": 1987.

6.012   Boylan, Jay H. "Hal in '2001: A Space Odyssey' [sic]: The Lover Sings His Song." JPC 18.4 (Spring 1985): 53-56.

Somewhat quirky but interesting short essay on HAL's singing "Daisy" at his death as "the perfect epiphany for the relationship between HAL (and by extension all machine technology) and humankind" (55).

6.013   Brosnan, John. Future Tense: The Cinema of Science Fiction. Full citation under Reference.

Primarily useful for its plot summaries and unabashed judgments of cinematic quality, plus interesting critical comments (passim) on 2001, THX 1138, and other relevant films.

6.014   Bukatman, Scott. "The Cybernetic (City) State . . . ": Important for Blade Runner;
        cited under Graphics.

6.015   ---. "Who Programs You? The Science Fiction of the Spectacle." In Alien Zone.
        Annette Kuhn, ed., cited above by title.

        Pages 202-207 deal usefully with D. Cronenberg's Videodrome, q.v. under
        Drama; SB stresses TV in Videodrome as a method of programming people, for
        social control.

6.016   Byers, Thomas B. "Commodity Futures: Corporate State and Personal Style in Three
        Recent Science-Fiction Movies." SFS #43, 14.3 (Nov. 1987): 326-39. Rpt. Alien
        Zone, cited above by title.

        The films are Alien, Blade Runner, and Star Trek II: The Wrath of Khan, to which
        TBB applies a very insightful Leftist analysis. Concludes that the corporate state
        is brought into question in Alien and Blade Runner, reinforced in Star Trek II;
        along the way there is useful commentary on machines, mechanistic structures,
        and mechanistic people. See this section, P. Fitting's "Futurecop" article.

6.017   Chevrier, Yves. "Blade Runner; or, The Sociology of Anticipation." Will Straw, trans.
        Robert M. Philmus, ed. SFS #32, 11.1 (March 1984): 50-60. "This essay is a
        modified (and also expanded) version of one that appeared under the equivalent
        French title in Esprit, No. 19" (February 1983): 138-43—Philmus's note.

        See for the politics and *mise en scène* of Blade Runner, contrasting the "utterly
        medieval disorder" of Los Angeles of 2019 with "the spotless and transparent
        world . . . portrayed in classical SF and in political fiction ([Y.] Zamiatin's We,
        [A.] Huxley's Brave New World, [G.] Orwell's 1984 [sic], and, in the cinema, [F.]
        Lang's Metropolis)" (52). Usefully places what "visual revolution" there is in
        Blade Runner into the context of art history, history of cinema, modernization,
        and Modernism (52-53 and passim).

6.018   Cinefantastique 20.1-2 (Nov. 1989). Copiously illus.

        The emphasis of this special double issue is on Tim Burton's first Batman movie
        (q.v. under Drama).

6.019   Colwell, C. Carter. "Primitivism in the Movies of Ridley Scott: Alien & Blade Runner."
        In Retrofitting Blade Runner, q.v. below, this section.

        On primitivism and technology in Alien and Blade Runner, with the replicants in
        Blade Runner being both high-tech and primitive. Caution: About four of CCC's
        comments are somewhat misleading.

6.020   Crow, John [H.], and Richard [D.] Erlich. "Mythic Patterns in Ellison's [and Jones's] A
        Boy and His Dog." Extrapolation 18 (May 1977): 162-66.

        Deals with both H. Ellison's novella and L. Q. Jones's film (listed under Fiction,
        and Drama, respectively). Briefly handles the "mechanization of the underworld"
        motif in both works. Also deals with the potentially fatal containment of the
        protagonist in the "wedding" sequence of the film.

6.021   Davis, Ken. "The Shape of Things to Come: H. G. Wells and the Rhetoric of Proteus."
        In No Place Else, q.v. under Literary Criticism, 110-24.

        A. Korda's film Things to Come (q.v. under Drama) is emphatically
        "Promethean": showing faith in logic, science, technology, and (social) control.
        Wells's The Shape of Things to Come, and his script for Korda's film, go beyond
        the Promethean to the "Protean," showing faith in the ability of all forms of life to
        change and adapt—and valuing individuality and freedom (117-18).

6.022 Desser, David. "Blade Runner: Science Fiction and Transcendence." Literature / Film
Quarterly 13 (1985): 172-79.

A "discussion of the film's atmosphere relating Blade Runner to Film Noir and of
the significance of the Christian symbolism of the film" (Quoting DD, "Do
Androids Dream of Ridley Scott?", 200).

6.023 ---. "Do Androids Dream of Ridley Scott?" Phoenix from the Ashes: The Literature
of the Remade World. Carl B. Yoke, ed. New York: Greenwood, 1987.

Nonmechanical nature of film replicants vs. androids of P. K. Dick's Do
Androids Dream ..., while "Both novel and film share the fundamental question
of what it means to be human" (199).

6.024 ---. "Race, Space and Class: The Politics of the SF Film from Metropolis to Blade
Runner." In Retrofitting Blade Runner, q.v. below.

Includes brief discussions of robots, technology, and the overt politics in
Metropolis, Blade Runner, Things to Come, The Time Machine, Alphaville, A
Clockwork Orange, THX 1138 (all listed under Drama), and other films.
Caution: DD does some questionable things with the Morlocks and Eloi in Time
Machine (with lesser problems with THX, and with J. F. Sebastian in Blade
Runner).

6.025 Doherty, Thomas. "Video, Science Fiction Fiction, and the Cinema of Surveillance."
Journal of the Fantastic in the Arts 2.2 (Summer 1989): 69-79. JFA special issue
on S. F. film, Brooks Landon, guest ed.

Covers a large number of films but esp. good on television and cinema in The
Running Man (q.v., under Drama).

6.026 Doll, Susan, and Greg Fallen. "Blade Runner and Genre: Film Noir and Science
Fiction." Literature / Film Quarterly 14 (1986): 89-100.

Cited in "Year's Scholarship": 1987.

6.027 Elkins, Charles, ed. "Symposium on Alien." SFS #22, 7.3 (Nov. 1980): 278-304.

A Marxist analysis of the ideological implications of Alien (q.v. under Drama).
Comments usefully on the android, Ash; the ship's computer, "Mother"; the
Company; and the "biological-mechanical" derelict alien spaceship seen early in
the film.

6.028 Fitting, Peter. "Futurecop: The Neutralization of Revolt in Blade Runner." SFS #43,
14.3 (Nov. 1987): 340-54.

Extended comparison and contrast of Blade Runner with the source novel, P. K.
Dick's Do Androids Dream of Electric Sheep? (cited under Drama and Fiction
respectively)—coming down strongly in favor of Dick's novel. Finds "a
fundamental contradiction at the core of the film; for in the novel ... there was
an ethical juxtaposition of the human and the mechanical, a valorization of life
and the living and a rejection of the machine," which is confused in the film's
sympathetic androids and the stress on their rather admirable "struggle to survive"
(343). See this section, T. Byers on "Commodity Futures."

6.029 Franklin, H. Bruce. "Don't Look Where We're Going: Visions of the Future in
Science-Fiction Films, 1970-82." SFS #29, 10.1, (March 1983): 70-80. Rpt.
Shadows of the Magic Lamp. George E. Slusser and Eric S. Rabkin, eds.
Carbondale: Southern Illinois P, 1985. Alien Zone, cited above.

Concentrates on two "great archetypal image[s] of the future" in SF films, "THE
WONDER CITY OF THE FUTURE and THE MARVELOUS FLYING

MACHINE," from Metropolis to Blade Runner, with most of the discussion on the more important of the fifty-two Anglo-American films "set wholly or in part in some distinctly future time which were released for general distribution from 1970 through . . . summer 1982" (71). See for contrast of the celebration of the "technocratic order" in Things to Come with an attack on that order—seen as a "totalitarian apparatus"—in such films as THX 1138, Ice, and A Clockwork Orange (72).

6.030   Geduld, Carolyn. Filmguide to 2001: A Space Odyssey. Bloomington, IN: Indiana UP, 1973.

Includes the credits for and an outline of 2001, a Kubrick filmography through 1971, and an extensive biblio. on the film. Important early handling of the question, as we will put it, "Where are the women (in 2001)?" See this section, the citation for J. Agel.

6.031   Giger, H. R. Giger's Alien: Cited under Graphics.

6.032   Glass, Fred. "Signs of the Times: The Computer as Character in Tron, War Games, and Superman III." Film Quarterly 38 (Winter 1984-85): 16-27.

Cited in "Year's Scholarship": 1985, which we follow in spelling War Games. See under Drama, TRON and Wargames.

6.033   Gordon, Andrew. "Science Fiction Film Criticism: The Postmodern Always Rings Twice." SFS #43, 14.3 (Nov. 1987): 386-91. Rev. Vivian Sobchack, Screening Space ....

Insightful review and sympathetic critique not only of Sobchack's book but of F. Jameson's essay on "Postmodernism..." (cited under Background).

6.034   Greenberg, Harvey R. "Reimagining the Gargoyle: Psychoanalytic Notes on Alien." In Penley et al., Close Encounters anthology; see under Penley, this section.

A professional psychoanalyst (and film critic) offers a close reading of Alien, including some controversial comments on the final confrontation between Ripley and the Alien.

6.035   Hall, Peter C., and Richard D. Erlich. "Beyond Topeka and Thunderdome: Variations on the Comic-Romance Pattern in Recent SF Film." SFS #43, 14.3 (Nov. 1987): 316-25.

Discusses a number of films set in wastelands created by nuclear holocausts, stressing A Boy and His Dog and Mad Max Beyond Thunderdome (films notable for mechanized underworlds).

6.036   Heldreth, Leonard G. "Clockwork Reels: Mechanized Environments in Science Fiction Films." In CW [213]-33. (See Abbreviations for CW).

See for Metropolis, Westworld, Futureworld; Logan's Run, THX 1138, A Boy and His Dog, and A Clockwork Orange.

6.037   Hughes, Philip. "The Alienated and Demonic in the Films of Stanley Kubrick: Cinemananalysis with a Freudian Technophobic Argument." Journal of Evolutionary Psychology 3 (April 1982): 12-27.

Cited in "Year's Scholarship": 1984, whose spelling we follow for "Cinemananalysis."

6.038 Hull, Elizabeth Anne. "Merging Madness: Rollerball as a Cautionary Tale." In CW [163]-80.

On W. Harrison's "Roller Ball Murder" (q.v. under Fiction) and N. Jewison's Rollerball (q.v. under Drama), emphasizing the film. "In Rollerball ... the essential plot conflict is no longer the agony of the individual man against himself," as in the story, "but the battle of an individual ... against external control by corporate society, control ... cinematically associated with the highly mechanized—and metaphorically mechanizing—game of rollerball" (166).

6.039 Huyssen, Andreas. "The Vamp and the Machine: Technology and Sexuality in Fritz Lang's Metropolis." New German Critique 24-25 (Fall-Winter 1981-82): 221-37. Coll. After the Great Divide: Modernism, Mass Culture, Postmodernism. Bloomington, IN: Indiana UP, 1986.

See for the sexual politics of Metropolis and their historical context in terms of (1) the debate over technology between the Expressionists and those championing The New Objectivity, (2) the history of the male imaging of technology as female, and (3) the conflict between capital and labor. An important essay.

6.040 Ingersoll, Daniel W., Jr. "Machines Are Good to Think ...": Cited under Literary Criticism.

6.041 Isaacs, Neil D. "Unstuck in Time: Clockwork Orange and Slaughterhouse-Five." Literature / Film Quarterly 1 (1973): 122-31.

Cited by J. Klinkowitz in "The Vonnegut Bibliography," q.v. above under Reference Works.

6.042 Jensen, Paul. "Metropolis." Film Heritage 3.2 (Winter 1967-68): 22-28.

Cited in New Film Index (q.v. under Reference) as an "Extended Analysis" of Metropolis; see Metropolis under Drama.

6.043 Johnson, William, ed. Focus on The Science Fiction Film: Cited citation above, under Reference.

Includes essays on Things to Come and 2001.

6.044 Kellner, Douglas, Flo Leibowitz, and Michael Ryan. "Blade Runner, a Diagnostic Critique." Jump Cut 19 (Feb. 1984): 6-8.

On ideological ambivalence in Blade Runner (cited biblio. in Retrofitting Blade Runner, q.v. this section, and "Year's Scholarship": 1985).

6.045 Kerman, Judith B. "Private Eye: A Semiotic Comparison of the Film Blade Runner and the Book Do Androids Dream of Electric Sheep[?]." Patterns of the Fantastic II. Donald M. Hassler, ed. Mercer Island, WA: Starmont, 1985.

A careful reading of both novel and film, esp. useful for the quest by the replicants for "incept date, morphology, and mortality" (73).

6.046 King, Stephen. Danse Macabre. 1980. New York: Berkley, 1982.

Cited in J. Egan's essay on "Technohorror" (q.v.). "The subtext of the technohorror film, King maintains, suggests 'that we have been betrayed by our own machines and processes of mass production'" (Danse Macabre 156, quoted Egan 141).

6.047 Klossner, Michael. Rev. The Complete James Bond Movie Encyclopedia, by Steven Jay Rubin. SFRA Newsletter #188 (June 1991): 33-34.

MK's first paragraph contains most of what one needs to know about machines in James Bond movies: generally, small machines good; big machines bad (cf. M. P. Esmond's "From Little Buddy to Big Brother" in TMG, cited under Literary Criticism).

6.048 Kuhn, Annette, ed. Alien Zone: Cited this section, by title.

6.049 Landon, Brooks. "Bet On It: Cyber/video/punk/performance." MR47/48: 245-51 (see under Literary Criticism, L. McCaffery, guest ed.).

Cyberpunk may be found in various media, with print less decorous than electronic media for delivering the cyberpunk message.

6.050 Leayman, Charles D. "Stephen King's 'Monkey's Paw' update a real shocker." Cinefantastique 20.1-2: 104, 119.

Rev. the horror film Pet Sematary (sic), in which CDL handles the film's speeding trucks as "weapons-on-wheels" that "implicitly evoke a rampant capitalism's oblivious intrusion on family, nature, time, and finally life itself," while the trucks remain quite literal machines (104).

6.051 Lofficier, Randy: "Tron: An Electronic Odyssey." Space Voyager #2 (1982): 38-45.

Cited in "Year's Scholarship": 1985.

6.052 Mathews, Jack. The Battle of Brazil. New York: Crown, 1987.

See for complex film history on Brazil (as told by a strong partisan for the dir. against the studio), for numerous comments on the film, and for a script with stills and illus.

6.053 McCaffery, Larry. "The Desert of the Real: The Cyberpunk Controversy": Cited under Literary Criticism.

6.054 Morley, Lewis. "Elements of Science Fiction and Violence in the Cinema: Robocop [sic]: A Marriage of Convenience." Rev. RoboCop. ASFR (Australian Science Fiction Review), 2nd Series, #12, 3.1 (Jan. 1988): [31]-34.

Finds the film derived from The Terminator and, like Terminator, "a blend of science fiction and violent action" (32). Comments usefully on RoboCop as "a product tailored for two different groups: those who would react to the satirical script and its underlying messages of social control, corruption and impersonal technology, and those who would enjoy and identify with gun-toting heroes who justifiably waste the bad guys, using maximum firepower" (34).

6.055 Moskowitz, Sam. Explorers of the Infinite: Shapers of Science Fiction. Cleveland, OH: World, 1963. Westport, CT: Hyperion, 1974.

Includes a discussion of R. U. R.: ch. 13, "Karel Capek [sic, no diacritic on the "C"]: The Man Who Invented Robots."

6.056 Newhouse, Edward. "Charlie's Critics." Partisan Review 3 (April 1936): 25-26.

Described in New Film Index (q.v. under Reference) as "An attack on critics who do not see Modern Times as a film of social consciousness." See Modern Times under Drama.

6.057   Newton, Judith. "Feminism and Anxiety in Alien." Part of the "Symposium on Alien." SFS #22, 7.3 (Nov. 1980). Rpt. Alien Zone, cited above by title.

See for Ripley as female hero against the mechanism of Mother, Ash, and the Alien (see also for the feminism of Alien and the limits to the film's radicalism).

6.058   Omni's Screen Flights / Screen Fantasies: The Future According to Science Fiction Cinema. Danny Peary, ed. Garden City, NY: Dolphin-Doubleday, 1984. Illus. Index. Introd. Harlan Ellison.

Substantial anthology of short pieces on a number of films of interest, including 1984 (1956 version), Alien, Battle Beyond the Stars, Buck Rogers, Death Race 2000, Fahrenheit 451, Flash Gordon, Forbidden Planet, Looker, Metropolis, THX 1138 and Blade Runner (an important essay by R. Silverberg), Wargames, Westworld—all listed under Drama.

6.059   Palumbo, Donald. "Loving that Machine; Or, The Mechanical Egg: Sexual Mechanisms and Metaphors in Science Fiction Films." TMG [117]-28 (see Abbrviations for TMG).

See for Star Trek [I]: The Motion Picture and such obvious candidates as Stepford Wives and Dr. Strangelove—and more subtle sexual images in films such as 2001, Star Wars [I] (A New Hope), and Close Encounters of the Third Kind. In the latter group, the hero becomes "the successful sperm-figure" moving "toward its rendezvous with the mechanical egg" (122-23 and passim).

6.060   Patalas, Enno. "Metropolis, Scene 103." In Penley et al., Close Encounters anthology, q.v. this section.

An extraordinarily useful short essay reconstructing Scene 103 of F. Lang's original Metropolis, a scene that explains the robot Maria as a reconstruction of Rotwang's lost love, Hel, who became wife to the ruler of Metropolis and mother to the film's hero.

6.061   Penley, Constance. "Time Travel, Primal Scene, and the Critical Dystopia." In Penley et al., Close Encounters anthology, q.v. this section. Rpt. Alien Zone. Annette Kuhn, ed., cited above by title.

See for The Terminator [1] and Aliens, both listed under Drama.

6.062   ---, et. al. Close Encounters: Film, Feminism, and Science Fiction. Minneapolis: U of Minnesota P, 1991.

Mostly an anthology of critical essays on film, including J. Bergstrom on "Androids and Androgyny," C. Penley on "Time Travel . . . ," H. R. Greenberg on Alien, and E. Patalas on "Metropolis, Scene 103" (all listed in this section); also includes R. Bellour essay on "Ideal Hadaly" in Villier's de l'Isle-Adam's novel The Future Eve (see under Literary Criticism); and the script for P. Wollen's film, Friendship's Death (see under Wollen, under Drama).

6.063   Persons, Dan. "Making the Blockbuster Sequel: RoboCop 2." Cinefantastique 21.1 (July 1990): 16-31.

A series of articles on several aspects of the RoboCop saga, including Irvin Kershner's view of "Robo" as "a metaphor for people in our society. They're becoming roboticized without knowing it" (22). Also see for development of the script.

6.064   Pohl, Frederik, and Frederik Pohl IV. Science Fiction: Studies in Film. Full citation under Reference.

Includes summaries and discussions of Metropolis, Things to Come, Forbidden Planet, Stanley Kubrick's SF through A Clockwork Orange, Westworld, Rollerball, and other films useful for the study of the human/machine interface in SF. Illus. with stills from the films discussed. No index; filmographic information given passim.

6.065   Retrofitting Blade Runner: Issues in Ridley Scott's Blade Runner and Philip K. Dick's Do Androids Dream of Electric Sheep? Judith B. Kerman, ed. Bowling Green, OH: BGU PopP, 1991.

Original anthology of essays, with annotated biblio. by W. M. Kolb. Includes A. Barlow's "Philip K. Dick's Androids . . . " (cited under Literary Criticism), David Desser's "Race, Space and Class . . ." (cited in this section). Rev. Jack Jakaitis, SFS #57, 19.2 (July 1992): 251-56. Richard D. Erlich, Extrapolation 33.4 (Winter 1992): 370-73.

6.066   Rogers, Dave. The Avengers. London: ITV Books/Michael Joseph, 1983.

Synopses from the 161 Avengers TV episodes aired between 1961 and 1969, some of which featured robot killers and various other machines for such things as mind control and weather control. Rev. Michael Klossner, FR #68 (June 1984): 40, our source for this entry.

6.067   "Rollerbrawl." Stan Hart, writer; Angelo Torres, artist. Mad #181 (March 1976): 4-[11].

Mad presents Rollerball as a commentary on contemporary society. Note opening words of the parody, among the spectators at a "Rollerbrawl" game: they explicitly relate violence in sports, rule by "the large corporations," and the destruction of individuality (three of the central themes of Rollerball) to 1976 America.

6.068   Rollin, Roger B. "Deus in Machina: Popular Culture's Myth of the Machine." Journal of American Culture 2 (Summer 1979): 297-308.

Argues that (Western, esp. American) "popular culture has begun to transform machines into archetypal heroes, villains, even gods, and gods, heroes, and villains into machines." Gives many examples from film and TV. Esp. useful for lesser-known works such as Breaking the Sound Barrier and Future Cop, and for its discussion of how "The Cars Are the Stars" in recent films.

6.069   Rose, Mark. "Machine." Ch. 6 of Alien Encounters. Full citation under Literary Criticism.

Includes an excellent discussion of "the opposition between man and machine" in the "narrative foreground" of 2001, and of the resolution of that opposition in the conclusion of 2001 (see 142-52).

6.070   Roth, Lane. "Ambiguity of Visual Design and Meaning in TV's Battlestar Galactica." Extrapolation 24 (Spring 1983): 80-87.

While the story-line of Battlestar Galactica clearly pits humans against the mechanical, the visuals for the series suggest that the humans and their robotic enemies have a good deal in common. See above under Drama, the entry for Battlestar Galactica.

6.071   ---. "Bergsonian Comedy and the Human Machines in 'Star Wars' [sic: quotation marks]." Film Criticism 4.2 (1980): 1-8.

Applies H. Bergson's theory from "On Laughter" (q.v. under Background) to the first Star Wars movie, now called A New Hope. Some of the comic business in the film is traditional Bergsonian superimposition of the mechanical upon the organic, more specifically upon the human. Much of the comedy, though, is from C-3PO and R2-D2. "The comic droids ... demonstrate the Bergsonian comic principles primarily though reversal—a machine acting like a person—and sometimes through double reversal—a machine acting like a person acting like a machine" (8). (Caution: Someone associated with Film Criticism consistently changed LR's "antinomy" ["opposition" or "contradiction"] to "antimony" [a "metallic chemical"], which might be confusing.)

6.072   ---.   "Metropolis, The Lights Fantastic: Semiotic Analysis of Lighting Codes in Relation to Character and Theme." Literature / Film Quarterly 6.4 (Fall 1978): 342-46.

See esp. for analysis of oppositions among Maria, the "robotrix" who impersonates Maria, and Rotwang.

6.073   ---.   "The Rejection of Rationalism in Recent Science Fiction Films." Philosophy in Context ll (1981), "Philosophy and Science Fiction," 3d essay, no pagination.

On Star Wars, Star Trek: The Motion Picture, and The Empire Strikes Back (all cited under Drama). Relates these films to Romantic rebellion: the spaceship "as a marvelous machine could aptly symbolize the material culmination of the Age of Reason .... In the context of the Science Fiction film, however, the spaceship signifies a denial of this philosophy." In the films he discusses, LR finds spaceships as obstacles or limitations, to be eliminated or transcended. See LR's notes for further readings.

6.074   Roud, Richard. "Anguish: Alphaville." Sight and Sound 34 (Autumn 1965): 164-66.

In praise of J.-L. Godard's Alphaville; includes comment about "Tarzan vs. IBM" as the title Godard wanted. Cited in New Film Index, q.v. under Reference. See under Drama, Alphaville.

6.075   Ryan, Michael, and Douglas Kellner. "Technophobia." From Camera Politica: Politics and Ideology of the Contemporary Hollywood Film. Bloomington, IN: Indiana UP, 1988. Rpt. Alien Zone, cited above.

Conservative technophobia in THX 1138 and Logan's Run versus more liberal or radical views of machines in Brainstorm, Silent Running, Star Trek: The Motion Picture, and, esp., Blade Runner (all listed under Drama).

6.076   Scott, Linda M. "'For the Rest of Us': A Reader-Oriented Interpretation of Apple's '1984' Commercial." JPC 25.1 (Summer 1991): 67-81.

A Kenneth Burkean/reader-response interpretation of a 60-second Macintosh commercial associating IBM with George Orwell's dystopian Oceania, and the Apple Macintosh with the human opposition symbolized by a hammer-throwing athlete: a young woman who throws a huge hammer into a telescreen image of Big Brother. The setting for the commercial "is at once mechanistic and organic" (73) and reminiscent of Alien and Bladerunner (q.v.)—earlier works by Ridley Scott, the producer-director of the "1984" commercial (see "1984" under Drama).

6.077   Science Fiction Studies #43 = Vol. 14, Part 3, Nov. 1987: The special issue on S. F. Film.

6.078   Semeiks, Joanna G. "Sex, Lawrence, and Videotape." JPC 25.4 (Spring 1992): 143-52.

JGS on D. H. Lawrence on technology, "the organic principle" vs. "the inorganic or mechanical principle"—with Lawrencian analysis applied to the videocamera (and other matters) in Steven Soderbergh's <u>sex, lies</u> and <u>videotape</u> (1989 [sic: lower-case throughout]).

6.079 Shelton, Robert. "Rendezvous with HAL: <u>2001/2010</u>." <u>Extrapolation</u> 28.3 (Fall 1987): 255-68.

Close reading of <u>2001</u> and <u>2010</u> as novels and films (see under Fiction, A. C. Clarke, titles under Drama), stressing Peter Hyams's changes in the film version of <u>2010</u> to get across a political message different from Clarke's in the novel <u>2010</u>. See for relationships among HAL, David Bowman, and Dr. Chandra.

6.080 Shay, Don. "<u>Blade Runner</u>—2020 Foresight": Cited under Graphics.

6.081 Slade, Joseph W. "Romanticizing Cybernetics in Ridley Scott's <u>Blade Runner</u>." <u>Literature / Film Quarterly</u> 18.1 (1990): 11-18.

Suggests "that humans are continuous with" our technology and that "technology is what makes humans human"; quoted in W. M. Kolb in his biblio. in <u>Retrofitting Blade Runner</u>, q.v. this section.

6.082 Sobchack, Vivian Carol. <u>The Limits of Infinity: The American Science Fiction Film, 1950-75</u>. South Brunswick, NJ, and New York: Barnes; London: Thomas Yoseloff, 1980.

Includes a selected biblio. of books, articles, and unpublished material; over 140 film stills; and a good index. Makes useful comments (mostly passim) about many films important for the study of the human/machine interface, esp. films featuring secure or dangerous containment in spaceships (see 68-77).

6.083 ---. <u>Screening Space: The American Science Fiction Film</u>. New York: Ungar, 1987. "Second, Enlarged Edition."

This is <u>The Limits of Infinity</u> enlarged with a "Preface to the Enlarged Edition," a new chapter (ch. 4, "Postfuturism"), and associated apparatus. The new chapter is heavily influenced by F. Jameson's essay, "Postmodernism, or The Logic of Late Capitalism," cited under Background, and deals with several relevant films, esp. <u>Close Encounters of the Third Kind</u>, <u>Blade Runner</u>, <u>Dune</u>, and a number of "marginal SF" films such as <u>Repo Man</u> and <u>Buckaroo Banzai</u>. See A. Gordon's rev. "The Postmodern...," cited above, this section.

6.084 Sontag, Susan. "The Imagination of Disaster." Coll. <u>Against Interpretation</u>. New York: Farrar, 1965/66. Farrar/Octagon, 1978. Rpt. <u>Science Fiction: The Future</u>. Dick Allen, ed. New York: Harcourt, 1971, 1983. <u>Science Fiction: A Collection of Critical Essays</u>. Mark Rose, ed. Englewood Cliffs, NJ: Prentice, 1976.

See this highly influential essay for a general introduction to SF films of the 1950s and 1960s and for some brief but excellent comments on "technological man" and the theme of mechanization.

6.085 <u>Stanley Kubrick's Clockwork Orange</u>. Stanley Kubrick, Andros Epaminondas, and Margaret Adams, eds. New York: Ballantine, 1972. Illus.

An attempt by Kubrick et al. "To make, as it were, a complete, graphic representation of the film [<u>A Clockwork Orange</u>], with the dialogue printed in the proper place in relation to the cuts, so that within the limits of still-photographs and words, an accurate . . . record of a film might be available" (3). The volume succeeds admirably.

6.086 <u>Star Trek, the Next Generation Manual</u>: Listed under M. Okuda, under Drama.

6.087   Stewart, Garrett. "Videology." In <u>Shadows</u> <u>of</u> <u>the</u> <u>Magic</u> <u>Lamp:</u> <u>Fantasy</u> <u>and</u> <u>Science</u> <u>Fiction</u> <u>in</u> <u>Film</u>. George E. Slusser and Eric S. Rabkin, eds. Carbondale, IL: Southern Illinois UP, 1985.

Video and film used for control in dystopian films.

6.088   Strick, Philip. "Philip K. Dick and the Movies." <u>Foundation</u> #26 (Oct. 1982): 15-21.

Primarily on Ridley Scott's film, <u>Blade</u> <u>Runner</u> (1982)—but with useful references to other works important for the study of the human/machine interface. Passes on news of other films "said to be in preparation" of works by Dick (17-18). Sees <u>Blade</u> <u>Runner</u> as the first serious effort in film to deal with the motif of humans struggling against more or less mechanical "human facsimiles" (16).

6.089   Telotte, J. P. "'The Dark Side of the Force': Star Wars and the Science Fiction Tradition." <u>Extrapolation</u> 24.3 (Fall 1983): 216-26.

Comments usefully on the rather complex handling of technology in the first two Star Wars movies, and in G. Lucas's <u>THX</u> <u>1138</u>.

6.090   Waters, Harry F. "TV's Record Crime Wave." <u>Newsweek</u> 6 May 1985: esp. 77B.

The section on "The Lows of Hi-Tech" comments briefly on the turning over of "the war against crime to machines," at least on such TV shows as <u>Knight</u> <u>Rider</u> (q.v. under Drama), <u>Airwolf</u> (which "stars a hopped-up helicopter"), and <u>Street</u> <u>Hawk</u> (which "stars an 'all-terrain attack' motorcycle that can hyperthrust to 300 mph and neutralize a killer tank with its 'particle beam' ray gun").

6.091   White, Matthew, and Jaffer Ali. <u>The</u> <u>Official</u> Prisoner <u>Companion</u>. London: Sidgwick, 1988.

Includes an "Episode Guide" to the seventeen episodes of <u>The</u> <u>Prisoner</u>, a chapter of "Notes, Anecdotes, and Nonsense," two chapters analyzing <u>The</u> <u>Prisoner</u>, rpt. of an interview with Patrick McGoohan, a brief McGoohan biography and filmography, an appendix giving "Sources of Information" about <u>The</u> <u>Prisoner</u> (including a biblio. and sources for videotapes), and an appendix giving excerpts from notable shooting scripts. See under Drama, <u>The</u> <u>Prisoner</u>.

6.092   Wood, Dennis. "No Place for a Kid: Critical Commentary on <u>The</u> <u>Last</u> <u>Starfighter</u>." <u>Journal</u> <u>of</u> <u>Popular</u> <u>Film</u> <u>&</u> <u>Television</u> 14 (1986): 52-63.

Cited in "Year's Scholarship": 1987.

6.093   Zukofsky, Louis. "<u>Modern</u> <u>Times</u>." <u>Kulchur</u> 1.4 (Winter 1961): 75-82.

Cited in <u>New</u> <u>Film</u> <u>Index</u> (q.v. under Reference Works) as an "Extended Analysis" of <u>Modern</u> <u>Times</u> (q.v. under Drama).

Graphic and Plastic Arts

7.001   Adams, Brooks. "R. M. Fischer." Art in America 78 (Feb. 1990): 167.

Rev. of exhibit at Jay Gorney gallery. BA describes three installations originally intended to be public art in terms that make technology (as Fischer uses it) seem sensual, even erotic. Thunderbird, a giant clock, is pictured.

7.002   Agee, William C. "Morton Livingston Schamberg: Notes on the Sources of the Machine Images." Dada/Surrealism #14 (1985): 66-80.

Schamberg's machine paintings and pastels are not nearly so abstract as once believed, being based on parts of specific machines. These works evolved more independently of Marcel Duchamp's and Francis Picabia's machine imagery than previously supposed. Although they speak to a pervasive attraction to the machine during the period, they lack the irony of the Dada stance.

7.003   Aldiss, Brian. Science Fiction Art. New York: Bounty, 1975 [Currey]. London: New English Library, 1975. U.S. Edn. by Crown, 1975.

On illustrations in SF. BA notes that "Science fiction is a literature of cities" (89, quoted in Wolfe 105).

7.004   Aloff, Mindy. Dance Department: Cited under Background.

7.005   Akira: Cited above, under Drama.

7.006   Animation (and related techniques): See citations under Drama.

7.007   Art into Life: Russian Constructivism, 1914-32. New York: Rizzoli; Seattle: Henry Art Gallery, 1990.

Exhibition catalogue. See below, S. Bann.

7.008   Ashbaugh, Dennis.

New York City artist who "composes canvas landscapes that attempt to visualize computer viruses," basing much of his work on the writings of W. Gibson and B.

Sterling — q.v. under Fiction (quoting J. Markhoff, "Art Invents . . . ," cited below, this section).

7.009   Aycock, Alice: Retrospective of Projects and Ideas, 1972-1983 (sic).   Stuttgart, Germany: Wurttembergischer Kunstiverein, 1983.

In English and German. Includes interview with Aycock and many black and white illus. of sculpture and drawings.

7.010   Bann, Stephen. The Tradition of Constructivism. New York: Viking, [1974].

From The Documents of Twentieth Century Art series.   See index for "Constructivism": an art movement in Russia around the time of the Revolution, associated with Vladimir Tatlin, Antoine Pevsner, and Naum Gabo—and with admiration for technology generally and machines in particular.   See in this section the entry for R. Goldberg.

7.011   Bass, Ruth. "Roger Brown." Art News 88 (Dec. 1989): 159.

Rev. of the show at New York's Phyllis Kind Gallery; notes bleakness that results from much of modern technology as depicted in Brown's cityscapes and landscapes.

7.012   Benjamin, Walter. "The Work of Art in the Age of Mechanical Reproduction."   Harry Zohn, trans. In WB's Illuminations. New York: Schocken, 1969. Hannah Arendt, ed., introd. 217-51.

A very important work.   Opposing Theodor Adorno, WB took a relatively optimistic view of the possibilities of art in the age of film, radio, and the phonograph—technological innovations that strip from art the "aura" given by uniqueness, thereby (potentially) liberating art from the bourgeois ruling elite. Where Adorno saw only commercial exploitation, WB saw the possibility—though hardly the inevitablity—of art truely open to politics.   Discussed in clear, concise prose by Raman Selden in A Reader's Guide to Contemporary Literary Theory (Lexington: The UP of Kentucky, 1989) esp. 36-37, which we have consulted.

7.013   Benson, Timothy O. "The Functional and the Conventional in the Dada Philosophy of Raoul Hausmann." In Dada/Dimensions, q.v. in this section.

Substantial essay, dealing with Hausmann's theories about and incorporation of new materials into visual art.   Hausmann holds that "The Dadaist does not translate something which today has a purely machine character . . . into another material" (138); note the "not."

7.014   Berkey, John. John Berkey, Painted Space. Text by Sharon Berkey.   Pittsburgh: Friedlander, 1991.

SF illustrations, generally "'hardware' art, mostly of space ships, shuttles, and futuristic mammoth land vehicles." Rev. Walter Albert, SFRA Newsletter #196 (April 1992): 20-21, our source for this entry, and whom we quote.

7.015   Bohan, Ruth L. "Joseph Stella's Man in Elevated (Train)." In Dada/Dimensions, q.v. in this section.

Deals with a series of works that merge "[Marcel] Duchamp's ironic detachment, his experiments with nontraditional materials, his sexual preoccupations, his concerns with the fourth dimension, and his fascination for the machine with Stella's own longstanding commitment to urban-technological themes" (188).

7.016   Bohn, Willard. "Picabia's Mechanical Expression and the Demise of the Object." The Art Bulletin 67 (Dec. 1985): 673-77.

The central form in Francis Picabia's watercolor entitled <u>Mechanical Expression</u> <u>Seen</u> <u>through</u> <u>Our</u> <u>Own</u> <u>Mechanical</u> <u>Expression</u>, which is labeled with the name of an exotic dancer, is based on a radiometer. See L. D. Henderson's follow-up article cited below, this section.

7.017 Bowlt, John E. "H2SO4: Dada in Russia." In <u>Dada/Dimensions</u>, q.v. in this section.

JEB finds Russian Dada had a more positivist interest in science than Dada elsewhere.

7.018 Bukatman, Scott. "The Cybernetic (City) State: Terminal Space Becomes Phenomenal." <u>Journal</u> <u>of</u> <u>the</u> <u>Fantastic</u> <u>in</u> <u>the</u> <u>Arts</u> 2.2 (Summer 1989): 43-63. <u>JFA</u> special issue on S. F. film, Brooks Landon, guest ed.

Among other projects, SB attempts to relate <u>Blade</u> <u>Runner</u> and other films to works and theories in the graphic and plastic arts, using analyses by F. Jameson, V. Sobchack, and others. The essay is unquestionably useful on individual works; Brooks Landon—a reliable authority—found the theoretical portions worthy of study.

7.019 Burnham, Jack. <u>Beyond</u> <u>Modern</u> <u>Sculpture</u>. New York: Braziller, 1969.

Note date of publication; see below, K. Hulten's <u>The</u> <u>Machine</u> <u>as</u> <u>Seen</u> <u>at</u> <u>the</u> <u>End</u> <u>of</u> <u>the</u> <u>Mechanical</u> <u>Age</u> (1968).

7.020 Burns, Jim. <u>Lightship</u>. Limpsfield, Surrey: Paper Tiger, 1986.

SF book covers "featuring futuristic machines, aliens, and cityscapes." Rev. Chris Morgan, <u>FR</u> #92, 9.6 (June 1986): 17, our source for this entry, and whom we quote.

7.021 Burns, Scott. <u>Design</u> <u>by</u> <u>Algorithm</u>. An exhibit by Scott Burns. Parkland College Gallery, Champaign, IL, Nov.-Dec. 1987. Lawrence Hall of Science, Berkeley, CA, June-Oct. 1988. Old Quarter Gallery, French Quarter, New Orleans, LA, March 1990-March 1991.

SB is an associate professor of general engineering at the U of Illinois, Urbana, who does "computer-based artwork derived from mathematical equations. . . . Each image may be thought of as a collection of 2.8 million very small colored dots," where each dot "represents the solution of a mathematical equation or process" (from one of SB's handouts on his art).

7.022 <u>Carplays</u>: Cited under Drama.

7.023 Cembalist, Robin. "Allen Wexler." <u>Art News</u> 91 (April 1992): 121.

Rev. of exhibit at Ronald Feldman Fine Arts. Sculptural environments set up a culture/nature dialogue without being antitechnology.

7.024 <u>Cincinnati</u> <u>Collects:</u> <u>The</u> <u>Corporate</u> <u>View</u>. "An Exhibition of Art from Area Corporate Collections at The Contemporary Arts Center [Cincinnati, OH], September 13-November 2, 1991."

Pieces of interest listed individually, with reference to "Cincinnati Collects." The catalog accompanying the exhibition is also entitled <u>Cincinnati</u> <u>Collects. . . .</u> The main (Fountain Square) entrance of The Contemporary Arts Center is marked by "Metrobot," a large electronic billboard, with a pay phone, suggesting a robot: an important introduction to the Center's artistic space.

7.025 Cyber Crush No. 4. Toms River, NJ: S.Q.P. Inc., with Grafinter Edicions (sic),
London, UK, [1991]. Bob Keenan et al., publishers.

Comic book significant for the following: (1) Jim Balen's cover showing a
chimera that is a four-eyed woman down to the waist and below that a mechanical
black widow spider; she is firing a long automatic weapon. (2) The final episode
of Hammer-Stein's War Memoirs, "Only Robots Left Alive!"; Hammer-Stein is a
robot, who will lead robots against robots after most of the humans are killed in
the war (cf., e.g., P. K. Dick's "The Defenders," cited under Fiction). (3) Sam
Slade, "Robo-Hunter," which features cute, insectoid robots.

7.026 Cyphers, Peggy. "Mary Lucier." Arts Magazine 65 (April 1991): 120.

Rev. of video installation at New York's Greenberg Wilson Gallery: techno-
industry destroys the natural world.

7.027 Dada-Constructivism: The Janus Face of the Twenties. London: Annely Juda Fine Art,
1984.

See above, this section, entry for S. Bann.

7.028 Dada/Dimensions. Stephen C. Foster, ed. Ann Arbor: UMI, 1985.

Anthology of essays on Dada, several of which are cited in this section.

7.029 Dean, Roger. Views. 1975. Limpsfield, Surrey: Dragon's World, 1985.

SF and fantasy art of Roger Dean, notably album covers for Yes, Paladin (a semi-
robotic horse for the LP Charge)—and insectoid flying machines. Rev. Chris
Morgan, FR #83 (Sept. 1985): 28, our source for this entry.

7.030 Decker, John, and Jim Postell. Inverse Square Law, 1991. Exhibited at Cincinnati
Collects (q.v.) "Courtesy the Kroger Company, Koster Gallery, Collection the
artist."

The title in the catalog is in mathematical form or a parody thereof. The work
suggests a two-string electronic harp.

7.031 Deichter, David. "When Worlds Collide." Art in America 78 (Feb. 1990): 121-27.

Discusses the Whitney's Image World: Art and Media Culture exhibition.
Touches on the desacralization of art through the use of mass media techniques,
as well as artists' use of communication media to criticize the society they usually
portray. See above, the entry for W. Benjamin.

7.032 Dimitrijevic, Nena. "Nam June Paik." Flash Art (International Edition) 144 (Jan./Feb.
1989): 130.

ND uses a rev. of exhibitions at London's Hayward Gallery and Nigel Greenwood
Gallery to put Paik's career into a critical framework, finding in Paik's work a
love/hate relationship with technology in which he is fascinated by it but places
the human spirit above it. Paik: "I want to make technology ridiculous." Paik's
oeuvre is in two parts: the early visions that "naturalize TV" into a transmitter of
Zen-inspired messages and the more recent "monuments to the meaningless flood
of television images which dominate our lives"—incuding Family of Robot
(1986), which ND finds a less anarchic version of the FLUXUS robot of 1964, K-
456.

7.033 Elderfield, John. "On the Dada-Constructivist Axis." Dada/Surrealism #13 (1984): 5-
16.

Constructivism arose from Dada, even through the former was very positivist and the latter, at least originally, nihilistic and destructive. Constructivists felt technological progress would lead to the perfection of individuals and society. (See in this section the entry for S. Bann.)

7.034 Escher, M[aurits] C. Ascending and Descending. Lithograph, 1960. Figure 6 in Gödel, Escher, Bach. By Douglas Hofstadter.

Rather geometrical and quite uniform "... monks trudge forever in loops" (Hofstadter [14], opposite Figure 6).

7.035 ---. Trappenhuis (House of Stairs). Dated XI/51. Printed by Baaker Baam, Holland, carrying copyright date of 1988, M.C. Escher c/o Cordon Art.

The creatures climbing up/down the stairs appear to be mechanical centipedes, except that they have only six legs, and the legs are humanoid.

7.036 ---. Waterfall. Lithograph, 1961. Figure 5 in Gödel, Escher, Bach. By Douglas Hofstadter (q.v., under Background).

The up/down waterfall turns a waterwheel; the composition balances geometrical and organic forms.

7.037 Erikson, John D. Dada: Performance, Poetry, and Art. Boston: Twayne, 1984.

Ch. 2, "In the Land of Jazz, Skyscrapers, and Machines: New York Dada," covers Francis Picabia, Marcel Duchamp, and Man Ray, and the genesis of machine imagery in their work, as well as touching on their ambivalence toward it. Ch. 7, "Dada Art and the Dynamics of the Uninhabitable Space," begins with a general discussion of the effect that the technology to mass produce images and objects had on the meaning of art and then proceeds to link that to machine imagery in Dada (see above, W. Benjamin). JDE differentiates between dehumanizing industry, concerned with equipment and created to produce consumer goods, and the human-created mechanical, which for Picabia and Duchamp symbolised transformation, metamorphosis, energy, and sexual function.

7.038 FASA Corporation 1991 Catalog (Summer). Chicago: FASA, 1991.

See any of the FASA catalogs for the imaging of BattleTech™ things in role-playing games, short story anthologies, handbooks, graphic novels, record sheets, and misc. products. A whole world of "-Techs" and "-Mechs," all registered trademarks and incredibly blatant in border-line fascistic power-appeals and phallic imagery (see esp. 18-19 of the 1991 issue).

7.039 Fisher, R. M. The Stations, 1986. Property of Arcorp., Inc., exhibited at Cincinnati Collects.

Seven pieces in "stainless steel, brass, aluminum" that look like boilers or machine cases without machines. Four of them are on three legs and three on four legs; all are round and squat, with conical tops.

7.040 "Five Painters and a Machine (Artists Interpret the Continuous Miner)." Fortune 11 Feb. 1980: 184 f.

7.041 Foster, Stephen C., ed.: See under Dada/Dimensions.

7.042 Freeman, Judi. "Bridging Purism and Surrealism: The Origins and Production of Ferdinand Leger's Ballet Mechanique." Dada/ Surrealism #15 (1986): 28-45.

Leger created his first film just as his painted imagery was shifting from explorations of machine age life to close-ups of fairly abstract objects. JF feels Ballet Mechanique needs to be considered within the context of traditional fine arts in the early 20th c. See Ballet méchanique (sic) under Drama.

7.043   Fry, Edward. "The Poetic Machines of Alice Aycock." Portfolio Nov.-Dec. 1981: 60-64.

Aspects of machinery and electronics both inspire Aycock's drawings and sculptural environments and inform their content. Includes photos and discussions of works like The Machine that Makes the World and How to Catch and Manufacture Ghosts.

7.044   Futurism: A Modern Focus. New York: Guggenheim Museum, 1973.

Futurism started as a movement among painters in Italy before World War I and produced a number of works celebrating machines. See Futurism volume for a view the movement from late in the 20th c.

7.045   Gardner, Colin. "Nam June Paik." Artforum 28 (1990): 181-82.

Rev. Paik's exhibit at the Dorothy Golden Gallery, Los Angeles. Concludes that Paik's video sculptures (illustrations of Alexander Graham Bell on 181) and etchings from the "Robot Portfolio" are potentially about "all forms of reification as received information" and the mindlessness and sameness of that information (181).

7.046   Giger, H. R. Giger's Alien. 1979. Beverly Hills, CA: Morpheus International, 1989. Text, photographs, and layout mostly by HRG and Mia Bonzanigo. Hugh Young, English trans. See copyright page for credits and complexities.

Note Giger's intention to express in the derelict ship in Alien (q.v. under Drama) "the biomechanical character of a space-ship built by non-humans" (24); his conception of the derelict's long-dead pilot "as one of my biomechanoids, attached to the seat so as to form a single unit" (34); the adult Alien as "insect-like and elegant" (58). See also for HRG's comments on the relation of Alien and H. R. Giger's Necronomicon (12 and passim)—and for the many plates and photographs.

7.047   ---. H. R. Giger's Biomechanics. Rpt. Beverly Hills, CA: Morpheus International, 1990. 12"x17". English language edn. Harlan Ellison, introd.

Advertised as reproducing nearly 300 of HRG'S works, combining biological images with the mechanical.

7.048   Gigliotti, Davidson. "The Allure of the Electronic: The Changing Vocabulary of Video Sculpture." Afterimage 17 (March 1990): 12-17.

Discusses the exhibition Video Skulptur retrospectiv und aktuell 1963-1989 mounted at the DuMont Kunsthalle, Cologne—an international survey of video art. Relevant works include some early interactive pieces, like those of Bruce Nauman and Les Levine, that conjure images of surveillance and more recent pieces dealing with the history and implications of communicating visually. The latter group includes Fabrizio Plessi's Materia prima, which compares disconnected video monitors with marble slabs as potential carriers of information, and Nam June Paik's VV-W, a huge double-sided pyramid of monitors which seductively combine the light with subliminal images.

7.049   Glowen, Ron. "Simulations of Nature." Artweek 20 (26 August 1989): 5.

Rev. of two installations at the Henry Gallery, U of Washington, Seattle. Mary Lucier's video installation plays on 19th-c. Romantic landscape traditions and the ambivalence born of the video camera's presence in the wilderness it records. Patrick Zentz's technological constructions transmit and simulate the outside environment inside the gallery—wind speed and direction, sounds, etc.

7.050 Goldberg, Roselee. <u>Performance Art</u>: <u>From Futurism to the Present</u>. New York: Abrams, 1988. Rev. and enlarged edition of RG's <u>Performance: Live Art, 1909 to the Present</u>. New York: Abrams, 1979.

History stressing first three decades of the 20th c. <u>PA</u> covers Italian Futurism's experimentation with machine noise as music, mechanical choreography and puppets, moving sets and mechanical costumes. RG finds Russian Futurism more political. The Constructivists announced the death of painting and supported art created in real space. Dada performance made less use of mechanized sets and costumes. Berlin Dadaists, however, demanded progressive unemployment through automation so workers could find the truth of and learn to experience life. In Holland, Schwitters argued for the equality of all materials, including equality among human beings, wire netting, and "thought pumps" (71). Bauhaus performances and ballets also combined art and technology, the human and the mechanical. Costumes aimed at the transformation of the human figure into a mechanical object, and choreography emphasized the dancers as objects. In the last third of the book, RG shows that many of these ideas came to the fore again in the 1940's and 50's at Black Mountain College, in the music of John Cage, and in Merce Cunningham's dances. More recently they have been extended by conceptualist, punk, live art, and other postmodernist performance art. See in this section the entry for S. Bann.

7.051 Goldsmith Arnold L. <u>The Golem Remembered, 1909-1980: Variations of a Jewish Legend</u>. Detroit: Wayne State UP, 1981.

Includes "12 unnumbered pages of illustrations, photographs (mostly from a Habima performance, from illustrations of Meyrink's novel, <u>Der Golem</u>, and from the best of the golem films)." Rev. Robert Plank, <u>SF&FBR</u> #6 (July-Aug. 1982): 9, our source for this citation, and whom we quote.

7.052 Graef, Manfred. "Toward A Cybernetic Art Corresponding to the Symbols of Our Early Ancestors." <u>Leonardo</u> 19.4 (1986): 293-96.

7.053 Grant, Daniel. "Art at the Borderline (Computer, Holographic and Xerographic Art: Pix Supplement)." <u>American Artist</u> 51 (Oct. 1987): 10.

7.054 Grimmett, Douglass and Chuck Carlton. <u>Robot Calendar 1985</u>. New York: Workman, 1984.

Features photos of robots in traditional '50s sci-fi themes. Rev. Russell Letson, <u>FR</u> #74 (Dec. 1984): 32, our source for this entry.

7.055 Hanhardt, John G. "Video Art: Expanded Forms." <u>Leonardo</u> 23 (1990): 437-39.

JGH discusses the works and artists shown in a 1988 exhibition of the same name that he curated for the Whitney at Equitable Center. He outlines the major directions in video art taken by seven video artists.

7.056 Heartney, Eleanor. "Paul Laffoley." <u>Art News</u> 88 (Dec. 1989): 166-67.

This show at New York's Kent Fine Art was "an odd mix of breathless futurism, technophilia, and muddled philosophy . . ." (166-67).

7.057 ---. "Sue Coe." <u>Art News</u> 88 (Dec. 1989): 158.

Coe's "Porkopolis" series at New York's Galerie Street Etienne, remarking on her use of the technology of the slaughterhouse as a metaphor for humanity's cruel disregard for the plight of the powerless in society.

7.058   Henderson, Linda Dalrymple. "Francis Picabia, Radiometers, and X-rays in 1913." The Art Bulletin 71 (Mar. 1989): 114-23.

Examines Picabia's watercolor Mechanical Expression Seen through Our Own Mechanical Expression in terms of the imagery and ideas inspired by the Crookes tube (used to produce x-rays) and the Crookes radiometer. LDH notes that the discovery of x-rays fired the public and cultural imagination well into the second decade of the 20th c.; in Picabia, they became part of his search for the invisible and for a higher reality as well as proof of the limits of human vision.

7.059   ---. "X-rays and the Quest of Invisible Reality in the Art of [Frank] Kupka, [Marcel] Duchamp, and the Cubists." Art Journal 47 (Winter 1988): 323-40.

Kupka also called by the French and Czech forms of "Frank." See LDH entry immediately above.

7.060   Hoenich, P. K. Robot Art. Haifa: Technion (Israel Institute of Technology, Faculty of Architecture and Planning), 1962.

7.061   Holt, Steven. "The Art of Design." Art News 89 (April 1990): 118-27.

New technology allows designers more aesthetic freedom.

7.062   Hofstadter, Douglas. Gödel, Escher, Bach: Cited under Background.

7.063   Huelsenbeck, Richard. Memoirs of a Dada Drummer. Joachim Neugroschel, trans. New York: Viking, 1974.

Section on Jean Tinguely (130-34) discusses his use of the machine to achieve motion, which the sculptor sees as the nature of existence, dooming all efforts to find the absolute. Through pseudo-machines like Homage to New York, which was intended to self-destruct before its audience at the Museum of Modern Art, Tinguely hopes to shock the viewer and skewer Western ideology's idea of stable values.

7.064   Hulten, K.G.P. Futurism & Futurisms. New York: Abbeville, 1986.

See entry for Futurism: A Modern Focus, cited above, this section.

7.065   ---. The Machine as Seen at the End of the Mechanical Age. New York: Museum of Modern Art, 1968.

Arguably the most useful work on machines in the graphic and plastic arts, plus designs for machines and real-world machines for a large section of Western history up to the late 1960s.

7.066   The Illustrated Blade Runner. David Scrogy, ed. San Diego: Blue Dolphin, 1982.

"Complete screenplay with over 350 selected storyboards"; cited by W. M. Kolb (whom we quote) in his Bibliography for Retrofitting Blade Runner, q.v. under Drama Criticism.

7.067   L'Illustrazione di Fantascienza e Fantasy in Italia—Italian SF & Fantasy Art. Milan: Editrice Nord, 1985.

Over 120 color plates, including a section on "Starships and Machines." Rev. Piergiorgio Nicolazzini, FR #81 (July 1985): 26, our source for this entry.

7.068   Jameson, Frederic. "Postmodernism, or The Cultural Logic of Late Capitalism.": Cited under Background.

7.069   Judas Priest: See under Music (for interesting cover art on albums).

7.070   Kraftwerk: See under Music (for interesting cover art).

7.071   Kluger, Jeffrey. "Painting By Numbers (Computer Art)." Discover 8 (Oct. 1987): 56.

7.072   Koyre, Alexander. From the Closed World to the Infinite Universe. Baltimore: Johns Hopkins P, 1957.

If in some sense all artists are realists, attempting to tell truth about the world, then the vision of the world they accept as true conditions their art. KA elucidates a change in vision crucial for artists who deal with forms in space.

7.073   Kyle, David. A Pictorial History of Science Fiction. London: Hamlyn, 1976.

Includes pictures of science fictional machines and related devices from 1871—a parachute? (17)—to the cover of the second issue of Science Fiction Monthly, featuring a highly angular, colorful space craft (163).

7.074   Lawrence, Sidney. "Clean Machines at the Modern." Art in America Feb. 1984: 127 f.

7.075   Lee, Stan [et al.]. The Power of Iron Man: The Enemy Within. New York: Marvel Comics / Crown: 1984.

Book rpt. of complete sequence of nine Iron Man episodes from March 1977 onwards. Hero dons a suit of high-tech armor to become Iron Man. Deals with question of physical strength attained through mechanical means opposed to human strength attained (paradoxically) through human vulnerability. Rev. Thom Dunn, FR #72 (Oct. 1984): 32.

7.076   Léger, Ferdinand. French artist (1881-1955), described in the Encyclopaedia Britannica (1974) Micropaedia entry for him as a "painter, deeply influenced by modern industrial technology, who developed 'machine art,' or a style characterized by monumental mechanistic forms in bold colours arranged in highly disciplined compositions" (VI.124). See in this section, Judi Freeman entry; see under Drama, Ballet mécanique.

7.077   Lemos, Peter. "Openhouse." Art News 89 (April 1990): 128-33.

Nigel Coates, one of the interior designers profiled, mixed aboriginal motifs with industrial fragments for "the latest in decadent chic" (129).

7.078   Light Years: Cited under Drama.

7.079   Machineworks: Vito Acconci, Alice Aycock, Dennis Oppenhiem. Philadelphia: Institute of Contemporary Art, U of Pennsylvania, [1981].

Catalog of the exhibition organized by Janet Kardon. These three artists were among the only ones in the late seventies to adopt a machine aesthetic as their approach to object making.

7.080   Mahoney, Robert. "Nam June Paik." Arts Magazine 64 (Feb. 1990): 101-2.

Rev. of exhibit in New York's Holly Solomon Gallery notes the figural aspect of many of Paik's works, including the way video monitors read as thought or brain activity in TV Eyes and Young Buddhas on Duratrans Bed. See also W. Robinson, cited below, this section.

7.081   Malina, Roger F. "Art in the Computer Age (SIGGRAPH 1989 Art Show, the Computer Museum, Boston)." Technology Review 92 (Oct. 1989): 71.

7.082   Mandelbrot, Benoît. Fractals: Form, Chance, and Dimension. San Francisco: Freeman, 1977.

Cited by Douglas Hofstadter as "a picture book of sophisticated contemporary research ideas in mathematics," in the Bibliography to Gödel, Escher, Bach, q.v., under Background.

7.083   Markhoff, John. "Art Invents A Jarring New World From Technology." The New York Times Sunday, 25 Nov. 1990: E-5.

On cyberpunk's influence on the plastic and graphic arts, opera (see under Music, VALIS, by T. Machover), television, and film.

7.084   McBride, Henry. "Love Among the Machines." Arts 4 (1946).

7.085   McNamara, Martin H. "Garden Technology." Landscape Architecture 81 (Mar. 1991): 26.

Nam June Paik's Video Arbor is illus. and discussed. Paik says it expresses the need for technology and nature, so often considered enemies, to work together.

7.086   Mead, Syd. "Designing the Future." Omni's Screen Flight / Screen Fantasies: The Future Acccording to Science Fiction Cinema. Danny Peary, ed. Garden City, NY: Doubleday, 1984. 122-313.

Includes one still and eight pre-production paintings for Blade Runner, by the visual futurist of the film.

7.087   ---. Oblagon: Concepts of Syd Mead. Tokyo: Kodansha Kabushiki-kaisha, 1985.

Includes 14 of SM's paintings for Blade Runner; cited by W. M. Kolb in his Bibliography for Retrofitting Blade Runner, q.v. under Drama Criticism.

7.088   Mechanika, an exhibit of thirty pieces of sculpture by "some 20 artists." Contemporary Arts Center, Cincinnati, OH. May-July, 1991.

Many of the works are animated. Includes Dennis Oppenheim's Disco Mattress, which does disquieting things with a Raggedy Ann doll, a Raggedy Andy doll, a mattress, and an electric saw. Rev. Jerry Stein, "'Mechanika' show plays visual tricks on viewer" (sic), Cincinnati Post 25 May 1991: 1C, 5C.

7.089   Meltzer, Bonnie. "Computers Should Be Seen As Artists' Tools Rather Than Enemies of the Arts." PC Week 9 Feb. 1988: 33.

7.090   Microman: Computers and the Evolution of Consciousness. See under Background, G. Pask, with S. Curran.

7.091   Mifflin, Margot. "Performance Art: What Is It and Where Is It Going?" Art News 91 (April 1992): 84-89.

This survey of current performance artists mentions Comfort Control Systems, a group dealing with the negative side of technology; Survival Research

Laboratories, which stages remote-controlled warfare between robots and machines; Blue Man Group (see P. Pacheco, this section); and Liz Young, who confines people in torture chamber-like settings in order to protest "governmental and psychological enslavement" (88).

7.092   Miller, Nancy. Matta, the First Decade. Waltham, MA: Rose Art Museum, Brandeis U, 1982.

On Roberto Sebastian Matta Echaurren (Robert Matta, b. 1911). Essays and interview in this exhibition catalog discuss Matta's break with Surrealism and the New York School over his interest in science, mathematical systems, and technology. Matta began to use futuristic imagery in 1943, partly in homage to Marcel Duchamp. From 1944 through the immediate post-war period, machine/human hybrids began to people Matta's art. Distorted by tension, terror, and anger, they reflect victimization and the horrors of war.

7.093   Milman, Esther. "Dada New York: An Historiographical Analysis." In Dada/Dimensions, q.v. in this section of the list.

Contains a wealth of biblio. material in text and notes.

7.094   Milner, John. Vladimir Tatlin and the Russian Avant-Garde. New Haven, CT: Yale UP, 1983.

Includes biblio.

7.095   Moore, Alan, Dave Gibbons, and John Higgins. Watchmen. New York: DC Comics, 1986, 1987.

For those unfamiliar with the graphic novel and its possibilities, Start Here. The science-fictional aspects of the work are very relevant, and Watchmen is both serious and complex. Rev. Darren Harris-Fain, Extrapolation 30.4 (Winter 1989): 410-12.

7.096   Moreno, Pepe. Contemporary artist working "on a computer-generated Batman story" set in a cyberpunkish future in which Bruce Wayne is dead but his spirit marches on in the form of an electronic Batman run by a supercomputer. See Darren Harris-Fain, rev. Mark Cotta Vaz's Tales of the Dark Knight: Batman's First Fifty Years ... (Extrapolation 31.3: 282).

7.097   "My Machine." Poster by General Cable Corporation, September 1944.

In a series of wartime posters for their workers. Transposes the military encomium to "My Rifle" to "My Machine," asserting the worker's oneness with the machine and gratitude toward it.

7.098   Onarato, Ronald J. "Wonder in Aliceland: Memory and Self in Aycock's Art." In Hugh M. Davies and Ronald J. Onorato, Sitings. La Jolla, CA: La Jolla Museum of Contemporary Art, 1986: 38-51. Illus. 120-23.

Essay in exhibition catalog covers Alice Aycock's gradual movement from work heavily dependent on traditions of Modernist and site-specific sculpture to work more based in personal memory and fantasy. Recent works reveal "Aycock's intention to express a less stable but so much more hopeful future life . . ." and suggest imagined environments with resemblances to construction sites, machines—even an alchemist's studio (45).

7.099   Onosko, Tim. Wasn't the Future Wonderful?: A View of Trends and Technology From the 1930s. New York: Dutton, 1979.

Mostly from Modern Mechanix (sic) magazine from 1930-37, but with some

others, including <u>The Technocrats' Magazine</u>. See for earnest discussions of such
topics as, "Is Man Doomed by the Machine Age" (18-23) and for text and
copious illustrations of the great future of mechanical civilization as seen from
the view of 1930s technophiles.

7.100   Overstreet, Robert M. <u>The Overstreet Comic Book Price Guide</u> (vt). 18th-20th edns.
Cleveland, TN. Overstreet, 1988. New York: Ballantine, 1989, 1990.

Provides a list of available comic books and includes abridged overview of the
history of comic books. See also Randall W. Scott's <u>Comic Books and Strips: An
Information Sourcebook</u> (Phoenix, AZ: Oryx. 1988).

7.101   Pacheco, Patrick. "I Came, I Saw, I Blew." <u>Art and Antiques</u> April 1992: 20.

Rev. describes <u>Tubes</u> at New York's Astor Place Theatre by performance artists
Blue Man Group as "a satirically funny romp through the alienated landscape of
the industrial and communication age." Among other things, the theatre is filled
with plastic tubing, and the three performers have a futuristic alien/android look:
they are bald and painted blue.

7.102   Patton, Phil. "How Art Geared Up to Face Industry in Modern America."
<u>Smithsonian</u> Nov. 1986: 156 f..

Various artists' works at Brooklyn Museum. See in this section, P. C. Phillips, C.
Willis.

7.103   Performance Art: See also, Indexes and listings under Drama.

7.104   Phillips, Patricia C. "Building Machines." <u>Artform International Magazine</u> Feb. 1987:
118-19.

Various artists' work at P.S. 1 in New York City, examining the way machines
have affected human life. "The designers did not simply appropriate machine
imagery, but looked to the concept of mechanization with originality, intelligence,
and some irony" (119).

7.105   ---. "The Machine Age in America, 1918-1941." <u>Artform International Magazine</u>
Feb. 1987: 118.

Various artists' works at Brooklyn Museum. See in this section, C. Willis.

7.106   Popper, Frank. <u>Origins and Development in Kinetic Art</u>. New York: New York
Graphic Society, 1968.

See for a necessarily mechanized art, popular in the middle and late 20th c.

7.107   Price, Aimee Brown. "A Conversation with Alice Aycock." <u>Architectural Digest</u> April
1983: 54-60.

Includes discussion of machine-based sculptures.

7.108   Reveaux, Tony. "Video's New Territory." <u>Artweek</u> 19 (Dec. 10, 1988): 5-6.

The natural world meets video in the installations of Doug Hall, Rita Myers, Dara
Birnbaum, and Mary Lucier at the San Francisco Museum of Modern Art.

7.109   Reynolds, Kay, and Ardith Carlton. <u>Robotech Art 1</u>. Norfolk, VA: Donning, 1986.
<u>Robotech Art 2</u>. 1987.

Features art from the Robotech cartoons, an animated series from Japan (1982-

83) that has appeared on US TV. First volume rev. Michael Klossner, FR #94 (Sept. 1986): 36, our source for the description of Art 1. See above under Fiction, the ROBOTECH™ entry for J. McKinney.

7.110 Rhodes, Anthony. Propaganda, The Art of Persuasion: World War II. Victor Margolin, ed. New York: Chelsea, 1976.

See for posters and films prominent in propaganda during WWII, many of which (appropriately for a high-tech war) featured things mechanical.

7.111 Rice, Shelley. "The Luminous Image: Video Installations at the Stadelijk Museum, (Amsterdam)." Afterimage 12 (Dec. 1984): 12-15.

Many artists are covered. Esp. relevant here are Robert Wilson's The Spaceman, which includes a mannequin spaceman hovering over a desert landscape and "creates a strange, bell-jar type of dreamworld that is . . . disconcerting" (14), and Tony Oussler's L7-L5, which uses technology to convey shattering futility.

7.112 Richardson, John Adkins. Modern Art and Scientific Thought. Urbana, IL: U of Illinois P, 1971.

Ch. 6, "Conformity as Rebellion—Expressionism, Dada, Surrealism," discusses the connection between World War I and the formation of Dada: not only the way in which "modern" society treated individuals like machines, but also the peculiarly intricate and often faintly ridiculous mechanical nature of the actual machines used in that war. The "plethora of useless mechanisms and displaced appliances in Dada art exudes a kind of gallows humor" (140). The last chapter notes Claes Oldenburg's use of household technology to comment upon "an implied impotence of industrial society" (169).

7.113 Riechardt, Jasia. Cybernetic Serendipity. New York: Praeger, 1969.

On computer art.

7.114 ---. Cybernetics, Arts, and Ideas. Boston: New York Graphic Society, 1971.

Described by D. Hofstadter as "A weird collection of ideas about computers and art, music, literature. Some of it is definitely off the deep end—but some of it is not." Some of the "not" is in JR's area of art. See Bibliography to Gödel, Escher, Bach (753), q.v., under Background.

7.115 ---. "Machines and Art." Leonardo 20.4 (1987): 367-72.

7.116 Robinson, Walter. "Nam June Paik." Art in America 75 (June 1987): 157.

Rev. of exhibition at New York's Holly Solomon Gallery. WR maintains Paik is famous for bringing together witty clichés from television and emblems of humanity, religion, nature, and vision—all of it mediated by avant-garde art. The new work in this show includes video paintings (video stills are airbrushed in canvas by computerized machines) and the 1986 Family of Robot, in which each figure in three generations of robots is constructed of stacked video monitors mounted in period housings. WR is especially taken by Baby, "a futuristic high-tech spectacle," and by the "impressive metaphor of consciousness" the flickering video screens provide in these figures. Color illus. of Grandfather.

7.117 Robot Calendar 1985. Douglass Grimmett and Chuck Carlton, makers. New York: Workman, 1984.

Photos of robots in traditional 1950s S. F. style. Rev. Russell Letson, FR 74 (Dec. 1984): 32, our source for this citation.

7.118 "The Robot Exhibit." American Craft 44 (April-May 1984): 14.

7.119 "Robots in Space." Mones (sic on spelling, and only one name). Illus. New York: Random, 1989.

A punch-out figure coloring book, with 10 punch-out figures of robots and accessories, plus pages to color, also featuring robots.

7.120 Rom™. Comic series from Marvel Comics Group. Stan Lee, publisher. Beginning December 1979.

We have examined issue 1.2, Jan. 1980. Rom, "The Greatest of the Space Knights" is a heroic robot, emphatically humanoid and masculine in body shape. See under Drama, RoboCop (where Real Manhood [our phrase] is a serious issue).

7.121 Rottensteiner, Franz. The Science Fiction Book: An Illustrated History. New York: Seabury Press, 1975. "A Continuum Book."

See for the illus., including movie stills and the covers of S. F. magazines, from a variety of national literatures that have produced SF: e.g., laboratories, Martian war machines, robots and the Golem, submarines and rocket ships.

7.122 Rubin, William S. Dada and Surrealist Art. New York: Abrams, [1968].

This exhaustive and well-illustrated volume features a number of artists (including Marcel Duchamp, Francis Picabia, Max Ernst, Robert Matta, René Magritte) who deal with machine imagery and/or the subversion of bureaucratic society—the latter being a stated aim of the Surrealist movement in its formative years. (For Matta's full name, see above, entry for N. Miller.)

7.123 ---. Matta. New York: Museum of Modern Art, [1957].

Exhibition catalog for an artist whose works are relevant for the theme of mechanization. See citations for WSR, above, and N. Miller.

7.124 Rush, Grace Under Pressure: See under Music for album cover.

7.125 Shay, Don. "Blade Runner—2020 Foresight." Cinefex #9 (July 1982): 1-71.

In a journal issue entirely "devoted to design, construction and photography in Blade Runner," this is a central article and the "Definitive article on production" of the film, with over 100 stills—all according to W. M. Kolb (whom we quote) in his biblio. for Retrofitting Blade Runner, q.v. under Drama Criticism.

7.126 Singer, Leslie. Zap! Ray Gun Classics. San Francisco: Chronicle P, 1991. Dixie Knight, photography.

Presents 97 pictures of rayguns and such, mostly from the 1950s, the golden age for zap weapons. Rev. Russell Letson, SFRA Newsletter #196 (April 1992): 44-45, our source for this entry. Letson refers his readers to Pierre Boogaerts's Robot (Futuropolis, 1978), which he refers to as a classic work on S. F. toys.

7.127 "Some Robot Fun for a Super Boy!" Birthday card from American Greetings, n.d. (ca. 1990).

A kind of mix-n-match, producing different robots.

7.128 Starship Troopers, cover: See above, under Fiction, R. A. Heinlein.

7.129   Starship Troopers. Game by Avalon Hill Game Company, Baltimore, 1976.

Game based on the novel by R. A. Heinlein (q.v. under Fiction); includes a statement by Heinlein.

7.130   Stokes, Charlotte. "Dadamax: Ernst in the Context of Cologne Dada." In Dada/Dimensions, q.v. in this section.

Discusses Max Ernst's use of imagery of the mechanical man, dressmaker's dummy, and science to lampoon contemporary fashion, sexual taboos, bourgeois pastimes, education, religion, natural science.

7.131   Tatlin. Larissa Alekseevna Zhadova, ed. Paul Filotas and Colin Wright, trans. New York: Rizzoli, 1988.

Selections from Vladimir Tatlin's art, manifestos, letters, and other writings. See for the work of an important avant-garde Russian artist in the 1920s, who tried to apply principles of engineering (and pure geometric forms) to constructed sculpture. See in this section, entry for S. Bann.

7.132   Taylor, Joshua C. America as Art. Washington, D.C.: Smithsonian Institution, 1976.

See for context of Futurism and other relevant movements in art.

7.133   Tomkins, Calvin. The Bride and the Bachelors: The Heretical Courtship in Modern Art. New York: Viking, 1965.

CT asserts that what the four artists profiled (Marcel Duchamp, John Cage, Jean Tinguely, Walter Rauschenberg) have in common is their focus on accepting the external world of the commonplace as it is rather than, as tradition would have it, organizing and interpreting the external world by presenting its objects as images or symbols in a work of art. The effect of removing the artist's control over media and reducing the imposition of self-expression on it is to obliterate the boundary between art and life. All four artists are fond of "the mundane objects of modern industrial society ... and in Cage's case the 'found sounds' of an urban, electronic environment ... " (3). The chapter on Tinguely discusses the ways in which the machines he builds from junk most often fail to work as planned, much to Tinguely's delight in their "freedom."

7.134   Tsai, Eugenie. "A Tale of (At Least) Two Cities: Alice Aycock's 'Large Scale Dis/Integration of Microelectronic Memories (A newly Revised Shantytown)'." Arts Magazine June 1982: 134-41.

Covers shift in Aycock's artistic vocabulary from architecture toward technology. Part of Aycock's intent is to explore the way disorientation can give rise to both terror and euphoria.

7.135   The Tubes. Remote Control: Cited under Music; see for album cover.

7.136   UDF Jet Engine. Property of General Electric Aircraft Engines. Exhibited at Cincinnati Collects (q.v. above).

A 1/4-scale model of an UnDucted Fan-jet engine. It was prominently displayed at Cincinnati Collects, listed in the catalog, and labelled as an art work.

7.137   Veber, Jean. Allégorie sur la machine dévoreuse des hommes (Allegory of the Men-Eating Machine). Ca. 1905.

Described by A. Huyssen as "an allegory of sexual intercourse" in which "the woman has appropriated the phallic power and activity of the machine" (under Drama Criticism, "Vamp" 77).

7.138   Viladas, Pilar. "Speaking in Metaphors." <u>Progressive/Architecture</u> Sept. 1983: 108-
13.

Photos and brief entries on Alice Aycock's <u>The Thousand and One Nights in the
Mansion of Bliss</u>, which "addresses the machinery of metaphysics (and vice
versa)" (110) and Issey Miyake's <u>Bodyworks</u>, in which garments are displayed on
cyborgs (115).

7.139   Vitz, Paul C., and Arnold B. Glincher. <u>Modern Art and Modern Science: The Parallel
Analysis of Vision</u>. New York: Praeger, 1984.

Thorough discussion of ways in which aspects of Modernist art were parallel to
scientific discoveries in or new conceptions of color, space, time, etc. Esp. note
ch. 5, "Space and Time," (107-41) with its discussion of how technological
hardware like stereoscopes and early cinematic devices influenced artists, notably
Marcel Duchamp, Frank Kupka (see above, entry for L. D. Henderson, "X-rays
and the Quest"), Giacomo Balla, and the Futurists. Also of interest in the closing
chapter is the speculation that art and science have recently lost their parallelism
largely because "the prestige and the moral standing of science have greatly
declined" (259). Science has been criticized for just such analytical/reductionist
leanings as attracted Modernist artists.

7.140   <u>Watchmen</u>: Cited above under Alan Moore.

7.141   Webb, Michael. "The Robots Are Here, The Robots Are Here!" <u>Design Quarterly</u> 121
(Spring 1983): 4.

7.142   Wilks, Mike, and Brian W. Aldiss. <u>Pile: Petals from St. Klaed's Computer</u>. New York:
Holt, 1979. Illus.

Sort of Dr. Seuss visits F. Lang's <u>Metropolis</u> (q.v. under Drama)—but with a
technological-rococo sensibility in the art work.

7.143   <u>William Gibson's Neuromancer: The Graphic Novel, Vol 1</u>. Tom De Haven and Bruce
Jensen, adaptation and graphics. Epic Comics, 1989.

Introduction by Gibson, who says the appearance of this graphic novel is true to
his vision for the straight novel (q.v. above under Fiction).

7.144   Willis, Carol. "Mechanisms of Culture: The Machine Age in America, 1918-1941."
<u>Architectural Record</u> Feb. 1987: 2.

Various artists' works at Brooklyn Museum. See in this section, P. Patton, P. C.
Phillips.

7.145   Wilson, Richard Guy, et al. <u>The Machine Age in America, 1918-41</u>. New York:
Abrams, 1986. A Times Mirror Book "Published in conjunction with a major
exhibition that will tour the country after opening at the Brooklyn Museum."

RGW and Dianne H. Pilgrim were the Exhibition Currators. Nine chapters:
"America and the Machine Age," "Machine Aesthetics," "Selling the Machine
Age," "The Machine in the Landscape," "Transportation Machine Design,"
"Architecture in the Machine Age" (all written by RGW), "Engineering a New Art"
(by Dickran Tashjian), "Design for the Machine" (Dianne H. Pilgrim), "The
Machine Age and Beyond" (RGW, DT, DHP). Illus. include L. Lozowick,
<u>Machine Ornament No. 2</u>; L. W. Hine, <u>Heart of the Turbine</u>; and H. Ferriss, <u>Study
for the Maximum Mass Permitted by the 1916 New York Zoning Code, Stage 2</u>.

7.146   Wooster, Ann-Sargent. "Why Don't They Tell Stories Like They Used To?" <u>Art
Journal</u> 45 (Fall 1985): 204-12.

Attempts to create a critical model for video art, which has too often been treated as "aberrant" TV. Covers Nam June Paik, Bruce Conner, Shalom Gorewitz—and includes biblio. citations.

7.147 Zabel, B. "Machine as Metaphor, Model, and Microcosm: Technology in American Art." Arts Magazine 57 (Dec. 1982): 100-105.

7.148 Zone, Ray. "Boltbeak: The Art of Basil Wolverton." JPC 21.3 (Winter 1987): 145-63.

Immediately relevant for "Robot Woman," Wolverton's version of the creation of "a beautiful mechanical woman . . . as a love object" (148).

7.149 Zhadova, Larissa Alekseevna, ed.: See above, this section, Tatlin.

Music

8.001   The Alan Parsons Project. <u>I Robot</u>. Arista, 7002, 1977.

"The story of the rise of the machine and the decline of man. Which paradoxically coincided with his discovery of the wheel . . . and a warning that his brief dominance of this planet will probably end, because he tried to create robot in his own image" (liner note).

8.002   Antheil, George. <u>Ballet méchanique</u>. First performance ca. 1925-26, with arrangements for performance made in conjunction with Virgil Thomson. Available in Phillips recording of Holland Festival live performance in 1970.

Composer denies that the piece is "an actual description" in pure sound "of factories and machinery" but instead warns of the dangers of mechanistic philosophy and esthetics. See under Drama, <u>Ballet méchanique</u>.

8.003   <u>Atomic Cafe</u>. Rounder, 1034, 1980. Charles Wolfe, prod. From the film <u>The Atomic Cafe</u> (1982).

The impact of the atomic bomb on US culture, in sound.

8.004   Brown, James. "Sex Machine." On <u>Love Peace Power: Live at the Olympia, Paris 1971</u>. Polydor, 314 513 39-2, 1971.

The singer is an unstoppable, perfect lover, as proficient as a machine.

8.005   The Buggles. "Radio Star." <u>Age of Plastic</u>. Island, 422-842849-1, 1979.

Bemoans the loss of the imagination and grandeur of radio drama when television became the most popular mass medium.

8.006   <u>Carplays</u>: Cited under Drama.

8.007   Dean, Roger. <u>Views</u>: Collection of art works including a number of reproductions of album covers, LP sleeves, and posters, cited under Graphic and Plastic Arts.

8.008   Delibes, L. Coppélia: Cited under Drama.

8.009   Devo. In performance, through 1982. E.g., from 1975-1977, Devo Live—The
            Mongoloid Years. Rykodisc, RCD 20209, 1992.

            Devo repeats the question of the "humanized" animals in H. G. Wells's Island of
            Dr. Moreau: "Are we not Men?" They answer, "We are Devo!" The animals in
            Dr. Moreau become less than human when they return to their animal forms;
            Devo's "mechanized musicians playing robot rock" (Erlich's notes) suggest a
            form of devolution in presenting humans as machines. Their early schtick is
            preserved on the videotape of Saturday Night Live for 14 Oct. 1978.

8.010   Dolby, Thomas. "She Blinded Me with Science." The Golden Age of Wireless.
            Capitol, C2-4609, 1980.

8.011   Downes, Geoff et al. Yes. "Machine Messiah." On Drama. Atlantic, SD 16019, 1980.
            Lyrics for the three parts of this song given on liner.

            Ironic or ambivalent celebration of the "Machine," as messiah, with an explicit
            allusion to William Blake's "satanic mills."

8.012   Edge, Graeme. The Moody Blues. "In the Beginning." 1969. Coll. on This Is the
            Moody Blues. London, XZAL 13344 TH, 1974.

            A brief cut featuring a dialogue between a contemporary Cartesian Man and a
            computer that tries to convince him that he is magnetic ink.

8.013   Glass, Philip. Kokaanisqatsi: Life Out of Balance. Antilles, ASTA 1, 1983.

            Tone poem of sorts, presenting "images" of a chaotic modern world.

8.014   Hofstadter, Douglas. Gödel, Escher, Bach: Cited under Background.

8.015   The Infernal Machine: See below under C. Rouse.

8.016   Ivey, Jean Eichelberger. Pinball. Folkways Records, FMS 33436, 1967.

            A symphonic work, not directly related to The Who's "Pinball Wizard" (q.v.
            below), using bells and such to evoke a pinball machine.

8.017   Jefferson Starship: See below under P. Kanter.

8.018   Judas Priest. "Electric Eye." On Screaming for Vengeance. [CBS] Columbia, BL
            38160 / FC 38160, 1982. Song written by Judas Priest's Glenn Tipton, Rob
            Halford, and K. K. Downing.

            The Singer of "Electric Eye" is a space-based unobserved observer—made of
            metal, with gleaming circuits, an AI perpetually keeping "the country clean" by
            constant surveillance of everyone; feeding upon our thoughts, the Eye grows in
            power. Note cover art, conceived by Judas Priest and executed by Doug Johnson:
            here a mechanical screaming eagle; cf. JP/Johnson cover on Defenders of the
            Faith (Columbia Records, 1984); cf. and contrast bronzed human(oid) head on
            Stained Class (design by Roslav Szaybo of CBS Records, photography by Ronald
            Kass [Columbia, 1978]). The combination of artwork, photography, lyrics, and
            music in Screaming for Vengeance and Defenders of the Faith produces a very
            strange amalgam of animal vitality, decadent kinkiness, and mechanization.

8.019 Kantner, Paul (music and lyrics), with Mickey Thomas (lyrics). "Modern Times." Jefferson Starship. <u>Modern Times</u>. RCA Stereo BZL1-3848. (c) notice with song lyrics: Little Dragon Music, 1981; for album: Grunt 1971 and RCA 1981.

Futuristic cover and liner notes in type resembling a computer-readable font of the period. Lyrics to "MT" concern freedom and machine guns. See also on this album "Alien" and "Stairway to Cleveland (We Do What We Want)."

8.020 Kraftwerk. <u>Die Mensch/Maschine</u> (<u>The Man/Machine</u> [slashes represent raised periods in original]). Electrola, 1C058-32843, 1978.

Includes "Die Roboter," "Spacelab," "Metropolis," and "Die Mensch / Maschine." Album described legitimately in Blue Angel, Inc., catalog as "Teutonic Techno-Rock." In addition to the "mechanical" aspects to the music, note the album cover and the pictures on the record jacket and labels. The cover gives the album's title in German, Russian, English, and French; the last is both a famous phrase in French and the title of a 1748 work by Julien Offroy de la Mettrie arguing the rigorously materialistic thesis that human beings are machines (see under Background entries for D. Hofstadter and J. Smart). The pictures suggest both S. Sontag's "technocratric" men (see under Drama Criticism) and a combined alumni of Hitler Youth and the more decadent cabarets of the Weimar Republic.

8.021 Landon, Brooks. "Bet On It: Cyber/video/punk/performance": Cited under Drama Criticism.

8.022 <u>Metropolis</u>. Giorgio Moroder, composer and prod. Pete Bellontte et al., lyrics. Columbia Records (CBS), CK 39526 (compact disc), 1984. "Original Motion Picture Soundtrack," from the Fritz Lang Film "Reconstructed And Adapted by Giorgio Moroder."

Music for re-release of Lang's <u>Metropolis</u> (q.v. under Drama). Note Jon Anderson singing "Cage of Freedom"—a lament for humankind trapped in a prison of our own making—and Moroder's instrumental, "Machines."

8.023 Miracles: See below, under Smokey Robinson.

8.024 Moody Blues: See above under G. Edge.

8.025 <u>Moonwalker</u> (music video): Listed under Drama.

8.026 Moraz, Patrick. <u>I</u>. Atlantic, SD 18175, 1976.

The guests in a hotel are united "in search of the ultimate experience"; the hotel building "is controlled by a sphere hovering overhead, within which is stored all information on the emotions, sentiments and sensations of all the people in the various rooms" (liner notes). See for surveillance, machine domination, and containment of the mental and emotional within something geometrically perfect, if not necessarily mechanical (the sphere).

8.027 <u>Music by Computers</u>. Heinz von Foerster and James W. Beauchamp, eds. New York: John Wiley, 1969.

Early book on music generated by computers, cited by D. Hofstadter in the Bibliography section of <u>Gödel, Escher, Bach</u>, q.v., under Background. Hofstadter says the book comes with "a set of four small phonograph records so you can actually hear . . . the pieces described" (748), if you have the proper equipment.

8.028   The New Grove Dictionary of Music and Musicians. Stanley Sadie, ed. 20 vols.
            London: Macmillan, 1980.

            Reference work including useful articles on electronic music, mechanism as a
            musical theme, Futurism in music, computers in music. See below, this section,
            entry for J. C. Waterhouse.

8.029   Offenbach, J. Tales of Hoffmann: Cited above, under Drama.

8.030   Pink Floyd. "Have a Cigar." "Welcome to the Machine." On Wish You Were Here.
            BMI, PC 33453, 1975.

            Esp. in context of the album, the songs present society as a machine within which
            individuals lose identity, and lose control to the desires of others; see below, Pink
            Floyd's The Wall.

8.031   ---. The Wall. Columbia, C2K3618, 1979.

            Mechanization of people within a machine-like society. See Pink Floyd entry
            above; see under Drama, Pink Floyd—The Wall.

8.032   The Police. Ghost in the Machine. A&M, SP-3730, 1981.

            Note esp. "Spirits in the Material World" (side 1, first cut) and "Rehumanize
            Yourself" (side 2, second cut).   One reviewer comments that "Rehumanize
            Yourself" describes "a totally mechanized society in which violence has become a
            'social norm'" (Jeff Callan, "Unabridged" supplement to The Miami Student
            [Miami University, Oxford, OH], 16 Oct. 1981: 2).

8.033   Reynolds, Malvina. "Little Boxes." On Pete Seeger's Greatest Hits. Columbia, CS
            9416, n.d.

            "You see, the machine says to all of us . . . 'If you want it cheap, take it like I
            make it—rectangular'" (Seeger's comments on record jacket).

8.034   Rouse, Christopher. The Infernal Machine. Brief symphonic work (ca. five minutes).
            Premiered Avignon, France, 1981. Available on Nonesuch, 79118-1, 1986. Our
            major source: Chicago Symphony Series, Leonard Slatkin, conducting. WGUC-
            FM, Cincinnati, OH, Saturday, 2 Feb. 1985.

            Music based on Jean Cocteau's play, La Machine infernale (The Infernal
            Machine, 1934), itself based on a rather Freudian reading of the legend of
            Oedipus in which the machinery of the human subconscious is the "destiny" that
            negates free will. Composer tried to suggest a great, self-sufficient machine,
            eternally in motion, not demonic in itself but potentially dangerous to people in
            its indifferent operation.

8.035   Rucker, Rudy. "Raising the Level." In "Cyberpunk Forum/Symposium," MR47/48:
            51-55 (see under Literary Criticism, L. McCaffery, guest ed.).

            Relates cyberpunk to punk rock—and information theory (53).

8.036   Rush. Grace Under Pressure. PolyGram (manufacturing and marketing [Mercury
            label]) / RCA Music Service (re-release dist.), R-153786, 1984.

            Liner shows a square with a picture of a U-clamp holding an egg; reverse of liner
            gives lyrics. Of immediate relevance, Neil Peart's lyrics to "The Body Electric":
            the story of the escape toward (if not to) freedom by an "android" who may
            symbolize a human being reduced to a computerized "humanoid."

8.037   ---. Signals. Polygram Records, C104831 (MCR4-1-4063: RCA Music Service Cassette), 1982.

Side One includes "The Analog Kid" and "Digital Man"; Side Two includes "The Weapon," "New World Man," and "Countdown."

8.038   Simon, Paul. Simon and Garfunkel. "The Sounds of Silence" (vt "The Sound of Silence"). On Wednesday Morning, 3 A.M. Columbia, CS 9049, n.d. Art Garfunkel's note gives the date of composition as 19 Feb. 1964. Authorized music and lyrics given in The Songs of Paul Simon (New York: Knopf, 1972).

Note people bowing and praying to a deified neon sign. Note also the use of this song in Mike Nichols's film The Graduate (1967): it is associated with Benjamin Braddock and an airplane, a "people mover," car keys, and a bus.

8.039   Slick, Grace (lyrics), and Jorma Kaukonen (music). The Jefferson Airplane. "Eat Starch Mom." On Long John Silver. Grunt, FTR-1007, 1972.

Lyrics on inner sleeve. Deals with America's love for things mechanical and lesser regard for things natural and human.

8.040   [Smokey Robinson and the] Miracles. "Love Machine." Love Machine. Motown, MOTCS-6048, 1975.

The singer is a "machine" who needs love in order to work.

8.041   Starlight Express: Cited under Drama.

8.042   Thomas, Pascal J. "Cyberpunk as roots music: an observation." In "Cyberpunk Forum/Symposium," MR47/48 62-64 (see under Literary Criticism, L. McCaffery, guest ed.).

Relates cyberpunk to punk rock and "celebration of non-intellectual, almost involuntary creation, born out of spontaneity and enjoyment rather than calculation. The Dyonisian side of culture, devoid of the respectability of accepted myths" (63).

8.043   Townshend, Pete (also Peter Townshend): See below under The Who.

8.044   The Tubes. Remote Control. A&M, SP-4715, 1979.

Album cover depicts a baby in front of a TV set; the set has a nipple attached, apparently signifying TV as the "nurturer" of the child. The music on the album deals primarily with television, including such songs as "TV Is King" and "Telecide."

8.045   VALIS. Opera by Tod Machover. Based on Philip K. Dick's VALIS. World première Pompidou Center, Paris, for the 10th Anniversay of the Center in 1987. American première MIT, June 1989.

Part II of opera relevant. VALIS = Vast Active Living Intelligent System; a character in this part of the opera, Sophia, may be a girl, an angel, or a hologram. Sophia is eventually exploded by a pink laser beam, taking with her the climactic scene, which fades into a coda with the hero, Phil, watching his TV set, waiting for a message that we assume would come from VALIS.

8.046   Van Halen. "1984." On 1984. Warner, R-160018, 1983, 1984.

This musical salute to the Orwellian year is done on a synthesizer. "1984" begins the album.

8.047   The Who. "Pinball Wizard." On <u>Tommy</u>. Decca-MCA, DXSW 7205, 1969.

From the opera by Peter Townshend et al. Unable to hear, speak, or see, Tommy can feel enough to get into the Tao of pinball; in more Western terms, <u>Tommy</u> gives us a Savior-figure who's really into pinball. The full opera was made into a film by Ken Russell (1975) and revived in the USA in 1992. See above, this section, J. E. Ivey.

8.048   Waterhouse, John C. "Futurism." <u>The New Grove Dictionary of Music and Musicians</u>. Stanley Sadie, ed. Vol. 7. London: Macmillan, 1980.

As in other arts, Futurism in music was a movement in the early 20th c. trying to present "subversively dynamic art inspired by the machine age." Extensive biblio.

8.049   Yes: Cited under Geoff Downes.

Background Reading

9.001 12-E: Disaster Transport. Roller coaster ride at Cedar Point, OH. In service since 1990.

You are on a suborbital flight to Alaska in a defective ship flown by an incompetent crew for a disreputable company. The attraction is entirely within a large building and (rather differently from the Disney version) calls attention to the machinery patrons are inside of. Not cyberpunk, but in the tradition that led to cyberpunk. See under Drama Criticism, J. Bierman, "Automated Theatre."

9.002 Adams, Henry. "The Dynamo and the Virgin (1900)." Ch. XXV of The Education of Henry Adams: An Autobiography. Henry Cabot Lodge, ed. Boston: Houghton, 1918. Rpt. Theme of the Machine, q.v. above under Anthologies and Collections.

In the Gallery of Machines at the Great Exposition of 1900, HA begins a meditation on force—force expressed spiritually, sexually, physically. Asserts that "the nearest approach to the revolution of 1900 [the scientific and technological revolution] was that of 310, when Constantine set up the Cross" (Education 382-83). Implies that in the new world after 1900, esp. in America, "the symbol of infinity," or of greatest force, would be neither Venus nor Virgin, fecundity nor deity, but the dynamo (380, 383-85). See H. G. Wells, "Lord of the Dynamos," above, under Fiction.

9.003 Akin, William E. Technocracy and the American Dream: The Technocrat Movement, 1900-1941. Berkeley: U of California P, 1977.

Includes extensive biblio. notes and a formal biblio. listing primary and secondary sources in books, articles, and unpublished materials. Traces the Technocracy movement back to its intellectual origins in the work of F. W. Taylor (cited below), Thorstein Veblen, and the Progressives, and forward to J. Burnham's The Managerial Revolution (see below). See for importance of the Technocrats in the early 1930s, and for some indication of their lasting influence. Important for study of eutopias and dystopias run by engineers and other technicians.

9.004 Aloff, Mindy. Dance Department. The Nation 17 March 1984: 329-32.

Mechanism in dance, or "machine esthetics."

9.005   Arendt, Hannah. On Violence. New York: Harcourt, 1969, 1970.

Parts II and III relevant; see esp. 38-39 for bureaucratic tyranny as "rule by Nobody," and 81-87 for the rebellion of human beings using our "faculty of action" against "the huge party machines" and the apparatus of the state. Many of the world machines in dystopian fiction may be literalizations of such machine metaphors.

9.006   ---. The Origins of Totalitarianism. 2nd enlarged edn. 1958. Cleveland: World, 1958.

Most relevant: Part Three: Totalitarianism, esp. ch. 11, part II ("Totalitarian Organization"), and ch. 12 ("Totalitarianism in Power"). See for possible real-world referents for the motif of individual human helplessness before the machine of the state.

9.007   Armstrong, D. M. A Materialist Theory of Mind. London: Rutledge; New York: Humanities P, 1968.

See esp. Part Three (ch. 17), "Identification of the Mental with the Physical"— DMA approves of doing so. See below, entry for R. Descartes and the works cross-referenced there. Note publication date: 1968 was an important year for radical ideas.

9.008   Asimov, Isaac, and Karen A. Frenkel. Robots: Machines in Man's Image. New York: Harmony, 1985.

Cited in "Year's Scholarship": 1986, and described as "A history of robots and their technological applications," presumably in the real world. Significant here for its coauthorship by IA.

9.009   "At Home in Chicago's Hancock Center." National Geographic 175.2 (Feb. 1989): 179.

"When winter winds bluster, John Hancock Center tenants need never step outside. An elevator ride brings them to most of life's basics . . . ." Cf. under Fiction (e.g.), B. Aldiss's "Total Environment," R. A. Heinlein's "Universe" and the generation-starship stories cross-referenced there, and R. Silverberg's The World Inside.

9.010   Barrett, William. Death of the Soul: From Descartes to the Computer. Garden City, NY: Anchor-Doubleday, 1986.

The author of Irrational Man: A Study in Existential Philosophy (1958) traces "the origins of modernism's persistent dualisms" back to R. Descartes's "vision of nature as a soulless machine and the human mind as a transcendent entity empowered to subjugate it." WB opposes "physicalism, behaviorism, and the more immodest claims" for AI, rejecting the computer as a "metaphor for the mind." Discussed by Rob Latham in his editorial in FR #97, 9.11 (Dec. 1986): 29, our source for this citation and whom we quote.

9.011   Barton, Marthalee, and Dwight W. Stevenson, guest co-eds. Technology and Pessimism special issue of Alternative Futures 3.2 (Spring 1980).

Esp. useful articles by E. Goodheart, S. Lyngstad, and L. Marx (all cited under Literary Criticism). The other articles, notably that by Richard Falk, provide useful real-world background.

9.012   Bear, Greg. "The Machineries of Joy." Early Harvest. Cambridge, MA: NESFA P, 1987. Coll. Tangents. New York: Quester-Warner, 1989.

A major SF author talks about the possibilities of computers. Rev. Jerry L. Parsons, SF&FBR 1990: 198, our source for much of this entry.

9.013   Beatty, Jack. "Trapped in the 'NASA-Speak' Machine." The New York Times Sunday, 9 March 1986.

Examines the relationships among "the dread of mechanism" as a literary theme, the space-shuttle Challenger disaster, bureaucracy, and language.

9.014   Benacerraf, Paul. "God, the Devil, and Gödel." Monist 51 (1967): 9.

An attempt to refute J. R. Lucas's arguments against the possibility of true AI, cited by D. Hofstadter in the Bibliography to Gödel, Escher, Bach. Described by Hofstadter as "All about mechanism and metaphysics, in the light of Gödel's work" (746). (Lucas and Hofstadter cited below).

9.015   Bergson, Henri. "Laughter." Ca. 1900. Available in various trans. Trans. by Presses Universitaires de France available in Comedy. Wylie Sypher, ed. Garden City, New York: Anchor-Doubleday, 1956.

The cause of laughter is the superimposition of the mechanical upon the organic, more specifically, upon the human. See for a simple introduction to HB on "vitalism" (one anthithesis to "mechanism"). See below, "Mechanism" and "Vitalism."

9.016   Bernal, J. D. The World, the Flesh and the Devil. London: Kegan Paul, 1929. In the series Today and Tomorrow.

Described by B. Stableford, Romance, as an early discussion of "cyborgisation" (160 [sic on spelling: British "s"]).

9.017   Bettelheim, Bruno. "Joey: 'A Mechanical Boy.'" Scientific American March 1959. Rpt. Man Alone, q.v. below.

A case study of an autistic boy who was convinced that he was a machine. (See L. Yablonsky, Robopaths, this section.) Joey creates for himself an "artificial, mechanical womb," initially an "electrical papoose."

9.018   "Biomechanics": See in the section on Drama, O. G. Brockett.

9.019   Boden, Margaret. Artificial Intelligence and Natural Man. New York: Basic Books, 1977.

Handles questions of free will and mind. Cited with praise by D. Hofstadter in the Bibliography to Gödel, Escher, Bach, q.v., this section.

9.020   Bolter, J. David. Turing's Man: Western Culture in the Computer Age. Chapel Hill, NC: U of North Carolina P, 1984.

Introd. to the social implications of computer technology, written for a literate general audience. Premise: ". . . technology is as much a part of classical and Western culture as philosophy and science[,] and these 'high' and 'lowly' expressions of culture are closely related"; Plato and pottery, R. Descartes and mechanical clocks—similarly, "the computer as a technological paradigm for the science, the philosophy, even the art of the coming generation" (xii).

9.021   Boorstin, Daniel J. The Discoverers. New York: Random, 1983.

Includes detailed discussion of real-world clocks and clockworks.

9.022   ---. The Lost World of Thomas Jefferson. 1948. Chicago: U of Chicago P, 1981.

> Develops with clarity and precision the static, pre-Darwinian, yet post-Ptolemaic, cosmology of the American Philosophical Society, which saw the universe as the perfectly designed machine of the "Supreme Workman." An important study of 18th-c. intellectual American mindset.

9.023   Bramson, Leon, and Michael S. Schudson. "Mass Society." Encyclopaedia Britannica: Macropaedia. 1974 edn.

> Good introd. to the hypothesized effects of mass society that may be the real-world referents in much pessimistic SF using the theme of mechanized societies and individuals. Includes a briefly annotated, selected biblio. of works on mass society from Alexis de Tocqueville's Democracy in America (1835) through the work of contemporary scholars.

9.024   Braverman, Harry. Labor and Monopoly Capital: the Degradation of Work in the Twentieth Century. New York: Monthly Review P, 1974.

> Includes a Marxist critique of Taylorism. See CW essay by G. Beauchamp, "Man as Robot" (listed under Literary Criticism) and entry below for F. W. Taylor.

9.025   Brod, Craig. Technostress: The Human Cost of the Computer Revolution. Reading, MA: Addison-Wesley, 1984.

> Deals with "technocentered" people trapped in "the 'mind as machine' metaphor" and without patience for human inferiorities to computers; notes that the technocentered have problems with the unpredictability and uncontrollability of sexual passion. Rev. Michael Rogers, Newsweek 6 Aug. 1984: 69, our source for this entry, and whom we quote.

9.026   Burnham, James. The Managerial Revolution: What Is Happening in the World. New York: The John Day Company, 1941.

> Mostly written in 1940, with some last-minute notes added in 1941, so "What Is Happening" includes the Great Depression (which JB saw continuing), the betrayal of socialist ideals in Russia, the Hitler-Stalin pact, and the start of World War II. Important for G. Orwell's Nineteen Eighty-four (q.v. under Fiction): for the division of the world into three competing superstates and (relevant here) the analysis of oligarchical collectivism with "managers" as the new ruling class.

9.027   Calhoun, Jim, and Bob Fogarty. "Electronic 'Jailer' Makes Home Prison." The Cincinnati Enquirer 16 Jan. 1985: A-1 f.

> On an experiment by the Kenton Fiscal Court in Kenton County, KY, to use the "In House Arrest" system to confine nonviolent, relatively well-to-do convicts in their homes. The system uses "a special bracelet that emits signals every 35 seconds." The prisoner pays for the system, which can be programmed to allow the prisoner to go to work. Cf. collars for "Risks" in F. Pohl and Jack Williamson's, The Reefs of Space (cited under Fiction).

9.028   Carlyle, Thomas. "Signs of the Times." Edinburgh Review #98 (1829). Coll. Thomas Carlyle: Critical and Miscellaneous Essays. 5 vols. London: Chapman and Hall, 1899. New York: AMS P, 1969. Centenary Edition of The Works of Thomas Carlyle. Vol. II (Vol. XXVII in the thirty-vol. Works).

> A very influential essay contrasting the "outward" vision of the world, translated into attempts to control nature and humans through "Mechanics," and the "inward" attempt of "Dynamics" to understand "the primary, unmodified forces and energies of man," which TC sees possessed of "a truly vital and infinite character" (Works 66 and 68 f.). In "the Mechanical Age" of early 19th-c.

Europe, people have "grown mechanical in head and in heart," with even philosophers organized into institutes that are "like so many ... hives" (59, 63, 62). Deals with the metaphor of "the Machine of Society" and compares "Mechanism" to "some glass bell" that "encircles and imprisons us" (66, 81, and passim). Discussed by L. Marx in ch. IV, sections 3 and 4, of Machine in the Garden (q.v. below).

9.029   "Cartesianism": See this section, entry for R. Watson.

9.030   Clark, Jennifer. "The American Image of Techonology from the Revolution to 1840." American Quarterly 39 (Fall 1987): 431-49.

Cited in "Year's Scholarship": 1987.

9.031   Cockburn, Cynthia. Machinery of Dominance: Women, Men, and Technical Know-How. Ruth Schwartz Cowan, foreword to US edn. London: Pluto, 1985. Boston: Northeastern UP, 1988.

Sociologist CC examines "technologies of production" in a number of workplaces in Britain and concludes that "women are to be found in great numbers operating machinery," even as in the electro-mechanical era of production, "But women continue to be rarities in those occupations that involve knowing about what goes on inside the machine. The electronic revolution [of the computerized workplace] is making little difference" in changing sexual inequalities (8, 11, 13). Contrast optimism of P. McCorduck, cited this section.

9.032   Comte, Auguste (more fully, I.-Auguste-M.-F.-X. Comte): Founder of the philosophical school of Positivism; see below, entries for H. Feigl and for C.-H. Saint-Simon.

9.033   Curry Tom et al. "Nowhere to Hide." Time 11 Nov. 1991: 34f.
Cover story. "Using computers, high-tech gadgets[,] and mountains of data, an army of snoops is assaulting our privacy" in the very real world of the early 1990s.

9.034   The Cyberpapacy: Role-playing game listed under Fiction.

9.035   Cyberspace: First Steps. Michael Benedikt, ed. Cambridge, MA: MIT P, 1991.

A hefty anthology of essays, largely Theoretical (sic: capital "T"), including speculation by Nicole Stenger on "electronic transcendence and cyber Sacred Space." Rev. James A. Connor, S.J., American Book Review 14.1 (April-May 1992): 7, our source for this citation, and whom we quote.

9.036   Davis, Douglas, et al. "Offices of the Future." Newsweek 14 May 1984: 72 f.

Subhead: "The computer is transforming the workplace—and, surprisingly, often making the space more human" (72). See in this section, entries for C. Cockburn and P. McCorduck.

9.037   Dawkins, Richard. "Selfish Genes and Selfish Memes." Excerpt from The Selfish Gene. New York: Oxford UP, 1976. Anthologized in The Mind's I, q.v. under Anthologies (124-44).

Living things as "survival machines" for genes, including the interesting subset of complex "purpose machines," which may be conscious, but don't need to be. Ultimately presents a belief not only in subjective consciousness but in the importance of the "meme," short for "mimeme," RD's new word for "a unit of cultural transmission."

9.038 Dennett, Daniel C. Brainstorms: Philosophical Essays on Mind and Psychology.
[Montgomery, VT]: Bradford Books, 1978. (Try also MIT P.)

Fairly early on AI, but a relatively recent entry into the debate over Mechanism
vs. Idealism (our formulation), from the approach of Materialism of the
physicalist variety (see below, the entry for R. Descartes). Essays coll. include
"Intentional Systems," "[B. F.] Skinner Skinned," "Artificial Intelligence as
Philosophy and as Psychology," "Why You Can't Make a Computer that Feels
Pain," and "Mechanism and Responsibility." No biblio. but useful notes and
index.

9.039 Descartes, Réne. The Philosophical Writings of Descartes. Trans. John Cottingham,
Robert Soothoff, Dugald Murdoch. 2 vols. Cambridge, UK: Cambridge UP,
1985.

Gives marginal page citations to Oeuvres de Descartes, ed. Ch. Adam and P.
Tannery, rev. edn. (1964-76), which we give below in square brackets. Does not
contain Geometry (1637) but does have the rest of the works that laid the
groundwork for a rigorously mechanistic view of the physical universe,
nonhuman animals, the human body, human thought, and, ultimately—though
emphatically not for RD—human beings. (In Geometry, RD presents analytic
geometry, where the world can be placed on Cartesian coordinates and described
algebraically. Truly Modern cities are placed on precisely those coordinates, and
we who grew up in them look for 0, 0 points as the "natural" way to begin
mapping the world.)

For RD on mathematical reasoning as the way to truth and for the assumption
that ". . . there is only one truth concerning any matter," see Discourse on the
Method, Part Two, I.120-21 [VI.19-22]. For RD's limitation of physics and
possibly science in general to what can be done with the "principles . . . of
geometry and pure mathematics," which can "explain all natural phenomena, and
enable us to provide quite certain demonstrations regarding them" (italics
removed), see Principles of Philosophy, Part Two, assertion 64: I.247 [VIIIA.78-
79].

For RD's granting that, prior to admitting the human soul, he had "described this
earth and indeed the whole visible universe as if it were a machine," see Principles
of Philosophy, Part Four, assertion 188: I.279 [VIIIA.315-16].

For mechanistic explanations of the human body and animals, and a word or two
on automata, see Treatise on Man, I.100-101 [XI.131-32]; Discourse on the
Method, Part Five, I.134 [VI.46], I.139 [VI.55-56], I.139-40 [VI.56-57];
Meditations on First Philosophy, II.58-59 [VII.84-87]. See also T. Hobbes's
objection to "I am a thinking thing," which Hobbes finds "Correct"—but
concludes that it "seems that the correct inference is that the thinking thing is
material rather than immaterial": Objections and Replies to Meditations on First
Philosophy: "Third Set of Objections with the Author's Replies," Second
Objection, II.122-23 [VII.172-75]; the classic insult is that with the soul RD
presents a "ghost in the machine," and Hobbes does his best to remove the
"ghost."

See in this section of the List, T. Hobbes; D. Hofstadter; J. R. Munson and R. C.
York; D. S. Robinson; C. Sagan, "Life"; J. C. J. Smart; B. de Spinoza; S. E.
Toulmin; R. A. Watson; R. S. Westfall.

9.040 Dick, Philip K. "The Android and the Human." Public Speech, Vancouver, BC, 1972.
Phillip K. Dick: Electric Shepherd. Bruce Gillespie, ed. Melbourne: Nostrilia,
1975.

Real-world machines are becoming more like humans, humans more like
machines. Discussed by A. Barlow, "Philip K. Dick's Androids," (esp. 76-77),
cited under Literary Criticism.

9.041   Dickson, David.   "Limiting Democracy: Technocrats and the Liberal State."
democracy (sic) 1.1: 61-79.

Most relevant essay in a highly relevant first issue: democracy indirectly shows
that the motif of hopelessness/helplessness in dystopian literature is at least
decorous in a world in which democracy is rapidly losing out to rule by experts.

9.042   Dreyfus, Hubert.   What Computers Can't Do: A Critique of Artificial Reason.   New
York: Harper, 1972.

Argues against the possibility of true AI.   Cited by D. Hofstadter in the
Bibliography to Gödel, Escher, Bach, q.v., this section.

9.043   Eaves, Morris.   "Blake and the Artistic Machine: An Essay in Decorum and
Technology."   PMLA 92 (Oct. 1977): 903-27.

On classic vs. Romantic aesthetics, and William Blake's idea of how "mechanical
order becomes artistic order" (ME's abstract).

9.044   Eichner, Hans.   "The Rise of Modern Science and the Genesis of Romanticism."
PMLA 97 (Jan. 1982): 8-30.

The temporary "replacement of the mechanical philosophy by an organic view of
the cosmos is one of the most significant features of Romanticism."   Explains
"why the Romantics felt compelled to attack the mechanical philosophy" of the
Scientific Age and "confirms [Morse] Peckham's findings that the new
organicism accounts for a large part of Romantic theory" (quotations from HE's
abstract).   An important introd. to mechanism vs. organicism: a debate of great
significance for machines and mechanized environments in the arts.

9.045   Eliade, Mircea.   The Myth of the Eternal Return (or, Cosmos and History).   France:
1949; English trans. 1954.   Willard R. Trask, trans.   Bollingen Series, No. XLVI.
Princeton, NJ: Princeton UP, 1971.

Summarizes EM's ideas on the social and psychological necessity for occasional
or periodic return to the formless, the chaotic.   See for the opposition of the
living (vital and comic) against the mechanical.   (See under Fiction, H. Ellison,
"Repent, Harlequin!")

9.046   Ellul, Jacques.   The Technological Society.   (La Technique ou l'enjeu du siècle, 1954).
John Wilkinson, trans.   New York: Knopf, 1964.   Rev. American edn.   New York:
Knopf, 1967.   Also, New York: Vintage, 1967.

Significant for its analysis of the replacement of "political man" by "the
technician" (Preface vii in 1967 Knopf edn.).   More significant for the analysis of
contemporary industrial society which JE encapsulates in ch. 1: the machine is
important because it "represents the ideal toward which technique strives.   The
machine is solely, exclusively, technique . . . .   [W]herever a technical factor
exists, it results, almost inevitably, in mechanization: technique transforms
everything it touches into a machine" (4)—and ours is a "technological society."
JE's more recent works include The Political Illusion (New York: Random, 1967),
and Le Système technicien (Paris: Calmann-Levy, 1977).   See V. Lauber,
"Efficiency and After," below.

9.047   Elsner, Henry, Jr.   The Technocrats: Prophets of Automation.   Syracuse, NY: Syracuse
UP, 1967.

Cited by W. E. Akin (q.v. above, this section) as "the standard account" of the
Technocracy movement (Akin 110).

9.048 Feigl, Herbert. "Positivism and Logical Empiricism." Encyclopaedia Britannica: Macropaedia. 1974.

See for a couple notable positivists (Ernst Mach is one) as critics of "the traditional mechanistic view of nature" (879), and for the philosophical basis of much of what is loosely called the "scientific" view of the world and attacked as mechanistic thinking and technophilia.

9.049 Firestone, Shulamith. The Dialectic of Sex: The Case for Feminist Revolution. New York: Morrow, 1970. London: Cape, 1971. London: Women's P, 1979.

In Feminism and Science Fiction (ch. 6), Sara Lefanu says that Firestone supports "the technological control of reproduction," empirical method, and "the progress of technology, whose ultimate goal is the building of the ideal in the real world." The important questions are who gets to say how and to what ends technology gets used. Lefanu asserts that much in feminist utopias in the late 1980s generally was heavily influenced by Firestone, and more specifically, that Woman on the Edge of Time is Marge Piercy's engagement "with Firestone's ideas on technology" (Indiana UP edn. 59; ch. 5).

9.050 Florman, Samuel C. Blaming Technology: The Irrational Search for Scapegoats. New York: St. Martin's, 1981. Earlier versions in Harper's, American Scholar, and Alternative Futures.

Ch. 1, 3 f. gives accusation by John Broomfield, historian: "bureaucratic technocracy" is to be blamed. SCF holds that technology as such isn't at fault for its political concomitants.

9.051 Foucault, Michel. Discipline and Punish: The Birth of the Prison. Alan Sheridan, trans. New York: Pantheon, 1977.

MF cites Jeremy Bentham's plan for an ideal prison, the Panopticon, in which the prisoner is constantly subject to surveillance; the motif of constant surveillance is very important in dystopian fiction where the world, in a sense, becomes a prison.

9.052 Fournier d'Albe, E. E. Hephaestus; or, the Soul of the Machine. London: Kegan Paul, 1925. In the series Today and Tomorrow.

Cited by B. Stableford, Romance.

9.053 Franklin, H. Bruce. War Stars: The Superweapon and the American Imagination. New York: Oxford UP, 1988.

The weapon-obsession aspect of "America as Science Fiction." See below, J. W. Gibson, The Perfect War. See above under Literary Criticism, HBF on "The Vietnam War as American Science Fiction and Fantasy."

9.054 Garrett, Garet. Ouroboros; the Mechanical Extension of Man. London: Kegan Paul, 1925. In the series Today and Tomorrow.

Cited by B. Stableford, Romance, as a good source from the period to see a strong "statement about the relationship of man and the products of his science" (160).

9.055 Gendron, Bernard. Technology and the Human Condition. New York: St. Martin's, 1977.

A three-part discussion of the benevolence and/or malevolence of technology. "Part One: The Utopian View" examines the contention that technology "will eliminate scarcity and disease, . . . improve communications and education, and . . . undermine aggression, prejudice," and other bad things. Notes that

"Utopians," who see technology as positive, see "major world problems as 'technical,' rather than as 'political' or 'ideological.'" "Part Two: The Dystopian View" examines the proposition "that technological growth in the long run generates or intensifies many more social evils than it reduces or eliminates." "Part Three: The Socialist View" presents the Socialists' insistence "that technological growth is a necessary condition for social progress," but is still "far from a sufficient condition for overall social progress" (3). BG finds the Socialist position most promising.

9.056 Gibson, James William. The Perfect War: Technowar in Vietnam. Harry Evans, ed. New York: Atlantic Monthly, 1986.

See above, H. B. Franklin, War Stars.

9.057 Giedion, Siegfried. Mechanization Takes Command. New York: Oxford UP, 1948.

According to Wolfe (12), MTC recounts the effects of 19th-c. technology on human behavior; GS reaches conclusions similar to those of L. Mumford in The Pentagon of Power (q.v. below).

9.058 Good, I. J. "Gödel's Theorem is a Red Herring." British Journal for the Philosophy of Science 19 (1969): 357.

Response to J. R. Lucas's arguments against the possibility of true AI (see Lucas entries below); cited by D. Hofstadter in the Bibliography to Gödel, Escher, Bach, q.v., this section.

9.059 Gunderson, Keith. Mentality and Machines. New York: Anchor-Doubleday, 1971.

Cited by D. Hofstadter as "A very anti-AI person tells why," in the Bibliography to Gödel, Escher, Bach, q.v., this section.

9.060 Halacy, D. S., Jr. The Robots are Here! New York: Norton, 1965.

Relatively early, nonfiction work dealing with such topics as the origin of the term "robot," robots as threats, literary robots, the history of real robots, robots in space, electronic brains, industrial robots, and speculations about the future of robots.

9.061 Hall, Ernest L., and Bettie C. Hall. Robotics: A User-Friendly Introduction. New York: Holt, 1985. See copyright page for complexities of ownership.

College textbook on real-world robots. Chapters include "An Introduction to Robotics," "History of Robotics," "Intelligent Robot Programming"—where the "Intelligent" modifies "Robot" (among other things, the chapter covers AI and Machine Intelligence), "Social Impact of Industrial Robots," "Responsible Technology," and "Robots Today and Tomorrow." The last chapter has five brief subsections beginning "Robots in" and supplies as objects of the "in" Medical and Patient Care Applications, Hostile or Remote Environments, Education, and Agriculture; the chapter begins with a section on Advances in Robot Intelligence and ends with Mobile Robots; the remaining sections are on Domestic and Entertainment Robots and what's just called The Military.

9.062 Haraway, Donna. "A Manifesto for Cyborgs: Science, Technology and Socialist Feminism in the 1980s." Socialist Review #80, 15.2 (March-April 1985): 65-107.

The cyborg exists today and offers utopian possibilities for the breaking down of categories, including such already breached categories as human/animal and human-animal/machine (66-69). Discussed in detail by I. Csicsery-Ronay in "The SF of Theory," listed under Literary Criticism.

9.063   Hayles, Katherine N.   Chaos Bound . . . : Cited under Literary Criticism.

9.064   Hobbes, Thomas.   Leviathan; Or the Matter, Forme and Power of a Commonwealth
Ecclesiaticall and Civil (sic on spelling). 1651. Available in numerous eds., e.g.
Michael Oakeshott, ed. Richard S. Peters, introd. New York: Collier; London:
Collier-Macmillan, 1962.

For TH's strong suggestion "that man is a machine, like every other part of
nature" (Peters 13), see esp. The First Part: Of Man, ch. 5, "Of Reason and
Science" and TH's famous definition of reason as "nothing but reckoning, that is
adding and subtracting, of the consequences of general names agreed upon for
the marking and signifying of our thoughts" (Oakeshott edn. 41). This part of
Leviathan also contains an elegant statement of TH's rigorous and frequent denial
of freedom: "And therefore if a man should talk to me of a round quadrangle . . .
or of a free subject; a free will; or any free, but free from being hindered by
opposition, I should not say he were in error, but that his words were without
meaning, that is to say, absurd" (43). See in this section of the List, R. Descartes;
D. Hofstadter; J. R. Munson and R. C. York; D. S. Robinson; C. Sagan, "Life"; J.
C. J. Smart; B. Spinoza; S. E. Toulmin; R. A. Watson; R. S. Westfall.

9.065   Hofstadter, Douglas R.   Gödel, Escher, Bach: An Eternal Golden Braid. 1979. New
York: Vintage-Random, 1980.

Includes an index and a highly useful biblio. See for M. C. Escher and for an
important discussion of formal ("mechanical") logic, Kurt Gödel, computers, AI,
and "some perspective on the battle" continuing between the successors of Johann
Michael Schmidt, proponent of soul, and Julien Offroy de la Mettrie, "author of
L'homme machine ('Man, the Machine'), and Materialist Par Excellence" (27).
Attacking most directly J. R. Lucas, DH comes down for the materialists, arguing
that ". . . reasoning is mechanizable" and true AI, and artificial will and desire, are
both possible and desirable (685 and passim).

9.066   "Idealism": See this section, entry for D. S. Robinson.

9.067   Ihde, Don.   "A Phenomenology of Man-Machine Relations." In Work, Technology,
and Education, q.v. below.

Focuses upon "a descriptive psychology of man-machine relations," starting with
the notion "that the machine. . . may be thought of as a 'means' of relating to the
world"—one of our major means in everyday life in industrial societies.

9.068   Jackson, Philip C.   Introduction to Artificial Intelligence. New York: Petrocelli
Charter, 1975.

AI work recommended for its "giant bibliography" by D. Hofstadter, in the
Bibliography to Gödel, Escher, Bach, q.v., this section.

9.069   James, William.   "The Ph.D. Octopus." William James: Writings 1902-1910. New
York: The Library of America, 1987.

Uses the phrase "tyrannical machines" to describe bureaucratic systems, quoted
by Lynne V. Cheney, Chairman (sic) of the National Endowment for the
Humanities in Tyrannical Machines: A Report on Educational Practices . . .
(Washington, DC: NEH, 1990).

9.070   Jameson, Fredric.   "Postmodernism, or The Cultural Logic of Late Capitalism." New
Left Review #146 (July-Aug. 1984): 53-94.

A revision or two short of being downright ovular, this essay is at least historically
seminal for the study by students of literature of postmodernism—which
cyberpunk may be the apotheosis of. See above under Literary Criticism the

entry for L. McCaffery, guest ed. for <u>Mississippi</u> <u>Review</u> nos. 47 and 48, and the
works cross-referenced there.

9.071 Kandel, Michael. "Introduction" to Stanislaw Lem, <u>Mortal Engines</u>. Coll. and trans.
Kandel. New York: Seabury, 1977. New York: Avon (Bard), 1982.

Includes an elegant survey of the historical and ideological sources (mostly
Romantic) of our fear of "artificial man" and "of man <u>made</u> artificial by Science
and through the mass society"; also includes intriguing comments on how
modern "Science . . . provides a guarantee that man . . . can never be . . . turned
into a cog of any social mechanism—and remain a man" (see esp. vii-xiv).

9.072 Kateb, George. <u>Utopia and Its Enemies</u>. (c) 1963. New York: The Free P of Glencoe
(A Division of The Macmillan Company), n.d. Also, London, UK, and Galt,
Ontario: Collier-Macmillan Ltd.

G. Orwell's <u>Nineteen Eighty-four</u> relegated to a brief appendix, but deals usefully
with E. M. Forster's "The Machine Stops," A. Huxley's <u>Brave New World</u>, Y.
Zamyatin's <u>We</u>, and, most esp., B. F. Skinner's <u>Walden Two</u>. See for (1) the
importance for utopian and antiutopian thought of real-world technology,
including techniques for psychological conditioning, and (2) metaphors of social
machinery, robots, and anthills.

9.073 Koestler, Arthur. <u>The Ghost in the Machine</u>. New York: Macmillan, 1968.

Includes a discussion of the hierarchical organization of life and an attack on the
"pseudoscience called Behaviourism" (5). Cf. and contrast S. Milgram's
discussion of hierarchy in <u>Obedience to Authority</u>, q.v. below; see entries below
for B. F. Skinner and J. B. Watson.

9.074 Krutch, Joseph Wood. <u>The Measure of Man: On Freedom, Human Values, Survival
and the Modern Temper</u>. (c) 1953, 1954. Indianapolis: Bobbs, n.d.

A popular work—no citations, no index—attacking contemporary incarnations of
the tradition running from T. Hobbes through R. Descartes to Charles Darwin,
Sigmund Freud, and K. Marx. "Hobbes proves that man is an animal; Descartes
proves that an animal is a machine." Hence, as perfected by the early 20th c. and
embodied in B. F. Skinner's <u>Walden Two</u> (q.v. under Fiction), ". . . Man is a
machine" (35); the attack on Skinner is a motif in <u>MoM</u>.

9.075 Lapp, Ralph E. <u>The New Priesthood: The Scientific Elite and the Uses of Power</u>. New
York: Harper, 1965.

REL is an atomic scientist who worked on the A-Bomb, and <u>TNP</u> is mostly a
historical narrative and analysis of the military and political implications of
atomic research. "It is the thesis of this book that democracy faces its most severe
test in preserving its traditions in an age of scientific revolution. . . . The danger
to our democracy is that national policy will be decided by the few [i.e. various
experts] acting without even attempting to enter into a public discourse on the
issues. If these few are the best technically qualified, then, according to an
updating of Plato's original definition, our democracy will become a timocracy"
(2-3). Immediately relevant, ch. 11, "The Tyranny of Technology."

9.076 Lasky, Melvin J. <u>Utopia and Revolution</u>. Chicago: U of Chicago P, 1976.

Contains useful comments (mostly passim) on the metaphors and imagery of
revolution and radical reform. Such metaphors for change (particularly the
organic image of birth) should be contrasted with the images of mechanism often
used to symbolize dystopian stasis. See below, the citation for G. Saccaro-Battisti.

9.077   Lauber, Volkmar. "Efficiency and After: The Dilemma of the Technicized Society."
Alternative Futures 2.4 (Fall 1979): 47-65.

Summarizes, places into its historical context, and extends the work of J. Ellul
(q.v. this section). See VL's notes for further readings. Discusses the opposition
of "technique" to political life, ideology, "spontaneity, creativity, [and] biological
rhythms" (56-7).

9.078   Leithauser, Brad. A Reporter at Large: "The Space of One Breath." The New Yorker
9 March 1987: 41 f. (for some 19 pages).

Very full report for laypeople on computer chess, history of chess automata (and
claims of such), new developments in computer chess, and applications of chess-
solving intelligence to the larger world. Significant that The New Yorker would
devote so much space to such esoteric subjects as Alan Turing's "abstract
universal computing machine" (68).

9.079   Livingston, Dennis. "Science Fiction Models of Future Order Systems." International
Organization 25 (Spring 1971): 254-70.

Perhaps as much literary criticism as political science, this essay handles the
political aspects of J. Brunner's Stand on Zanzibar, G. Orwell's Nineteen Eighty-
Four (both cited under Fiction), and a number of other works of immediate or
secondary interest, including Poul Anderson, "Un-Man"; Fritz Leiber, Gather
Darkness!; Andre Mauris, "The War Against the Moon"; Frederik Pohl and C. M.
Kornbluth, The Space Merchants; Mack Reynolds, "The Five Way Secret Agent";
and R. Theobald and J. M. Scott, Teg's 1994: An Anticipation of the Near Future.
Refers briefly to other S.F. works, including "prophetic novels" by H. G. Wells
and R. A. Heinlein. Deals well with politically and socially significant
technology.

9.080   Loeb, Harold. Life in a Technocracy: What It Might Be Like. New York: Viking,
1933.

Cited by Sargent (1988) as a nonfiction work, and a borderline utopian work
under his criteria. Describes the positive changes under technocracy. See this
section, Technocracy . . . .

9.081   Lucas, J. R. "Minds, Machines, and Gödel." Philosophy 36 (1961): 112. Rpt. Minds
and Machines and Modeling of Mind (see below).

Argued against at length by D. Hofstadter in Gödel, Escher, Bach, q.v., this
section. (See above, entries for P. Benacerraf and I. J. Good.)

9.082   ---. "Satan Stultified: A Rejoinder to Paul Benacerraf." Monist 52 (1968): 145.

Cited by D. Hofstadter in the Bibliography to Gödel, Escher, Bach, q.v., this
section. See above, entry for Benacerraf.

9.083   Man Alone: Alienation in Modern Society. Eric and Mary Josephson, eds. New York:
Dell, 1962.

A collection of essays and selections, "from Karl Marx to James Baldwin, from
Dostoyevsky to Ignazio Silone," on alienation. Includes B. Bettelheim, "Joey"
(q.v. this section) and selections from L. Mumford, C. Wright Mills, and William
H. Whyte. An excellent introd. to the concept of alienation, an important theme
in much dystopian fiction.

9.084   Mandel, Ernest, and George Novack. The Marxist Theory of Alienation. New York:
Pathfinder, 1970.

An original introd. and rpts. of three essays by EM and GN. Note the cover of TMTA: "Detail of a fresco by Diego Rivera. This panel . . . was inspired by an actual punch press which was operated by manacled workers whose hands were automatically pulled back by the handcuffs each time the press descended" (cover note on copyright page). The essays develop systematically the causes of alienation symbolized by the picture on the cover.

9.085   Marcuse, Herbert. An Essay on Liberation. Boston: Beacon, 1969.

"Is it still necessary to state that not technology, not technique, not the machine are the engineers of repression, but the presence, in them, of the masters who determine their number, their life span, their power, their place in life, and the need for them? Is it still necessary to repeat that science and technology are the great vehicles of liberation, and that it is only their use and restriction in the repressive society which makes them into vehicles of domination?"—Quoted by P. Fitting in "Futurecop" essay, q.v. under Drama Criticism.

9.086   Marx, Karl. "Machinery and Large-Scale Industry." Ch. 15 of Book I (i.e., the first volume) of Capital: A Critique of Political Economy (in Part Four). 1867. Frequently trans. and rpt., e.g. Ben Fowkes, trans. Ernest Mandel, introd. New York: Vintage-Random, 1976.

See esp. section 3 of the chapter, "The Most Immediate Effects of Machine Production on the Worker," and section 4, "The Factory." Includes descriptions and analyses of working with machines in the UK in the middle of the 19th c. and a very important comment on two possible relationships between humans and machines in a factory: "In one, the combined collective worker appears as the dominant subject . . ., and the mechanical automaton [i.e., the machine] as the object; in the other, the automaton itself is the subject, and the workers are merely conscious organs, co-ordinated with the unconscious organs of the automaton, and together with the latter subordinated to the central moving force. The first description is applicable to every possible employment of machinery on a large scale, the second is characteristic of its use by capital, and therefore of the modern factory system" (544-45; 2nd paragraph of 15.4). For application of KM's insight to industry in general, see E. S. Rabkin, "Irrational Expectations" (162-63), cited under Literary Criticism.

9.087   Marx, Leo. The Machine in the Garden: Technology and the Pastoral Ideal in America. New York: Oxford UP, 1964, 1970. Rpt. as A Galaxy Book paperback, 1967.

The "garden" is America, the New World; the machine is urban culture in general and technology in particular. (An application of LM's work may be found in K. Blair's analysis of Star Trek, q.v. under Drama Criticism.)

9.088   "Materialism," Mechanism, Mechanical Materialism, Physicalistic Materialism: See below, this section, entry for John J. C. Smart.

9.089   McCarthy, John. "Ascribing Mental Qualities to Machines." Philosophical Perspectives in Artificial Intelligence. Martin Ringle, ed. New York: Humanities P, 1979.

Cited by D. Hofstadter in the Bibliography to Gödel, Escher, Bach, q.v., this section. Hofstadter lists "beliefs, desires, intentions, consciousness . . . free will"— the AI basics—for the "mental qualities" refered to in JM's title.

9.090   McCorduck, Pamela. The Universal Machine: Confessions of a Technological Optimist. New York: McGraw Hill, 1985.

Sequel to PM's Machines Who Think (1979), as a history of AI. See for a chatty, technophilic, entertaining placement of computers in Western history and their social context in the mid-1980s. Summarized by R. Latham in his editorial in FR #97, 9.11 (Dec. 1986): 29. (See entry for C. Cockburn, this section.)

9.091 McDougall, Walter A. The Heavens and the Earth: A Political History of the Space Age. New York: Basic Books, 1986.

Rev. Gene Lyons, "Athens Vs. Sparta," Newsweek 27 May 1985: 82. According to Lyons, a study of technocracy in the USA and USSR, with the primary focus on the military/space-race/technological aspects. Takes a kind of mystic turn at the end, rejecting "'the technocratic promise'" and calling for a return to God.

9.092 McGrath, Peter. "A Republic of Technology." Newsweek 19 May 1986: 65.

Essay in "Ideas" subsection of "Society" section, meditating on recent failures in the US space program and on "the centrality of technology in the American imagination" from the 19th c. on. References to Walt Whitman, Henry David Thoreau, Herman Melville, Charles Chaplin, and others—and, preeminently, Daniel Boostin's 1970s trilogy The Americans.

9.093 Mechanism, "Mechanical Materialism," Physicalist Materialism, "Materialism": See this section, entry for John Jamieson Carswell Smart, "Materialism."

9.094 Mechanism, Vitalism: See in this section the entries for Carl Sagan, J. Ronald Munson and Richard Charles York, and Stephen E. Toulmin.

9.095 Melville, Herman. Moby Dick. First British Edn.: London: Bentley, October 1851. First American Edition: New York: Harper & Brothers, November 1851. Frequently rpt.

See for literal machines, machine imagery, Ahab as "the perverted, monomaniac incarnation of the Age of Machinery," a "whaling world" in which "man's primary relation to nature is technological," and the possibility of a textile-mill universe (quotations from section 3 of ch. 5, L. Marx, The Machine in the Garden, q.v., this section of the List).

9.096 ---. "The Paradise of Bachelors and The Tartarus of Maids." Harper's April 1855. Frequently rpt., including Great Short Stories of Herman Melville. Ed. Warner Berthoff. New York: Perennial-Harper, 1969.

"The Tartarus of Maids" is a Berkshire Hills paper-mill, where machinery "stood menially served by human beings" (Perennial 219).

9.097 Merchant, Carolyn. The Death of Nature: Women, Ecology and the Scientific Revolution. San Francisco: Harper, 1980.

Cited by Phyllis J. Day in her article "EarthMother/WitchMother: Feminism and Ecology Renewed" (Extrapolation 23 [Spring 1982]: 12-21). "According to Merchant, the new mechanistic ordering of the universe brought by the scientific revolution provided a new perspective on the place of humankind in nature" (Day 18)—a place of dominion within a mechanism, rather than a cellular function in a cosmic organism.

9.098 Merton, Robert K. "Bureaucratic Structure and Personality." Coll. Merton, Social Theory and Social Structure. Glencoe, IL: Free P, 1957 Ch. VI: 195-206.

On bureaucracy, the apparat that may be the real-world referent of some of the imagery of machines in pessimistic SF.

9.099 Mettrie: Julien (Offroy) de La Mettrie: See in this section entries for D. R. Hofstadter and J.C.J.S. Smart, and, under Music, the entry for Kraftwerk.

9.100 Metzger, Robert A. "On Autopilot." Aboriginal S. F. #24 (Nov.-Dec. 1990): 42 f.

On the work of Rodney Brooks of the MIT Insect Lab on small, simple, cockroach-like robots for research on Mars. The little robots would use low-level AI, not like conscious human thinking but like the great majority of our actions, like walking and most driving of cars: figuratively "on autopilot."

9.101 Michels, Robert. Political Parties: A Sociological Study of the Oligarchic Tendencies of Modern Bureaucracy. 1915. Eden Paul and Cedar Paul, trans. New York: Free P, 1962, 1966. London: Collier-Macmillan, 1962.

From his study of the bureaucratization of the German Social Democratic Party and other European socialist parties (the most democratic parties in Europe), RM inferred the "iron law of oligarchy." That is, all large organizations, however democratic in ideology, tend to fall under the control of a small group of knowledgeable, experienced, and energetic people who hold and seek to retain power. RM uses without apology mechanical metaphors for political phenomena in the bureaucratized state.

9.102 Milgram, Stanley. Obedience to Authority. New York: Harper, 1974.

See esp. chs. 10, 11, and 15. SM opposes autonomy to being in "the agentic state" and holds groups in extreme agentic states to "consist not of individuals but automatons" (181).

9.103 Miller, Marc S. "New Toys for Robocop [sic: lower-case "c"] Soldiers." The Progressive 52.7 (July 1988): 18-21.

High-tech weapons for future "Low-Intensity Conflict," including "PITMAN, a 200-pound 'exoskeleton' for low-intensity warriors": described as "thinking armor, powered to move with its wearer" (20)—cf. the armor in R. A. Heinlein, Starship Troopers, and J. Haldeman, The Forever War (cited under Fiction).

9.104 Mills, C. Wright. The Power Elite. New York: Oxford UP, 1956.

See for powerlessness of individuals in real-world mass societies.

9.105 Minds and Machines. Alan Ross Anderson, ed. Englewood Cliffs, NJ: Prentice-Hall, 1964.

Collection of essays on AI. Cited by D. Hofstadter in the Bibliography to Gödel, Escher, Bach, q.v., this section.

9.106 The Mind's I: Fantasies and Reflections on Self and Soul. Douglas R. Hofstadter and Daniel C. Dennett, composers and arrangers.

Cited under Anthologies. See for readings (including a great deal of material by the "composers") on philosophical issues dealt with by a number of SF works dealing with human consciousness, AI, the mind/body problem, and free will vs. determinism.

9.107 Minsky, Marvin L. "Matter, Mind, and Models." In Semantic Information Processing. Marvin L. Minsky, ed. Cambridge, MA: MIT P, 1968.

D. Hofstadter cites this as an important article by an important worker in AI, in the Bibliography to Gödel, Escher, Bach, q.v., this section.

9.108   The Modeling of Mind: Computers and Intelligence.   Kenneth M. Sayre and Frederick J. Crosson, eds. New York: Simon (Clarion Books), 1963.

Early anthology of speculations on AI by a number of major thinkers, including Ludwig Wittgenstein; cited by D. Hofstadter in the Bibliography to Gödel, Escher, Bach, q.v., this section.

9.109   Mouzelis, Nicos P. Organisation [sic: British spelling] and Bureaucracy: An Analysis of Modern Theories. London: Routledge, 1967.

Summarizes many important recent theories on bureaucracy and how life in an apparat leads to alienation and feelings of helplessness. Holds that the "concentration of the means of administration" (of which monopolizing the means of production is only a special case) leads to oligarchic control in which each individual "becomes a simple cog in a machine, a well disciplined and regulated automaton." See this section, R. Michels, Political Parties.

9.110   Mumford, Lewis. "The Mechanical Routine." Technics and Civilization. New York: Harcourt, 1934. Rpt. Man Alone: Alienation in Modern Society. Eric and Mary Josephson, eds. New York: Dell, 1962.

An examination of the effects on people of increased mechanization and scheduling. LM examines the subjugation of humans to the time clock (regardless of individual needs), the phenomenon of time-saving devices as a source of stress, the deskilling of the workforce where tasks are automated, the imposition of the necessity for collective action and not self-sufficiency. Lack of social evaluation of new technology yields stress and tension on humans, which LM finds very detrimental.

9.111   ---. The Myth of the Machine. Vol. l, Technics and Human Development, 1966, 1967. Vol. 2, The Pentagon of Power, 1964, 1970. New York: Harcourt, 1970.

With the application of mathematics and the physical sciences to technology, we have entered a new relationship to technics. "With this new 'megatechnics' the dominant minority will create a uniform, all-enveloping, super-planetary structure, designed for automatic operation. Instead of functioning actively as an autonomous personality, man will become a passive, purposeless, machine-conditioned animal whose proper functions, as technicians now interpret man's role, will either be fed into the machine or strictly limited and controlled for the benefit of de-personalized, collective organizations" (Vol. 1, ch. 1, 3). Cf. J. Ellul, cited this section.

9.112   ---. "Utopia, The City and The Machine." In Utopias and Utopian Thought. Frank E. Manuel, ed. Cambridge: Riverside & Houghton, 1966. (Augmented rpt. of article in Daedalus Spring 1965.)

Traces the rise of the "utopian" city to the institution of the army: "the collective human machine, the platonic model for all later machines." The price of the urban utopia was "total submission to a central authority, forced labor, lifetime specialization, inflexible regimentation, one-way communication, and readiness for war" (15, 17).

9.113   Munson, J. Ronald, and Richard Charles York. "Nature, Philosophy of." Encyclopaedia Britannica: Macropaedia. 1974.

Under "The Nature of Biological Systems" briefly handles Vitalism, Mechanism, and Organicism—the last a theory holding "that organisms must be interpreted as functioning wholes and cannot be understood by means of physics and chemistry alone" (873-74). Vitalism is dead, but simplistic Mechanism may be ailing: although "Few scientists today call themselves organismic biologists . . . . most antireductionists subscribe at least to part of the organismic doctrine, in particular to its wholistic claim" (873)—and our impression is that the systems approach to biology is now more respectable than any kind of reductionism. (The whole equals not only the sum of its parts but their relationships.) Article ends with a very extensive, analytical, annotated biblio. (876-77). See in this section of the List, R. Descartes; T. Hobbes; D. Hofstadter; D. S. Robinson; C. Sagan, "Life"; J. C. J. Smart; B. de Spinoza; S. E. Toulmin; R. A. Watson; R. S. Westfall.

9.114   Newton, Sir Isaac: See below, entry for R. S. Westfall.

9.115   Nugent, William R. "Virtual Reality: Advanced Imaging Special Effects Let You Roam in Cyberspace." JASIS: Journal of the American Society for Information Science 42.8 (Sept. 1991): 609-17.

A substantial review article examining aspects of virtual reality work ranging from their philosophical and psychological bases, through literary embodiment in the works of W. Gibson (see under Fiction), to political issues. See below, J. Romkey entry.

9.116   Pask, Gordon, with Susan Curran. Microman: Computers and the Evolution of Consciousness. New York: Macmillan, 1982. Numerous significant illus. provided by Millions Design. See copyright page for prod. history and brief credits.

Includes chapters on "Computers Come of Age," "The Threatening Computer," "Computers, Consciousness and Conflict," "Maverick Machines," "The Best and Worst of Possible Worlds," and "Metamorphosis of Machines and Man" (we have regularized the capitalization). Among the "Best and Worst" future worlds envisioned (ch. 11) are "Micro-freak societies" of computer hackers living in "their abstract world" (202) and "Anthill cultures"—like the micro-freaks, but without micro-freak diversity: "Anthill citizens are sadly uniform" (204).

9.117   Peck, Keenen. "High-Tech House Arrest." The Progressive 52.7 (July 1988): 26-28.

"Each day and night, the movements of hundreds of Americans are electronically monitored by local and Federal authorities" in the increasingly popular program of "electronic home detention." The "Orwellian" possibilities are noted by KP (26); more direct analogies would be the handling of "Risks" in F. Pohl and J. Williamson's The Reefs of Space and convicts in the film The Running Man (cited under Fiction and Drama respectively).

9.118   "Peddling Big Brother." Elmer-Dewitt, Philip, by-line writer. "With reporting by John Dunn, Sydney and Narunart Prapanya, Bangkkok." Time 24 June 1991: 62.

"Foreign governments are snapping up surveillance systems that are produced—but proscribed—in the West," says the subheadline; most impressive is a personal I.D. system now in use in Thailand keyed into a "population data base" that allows, in theory, linking independent government data bases to produce in one dossier all the information the government has on an individual. See for real-world referents for motif of governmental surveillance by computer.

9.119   Pennist, Elizabeth. "Neural Nets Are Sparking Heated Debates Among Their Enthusiasts" and "Of Great God Cybernetics And His Fair-Haired Child." The Scientist 14 Nov. 1988: 1 f.

"The advantage of neural networks" in advanced computers "over AI is that they 'think' like a real brain, instead of performing computations in a linear sequence" (5). See for recent in-fighting among computer scientists, and esp. for the notable little tale of how " . . . the great god Cybernetics begat two promising daughters" and how those daughters "vied for the attention of the Dark Prince DARPA" (the US agency funding advanced research projects with national security possibilities); this tale of personified AI and Neural Networks combines myth with fable, folktale, and allegory and, significantly, was written by Seymour Papert, emphatically a scientist and not a writer of SF.

9.120   Pirsig, Robert M. <u>Zen and the Art of Motorcycle Maintenance</u>. New York: Morrow, 1974. Toronto: Bantam, 1975.

A best-selling attempt to show how a world split into "hip and square, classic and romantic, technological and humanistic" can be reunited through a proper appreciation of "Quality," a "real understanding" of which "<u>captures</u> the System, tames it, and puts it to work for one's own personal use . . ." (Bantam edn., 200). Since "the System" is mostly technology and the intellectual approach to the world underlying technology (14-15), the analysis offered by <u>ZAMM</u> is quite useful for an introd. to the philosophical oppositions RMP has indentified—even if Quality, thus far, has failed to synthesize the oppositions and contradictions of Western culture. (See below, the entries for T. Roszak.)

9.121   Porush, David. "Prigogine, Chaos, and Contemporary Science Fiction." <u>SFS</u> #55, 18.3 (Nov. 1991): 367-86.

A presentation for layfolk of the basics of Ilya Prigogine on chaos theory: an attempt to reconcile, among other things, the determinism of Newtonian mechanics with the unpredictability obvious in a complex universe. Also useful for A. A. Attanasio's <u>Radix</u> and some cyberpunk and associates: Lewis Shiner's <u>Deserted Cities of the Heart</u> (1988), B. Sterling's "Cicada Queen" and <u>Schismatrix</u>, and Sterling and W. Gibson's <u>The Difference Engine</u> (consult Fiction).

9.122   <u>Presence: Teleoperators and Virtual Environments</u>.

Quarterly journal published by MIT P, beginning January 1992, devoted to real-world work in long-distance manipulation and the architecture of virtual worlds.

9.123   Randall, John Herman, Jr.   <u>The Making of the Modern Mind: A Survey of the Intellectual Background of the Present Age</u>. Boston: Houghton, 1926. New York: Columbia UP, 1976.

See for its telling well and simply the story of the rise of "The mechanical interpretation of Nature" and the subsequent vision of a "Newtonian World-Machine" in the 17th and 18th c.s, and of "The Romantic Protest Against the Age of Reason" and its mechanistic worldview in the 19th c.: see esp. chs. X-XI, XVIII-XIX, XXI. The discussion of "Philosophic Reactions to the Growing World of Mechanism" (ch. XXI) includes generous quotations from Victorian and more recent poetry.

9.124   Reichardt, Jasia. <u>Robots: Fact, Fiction, and Prediction</u>. New York: Viking, 1978.

A general discussion of robots. See JS entries under Graphics.

9.125   Reiter, Carla. "Toy Universes." <u>Science 86</u> June 1986.

Popular account of development in computer science of "miniature computer universes" to study systems sufficiently complex to mimic biological evolution in their adaptive ability; these model universes offer the promise of discovering "general principles that govern all complex systems, from evolving . . . species to thinking machines" (55).

9.126   Rheingold, Howard. <u>Virtual Reality</u>. New York: Summit, 1991.

Described by W. D. Stevens as "an excellent exposition on the development and potential use of this emerging technology," one which creates an electronic, cybernetic reality. Note recent work on the "DataGlove," bringing to reality a motif that runs from Nordic myths through the hands of Rotwang (<u>Metropolis</u>),

Dr. Strangelove (<u>Dr. Strangelove</u>), H. Ellison's "Demon," <u>Luke Skywalker</u>, and others (see Drama section of List and entries under "hand" in Keyword Index).

9.127 Robinson, Daniel Sommer. "Idealism." <u>Encyclopaedia Britannica: Macropaedia</u>. 1974.

Brief summary of Idealism in Western and Eastern philosophy, with an extensive annotated biblio. (193-94). See for a major alternative to Materialism, the ground philosophy for Mechanism. See in this section of the List, R. Descartes; T. Hobbes; D. Hofstadter; J. R. Munson and R. C. York; C. Sagan, "Life"; J. C. J. Smart; B. de Spinoza; S. E. Toulmin; R. A. Watson; R. S. Westfall.

9.128 Rogers, Michael. "Home, Smart Home." <u>Newsweek</u> 3 Nov. 1986: 58-59.

On currently available "smart" homes. Explicitly refers to Ray Bradbury's automated house in "There Will Come Soft Rains," and notes that "Bradbury's house simply wasn't smart enough": the new "IntelliHome" is more sophisticated and would know when there were no humans around to serve.

9.129 ---. "Robots Find Their Place." <u>Newsweek</u> 28 March 1988: 58-[59].

In the Technology subsection of <u>Newsweek</u>'s Society section. An update on robot technology in the real world, as of early 1988, with references to S. F. robots and the news that most robot builders have scaled down their expectations and claims: "'The more we tried to build humanlike machines, the more we admired what a human is,' says David Nitzan of SRI International" (58).

9.130 Romkey, John. "Whither Cyberspace?" <u>JASIS: Journal of the American Society for Information Science</u> 42.8 (Sept. 1991): 618-20.

Brief article on cyberspace in S. F. and virtual reality in our world. See above, W. R. Nugent on "Virtual Reality."

9.131 Roszak, Theodore. <u>The Making of a Counter Culture: Reflections on the Technocratic Society and Its Youthful Opposition</u>. Garden City, NY: Doubleday, 1969 (both hardcover and Anchor paperback edns.). "Portions of chapters I, II, IV, V and VI originally appeared in <u>The Nation</u> in March and April 1968 and have been revised for publication in this volume."

In Modern society, all are "locked into" a figurative "leviathan industrial apparatus" ruled by possessors of "technical expertise" who justify their rule by appeals to "Reason, material Progress, [and] the scientific world view." In a resurgence of the Romantic movement, "by way of a dialectic [Karl] Marx could never have imagined, technocratic America produces a potentially revolutionary element among its young": the counterculture of the 1960s and its opposition to technocracy (Anchor edn., 21, 146, 34). See for real-world referents for fictional mechanized environments. (See entries for TR, under Fiction, and for R. Pirsig, this section.)

9.132 ---. <u>Where the Wasteland Ends</u>. Garden City, NY: Doubleday, 1972.

The "wasteland" has been produced by the lack of discipline in our use and acceptance of technology; TR seeks to transcend, and thereby end, the wasteland (Wolfe 12).

9.133 Saccaro-Battisti, Giuseppa (also, Giuseppa Saccaro Battisti). "Changing Metaphors of Political Structures." <u>Journal of the History of Ideas</u> 44 (Jan.-March 1983): 31-54.

Originally scheduled to appear in revised and expanded form in <u>CW</u>, this essay includes a highly relevant and important discussion of metaphors "describing the socio-political structure as a machine" or "comparing this structure to the human body" (33).

9.134   Sacks, Oliver. The Man Who Mistook His Wife for a Hat and Other Clinical Tales. NY: Summit Books, 1985.

Coll. of articles published 1970-85, giving case studies of psychiatric patients with right-brain neuropathologies, pathologies so bizarre and resulting in such specific dysfunctions that the study of them is bringing neuropsychology close "to the very intersection of mechanism and life, to the relation of physiological processes to biography" (xiv).   See above in this section, the entries for Mechanism and R. Descartes, and the works cross-referenced for those entries.

9.135   Sagan, Carl. "Life." Encyclopaedia Britannica: Macropaedia. 1974.

Under the subsection "Life on Earth," briefly handles "Mechanism and vitalism," endorsing strongly the victorious mechanist position that ". . . all organisms are made of atoms and nothing else . . ." and can be explained in detail and "solely by physics and chemistry" (894-95). See in this section of the List, R. Descartes; T. Hobbes; D. Hofstadter; J. R. Munson and R. C. York; D. S. Robinson; J. C. J. Smart; B. de Spinoza; S. E. Toulmin; R. A. Watson; R. S. Westfall.

9.136   Saint-Simon, Claude-Henri de Rouvroy, Conte de. Oeuvres (Works). 6 vols. Paris: Editions, Anthropos, 1966.   There is also a 47-vol. set of the works of Saint-Simon and Barthélemy-Prosper Enfantin (1865-78).

Saint-Simon (1760-1825) was an early proponent of "a governing scientific and technocratic elite" (B. Lyau, "Technocratic Anxiety . . ." 296 [part of citation], 277 [quote], cited under Literary Criticism).   Most relevant here, Lettres d'un habitant Genéve à ses contemporains (1803, "Letters of a Genevan to His Contemporaries"), calling for scientists to take the social niche of priests; Du Système industriel (1820-21) and Catèchisme des industriels (1823-24, both more or less "Concerning the Industrial System").

9.137   Schafer, Roy.   "Narration in the Psychoanalytic Dialogue."   Critical Inquiry 7 (Autumn 1980): 29-53.

Briefly and clearly summarizes Sigmund Freud on humans as beasts and machines (see esp. 32-33).

9.138   The Science in Science Fiction. Peter Nicholls, gen. ed. David Langford and Brian Stableford, contributors. New York: Knopf, 1983.

Deals directly with a number of S. F. narratives. Useful sections on generation starships, space habitats, alien societies (including social insects), "Intelligent Machines" (including cyborgs and [AI] robots), "Pantropy" (adapting humans to alien environments), and eutopias and dystopias.

9.139   Searle, John R. "Minds, Brains, and Programs." The Behavioral and Brain Sciences 3 (1980): 417-24. Followed by "Open Peer Commentary."

Looks at the question, "'Could a machine think?' On the argument advanced here only a machine could think, and only very special kinds of machines, namely brains and machines with internal causal powers equivalent to those of brains. And that is why strong AI—the idea that a properly programmed computer (showing AI) can "understand and have other cognitive states"—"has little to tell us about thinking, since it [strong AI] is not about machines but about programs, and no program by itself is sufficient for thinking."   Thinking requires intentionality, and intentionality is "a biological phenomenon" (from JRS's abstract, opening paragraph, and penultimate paragraph).

9.140 Segal, Howard P. <u>Technological</u> <u>Utopianism</u> <u>in</u> <u>American</u> <u>Culture</u>. Chicago: U of Chicago P, 1985.

Deals with 25 works from 1833-1933 "predicting that technology would transform the U.S. into a utopia." Cited in "Year's Scholarship": 1986, our source for this entry, and whom we quote.

9.141 Selnow, Gary. "The Fall and Rise of Video Games." <u>JPC</u> 21 (Summer 1987): 53-62.

Examines three surveys significant for real-world "video game playing as one form of human-machine interaction," tentatively concluding (among other things) that for the "more avid [and young] arcade enthusiasts there is a real sense of companionship" while playing video games, that the games seem to have "filled a variety of roles generally observed in human relationships" (54, 59).

9.142 Shaiken, Harley. <u>Work</u> <u>Transformed:</u> <u>Automation</u> <u>and</u> <u>Labor</u> <u>in</u> <u>the</u> <u>Computer</u> <u>Age</u>. New York: Holt, 1984.

Rev. Michael Kazin, <u>The</u> <u>Nation</u> 6 April 1985: 406-9. <u>WT</u> describes, in Kazin's words, "the uneven application of theoretically dazzling systems with names like CAD/CAM (Computer-Aided Design/ Computer-Aided Manufacturing), TOPS (Total Operations Planning System) and Numerical control." Notes necessity for human supervision, making "the fully automated factory" a possibility "only in the realm of science fiction" (Kazin). Rev. implies that TOPS necessitates preliminary time-and-motion studies and constant "computerized scheduling" of operations. <u>WT</u> explicitly deals with political implications of automation.

9.143 Sheckley, Robert. <u>Futuropolis:</u> <u>Impossible</u> <u>Cities</u> <u>of</u> <u>Science</u> <u>Fiction</u> <u>and</u> <u>Fantasy</u>. 1978. New York: A & W Publishers, 1978.

Pictures with explanatory text of many proposed (and sometimes built) or envisioned cities, ranging from a plan by Dinocrates, architect to Alexander the Great, to photographs of real cities to comic book art to SF illustration to illustrations for recent proposals for space colonies. Most of the imagined cities are highly mechanized and will be viewed by different people as eutopian, dystopian, hellish, heavenly, and most stops between.

9.144 Simons, Geoff. <u>Are</u> <u>Computers</u> <u>Alive?</u> <u>Evolution</u> <u>and</u> <u>New</u> <u>Life</u> <u>Forms</u>. Cambridge, MA: Birkhauser Boston, 1983.

GS believes computers are, in a sense, alive, since they can reason, evolve, and "express both creativity and free will." Rev. W. D. Stevens, <u>FR</u> #69 (July 1984): 44, our source for this entry, and whom we quote.

9.145 Skinner, B. F. <u>Beyond</u> <u>Freedom</u> <u>and</u> <u>Dignity</u>. New York: Knopf, 1971.

BFS denies the existence of "autonomous man" and asserts the current existence of a "technology of behavior" (conditioning) which should be used rationally and systematically. BFS's opponents see him proposing a view of humans-as-automata and recommending for us a dystopia of totalitarian control. BFS and the whole school of Behaviorism are favorite targets in a fair amount of pessimistic S. F. and dystopian satire. (See entry below for J. B. Watson.)

9.146 Smart, John Carswell Jamieson. "Materialism." <u>Encyclopaedia</u> <u>Britannica:</u> <u>Macropaedia</u>. 1974.

Begins with defining a paradigmatic "mechanical Materialism," where What Is is matter, matter understood as a collection of minute hard particles, possibly moving through a void—a classic atomist paradigm immediately modernized "to cover anyone who bases his theory on whatever it is that physics asserts ultimately to exist": "physicalistic Materialism" (611). Note discussion of R. Descartes's "doctrine that animals are automata," applied by Julien (Offroy) de La Mettrie to humans in his unequivocally titled L'Homme machine, 1747, trans. English Man a Machine, 1750 (612). Bringing the discussion to the late 20th c., the article deals with computers and the question of "real" AI (614). Includes a useful analytical, lightly annotated biblio. See in this section of the List, R. Descartes; T. Hobbes; D. Hofstadter; J. R. Munson and R. C. York; D. S. Robinson; C. Sagan, "Life"; B. de Spinoza; S. E. Toulmin; R. A. Watson; R. S. Westfall.

9.147   Soleri, Paolo. Arcology: The City in the Image of Man. Cambridge, MA: MIT P, 1970.

Presents PS's ideas for a real-world civilization based in "a structure called an arcology, or ecological architecture." Allowing humankind to function in the physical universe ("an immense megamachine"), an arcology is a city viewed as a huge organism, preferably one including a computer brain as well as the interacting organic brains of its human inhabitants. (PS's idea of an arcology is modified and given fictional life in Larry Niven and Jerry Pournelle's novel, Oath of Fealty [1981], in which an arcology is an antibureaucratic environment.)

9.148   Soloflex TV commercial, June 1985.

Voice-over explicitly identifies human body as a machine, with the point illustrated by what appear to be (and perhaps are) computer graphics putting in motion the famous sketch by Leonardo da Vinci showing the geometric regularities of the male physique by putting the figure of a man inside a circle and square.

9.149   Spinoza, Benedict de (also Benedictus and Baruch, and Despinoza). Ethica in Ordine Geometrico Demonstrata ("Ethics, Presented in the Manner of a Geometrical Proof" [our trans.], written 1662-75, publ. 1677). Available with other relevant works and extensive apparatus in The Collected Works of Spinoza. Edwin Curley, ed. and trans. Vol. 1. Princeton: Princeton UP, 1985.

Extends, and modifies, R. Descartes's mechanism from matter and body to include mind and even God, for a totally deterministic system. In his Tractatus Theologico-Politicus ("A Theologico-Political Treatise," written 1665-70, publ. 1670), BdS advises rulers against treating human beings as if we were "beasts or puppets" (ch. 20; R. H. M. Elwes trans.); but BdS became notorious—unjustly— for the idea that nonhuman animals are machines, and sees humans as part of a nature that is pantheistic but material and radically unfree. For soul "acting according to certain laws, like a spiritual automaton," see The Emendation of the Intellect, paragraph 85 (Curley 37). For humans as highly sophisticated mechanisms (our word), see esp. Ethics Part III, Preface and scholium (i.e., note) to proposition 2 (Curley 491-92, 494-97). See in this section of the List, R. Descartes; T. Hobbes, D. Hofstadter; J. R. Munson and R. C. York; D. S. Robinson; C. Sagan, "Life"; J. C. J. Smart; S. E. Toulmin; R. A. Watson; R. S. Westfall.

9.150   Sullivan, George. Rise of the Robots. New York: Dodd, 1971.

History of robots; their function as industrial robots; intelligent robots; the future of robots.

9.151   Survival Research Laboratories, performance art group: Cited under Drama.

9.152   Taylor, Frederick W. The Principles of Scientific Management. New York: Harper, 1911. New York: Norton, 1967.

To its enemies, "scientific management" meant reducing workers to automata doing their jobs in the manner their bosses' hired experts ruled most efficient. In mechanized industries, this meant fitting workers ever more perfectly to the rhythm of the machines. For further readings on FWT and Taylorism, see C. H. Rhodes, "Frederick Winslow Taylor's System of Scientific Management," cited under Literary Criticism; see also under Literary Criticism, "Man as Robot," the CW essay by G. Beauchamp.

9.153 Technocracy: Technological Social Design. Savannah, OH: Technocracy, Inc., 1975.

Literature on the Technocracy movement is available cheaply from Continental Headquarters, Technocracy, Inc., Savannah, OH 44874. This pamphlet provides a simple introd. to Technocracy and briefly outlines how the "Technate of North America" will be run after the technocrats take over. (See under Literary Criticism, W. W. Wagar, "the Steel-Gray Saviour" [sic on British spelling].)

9.154 Technology and Pessimism. Special issue of Alternative Futures.

Listed this section, under Marthalee Barton and Dwight W. Stevenson, guest co-eds.

9.155 Toulmin, Stephen E. "Science, Philosophy of." Encyclopaedia Britannica: Macropaedia. 1974.

Handles debate among Mechanists, Vitalists, Idealists, and others involved in the struggle for how educated people would model the world (see esp. 379-81). Includes an extensive, briefly annotated, biblio. (393). See in this section of the List, R. Descartes; T. Hobbes; D. Hofstadter; J. R. Munson and R. C. York; D. S. Robinson; C. Sagan, "Life"; J. C. J. Smart; B. de Spinoza; R. A. Watson; R. S. Westfall.

9.156 Turing, A. M. "Computing Machinery and Intelligence." Mind #236, 59 (1950), excerpted in The Mind's I, q.v. under Anthologies.

See for what is now called "The Turing Test" for AI, or machine intelligence: "The Imitation Game" AMT thought up, wherein a machine tries to convince a human being that it is a woman.

9.157 Turkle, Sherry. The Second Self: Computers and the Human Spirit. New York: Simon, 1984. New York: Touchstone-Simon, 1985.

Rev. Susan Chace, The Nation 22 Sept. 1984: 248-50. Chace acknowledges ST an "anthropologist of 'computer cultures,'" looking at "a dramatic shift" in human self-perception: from seeing nonhuman animals as "'our nearest neighbors in the known universe'" to computers vying for this position. Moving through subcultures of heavy users, ST illustrates "a growing tendency to regard the mind as 'mechanized'" (Chace 248). Rev. Michael Rogers, Newsweek 6 Aug. 1984, who finds the book pretty positive even with the "'mind as machine'" model, since ST found many people using "computers to establish identity and gain self-awareness, or to achieve a feeling of mastery over their lives" (Rogers 69). For historical context on the "mind as machine" issue, see in this section the entries for R. Decartes, Materialism, Mechanism, and B. Spinoza, and the works cross-referenced there.

9.158 Turner, Victor. "Passages, Margins, and Poverty: Religious Symbols of Communitas." Worship 46 (Aug.-Sept. 1972): 390-412; (Oct.): 432-94. Coll. as ch. 6 of Dramas, Fields, and Metaphors: Symbolic Action in Human Society. Ithaca, NY: Cornell UP, 1974.

Turner's discussion of structure vs. communitas ("community"), is significant for a study of clockwork societies: the rebels opposed to such machine-worlds are necessarily outsiders, "liminal" characters.

9.159   ---. The Ritual Process: Structure and Anti-Structure. 1969. Ithaca, NY: Cornell UP, 1977.

See chs. 3-5 for structured, hierarchical society vs. communitas ("community"): society as an "essential We" (Martin Buber's phrase). Exaggerations and perversions of structure and communitas may be the real-world referents of mechanical and hive worlds in dystopian SF.

9.160   Vitalism, Mechanism: See in this section the entries for C. Sagan, J. R. Munson and R. C. York, and S. E. Toulmin.

9.161   Wagar, W. Warren, "The Steel-Gray Saviour": Cited and annotated under Literary Criticism.

9.162   "A War on French Computers." Newsweek 28 April 1980: 56.

Brief report including mention of the French underground organization CLODO: "the Committee for the Liquidation or Deterrence of Computers." This group sees real-world computers as "the favorite instrument of the powerful. . . . used to classify, control, and to repress."

9.163   Watson, John B. "Psychology as the Behaviorist Views It." The Psychological Review 20 (March 1913): 158-77.

Classic statement of the Behaviorist view that "the prediction and control of behavior" is "psychology's sole task." See also JBW, Psychology from the Standpoint of a Behaviorist (1919), and his work for lay readers, Behaviorism (1924, 1925; rev. edn. 1930). JBW's name is preserved and much of his philosophy followed in the World State of A. Huxley's Brave New World (q.v., under Fiction). See this section, the entry for B. F. Skinner.

9.164   Watson, Richard A. "Cartesianism." Encyclopaedia Britannica: Macropaedia. 1974.

Elegant summary of Cartesian thought from slightly after Rene Descartes, "the father of modern philosophy" (968), through Benedict de Spinoza's mechanistic approaches to understanding the physical universe, human beings, and other animals, up to Noam Chomsky and contemporary forms of "the old Cartesian questions: how can machines think? That is, how can computers be self-conscious"—in the formulation we use, possess AI? (970). See in this section of the List, R. Descartes; T. Hobbes; D. Hofstadter; J. R. Munson and R. C. York; D. S. Robinson; C. Sagan, "Life"; J. C. J. Smart; B. de Spinoza; S. E. Toulmin; R. S. Westfall.

9.165   Weiss, Paul. "Love in a Machine Age." In Dimensions of Mind. Sidney Hook, ed. New York: New York UP, 1960.

Argues "that we recognize feelings in others because they move and emote as we do when we are feeling. . . . [S]ince robots have the capacity to accurately counterfeit our movements, we must attribute to them the same feelings when the movements are convincing" (we quote James Bierman, "Automated Theatre," q.v. under Drama Criticism). See for debate on AI and the potential humanity of robots.

9.166   Weizenbaum, Joseph. Computer Power and Human Reason. San Francisco: W. H. Freeman, 1976.

Cited by D. Hofstadter as "A provocative book by an early AI worker who has come to the conclusion that much work in computer science, particularly in AI, is dangerous" (755)—in the Bibliography to Gödel, Escher, Bach, q.v., this section.

9.167 Welsford, Enid. The Fool: His Social and Literary History. 1935. Garden City, NY: Doubleday, 1961.

The fool, Harlequin, Trickster, and Lord of Misrule have often been used by wise societies as antidotes for the stagnation and oppression threatened or achieved by too much social order. EW's work is the classic investigation of the role of the fool. (Note the Jester in A. C. Clarke's, City and the Stars, and H. Ellison's Harlequin hero in "Repent, Harlequin!"; both works cited under Fiction.)

9.168 Westfall, Richard S. "Newton, Sir Isaac." Encyclopaedia Britannica: Macropaedia. 1974.

See for influence on Newton of R. Descartes "and the other mechanical philosophers" (17), combined with elements of Hermetic philosophy. Newton used "transpositions of the occult sympathies and antipathies of Hermetic philosophy . . . . as a modification of the mechanical philosophy that rendered it subject to exact mathematical treatment . . . [offering] a bridge to unite the two basic themes of 17th-century science—the mechanical tradition . . . and the Pythagorean tradition, which insisted on the mathematical nature of reality" (19). We will add that the Cartesian view cited by RSW "of nature as an intricate, impersonal, and inert machine" (17) was strengthened by Newton and add the concept of the microcosm: if "Man-the-Microcosm" by definition embodies in little the Macrocosm of the universe, then a mechanical universe implies mechanical humanity; if universe and humans are machines, the mediating terms of Society and State might be also—for a wholly mechanistic world where all is determined (or where Humanity, Society, and the State are machines that can be tinkered with: a revolutionary idea). See below in this section, the entry for G. Wills. See also in this section of the List, R. Descartes; T. Hobbes; D. Hofstadter; J. R. Munson and R. C. York.

9.169 Wheeler, William Morton. "The Ant-Colony as an Organism." Journal of Morphology 22.2 (1911): 307-25.

Early and influential statement on insect colony as organism. Cited by D. Hofstadter in the Bibliography to Gödel, Escher, Bach, q.v., this section. See above under Literary Criticism, T. Dunn and R. Erlich, "The Mechanical Hive" and ". . . Beehives and Mechanization."

9.170 Whyte, William H. The Organization Man. 1956. Garden City, NY: Doubleday, Anchor, n.d.

A serious discussion of "Organization Man" as a new and significant variety of H. sapiens sapiens. WHW's book was highly influential in the later 1950s and early 1960s and is still quite useful for an analysis of the bureaucratization of real life and the idea of the "Organization Man" in fiction.

9.171 Wiener, Norbert. "The Brain and Machine." In Dimensions of Mind. Sidney Hook, ed. New York: New York UP, 1960,.

Computers "with second-generation functions (that is the ability to program or reprogram themselves) could take on a responsiveness akin to feelings" (quoting J. Bierman, "Automated Theatre," q.v. under Drama Criticism). See for AI debate.

9.172 ---. Cybernetics: or, Control and Communication in the Animal and the Machine. Cambridge, MA: MIT P, 1948.

The introduction of the new science of cybernetics to the general scientific community and to a fairly wide popular audience. Note well the early yoking in cybernetics of communication and control, animal and machine.

9.173 Willey, Basil. Ch. V, "The Philosophical Quest for Truth—Descartes," and ch. VI, "The Philosophical Quest for Truth—Hobbes." In The Seventeenth Century Background. New York: Columbia UP, 1935. Garden City, NY: Anchor-Doubleday, 1953.

On the effects on "literary developments in England after the middle of the seventeenth century" of the methodical thinking of R. Descartes and "the perfection of his mechanised [sic] universe" (94-95 of Doubleday rpt.). Also treats the influence of the militant materialism and determinism of T. Hobbes (Descartes and Hobbes cited above, this section).

9.174 Wills, Gary. Part Two, "A Scientific Paper," ch. 7. In Inventing America: Jefferson's Declaration of Independence. Garden City, NY: Doubleday, 1978. Vintage-Random, 1979: [93]-110.

On the liberating aspects of the Newtonian vision of a clockwork universe. See for a relatively simple introd. to the literally revolutionary effect of a mechanistic vision of the universe, society, and human beings. See above, entry for R. S. Westfall on I. Newton.

9.175 Winner, Langdon. Autonomous Technology: Technics-out-of-Control as a Theme in Political Thought. Cambridge, MA: MIT P, 1977.

Wolfe cites this work as an excellent survey of the subject identified in its subtitle (see Wolfe under Literary Criticism). Cf. J. Ellul and L. Mumford, works cited this section.

9.176 Work, Technology, and Education: Dissenting Essays in the Intellectual Foundations of American Education. Walter Feinberg and Henry Rosemont, Jr., eds. Urbana, IL: U of Illinois P, 1975.

Immediately relevant: Kenneth D. Benne, "Technology and Community: Conflicting Bases of Educational Authority"; Marx Wartofsky, "Art and Technology: Conflicting Models of Education? The Uses of a Cultural Myth"; Don Ihde, "A Phenomenology of Man-Machine Relations" (q.v. this section). Taken all together, these essays attack contemporary American schools as places where the human soul is just "another element to be shaped, molded, and conditioned to the requirements of machine production" (Introduction 11).

9.177 The World of Tomorrow. Lance Bird and Tom Johnson, producers. USA: TV Lab of WNET/Thirteen, 1984. Documentary in the PBS series Non-Fiction Television. 60 minutes. Jason Robards, narrator.

Intelligent commentary on the 1939 New York World's Fair (with some references to the Fair's second year). See for the Fair grounds themselves making up "a color-coded city: bright, rational, completely planned" and for the Fair's presentation of "the world science could make for us." Archival footage includes a scene with a primitive robot by Westinghouse; narration and intercutting with newsreels from the Depression and early Second World War stress Fair's combination of "science" with "magic," and with "illusion" (all quotations from Robard's voiceover).

9.178 Yablonsky, Lewis. Robopaths: People as Machines. 1972. Baltimore: Penguin, 1972, 1973.

Contains a number of references to literature, theater, and film. Concentrates on robopathology: people becoming mechanized—losing compassion and other positive emotions. Talks of the state as machine and of "social machines" like corporations and many schools and families. This book can be viewed legitimately as a polemical extension of the observations of B. Bettelheim, "Joey: A Mechanical Boy" (see above, this section).

9.179 York, Neil Longley. <u>Mechanical Metamorphosis: Technical Change in Revolutionary America</u>. Westport, CT: Greenwood P, 1985.

During the revolutionary period, "embryonic" American technology was significant "within the framework of the complex social, economic, and cultural events" of the time. Cited in "Year's Scholarship": 1987, our source for this entry, and which we quote.

9.180 Young, Michael. <u>The Rise of the Meritocracy, 1870-2033: The New Elite of Our Social Revolution</u>. London: Thames and Hudson, 1958. NY: Random, 1959.

A fictional monograph by a sociologist of the 21st c. putting the British social disturbances of 2033 into the context of the rise of the meritocracy: the new hierarchical system in the UK in which membership in the ruling class is ultimately decided by intelligence (as measured—and, in theory, soon to be predicted—by psychologists). Posits a future world in which great competition among nations requires England to become a techno-scientific culture of great efficiency.

9.181 Zins, Daniel L. "Rescuing Science from Technocracy . . .": Cited under Literary Criticism.

Author Index

A

Abernathy, Richard, 3.001
Abrahm, Paul M., 4.001
Abrash, Merritt, 4.002 4.003, 4.004, 4.005, 6.001
Ackerson, Duane, 3.002
Adams, Brooks, 7.001
Adams, Douglas, 3.003, 3.004, 3.005
Adams, Henry, 9.002
Agee, William C., 7.002
Agel, Jerome, 6.002
Akin, William E., 9.003
Alan Parsons Project, The, 8.001
Aldiss, Brian W., 2.002, 3.006-3.021, 4.006, 4.007, 4.008, 7.003, 7.142
Aldridge, Alexandra, 4.009, 4.010, 4.011, 4.012, 4.013
Aldridge, Ray, 3.022
Alfven, Hannes, 3.426
Ali, Jaffer, 6.091
Allen, Dick, 3.023
Aloff, Mindy, 7.004, 9.004
Alterman, Peter S., 4.014
Altman, Mark A., 1.001, 6.004

Anderson, Alan Ross, 9.105
Anderson, Kevin, 3.024, 3.025
Anderson, Poul, 3.026, 3.027, 3.028
Andreissen, David, 3.029
Annan, David, 6.005
Antheil, George, 8.002
Anthony, Piers, 3.030, 3.031, 3.032
Appel, Benjamin, 3.033
Aramaki, Yoshio, 3.034
Arendt, Hannah, 9.005, 9.006
Armstrong, D. M., 9.007
Aronica, Lou, 2.019
Ashbaugh, Dennis, 7.011
Asimov, Isaac, 2.004-2.006, 2.016, 3.035-3.059, 3.061, 9.008
Asimov, Janet, 3.059, 3.060, 3.061
Astel, Richard, 3.062
Astor, John Jacob, 3.063
Attanasio, A. A., 3.064
Auden, W. H., 3.065
Aycock, Alice, 7.008

Index compiled by D. Scott DeLoach, with Richard D. Erlich.

B

Bachman, Richard, 3.452
Bailey, J[ames] O., 4.015
Bailey, K. V., 4.016
Baker, Robert S., 4.017
Ball, Margaret, 3.551
Ballard, James Graham, 3.066-3.069
Bann, Stephen, 7.009
Barlow, Aaron, 4.018
Barnes, Steven, 3.592
Barrett, David, 2.013
Barrett, William, 9.010
Barron, Neil, 1.002
Barth, John, 3.070
Barthelme, Donald, 3.071
Barton, Marthalee, 9.011
Bartter, Martha A., 4.019
Bass, Ruth, 7.010
Bass, T. J., 3.072
Bates, Harry, 3.073
Baudrillard, Jean, 4.020
Baum, L. Frank, 3.074
Baxter, John, 1.003, 6.006
Bayley, Barrington J., 3.075, 3.076, 3.077
Bear, Greg, 3.078-3.082, 9.012
Beason, Doug, 3.025
Beatty, Jack, 9.013
Beauchamp, Gorman, 4.013, 4.021-4.026
Beauchamp, James W., 8.027
Benford, Gregory, 3.192
Bellamy, Edward, 3.083
Bellour, Raymond, 4.027
Benacerraf, Paul, 9.014
Benét, Stephen Vincent, 3.084, 3.085
Benedikt, Michael, 9.035
Benford, Gregory, 3.086, 3.087, 3.088, 3.089
Beresford, John Davis, 3.090
Berger, Harold L., 4.028
Bergson, Henri, 9.015
Bergstrom, Janet, 6.007
Berman, Jeffrey, 4.029
Bernal, J. D., 9.016
Berry, Stephen Ames, 3.091
Bester, Alfred, 3.092, 3.093
Bethke, Bruce, 3.094
Bettelheim, Bruno, 9.017
Bierce, Ambrose, 3.095
Bierman, James H., 6.008, 6.009
Biggle, Lloyd, Jr., 3.096
Biles, Jack I., 4.030
Binder, Eando, 3.097, 3.098
Bird, R. P., 3.099

Bishop, Michael, 3.100, 3.101
Blackford, Russell, 4.031, 4.032
Blackney, Jay D., 3.102
Blair, Eric, 3.602
Blair, Karen, 6.010
Bleiler, E. F., 4.033
Blish, James, 3.103-3.106
Boden, Margaret, 9.019
Bohan, Ruth L., 7.015
Bohn, Willard, 7.016
Bolter, J. David, 9.020
Bond, Nelson S., 3.107
Bone, J. F., 3.108
Boorman, John, 3.109
Boorstin, Daniel J., 9.021, 9.022
Boruszkowski, Lilly Ann, 6.011
Boucher, Anthony, 3.110
Bova, Ben, 3.111-3.115
Bowker, Richard, 3.116
Bowlt, John E., 7.017
Boyd, John, 3.117
Boylan, Jay H., 6.012
Brackett, Leigh, 3.118
Bradbury, Ray, 3.119-3.129
Bradley, Linda C., 4.034
Brady, Charles J., 4.035
Bramson, Leon, 9.023
Brand, Thomas, 3.131
Brautigan, Richard, 3.130
Braverman, Harry, 9.024
Brennan, John P., 4.036
Brians, Paul, 1.005, 1.012
Brigg, Peter, 4.037
Brin, David, 3.132, 3.133
Brink, Carol Ryrie, 3.134
Brod, Craig, 9.025
Broderick, Damien, 3.135
Broege, Valerie, 4.038-4.041
Broer, Lawrence, 4.042
Brosnan, John, 1.006, 6.013
Brown, Frederic, 3.136
Brown, James, 8.004
Brunner, John, 2.008, 3.137-3.141
Brust, Steven, 3.142
Bryant, Edward, 3.143-3.145
Budrys, Algis, 3.146, 3.147
Buggles, The, 8.005
Bukatman, Scott, 4.043, 4.044, 6.014, 6.015, 7.018
Bunch, David R., 3.148
Bunting, Eve, 3.149
Burgess, Anthony, 3.150, 4.045

Dennett, Daniel C., 9.038, 9.106
Dent, Guy, 3.242, 3.243
Descartes, Réne, 9.039
Desser, David, 4.060, 6.022, 6.023, 6.024
Devo, 8.009
Dick, Philip K., 3.244-3.269, 4.061, 4.174,
   9.040
Dicks, Terrance, 3.270-3.272
Dickson, David, 9.041
Dickson, Gordon R., 3.273, 3.274
Dimitrijevic, Nena, 7.032
Disch, Thomas M., 3.275, 3.276
Doherty, Thomas, 6.025
Dolby, Thomas, 8.010
Doll, Susan, 6.026
Downes, Geoff, 8.011
Drake, David, 3.277
Dreyfus, Hubert, 9.042
Dunn, Thomas [P.], 1.007, 1.024, 4.062, 4.063,
   4.064
Duprey, Richard, 3.278
Dwiggins, William Addison, 3.279

E

Eaves, Morris, 9.043
Edge, Graeme, 8.012
Edwards, Paul, 3.280
Effinger, George Alec, 3.281-3.285, 3.286,
   3.287
Egan, Greg, 3.286
Egan, James, 4.065
Eichner, Hans, 9.044
Eizykman, Boris, 4.066
Eklund, Gordon, 3.287
Elder, Michael, 3.288
Elderfield, John, 7.033
Elgin, Suzette Haden, 3.289
Eliade, Mircea, 9.045
Elkins, Charles, 4.067, 6.027
Ellison, Harlan, 2.014, 3.145, 3.290-3.297,
   3.700
Ellul, Jacques, 9.046
Elsner, Henry, Jr., 9.047
Emshwiller, Carol, 3.298
Erikson, John D., 7.037
Erlich, Richard D., 1.007, 1.024, 4.063, 4.064,
   4.068, 4.069, 4.070, 6.020, 6.035
Escher, Maurits C., 7.035, 7.036
Esmonde, Margaret P., 4.071
Etzler, John Adolphus, 3.299
Evans, Arthur B., 4.072

F

Fairman, Paul W., 3.300, 3.301
Fallen, Greg, 6.026
Farber, Sharon, 3.302
Farca, Marie C, 3.303, 3.304
Farmer, Philip José, 3.305-3.308
Faust, Joe Clifford, 3.311
Feigl, Herbert, 9.048
Feinberg, Walter, 9.176
Fekete, John, 4.074
Felice, Cynthia, 3.310
Ferman, Edward L., 2.018
Filotas, Paul, 7.131
Finch, Sheila, 3.311, 3.312
Fine, Stephen, 3.313
Firestone, Shulamith, 9.049
Fischlin, Donald, 4.075
Fisher, Judith L., 4.076
Fisher, Lou, 3.314, 3.315
Fisher, R, M., 7.039
Fitting, Peter, 4.077, 6.028
Florman, Samuel C., 9.050
Fogarty, Bob, 9.027
Forster, E. M., 3.316
Förster, Werner, 4.078
Forward, Robert L., 3.317
Foster, Alan Dean, 3.318-3.325
Foster, Stephen C., 7.038, 7.041
Foucault, Michel, 9.051
Fournier d'Albe, E. E., 9.052
Frank, Frederick S., 4.079
Franklin, H. Bruce, 4.080-4.082, 6.029, 9.053
Frayn, Michael, 3.326
Frazier, Robert, 3.327
Freeman, Judi, 7.042
Frenkel, Karen A., 9.008
Fresco, J., 3.446
Friedman, Jerrold David, 3.331
Fromm, Erich, 4.083
Fry, Edward, 7.043

G

Gaar, Alice Carol, 4.084
Gakov, Vladimir, 1.012
Gallagher, Edward J., 4.085, 4.086
Gallagher, Steven, 3.217
Galouye, Daniel F., 3.328
Gardner, Colin, 7.045

Title Index

Index compiled by D. Scott DeLoach, with Richard D. Erlich.

Ringworld Engineers, 4.254
"Rise of Modern Science and the Genesis of
   Romanticism, The", 9.044
*Rise of the Meritocracy, 1870-2033: The New
   Elite of Our Social Revolution, The*, 9.180
Rise of the Robots, 9.150
Rite of Passage, 3.599
*Ritual Process: Structure and Anti-Structure,
   The*, 9.159
Road Warrior, The,, 5.165
"Roads Must Roll, The", 3.385
Robert A. Heinlein: America as Science Fiction,
   4.080
"Robert Silverberg's The World Inside", 4.004
RoboCop, 3.588, 5.224
RoboCop 2, 5.225
Roboman, 5.226, 5.331
Robopaths: People as Machines, 9.178
"Robot", 5.102
Robot Adept, 3.032
Robot Art, 7.060
Robot Calendar 1985, 7.054, 7.117
"Robot Empire, The", 3.519
"Robot Ethics and Robot Parody....", 4.234
"Robot Exhibit, The", 7.118
Robot in the Closet, The, 3.349
Robot Jox, 5.228
Robot of Regalia, The, 5.229
Robot People, The, 3.149
Robot Rabbit, 5.230
Robot Romance, 3.509
Robot Visions, 2.005
Robot vs. the Aztec Mummy,The, 5.231
"Robot's Return", 3.862
Robot, The, 5.227
Robot: The Mechanical Monster, 6.005
Robot-bot-bot, 3.461
Robotech Art 1, 7.109
Robotech Art 2, 7.109
ROBOTECH™ SERIES, 3.559;
Robotics: A User-Friendly Introduction, 9.061
Robots and Empire, 3.054
*Robots, Androids, and Mechanical Oddities:
   The Science Fiction of Philip K, Dick*, 2.034
"Robots Are Here, The Robots Are Here!,
   The", 7.141
Robots are Here!, The, 9.060
"Robots Find Their Place", 9.129
Robots Have No Tails, 3.466
"Robots in Science Fiction", 4.131
"Robots in Space", 7.119
Robots of Dawn, The, 3.055

Robots: Fact, Fiction, and Prediction, 9.124
"Robots: Low-Voltage Ontological Currents",
   4.007
Robots: Machines in Man's Image, 9.008
"Robots: Three Fantasies and One Big Cold
   Reality", 4.173
Rocheworld, 3.317
"Rock On", 3.156
Rocketeer, The, 5.232
Rod of Light, The, 3.076
*Roderick at Random or Further Education of a
   Young Machine*, 3.766
*Roderick, Or the Education of a Young Ma-
   chine*, 3.766
Roderick's Progress, 3.766
"Roger Brown", 7.010
Roger Corman's Frankstein Unbound, 5.233
Roger Zelazny, 4.261
Rogue Bolo, 3.476
Rogue Golem, 3.443
"Roller Ball Murder", 3.378, 4.113
Rollerball, 5.234
"Rollerbrawl", 6.067
"Romantic Critique of Industrial Civilization,
   The", 4.089
"Romanticizing Cybernetics in Ridley Scott's
   Blade Runner", 6.081
Rom™, 7.120
*Round Trip to the Year 2000 or a Flight
   Through Time, A*, 3.212
Runaway, 5.235
Runaway Robot, The, 3.237
Running Man, The, 3.451, 5.236
Running Silent, 5.245

S

"S-F: Science Spéculative Stochastique Fic-
   tion", 4.066
Sagan om dem stora datamaskinin, 3.426
Sailing To Byzantium, 3.744
"Sales Pitch", 3.261
"Sam Hall", 3.028
"Sanatorium of Dr. Vliperdius, The", 3.505
"Sandman, The", 3.403
"Satan Stultified: A Rejoinder to Paul
   Benacerraf", 9.082
*Satan: His Psychotherapy and Cure by the
   Unfortunate Dr. Kassler*, 3.510
"Satin", 3.350
Saturn 3, 5.238
"Scanners Live in Vain", 3.771

Keyword and Theme Index

A

action, 3.040, 3.792, 6.054, 9.005, 9.158
actor, 5.052, 6.008
actor, robot, 3.579
Adam, 3.081, 3.701, 3.877
adolescent, 3.409, 5.017, 5.159, 5.276, 5.328
adult, 3.758
adventure, 3.097, 3.105, 3.180, 3.182, 3.445, 3.877, 4.254, 5.011, 5.038, 5.039, 5.157, 5.244, 5.247, 5.314, 5.324
advertising, 3.624, 3.626
afterlife, 5.010, 5.094
agentic state, 9.102
aggression, 9.055
agrarian society, 3.069, 3.118
agriculture, 9.061
AI (artificial intelligence), 2.005, 2.025, 2.029, 2.035, 3.004, 3.013, 3.045, 3.064, 3.078, 3.080, 3.087, 3.094, 3.095, 3.099, 3.123, 3.152, 3.171, 3.185, 3.194, 3.197, 3.199, 3.207, 3.210, 3.238, 3.275, 3.310, 3.317, 3.321, 3.334, 3.336, 3.337, 3.375, 3.382, 3.383, 3.391, 3.419, 3.435, 3.344, 3.424, 3.468-3.470, 3.487, 3.508, 3.510, 3.530, 3.531, 3.541, 3.545, 3.565, 3.575, 3.637, 3.640, 3.663, 3.670, 3.703, 3.708, 3.728, 3.750, 3.754, 3.772, 3.804, 3.806, 3.820, 3.833, 3.844, 3.845, 3.846, 3.875, 3.889, 4.046, 4.048, 4.132, 4.180, 4.244, 4.246, 4.247, 5.008, 5.153, 5.154, 5.168, 5.243, 5.299, 8.018, 9.010, 9.038, 9.042, 9.058, 9.059, 9.061, 9.065, 9.067, 9.089, 9.100, 9.105, 9.106, 9.107, 9.108, 9.119, 9.139, 9.146, 9.156, 9.164, 9.165, 9.166, 9.171; see also computer(s), computer, sentient, consciousness, cybernetics, sentience, and thinking.
AI, history of, 9.090
AI tank, 3.476
airplane, 3.328, 4.033, 5.249, 8.038
album cover, 7.029, 8.007, 8.020, 8.044
alien, 3.010, 3.045, 3.170, 3.171, 3.172, 3.231, 3.317, 3.366, 3.401, 3.412, 3.462, 3.484, 3.524, 3.608, 3.629, 3.708, 3.814, 3.855, 3.859, 4.180, 5.015, 5.065, 5.133, 5.186, 5.257, 5.288, 6.003, 6.016, 6.019, 6.027, 6.029, 6.034, 6.057, 7.020, 7.046, 7.101, 9.138

Index compiled by D. Scott DeLoach, with Richard D. Erlich.

fantasy, 3.207, 3.295, 3.408, 3.425, 3.642,
3.659, 3.805, 3.856, 3.893, 4.031, 4.082,
4.124, 4.173, 4.263, 5.205, 5.231, 5.306,
5.328, 7.067, 7.098, 9.143
fantasy, romantic, 5.105
fantasy art, 7.029
Faust, 3.111, 3.370
feeling(s), 3.411, 3.428, 3.574, 3.829, 5.216,
5.272, 5.280, 9.109, 9.165, 9.171; see also
emotion(s).
female, dangerous, 3.394, 5.047, 5.180
feminism, 3.312, 4.111, 4.162, 6.057, 6.062,
9.062, 9.097
fighting suit: See suit, fighting.
figurehead, 3.264
film, 1.003, 1.006, 1.014, 1.017, 1.018, 1.021,
1.022, 1.023, 1.025, 1.027, 1.028, 1.029,
1.043, 3.336, 3.451, 6.002, 6.003, 6.005,
6.006, 6.008, 6.016, 6.020-6.030, 6.035,
6.037, 6.038, 6.045, 6.046, 6.064, 6.068,
6.071, 6.079, 6.081-6.088, 6.091, 7.012,
7.018, 7.083, 7.086, 7.087, 7.110, 7.125,
8.022, 8.047, 9.178; see Section 5.
film noir, 5.016, 5.044, 6.022
first contact, 3.025, 3.608, 4.048, 5.116, 5.269,
3.814
flexibility, 3.873, 4.014
flying saucer, 5.032, 5.162
fool, 5.270, 9.167
forest, 3.480, 4.257, 5.103, 5.245
Frankenstein, 3.072, 3.146, 3.185, 3.403, 4.023,
4.050, 4.197, 5.044, 5.159, 5.188, 5.233,
5.323, 5.328
free will, 3.042, 3.358, 3.823, 4.228, 4.260,
5.250, 8.034, 9.064, 9.089, 9.106, 9.144; see
also determinism.
freedom, 3.138, 3.239, 3.336, 3.480, 3.498,
3.533, 3.793, 3.806, 4.026, 4.053, 4.168,
4.183, 4.193, 4.231, 5.246, 5.269, 5.279,
5.301, 6.021, 7.061, 7.132, 8.022, 8.036,
9.064, 9.074, 9.145
Freud, 4.152, 6.037, 8.034, 9.074, 9.137
frontier, 3.103, 5.157
funk, 3.336, 3.872, 5.044, 5.116, 5.183, 5.236,
5.323
future, 3.200, 3.336, 3.386, 3.392, 3.402, 3.413,
3.446, 3.477, 3.508, 3.562, 3.590, 3.607,
3.611, 4.094, 4.107, 4.171, 4.252, 5.027,
5.050, 5.125, 5.233, 5.246, 5.301, 5.302,
5.311, 6.029, 7.086, 7.096, 7.098, 7.099,
9.036, 9.060, 9.079, 9.103
futurism, 7.044, 7.050, 7.056, 7.064, 8.028,
8.048

G

gadget, 3.283, 3.451, 3.473, 3.633, 3.805,
5.021, 5.030, 5.218, 5.244, 9.033
Gaia, 3.042, 4.092
game(s), 3.047, 3.071, 3.203, 3.227, 3.332,
3.379, 3.419, 3.592, 3.680, 3.712, 5.234,
5.300, 5.314, 5.326, 6.038, 6.067, 7.038,
7.129, 9.141, 9.156; see also play.
garden, 3.187, 3.193, 3.790, 3.793, 5.050,
5.161, 6.010, 9.087, 9.095
generation starship, 3.145, 3.488, 3.543, 3.651,
3.817, 3.827, 3.857, 4.210, 5.262, 5.287,
9.138; see also environment, total.
genetic engineering, 4.040
genius, 3.178, 3.573, 3.732, 5.173
geometry, 5.013, 9.039
ghost, ghost in the machine, 3.372, 3.464,
3.734, 4.128, 5.125, 8.032, 9.039, 9.073
gigabit space, 3.078, 3.332, 3.333, 3.375, 3.391,
3.567, 3.570, 3.586, 3.612, 3.884; see also
cyberspace.
gimmick, 5.236
gizmo, 3.261; see also gadget.
god, 3.005, 3.007, 3.053, 3.072, 3.079, 3.136,
3.194, 3.274, 3.321, 3.352, 3.828, 3.843,
3.891-3.893, 4.099, 5.101, 5.212, 5.277,
9.014, 9.091, 9.119, 9.149
god, clockwork, 3.457
god, computer: see computer god(dess).
god, machine, 3.138, 3.298, 3.333, 3.850,
4.138, 4.262, 5.035, 5.283, 6.068
god, nuclear, 4.081
god, voodoo, 3.334
god mechanism, 3.579
goddess, 3.561
goddess, computer: see computer god(dess).
godhead, 3.729, 3.791, 4.223, 5.082
golem, 3.443, 3.498, 4.172, 4.178, 5.121, 7.051,
7.121
gothic novel, 3.348, 3.351, 3.403, 4.079, 5.014,
5.095
grandparents, 3.121, 3.710
graphic, 6.085, 7.018, 7.065, 7.093
graphic art, 7.083, 7.095; see Section 7.
graphic novel, 5.012, 5.135, 7.038, 7.142; see
also comic book.
graphics, computer, 7.021, 9.148
gravity, 3.302, 3.634, 3.652, 3.719, 4.037
group mind, 3.460, 3.654

H

machine, peace, 3.718
machine, pleasure, 3.536, 5.029; see also sex
 entries.
machine, political, 9.005; see also machine of
 the state.
machine, self-replicating, 3.243
machine, small, 5.032, 5.162, 5.235
machine, social, 3.186, 3.872, 4.194, 8.031,
 9.072
machine, space-time, 3.142, 5.099
machine, superiority of, 3.878
machine, survival, 9.037
machine, teaching, 3.287
machine, thinking, 4.071, 9.125; see also AI.
machine, threatening, 5.235; see also threat.
machine, time, 3.852, 5.307
machine, ultimate, 3.014, 3.160-3.162, 3.316,
 5.265
machine, war, 3.558, 3.659, 3.796, 7.121; see
 also machine, fighting.
machine age, 4.015, 4.105, 5.028, 5.052, 7.019,
 7.042, 7.065, 7.099, 7.105, 7.143, 8.048,
 9.028, 9.165
machine art, 4.182, 7.076
machine as human, 3.721, 3.890
machine civilization, 3.088, 3.316, 3.404, 3.481
machine consciousness; see AI.
machine culture, 3.086
machine eutopia, 3.213
machine evolution: See evolution entries.
machine god: See god, mechanical and other
 god entries.
machine of the state, 3.417, 3.503, 3.648, 9.006,
 9.178
machine revolt, 3.279
machine rule, 3.312; see also machine takeover
 and robot rule.
machine takeover, 3.064, 3.085, 3.185, 3.460,
 3.765, 4.189; see also computer rule, machine rule.
machine-based sculpture, 7.107
machine/hive/organism metaphor, 3.534
machinery, alien, 3.612-3.616, 3.618, 5.014,
 5.123, 5.312
mad(ness), 3.285, 3.300, 3.425, 3.465, 3.510,
 3.567, 4.051, 5.165, 5.166, 6.038
magic, 3.030, 3.209, 3.227, 3.408, 3.542, 3.555,
 3.735, 3.786, 3.812, 5.187, 5.215, 5.288,
 5.328, 6.029, 9.177
man, 3.191, 3.246, 3.290, 3.366, 3.403, 3.412,
 3.425, 3.439, 3.453, 3.459, 3.464, 3.497,
 3.501, 3.539, 3.552, 3.554, 3.572, 3.579,

3.601, 3.612, 3.619, 3.628, 3.681, 3.828,
 3.830, 3.849, 4.057, 4.061, 4.130, 6.004,
 6.039, 6.049, 6.068, 7.120, 8.001, 8.009,
 8.020, 9.028, 9.067, 9.074, 9.083, 9.134,
 9.148; see also men, woman, and women.
man, artificial, 9.071
man, clockwork, 3.596
man, last, 3.293
man, mechanized, 3.267
man as machine, 9.064
man-machine interface, 3.864
management, scientific: See scientific management.
managerial society, 4.083
manipulation, 3.015, 3.404, 3.653, 3.791, 3.831,
 3.833, 3.836, 4.117, 4.255, 5.193, 9.122
manipulation, economic, 3.249
mannequin, 3.594, 7.111
marriage, 3.069, 3.210, 3.335
Mars, 3.122, 3.252, 3.568, 3.682, 3.841, 4.170,
 4.194, 5.101, 5.144, 5.325, 9.100
Marx, Karl, 4.185, 4.252, 4.253, 6.010, 6.027,
 9.024, 9.028, 9.074, 9.084, 9.086, 9.087,
 9.131
mass production, 6.046
master, 3.053, 3.073, 3.146, 3.173, 3.175,
 3.176, 3.256, 5.084
master/slave society, 3.517
materialism, 3.219, 9.038, 9.088, 9.127, 9.146,
 9.173
mathematics, 3.047, 3.180, 3.337, 3.494, 7.021,
 7.030, 7.082, 7.092, 7.131, 9.111, 9.168
matriarchy, 3.107, 3.163
matrix, 3.335, 3.336, 3.544, 3.635
matter, 5.155, 5.158, 9.107, 9.146, 9.149
maze, 5.116
mechanical god: See god, mechanical.
mechanical house, 3.124
mechanical insect, 3.327
mechanical womb: See womb, mechanical.
mechanism, 3.259, 3.307, 3.574, 3.626, 3.753,
 3.815, 3.890, 4.070, 4.074, 4.198, 5.038,
 5.039, 5.159, 6.057, 7.112, 7.143, 8.028,
 9.004, 9.013-9.015, 9.028, 9.044, 9.076,
 9.088, 9.113, 9.127, 9.134, 9.135, 9.149
mechanism, sexual, 6.059
mechanism, social, 9.071
mechanism, societies as, 4.003, 3.626, 8.002
mechanism v. idealism, 9.038
mechanism v. organism, 3.153, 4.074, 4.183
mechanistic, 3.385, 4.036, 6.016, 6.076, 7.076,
 9.039, 9.123, 9.164

S

Satan, 3.174, 3.450, 3.510, 4.002, 5.001, 9.082
Satanic mills, 8.011
satellite, 3.086, 3.484
satellite, artificial, 5.252
satire, 3.004, 3.070, 3.153, 3.212, 3.313, 3.354,
    3.358, 3.503, 3.611, 3.626 3.805, 4.031,
    4.055, 4.063, 4.168, 4.189, 4.221, 4.259,
    4.260, 5.214, 9.145
savior (computer as), 3.140 4.242, 5.301, 5.304,
    8.047, 9.153; see also messiah.
science, 3.008, 3.073, 3.204, 3.542, 3.555,
    3.597, 3.627, 3.805, 3.849, 4.003, 4.012,
    4.057, 4.067, 4.096, 4.102, 4.154, 4.264,
    5.021, 5.233, 5.328, 6.021, 7.017, 7.092,
    7.130, 7.138, 9.020, 9.039, 9.044, 9.062,
    9.064, 9.071, 9.085, 9.121, 9.136, 9.138,
    9.143, 9.155, 9.168, 9.172, 9.177, 9.181
science, computer, 3.234, 9.125
science, mechanistic, 4.009
scientific management ("Taylor System"),
    3.296, 3.808, 3.883, 4.011, 4.024, 4.191,
    9.152
scientism, 4.012
scientist, 3.147, 3.149, 3.204, 3.218, 3.300,
    3.692, 3.718, 3.726, 3.851, 4.221, 4.225,
    4.264, 5.017, 5.019, 5.027, 5.053, 5.059,
    5.078, 5.151, 5.167, 5.213, 5.288, 5.331,
    9.075, 9.113, 9.119
scientist, computer, 3.199
scientist, mad, 5.020, 5.231, 5.309
scripture, 3.586, 3.524, 3.587, 7.009, 7.019,
    7.088, 7.098, 7.131
sculpture, machine-based, 7.107
secret agent, 3.347
seedship, 3.022, 3.191, 3.407, 3.606, 3.752,
    3.776, 3.835, 3.870
semiotic, 6.045, 6.072
sentience, 3.335, 3.435, 3.608 3.701; see also
    AI.
servant, 3.024, 3.275, 3.331, 3.351, 3.534,
    3.563, 3.623, 4.023, 5.084
servant, robot, 3.314, 5.025, 5.178, 5.189
serve, 3.250, 3.268, 3.292, 3.362, 3.386, 3.534,
    3.681, 3.759, 3.877, 4.055, 5.109, 9.128
servo-mechanism, 3.458
setting, 3.192, 3.251, 3.348, 3.416, 3.438,
    3.451, 3.534, 3.592, 3.631, 3.872, 4.029,
    4.170, 6.076, 7.091; see also mise en scène.
setting, corporation, 3.447
sex, 3.067, 3.130, 3.368, 3.532, 3.601, 3.740,
    3.762, 3.781, 3.858, 4.153, 5.115, 5.246,
    5.328, 6.059, 6.078, 7.037, 7.130, 7.136,
    8.004, 8.040, 9.002, 9.025
sex, computer: See computer love and sex.
sex, cybernetic, 3.667
sex, machine-mediated, 5.048, 8.004
sex, mechanized: See mechanized sex.
sex, space travel by, 3.779
sexual conditioning, 3.276
sexual desire, 3.018
sexual politics, 6.039
sexuality, 3.218, 3.220, 3.520, 4.039, 6.039
ship, 3.079, 3.104, 3.170, 3.177, 3.183, 3.214,
    3.216, 3.231, 3.273, 3.324, 3.342, 3.387,
    3.391, 3.401, 3.421, 3.435, 3.437, 3.460,
    3.486, 3.568, 3.608, 3.651, 3.711, 3.715,
    3.716, 3.719, 3.726, 3.750, 3.752, 3.778,
    3.835, 3.848, 4.016, 4.254, 4.256, 5.014,
    5.033, 5.082, 5.116, 5.138, 5.142, 5.187,
    5.201, 5.255, 5.274, 6.005, 6.027, 6.073,
    6.082, 7.014, 7.020, 7.046, 7.073, 9.001
simstim, 3.336-3.338, 3.858
simulacra, 3.244, 3.248, 3.249, 3.254, 3.262,
    4.020; see also android(s) and replicant.
simulacrum president, 3.264
simulation, 3.592
simulation, computerized, 3.155
slave, 3.019, 3.047, 3.454, 3.751, 4.015, 4.159,
    5.044, 5.045
sleep, 3.199, 3.251, 3.834, 3.853, 5.320
socialist, 9.026, 9.055, 9.062, 9.101
society, 3.100, 3.102, 3.117, 3.133, 3.150,
    3.269, 3.332, 3.355, 3.375, 3.393, 3.404,
    3.431, 3.456, 3.468, 3.483, 3.503, 3.552,
    3.554, 3.634, 3.653, 3.754, 3.779, 3.831,
    3.847, 4.011, 4.024, 4.036, 4.130, 4.159,
    4.166, 4.258, 5.016, 5.225, 5.264, 5.327,
    7.031, 7.057, 7.112, 7.122, 8.030, 9.028,
    9.046, 9.077, 9.083, 9.085, 9.092, 9.110,
    9.158, 9.159, 9.168, 9.174
society, agrarian, 3.069, 3.118
society, automated, 4.056
society, closed, 4.021
society, contemporary, 6.067
society, corporate managerial, 4.083, 6.038
society, hive: See hive.
society, industrial, 4.124, 4.153, 4.252, 5.185,
    7.132, 9.046, 9.067
society, machine (dependent), 3.217, 3.389
society, mass, 9.023
society, master/slave, 3.517
society, mechanized, 3.107, 3.885, 9.023
society, perfection in, 7.033

society, pleasant, 4.170
society, Taylorized: See scientific management.
society, technological, 4.237, 5.155
society, totalitarian, 3.552, 5.003
sociology, 4.004, 6.017
software, 3.485, 3.547, 3.605, 3.663, 3.727,
    3.731, 3.777, 3.804
soldier, 3.099, 3.280, 3.534, 9.103; see also
    warrior.
soldier, insect, 3.558
soldier, toy, 3.257
son, 3.768
soul, 3.062, 3.076, 3.231, 3.273, 3.305, 3.420,
    3.574, 4.250, 5.077, 9.010, 9.065, 9.106,
    9.149, 9.176
Soviet S.F., 1.012
space, 3.001, 3.233, 3.324, 3.477, 3.527, 3.626,
    3.781, 3.855, 5.005, 5.116, 5.133, 5.167,
    5.254, 5.255, 6.006,, 6.008, 6.024, 6.065,
    7.072, 7.119, 7.120, 7.138, 8.018, 8.020,
    9.035, 9.036, 9.060, 9.092
space capsule, 5.222
space colony, 3.406, 3.734, 9.143
space pilots, 3.556, 3.557
space shuttle, 3.278, 7.014, 9.013
space station, 3.302, 3.561, 3.643, 3.644, 3.646,
    3.804, 5.017
space travel by cities, 3.103, 3.105
spacecraft, 3.015, 3.193, 3.194 3.251, 3.386,
    3.606, 5.260, 5.269, 5.281; see also genera-
    tion starship.
spacecraft, organic, 3.010
space/time machine, 3.142
spacemen, 7.111
spaceship: See ship, starship, and spacecraft.
spaceship, quantum drive, 3.191
spacesuit, 3.791; see also suit.
Spengler, 4.125, 4.157
sperm-figure, 6.059
spider (robot), 3.079, 3.194, 3.520, 7.025
Spinoza, 9.149, 9.164
spirit, 3.629, 3.735, 3.753, 3.795, 7.096, 8.032,
    9.002, 9.157
spy(ing), 3.364, 3.539
stagnation, 3.834, 9.167
star, 5.082, 6.016
starship, 3.196, 3.214, 3.373, 3.386, 3.387,
    3.597, 3.600, 3.708, 5.284, 7.067; see also
    generation starship and spacecraft.
stasis, 3.312, 3.831, 4.253, 5.264, 9.076
state, 3.028, 3.354, 3.414, 3.743, 3.808, 3.890,
    4.026, 4.208, 6.016, 9.041, 9.139, 9.163,

9.168
state as machine: See machine of the state.
structural analysis, 4.116
structure, bureaucratic, 9.098
structure, mechanistic, 6.016
structure v. communitas, 9.158, 9.159
submarine, 3.308, 5.143, 7.121
subterranean: See underground and underworld.
suicide, computer, 3.839
suit, 5.121, 5.292; see also spacesuit.
suit, diving, 5.009, 5.090, 5.160
suit, fighting, 3.360-3.362, 3.386, 5.135
suit, protective, 3.325, 3.361, 5.121, 5.292
supercomputer: See computer.
superimposition, 3.726, 5.011, 5.015, 5.031,
    5.050, 5.083, 5.094, 5.143, 5.274, 6.071,
    9.015
surface, 3.247, 3.260, 3.266, 3.429, 3.562,
    3.812, 3.852
Surrealism, 7.042, 7.092, 7.112
surveillance, 3.024, 3.204, 3.227, 3.411, 3.632,
    3.639, 3.708, 3.734, 3.893, 5.003, 5.009,
    5.170, 5.203, 5.214, 5.215, 5.298, 5.313,
    6.025, 7.048, 8.018, 8.026, 9.118
survival, 3.238, 3.245, 3.406, 5.301, 9.074
symbiosis, 3.009, 3.240, 3.836
synsect, 3.508; see also robot, miniscule.
synthetic organism, 3.561

T

takeover: See rule by machines.
tank, 3.251, 3.394, 3.766, 3.849, 6.090
tank, ant (metaphorical), 3.260
tank, battle, 3.476, 3.732, 6.090; see also truck.
Taylor System: See scientific management.
teaching, 3.061, 3.096, 3.234, 3.250, 3.287,
    3.289, 3.531, 3.622
technician, 3.173, 3.833, 5.222, 9.003
technique, 9.046, 9.077, 9.085
technocracy, 3.103, 3.227, 3.410, 3.413, 3.833,
    3.851, 4.017, 4.030, 4.056, 4.137, 4.206,
    4.242, 4.264, 5.102, 5.298, 5.304, 5.305,
    9.003, 9.047, 9.080, 9.091, 9.131, 9.136,
    9.153, 9.181
technohorror, 6.046
technology, 3.001, 3.012, 3.067, 3.084, 3.112,
    3.154, 3.161, 3.177, 3.179, 3.238, 3.265,
    3.275, 3.299, 3.309, 3.326, 3.331, 3.370,
    3.380, 3.408, 3.425, 3.456, 3.486, 3.504,
    3.581, 3.599, 3.601, 3.606, 3.607, 3.609,
    3.636, 3.735, 3.779, 3.811, 3.819, 3.826,

About the Compilers

RICHARD D. ERLICH is Professor of English at Miami University, Oxford, Ohio. His previous publications include *The Mechanical God* (Greenwood Press, 1982), and *Clockwork Worlds* (Greenwood Press, 1983).

THOMAS P. DUNN is Professor Emeritus of English at Miami University, Oxford, Ohio. His previous publications include *The Mechanical God* (Greenwood Press, 1982), and *Clockwork Worlds* (Greenwood Press, 1983).